LAURENCE
GARDNER

BESTSELLING AUTHOR OF
BLOODLINE OF THE HOLY GRAIL AND *THE MAGDALENE LEGACY*

THE
GRAIL
ENIGMA

THE HIDDEN HEIRS OF JESUS
AND MARY MAGDALENE

D1635383

HARPER
element

HarperElement
An Imprint of HarperCollins*Publishers*
77–85 Fulham Palace Road,
Hammersmith, London W6 8JB

The website address is: www.harpercollins.co.uk

and *HarperElement* are trademarks of
HarperCollins*Publishers* Ltd

First published by HarperElement 2008
This edition 2009

2

© 2008 Laurence Gardner

A catalogue record of this book is
available from the British Library

ISBN 978-0-00-726696-8

Printed and bound in Great Britain by
Clays Ltd, St Ives plc

Mixed Sources
Product group from well-managed
forests and other controlled sources
www.fsc.org Cert no. SW-COC-1806
© 1996 Forest Stewardship Council

FSC is a non-profit international organisation established to promote the
responsible management of the world's forests. Products carrying the FSC
label are independently certified to assure consumers that they come
from forests that are managed to meet the social, economic and
ecological needs of present and future generations.

Find out more about HarperCollins and the environment at
www.harpercollins.co.uk/green

Contents

PART II **Denouncement of Women
and the Papal Succession**

PART IV   Grail Heritage and the Arthurian Tradition

Colour Plates

Illustrations, Maps and Charts

Illustrations

Maps

Charts

Acknowledgements

Through a period that now amounts to more than 20 years of continued research, so many institutions, museums, libraries and individuals have assisted my work that to list them all would almost constitute a book in itself. I must, however, nominate some for particular thanks for their help in tracing works of literature and art that have been of singular benefit to my endeavour. These include the British Library, the British Museum, the Bibliothèque Nationale de France, the Bibliothèque de Bordeaux, the Louvre Museum, the Vatican Archive, the Royal Irish Academy, the National Library of Scotland, the Ashmolean Museum, the Bodleian Library, the Warburg Institute, Birmingham Central Library, Devon County Library, Somerset County Library, the Fitzwilliam Museum and the National Library of Wales. I am also grateful to Prince Michael of Albany, the Stewart Archive and various Templar and chivalric organizations whose contributions have greatly aided the project.

I am most thankful to my wife Angela, whose tireless support has helped bring this work to fruition, and to my son James for his continued encouragement. My express gratitude is similarly due to my literary agent Andrew Lownie, publicity agent Jennifer Solignac, foreign rights agent Scarlett Nunn, website manager Karen Lyster, artistic consultant Peter Robson, technical advisor Tony Skiens, and business manager Colin Gitsham. Special thanks also to commissioning editor Katy Carrington, the directors and staff of HarperElement Publishers, and the book's editor Matthew Cory.

My appreciation must also be given to all the media producers and programme hosts who have enabled my numerous broadcasts over the years, along with the many magazine and journal editors, congress hosts and conference organizers who have been so supportive of my work in the international arena. I must similarly give due credit and thanks to the extensive list of publishers who have made my books available in so many different languages worldwide.

Since this book is very much a synthesis of interrelated subject matter, I am greatly beholden to those specialist authors whose individual scholarship in their respective fields has facilitated the coverage of specific aspects. Their personal expertise and pre-eminent published works have been invaluable. And, finally, I must convey my gratitude to all those readers who have followed and encouraged my work over the years, especially those who have written to me with useful comments and contributions.

Laurence Gardner
http://www.graal.co.uk

Introduction

Eleven years ago, in *Bloodline of the Holy Grail*, I introduced a series of previously unpublished genealogical charts concerning the descendant family of Jesus Christ. Along with these were the details of some other historically connected dynastic successions. The book itself was wide ranging in its discussion of subjects, from Darwinian theory to 20th-century current affairs. In the course of this, matters were addressed regarding Old Testament history through to the British Empire, the Second World War and beyond. Consequently, the coverage of the central theme of the book was perhaps somewhat limited, with information relating to the immediate messianic lineage and its persecution by the Church occupying only about a third of the book. In 2005, some edited snapshots from this sequence were repeated in *The Magdalene Legacy*, and this has led to a great many requests for further information. It is this dynastic section, in parallel with the rise of the Church, which is now expanded to fill this current edition – a 500-year record of documented accounts that reveal the hidden descent from Jesus.

Onwards from 1996, I have received many thousands of letters and e-mails in response to *Bloodline* and subsequent published works, but throughout the years the most popular subject of question and debate has always been the matter of Jesus' three offspring and their descendants. During the last decade, use of the Internet has grown exponentially, and one of the Web's most active subject areas is that of family genealogy. A search for the word 'genealogy' in Google now brings up nearly 40 million site entries. In this context, a large number of family trees have been produced around the world using the charts from *Bloodline of the Holy Grail* as source material. By virtue of the sheer breadth of the book's chronological content, so much of what *Bloodline* conveyed in genealogical terms was simply the end result of my investigations. There was no space to discuss in any depth the routes of detection which led to those results; neither did the book contain any detailed analysis or explanation of the primary source texts. In *The Grail Enigma*, these matters are now addressed for the benefit of previous and new readers alike. This book will take its readers on a step-by-step journey of discovery, following the individual paths of documentary evidence, noting and acknowledging all the relevant primary and secondary sources in the process.

In treading this 500-year path again, I have now been able to include a great deal of additional information. By concentrating on 1st–6th century events considerable expansion has been possible of items that were previously introduced, but which were not given the space that they warranted. Alongside this, I have now had the opportunity to study texts that were not readily available in the early 1990s. In particular, I have been able to add substantially to the generational information so that a much clearer picture of the bloodline descent is now presented, adding in hitherto unknown individuals. This has resulted in a revised and more concise genealogical table for the early centuries of the lineal progression. Meanwhile, for those readers who might wish to view the wider picture, the precursory and associated charts are to be found in *Bloodline of the Holy Grail*.

In following its course of enacted history and retrospective literature, *The Grail Enigma* is compiled in four themed sections, with each part structured to focus on particular aspects of the ongoing story.

Part I:
Forbidden Writings and the Heirs of Jesus

In order to set the scene for the events which are described in this book, a number of subjects are now discussed which were not touched upon originally. This enables us to understand better why the descendants of Jesus and his brother James were perceived as such a threat to the Church authorities, while also giving us an insight into why the punitive measures that were enforced might have been deemed necessary to circumvent that threat.

Notwithstanding the interest which has prevailed in this subject as a result of *Bloodline* and the associated research of other writers, it is a fact that since 2003 the readership audience has broadened considerably as a result of Dan Brown's novel, *The Da Vinci Code*. This work has not only brought the concept of Jesus' marriage to Mary Magdalene and the messianic lineage into a wider public arena, but aspects of the novel have also stirred an interest in such matters as Church evolution and New Testament gospel selection. There is now a far greater awareness of the fact that many early Christian texts were tactically sidelined because they contained information that was contrary to ecclesiastical requirement. Since the process of compiling and producing the canon was closely connected to the Church's vindictive strategy against the messianic bloodline, we shall be unravelling and considering the selection process as it was detailed in the Vatican archive. At the same time, we shall see how and why it was that even the New Testament books which are now so familiar were doctored and edited so as to comply with the desired objective.

In essence, this narrative is the story of two parallel, but competitive church movements: the Nazarene Church of Jesus and the Catholic Church of Rome. It is an account of Messianic Succession versus Apostolic Succession, and we are destined to meet with characters on each side of the conflict in their concerted attempts to gain supremacy during the rise of Christendom. On one side we have a descent of dedicated missionaries and a line of powerful kings, while on the other are the popes and the might of the Roman Empire. From the very outset at the time of Jesus' crucifixion, it is an account of intrigue, conspiracies, fraud, hypocrisy and violent persecution as documented by the historians and chroniclers of the era.

Part II:
Denouncement of Women and the Papal Succession

As we move throughout the realms of Christendom, from the Holy Land, to Syria, Egypt, Greece, Asia Minor, Rome, Gaul, and to ancient Britain, we discover that for hundreds of years the Christianity of one country was never the same as that of another. The randomly diverse belief structure of Christianity was never a cohesive, unified whole. The national leaders of the Catholic branch were severely at odds with each other, and their Councils, Synods and papal elections became battlegrounds with, on occasions, no shortage of blood spilled. Opposing them in the non-Catholic groups were the Nazarenes, Arians, Nestorians and many other sects including the influential Celtic movement in Britain.

Inherent in all these conflicts of opinion were numerous matters of constant disagreement, among the foremost of which was the position of women in Church and community society. Even within some branches of early Christianity there was a goddess culture, especially in those streams which evolved alongside the Druidic priesthood in Britain and Gaul. The only branch to set itself firmly and forcefully against any female involvement was the Catholic sector, wherein women were totally excluded and rules of celibacy were imposed on its clergy. And it is here that we discover one of the greatest hypocrisies when the truth is unveiled about formally acknowledged brothels within the Vatican. Despite all the supposed rules and regulations, the individually documented sex lives of the popes and cardinals provide an extraordinary revelation of the reality behind the scenes.

Part III:
Church Evolution and the Bloodline Descent

The concept that Jesus and Mary Magdalene were married is by no means a product of our modern era, even though it has gained a renewed press and media interest in recent times. In 1946, in his book *King Jesus*, the scholar Robert Graves had discussed the marriage of Jesus and Mary, even describing the ceremony. Prior to that, in 1931, DH Lawrence had written along similar lines in *The Man Who Died*. Of much greater importance than any of these latter-day works, however, are the testimonies of more ancient times.

During the Dark Ages, historians and Roman Church scribes had written about 'those in the bloodline of Jesus from his mother'. Through the medieval era into the Middle Ages, Mary Magdalene was referred to as the 'Bride of Christ'. Their descendants were known as the *Desposyni* (the Heirs of the Lord). In the light of such records, the event of the marriage itself is not really open to question, especially since it is detailed on four occasions in the Bible. More intriguing, however, is the story of their offspring, and of the great lengths to which the Roman emperors and popes went to suppress their legacy. This began with the 1st-century edict that 'not one must be left among them'.

Part IV:
Grail Heritage and the Arthurian Tradition

Gradually, as the Church managed to overawe the *Desposyni* inheritors through a centuries-long programme of intimidation and persecution, their supporters (classified as felons and heretics) became ever more wary and covert, manifesting in the nature of an underground stream of dedicated adherents. They began to communicate by way of secret signs and watermarks, moving the story of the tormented Blood Royal (the *Sang Réal*) into the romantic literature of the Holy Grail. Paramount in this scribal process were monks of the Cistercian Order, along with the Knights Templars who were attached to the Cistercians, and chroniclers of the houses of Provence, Aquitaine, Champagne and Anjou. Their writings portrayed individual characters of the Grail Family in descent from Jesus and his brother James, culminating in the legends of King Arthur and the quest for the lost heritage of the *Sangréal*.

This, then, is the overall period to which our current investigation relates – an account of the various desposynic heirs in succession from the time of Jesus to the era of King Arthur. Alongside the Bible itself, we shall be considering numerous texts that were discounted for New Testament inclusion, and a variety of chronicles, annals and reports of varying national and religious origins, dating from the Dark Ages to medieval times. These are pieced together with, and weighed against, items from the Vatican archive concerning the perceived need for restrictive edicts and decrees leading ultimately to the great Inquisition. What emerges is the continuous story of a prolonged strategy of subjugation against the messianic inheritors – those men and women whose legacy constitutes *The Grail Enigma*.

Laurence Gardner
Exeter, 2007

[*Please note:* All biblical citations in this work are given from the King James Authorized Version unless otherwise stated.]

PART I

Forbidden Writings
and the Heirs of Jesus

Forging the Testament

The Historical Jesus

It is claimed that history is written by its winners, and to a certain extent this is true. Invaders often rewrite the histories of conquered nations, and most royal dynasties have revised the histories of their predecessors, discarding previous records. There are, however, many instances where parallel histories coexist, particularly those which record episodes of battle and conflict. There is an English history of the 1314 Battle of Bannockburn and an alternative Scottish history of the same battle; there is an English history of the 1415 Battle of Agincourt and another, differing, French history. Opposing factions have always had their own viewpoints of the events being recorded.

In large measure, historical accounts depend on the identity of their writers, who might have been participants or eyewitnesses, or, alternatively, totally divorced from the events, perhaps compiling their records some time afterwards. In all cases, 'history' does not constitute the events of the past; it constitutes the 'records' of those events, and records vary in accordance with individual perspective, vested interest and interpretation.[1]

Written history cannot always be regarded as provable fact, and it becomes progressively harder to prove as more time elapses from the event in question. Most history derives from individual items of documentary evidence and we usually take them on board, without question, if they are a part of academic culture. But the picture can change with new discovery; archaeological relics are also records of past events, and previously unknown texts and artefacts are often found in uncatalogued archival storage. Sometimes historical tradition is overturned by such revelatory finds, but all too often they are ignored because they conflict with preferred establishment dogma.

In this context, the biblical scriptures are records of past events like any other, and are therefore defined as history. Whether they are accurate or wholly factual is another matter. The New Testament, with which *The Grail Enigma* is concerned, is a compilation of Christian documents, and scholars are in general agreement that these canonical gospels were written some decades after the events which they portray.

Since the gospels are of specifically Christian origin, it is evident that the Romans would not necessarily have written about Jesus and his apostles in a positive manner, as is made clear in *The Annals of Imperial Rome*, which describe Jesus' mission as a 'shameful practice'. The *Annals* cement Jesus in history outside his Christian portrayal, and in this manner the existence of Jesus Christ as a real figure of the era is confirmed by a parallel record from his enemies, whose perception of his character was entirely different from that of the gospel writers. His followers are described in the Roman annals as being 'notoriously depraved'; his beliefs are stated to have been a 'deadly superstition', and his sentence of execution by the governor of Judaea, Pontius Pilate, is documented in 1st-century Roman history as well as in the Christian gospels.[2]

In the Jewish archive, we find that Jesus is also mentioned twice in the *Antiquities of the Jews*. Compiled in about AD 92, this chronicle relates that Jesus began his ministry during the reign of Tiberius Caesar, in the period AD 26–35 when Pilate was the Roman governor in Jerusalem. This locates Jesus firmly within the historical fabric of the era, but without any mention of his divinity. When discussing the early establishment of the Christian movement, the Hebrew narrative refers to 'James, the brother of Jesus who was called Christ'. This supports the Roman *Annals* which also identify Jesus as being the Christ (from the Greek word *christos* meaning 'king').[3]

In another *Antiquities* entry, Jesus is referred to as 'a wise man and a teacher … who drew to him many of the Jews in addition to many of the Gentiles'. The chronicle further states that 'when Pilate, at the suggestion of the principal men among us, had him condemned to be crucified, those that had loved him from the first did not forsake him'.[4]

Overall, there is firm documentary evidence, from both Roman and Jewish sources, as well as the Christian scriptures, that Jesus was present in Judaea during the reign of Emperor Tiberius; that he was a teacher with a significant following; that he was considered to be the Christ, and that he was sentenced to execution by Pontius Pilate.

A Hybrid Canon

From the 4th century onwards, Christianity became the established religion of Rome, and the Catholic Church (the Church of Rome) was inaugurated. Many changes were made to bring the 'deadly superstition' into line with imperial requirement but, at this point, it is useful to consider the divergent opinions of Christians themselves as applicable to their faith. From the time that the original apostles and disciples began their missions beyond their homeland of Judaea, Christianity evolved in distinctly separate ways in different countries. These countries were as widely spread geographically as Syria, Asia Minor (essentially Turkey), North Africa, Greece, Britain, France and, of course, Rome. There were so many regional groups and movements that the actual nature of Christianity at this time is difficult to define except that, in one way or another, it was centred on the ministry of Jesus.

There were appointed leaders of the mission in each country, but the overall effort was not especially well coordinated, and when the leaders did come together they were not always in agreement about every aspect of their religion. This occurred because different documents of record were produced, or favoured, in each region, and the various belief structures were focused on different points of emphasis. For instance, some perceived Jesus as the son of God; others felt he was an earthly messiah, and many thought he was an intuitive prophet. Some factions upheld the notion of the virgin birth; others denied it absolutely, and there were constant disagreements concerning the extent to which the Judaism of Jesus should influence Christianity. If it can be said that the constitution of the Church of Rome achieved a unified end, then that achievement arose from confronting these disagreements in order to produce a doctrinal canon and a commonly regulated set of ground-rules for the Faith. Those bishops and leaders who did not agree with the decisions were either reluctantly brought into line or henceforth excluded from the self-styled orthodox movement.

In essence, what emerged was a religion based on the opinions of the most influential Church Fathers, along with a modicum of debated compromise. Into this were amalgamated various aspects of pagan belief in order to ease the conversion for hitherto non-Christians of the Empire. The resultant new Christianity was either good or bad news depending on one's perspective. Either way, however, it was in many respects far removed from anything that Jesus himself might have recognized.

The Early Years

Jesus, we are told in the New Testament, began his ministry in the year AD 29 – 'the fifteenth year of the reign of Tiberius Caesar' (as given in Luke 3:1) – and was sentenced to crucifixion in AD 33. The religious movement which sprang from his teachings acquired the name Christianity 11 years later in Antioch, Syria.[5] For many generations the Christians were persecuted throughout the Roman Empire. Then, in AD 313, Emperor Constantine relaxed the pressure and subsequently proclaimed Christianity as the new State religion of Rome. Later, in AD 397, the selected books of the New Testament canon were confirmed by the bishops of the emergent Church, which had assumed the name Catholic, meaning 'universal'.

The time-span between the crucifixion of Jesus and the final selection of the canonical text was 364 years. To put this into a latter-day perspective, from the present date this number of years would take us back to 1642 when the Stuart King Charles I was on the throne of Britain. This was the year of Galileo's death in Italy, and the year when Georgeana (now York, Maine) became the first incorporated city in America, 133 years before the War of Independence. If Jesus had been crucified in 1642, then 2006 would be the equivalent year in which the New Testament was confirmed.

During the early centuries of Christianity, countless literary works were produced to promote and uphold the Faith but, in the final event, only 27 documents were approved by the Catholic bishops, and even they were subject to editing and amendment before being considered wholly suitable. These now familiar works served to project a divine and elusive image of Jesus as required by the new Church of Rome, but in contriving this the bishops managed to subvert and override many of the beliefs of the original Christians. In this newly structured version of the Faith, the humanity of Jesus and the female element of his mission were subsumed by an ecclesiastical department of the imperial regime.

Fortunately, the texts of numerous Christian documents produced between the time of Jesus and the days of Constantine are still accessible. This makes it possible to determine what Christianity once was, as against what it became. The official ecclesiastical view is that a majority of these documents cannot be considered authentic because they were not approved by the Council in AD 397.[6] The fact that the early Christians considered their documents appropriate to their belief was discounted on the basis that the original religion of Jesus was not itself authentic since Jesus was a Nazarene Jew and did not follow the rule of Rome!

What we have here is a situation whereby the revised 4th-century style of Christianity was not established because of Jesus, but almost in spite of him. In practical terms, the very purpose of Christianity as a diversely scattered fellowship was nullified by the new regime. The emperors had long been revered as deities on Earth and, in this respect, the figure of Jesus had posed a significant challenge for Constantine in Rome (AD 312–337). He pointed out to the Christians that it was he who had secured their freedom within the Empire, and that it was he, not Jesus, who should henceforth be regarded as the true Saviour of the Faith. Christians of the original schools were therefore faced with the choice of being free or being persecuted. As a result, their long-standing ideals were mostly forsaken – handed over on a plate to be devoured by Jesus' Roman adversaries. Christianity was no longer a way of life based on the teachings of Jesus; it had become an institutionalized religion governed by the doctrines of the Church.

A Matter of Dates

Although opinions differ, it is generally considered by theologians that the first gospel of the New Testament to be compiled was that of Mark. Assumed to have been written in about AD 66, it is said to contain the earliest Christian references to Jesus.

More than half of the New Testament books are letters attributed to St Paul. Another two are letters of St Peter, while others are letters credited to James, John and Jude. In all, these amount to 21 of the overall 27 books of the canon. Irrespective of James, John and Jude, however, we know from *The Annals of Imperial Rome* that some Christian leaders were sentenced in Rome by Emperor Nero in AD 64.[7] This was the episode during which Catholic tradition records the executions of Peter and Paul, but it was two years before the Mark gospel is thought to have been written. The possible conclusions are that: a) Catholic tradition in this regard is incorrect; b) Mark has been incorrectly dated; c) the letters of Paul and Peter are older than the gospel of Mark, or that d) these letters were spuriously introduced or wrongly attributed. The most baffling element is that, when it comes right down to it, we do not actually know who wrote the letters, nor indeed who wrote the four canonical gospels. We only know the names which have been ascribed to them.

The most likely candidate for an authentic authorship is the gospel of Luke. But Luke was not listed as an apostle of Jesus, neither was he a Jew of Jesus' immediate fraternity. Luke was a Syrian physician from Antioch who wrote his account of Jesus' life in about AD 80.[8] He is also reckoned to have written The Acts of the Apostles, wherein there are many aspects of literary and linguistic similarity. Not the least of these is that both Luke and The Acts begin with prefaces addressed to a certain Theophilus.[9]

Although there is enough evidence to suggest a common authorship for these two New Testament books, it is simply a conjecture that the author was Luke because there is no mention to this effect in either account. What we do know, however, is that the author was not writing from first-hand experience of Jesus' ministry; he was writing from a position of tradition and belief, and he stated this to be the case in his opening to the Luke gospel:

> Forasmuch as many have taken in hand to set forth in order a declaration of those things which are most surely believed among us, even as they delivered them unto us, which from the beginning were eyewitnesses and ministers of the word, it seemed good to me also ... to write unto thee in order, most excellent Theophilus, that thou mightest know the certainty of those things.[10]

It is clear from this that the author was writing a second-hand account passed down to him from others whom he called 'eyewitnesses'. It is commonly thought that Luke's source of information was Mark – or at least the gospel of Mark, much of the content from which is included within the gospel of Luke – but we know from the biblical lists that Mark was also not an apostle of Jesus. Neither was he an eyewitness to Jesus' ministry.

As with Luke, the gospel attributed to Matthew contains numerous verses that appear in Mark, which indicates that either Mark was the primary text or that all three gospels derived independently from the same original source. Since the Matthew gospel appears to have been written some decades after Jesus' crucifixion, it is generally felt that its author was not the apostle Matthew whose name the gospel is presumed to carry.[11]

Whatever the case, these things are all matters of speculation. Whichever gospel came first, there are such similarities between Matthew, Mark and Luke that they are classified as the three Synoptic Gospels (from the Greek, *syn-optikos* – '[seeing] with the same eye'). This is the case even though they do not concur in many respects and each contains items of narrative which are not present in the others. By virtue of their compilation styles, the consensus of historical opinion is that Mark (the shortest of the three) was undoubtedly the first to be written, and that Matthew and Luke were partially copied from Mark, while also including additional information from some other source. The similarities and discrepancies are discussed later when we take a more detailed look at the synoptic gospels (*see* page 44), together with the gospel of John, which has a distinctly separate origin.

Ancient Texts

Notwithstanding all tradition and scholarly opinion concerning the authorship dates of the canonical gospels, the fact is that not one single original manuscript is available for analysis. The earliest complete canonical texts date from the 4th century. They are considered to be copies from older originals, but this cannot be proved except by way of circumstantial evidence.

The relevance of this is that various other gospels and Christian texts do exist from earlier times in the 2nd and 3rd centuries. Although these documents are older than the oldest extant canonical texts, they too are stated historically to be copies from much earlier originals. In the light of this, it is difficult to comprehend how the

Church can persist in maintaining that its own selected and approved texts are more authentic than the rest when there is no confirmation of this available. Perhaps the gospels of Matthew, Mark, Luke and John are indeed older than the non-canonical gospels of Peter, Thomas, Philip and others – but they might not be. The most important fact to note is that all these individual texts were in Christian usage before the New Testament was compiled and, historically, they are equally valid as evidence of Christian beliefs and practice in the days prior to Roman intervention.

The very oldest biblical compilation held in the Vatican Library dates from no earlier than the 4th century and is known as the Vatican Codex (the *Codex Vaticanus*).[12] These manuscripts, written in Greek, are bound in a series of 759 papyrus folios with two or three columns to a page. Additionally there are 30 dubious folios from a later date that were added in the 16th century to replace some that were missing from the original collection. There have long been disputes as to the origin of the Vatican Codex, but the most common opinion is that it was produced in Egypt.[13]

One surprising revelation that emerges from this work occurs in the gospel of Mark. Although Mark is generally considered to have been the synoptic model for Matthew and Luke, this earliest known version of Mark is somewhat shorter than the text with which we are now familiar. The *Vaticanus* book ends at chapter 16 verse 8, whereas the canonical version of Mark continues for a further 12 verses. This is the sequence which relates to the resurrection and subsequent ascension of Jesus after his crucifixion. It is now generally considered that these final verses were appended as spurious additions. We know that this occurred before AD 339 since the Church Father, Eusebius of Caesarea (who died in that year), wrote that he did not consider the verses of Mark 16:9–20 to be authentic.[14]

Another 4th-century text from which the additional verses of Mark are missing is the Sinai Codex (*Codex Sinaiticus*). Dating from the same period as the Vatican Codex, these substantially fragmented manuscripts were found at St Catherine's monastery in Sinai through a series of discoveries in the late 1800s, and are now in the British

Museum, London. Once again the codices are written in Greek, but unlike the papyrus leaves of the *Codex Vaticanus*, the books are written on parchment and their place of origin is unknown.[15]

A significant feature of the *Sinaiticus* work is that its text differs in many instances from the contemporary *Vaticanus* edition. The Catholic archive states that 'it cannot be derived from the same immediate ancestor'[16], so we are looking (probably in both cases) at 4th-century interpretations of earlier documents, not at facsimile copies. It is plain that differently interpreted biblical scriptures were produced for different regional cultures, and it was not until the Catholic canon was formulated that the New Testament was hammered into its now familiar form.

An interesting entry in Paul's first epistle to the Corinthians refers to 'the gospel' that he was preaching,[17] and there are many instances in his letters where he implies a knowledge of events contained in the canonical gospels. If, according to the accepted compilation dates of these documents, Paul was preaching before they were written, then clearly there was another source for his information. The English (or more correctly Anglo-Saxon) term 'gospel' stems from the Greek *eu-aggelos* (bringing good tidings), which may lead us to believe that Paul might have been referring to an oral tradition rather than a written gospel.

Many of the sayings of Jesus – as reported in the gospels of Matthew, Mark and Luke – are repeated word for word, even to the detail of their parenthesized elements.[18] Moreover, a good many of these entries also appear in the non-canonical gospel of Thomas, which actually adds to them giving a total of 114 sayings purportedly spoken by Jesus.

The gospel of Thomas was a vital handbook for the early Christians although it was not selected by the bishops for the New Testament. There were a number of reasons for its exclusion, not the least of which was that it dealt specifically with the teachings of Jesus, and made no mention of his birth, death and resurrection which became so crucial to the Roman portrayal of the Faith in later times. It also contradicted the new Catholic teaching that Jesus was only accessible by way of adherence to the Church. In contrast, Thomas made the point that the spirit of Jesus was everywhere; Jesus said: 'Split a piece of wood, and I am there. Lift up a stone, and you will find me.'[19]

Additionally, the gospel of Thomas contained an item concerning Mary Magdalene in which Peter complained about her presence in the apostolic fraternity of males. In response, Jesus confided that she would become an equally living spirit in their company.[20] But there was no room for anything concerning female equality in the newly devised, male-dominated Church of Rome. As a consequence of this – along with the 4th-century notion that access to Jesus was a strict prerogative of the bishops – the gospel of Thomas was deemed inappropriate for the canon.

It has been argued recently that Thomas does not have the same provenance of antiquity as the canonical gospels, but this is simply not so. Extant Greek manuscript sections of Thomas date from around AD 200 (well over a century earlier than any canonical manuscript). In addition, the gospel of Thomas is known to have existed in Syriac or Aramaic writing in the second half of the 1st century.[21] It stems from precisely the same era attributed to the gospel of Mark, and might indeed have been one of that gospel's original sources. A comparison of the sayings in Thomas with their parallels in Matthew, Mark and Luke has led linguistic scholars to deduce that the Thomas verses have a more primitive construction. Also that this gospel more closely resembles the ultimate key source for the synoptic gospels – an earlier gospel now known as 'Q' (relating to the Teutonic word *quelle*, meaning 'source').[22]

The Gospel and the Grail

Dating from about AD 50, the 'Q' gospel was not a narrative account of Jesus' life, nor anything that would suggest the birth of a new religion. It was a comprehensive list of Jesus' philosophies directed against the ruling elite of Jerusalem and presented as a series of social codes referred to as The Way.[23] This was a doctrinal theme of the Essene community of Qumrân, near Jericho, where the first Dead Sea Scrolls were discovered in 1947. [For more on the Essenes and to Jesus' association with this scholarly sect, *see* page 83.]

Individual extracts from 'Q' appear in other documents including Thomas and the synoptic gospels, but no complete manuscript has yet been discovered. Since Matthew and Luke jointly contain 250 items from 'Q' that are not in Mark, it is possible that each of the writers used 'Q' independently as a reference source, rather than copying from Mark as has been commonly supposed.[24]

Like the gospel of Thomas, 'Q' provides a unique insight into the mind-set of the early Christians who did not regard the death and resurrection of Jesus to be a feature of their religion. Since the original gospel of Mark did not include the resurrection, it is worth pursuing this line of inquiry by looking at the work of the persecuted Christians in Rome. Was the resurrection important to their beliefs, or was it a later item of enforced Church doctrine?

Beneath the streets of Rome, the catacombs of the era before Emperor Constantine hold the remains of more than six million Christians. Laid in a single row the passages would extend for 550 miles (880 km). These underground rooms and passages contain the earliest known examples of Christian artwork. Even the chambers used for interment in the 1st and 2nd centuries carry some decoration. Fish and doves were common symbols of the Faith, and although there are many pictures of Jesus and the apostles, there are no direct portrayals of Jesus' resurrection. Even within the Christian community of Rome, it can be seen that this did not carry the weight of importance that was subsequently applied by the new Church. All evidence points to the fact that the precepts of true Christianity were the philosophies of The Way as taught by Jesus; they were not about venerating Jesus for his own divine sake.

Interestingly, *The Catholic Encyclopedia* confirms that the most common recurring theme in the catacomb drawings is a grapevine.[25] In the Old Testament, the sovereignty of Israel is expressed in Psalm

80 as a growing vine. For this reason, grapes and vines have often been used in artwork to demonstrate life, growth and generational progression.

From the book of Genesis onwards, there are constant references to vineyards and lineal descent, with the repeated assertion, 'Be fruitful, and multiply'. In Isaiah 5:7, Israel and the Royal House of David are described as the Lord's 'cherished plant'. And in John 15:10, referring to his ancestry from King David, Jesus makes the claim: 'I am the true vine'. It is for this reason that, in terms of allegorical fine art, Jesus has often been painted in conjunction with a wine press.[26]

The vine was not only the most depicted emblem of the early Christians; vines and grapes (the fruit and seeds of the vine) remained, for hundreds of years, the most important symbols of the esoteric church of Jesus that persisted despite the wide-scale Catholic domination. Another prominent symbol was a cup or chalice, and the two images combined were known as the Vessel and the Vine. The relevance of this symbolism is looked at in greater detail later (see page 181) but, in simple terms, they alluded to the eternal blood of Jesus as determined when he passed the cup of wine to his apostles at the Last Supper. Jesus made the point that he was offering the 'fruit of the vine', saying, 'this is my blood'.[27] This imagery is synonymous with the familiar Church sacrament of the Eucharist – the communion ritual of the chalice and the wine.

It is not surprising that Christianity inherited the symbolism of cups and grapes because the Faith had evolved from Nazarene Judaism and these were common emblems of heritage. They appeared on Judaean coins of the 1st century BC, and would have been familiar to Jesus and his disciples. The same designs have been reintroduced for some modern Israeli coins. In Israelite terms, the chalice represented the Omer Cup of Temple ceremony (an omer being a unit of measurement).[28]

Outside the Catholic Church, the chalice and the wine (as determined by the inheritors of original Christianity) were similarly related to the perpetual blood of Jesus, but in more explicit terms.

Cup and Vine coins of ancient Judaea, and their recent counterparts

They symbolized a vine from King David growing through Jesus and beyond – a progression of the royal line spreading its branches as defined in the book of Ezekiel 19:10, which states: 'Thy mother is like a vine in thy blood, planted by the waters; she was fruitful and full of branches.' The same terminology was used in the adventurous lore of the Holy Grail. In the romance of *Parzival* by the 13th-century Bavarian knight Wolfram von Eschenbach, it is said of the Grail Queen that she 'bore the perfection of earthly paradise, both roots and branches. It was a thing men call the Grail'.[29]

There is absolutely nothing in the gospels of Thomas or 'Q' to indicate the notion that Jesus died for people's sins and rose again, but the early Christians who used these books clearly believed in a different concept of his perpetual existence. In fact, so too did the Romans and, as we shall discover (*see* page 81), it is documented from imperial times that the emperors took the most extreme measures to persecute and exterminate those messianic dynasts whom they called the Heirs of the Lord.

From Rags to Riches

Shot in the Foot

To gain an insight into the extreme change of attitude to Christianity taken by Constantine and his officials, it helps to understand how Christians and their 'deadly superstition' were perceived by the Romans in earlier times.

The Senate and its ambassadors were able to claim religious supremacy over the Christians following Rome's military conquest and destruction of Jerusalem by the legions of General Titus in AD 70. Just two years after the mass slaughter of Christians by Nero, a Jewish revolt had erupted against the Roman overlords of Judaea in AD 66. As far as the Romans were concerned, Christianity was born out of liberal Judaism, and was perceived as a Jewish cult which shared the same God. This God was traditionally reckoned to be the all-powerful protector of the Israelite nation, and yet, to the Romans, their Roman gods were clearly more powerful because, following the crushing of the four-year revolt, the Judaeo-Christian God was seen to have been defeated.

Joseph ben Mattathias, a Pharisee scholar, was one of the leading figures of the Judaean rising. Better known these days by his Romanized name, Flavius Josephus, he was the appointed military commander of Galilee, and in the years subsequent to the revolt, he wrote *The Wars of the Jews* (AD 78) and its companion edition, *The Antiquities of the Jews* (AD 92). By comparing his work with *The Annals of Imperial Rome*, the parallel histories of the Jews and Romans give us first-hand perspectives from the two opposing cultures.

Some time later, in AD 132, the Israelites rebelled again, this time under the leadership of Simon bar Kochba, a prince of Israel. He assembled a large army of local volunteers, together with professional mercenaries from abroad, and his battle plan included many guerrilla operations, some of which made use of tunnels and underground chambers beneath Jerusalem. Within a year, Jerusalem was recaptured from the Romans, following which a Jewish administration was established and maintained for a further two years. Outside the city, the struggle continued and the Jewish strategy depended on gaining military assistance from Persia. At the point when the Persian forces were preparing to set out for the Holy Land, Persia was invaded and so its troops had to stay and defend their own territory. Consequently, Simon bar Kochba and his followers were not able to counter the advance of the twelve Roman legions which had regrouped in Syria at the command of Emperor Hadrian, and Simon's men were overwhelmed at Battin, west of Jerusalem, in AD 135.[1] Once again, the superiority of the Roman gods seemed to be demonstrated, and the god of the Jews and Christians was ridiculed throughout the Empire.

The prevailing religion of imperial Rome was polytheistic (observing many gods), and had emanated largely from the worship of natural deities such as those of the woods and waters. As Rome had grown to statehood, the gods of her Etruscan and Sabine neighbours were incorporated. These included Jupiter, the sky god, and Mars, the god of war. Some Grecian cults were also embraced, as evidenced by the hedonistic rituals of Dionysus/Bacchus, the god of wine. Additionally, in spreading eastwards, the Roman Empire had adopted the Persian veneration of Mithras, the god of light, truth and justice.

Religion in 2nd-century Rome was, in essence, a hotchpotch of glued-together aspects of so many cults and creeds that there was no overall uniformity. Astrologers, magicians, herbologists, mystics, physicians, musicians and theosophists of all kinds descended upon the imperial capital, each adding their cultural traditions to an already complex set of beliefs.[2] Christianity was among these diverse movements but, where the other religious proponents flaunted their faith by way of the healing and entertainment they offered, the Christians kept very much to themselves and held their meetings in private. They did not seek the company of the rich and famous, preferring to associate themselves with the poor and more lowly end of society. A Roman report from the 2nd century reads: 'They exclude from their fellowship the wise and good, and consort only with the ignorant and sinful'.[3] All of this engendered a deep suspicion, even a fear, of their separatist motives, and this gained the Christians a repu-tation as of being somehow menacing and subversive.

Eventually, in order to consolidate the various Roman cults into a cohesive format, the Syrian solar religion of *Sol Invictus* (the uncon-quered and unconquerable sun) became the all-encompassing belief in Rome. Its vision of the sun as the ultimate giver of life enabled all other beliefs (with the exception of Christianity and Judaism) to be subsumed, with the Emperor as the presumed earthly incarnation of the godhead.

By the time of the Bar Kochba revolt, significant divisions had appeared in the Christian movement. Although a suppressed under-ground society in Rome, they maintained the tradition of appointing bishops to lead them and, from AD 136, Hyginus was their bishop in Rome. Hyginus was at odds with some of the bishops in other lands, the main dispute between the various factions concerning the matter of Jesus' personal divinity. There were two predominant groupings in the debate: the followers of Hyginus, who had spread into parts of Gaul (later France), Spain and North Africa, while the alternative Nazarene sect was scattered through Asia and the Middle East, and also, to a lesser extent, in Britain and Gaul. In essence, the Hyginus Christians followed teachings that were said to have emanated from St Paul, whereas the Nazarenes preferred the more direct teachings of Jesus and his brother James, who had been the first Nazarene bishop in Jerusalem.

During this period of Christian history, a number of powerful figures emerged in the ranks outside Rome, not the least of whom was Irenaeus, the Bishop of Lyon in Gaul. In about AD 177, he challenged the Nazarene concept that Jesus was a man and not of divine origin as the Hyginus teaching implied. He also condemned the Nazarenes for preaching the gospel of Matthew, which he considered to be Jewish rather than Christian. In endeavouring to enforce his opinion, Irenaeus went so far as to pronounce in his treatise *Adversus Haereses* (Against Heresies) that Jesus was himself a heretic who had been practising the wrong religion! Jesus, he claimed, was personally mistaken in his beliefs. Additionally, he wrote of the Nazarenes, whom he classified as *ebionites* (a transliteration from Aramaic, meaning 'poor'):

> They, like Jesus as well as the Essenes and Zadokites of two centuries before, expound upon the prophetic books of the Old Testament. They reject the Pauline epistles, and they reject the apostle Paul, calling him an apostate of the law.[4]

The Nazarenes recognized the absurdity that Jesus' teachings should take second place to those of Paul. In retaliation, they denounced Paul as having been a 'renegade and a false apostle', claiming that his idolatrous writings should be rejected altogether. Thus, even 222 years before the New Testament was compiled, the original Christians were themselves divided in opinion as to which scriptural texts they preferred.

Notwithstanding the nature of the dispute itself, the Roman authorities had come to realize that Christians at large were an argumentative lot, who could not even agree among themselves, and they were therefore perceived as a threat to structured, law-abiding society. The subject came up for Senate discussion, and the senators were told how a Christian revolt in AD 64 had led to the great fire of Rome. In reality, the unbalanced Emperor Nero was himself suspected of having caused the fire but, with so much time having passed since the event, the truth of the fire was forgotten. Once again, the Christians were accused of anti-social behaviour and, with vociferous and argumentative characters such as Irenaeus in their ranks, it was easy to condemn the Christians anew. By declaring that Jesus had been mistaken in his beliefs, Irenaeus had caused Christians to fight amongst themselves, thereby creating disturbances within the Empire. In effect, he had shot his own religion in the foot by drawing attention to it so soon after the Bar Kochba revolt in Jerusalem. From this point, the Roman persecution of Christians began in earnest.

Persecution

In places as far apart as Rome, Lyon and Carthage, Christians were rounded up in their thousands to be burned alive or devoured by animals in public amphitheatres.[5] It is from this period that we find the recorded names of many of the martyrs, including, interestingly, individual stories of women as well as men. In later times (*see* page 119), women were excluded from active Christian practice, but eyewitness reports confirm the Romans' fear of Christian women in that era. There was no gender discrimination whatever in their brutal attempts to decimate the movement. Blandina, for example, was tied in a net and trampled by a bull in the arena at Lyon. Perpetua was slain in Carthage by a gladiator, and Felicitas was ravaged by a wild beast and then executed.[6]

Of more concern to the Romans than internal Christian arguments or their perceived general behaviour was that Christianity, in its various forms, was actually gaining international popularity and had the potential to undermine the disciplines of the Empire. In particular, the notion of Jesus' divinity within the Pauline doctrine posed a significant threat to the authority of the emperors who were deemed to be gods in their own right.

A number of texts containing attacks against Christians have been preserved from this era, among the more objective and reasoned of which is a polemic entitled *The True Discourse* by the philosophical observer Celsus. Writing in about AD 178, he appears to have been on good enough terms with the Christians in Rome, but he simply could not comprehend the logic of their support for a Jewish messiah who had failed in his mission and ended up betrayed and crucified. Celsus claimed this was hardly the mark of a worthy leader and constituted a most disappointing performance by a man reckoned to be the son of a god. He was also baffled by the strange and diverse nature of Christianity, which had no cohesion in its ranks. He wrote: 'There is a lack of unity among themselves. So many sects, and all so different. They have nothing in common save the name Christian.'[7]

There was no bitterness or malice in the work of Celsus, just considered observations, but at the far end of the scale were some extremely vicious assaults, one of which emanated from around AD 225. It is included within a work entitled *The Octavius of Marcus Minucius Felix*, and it provides a good example of how Roman propaganda was contrived to slander Christians as diabolical creatures, not fit to be citizens of the imperial domain. It is almost inconceivable that just 100 years later Constantine would be hosting the first ecumenical Council of Nicaea (AD 325), with himself the newly proclaimed head of the Christian Church. In putting the case against Christianity, the *Octavius* reads:

And now, as wickeder things advance ... those abominable shrines of an impious assembly are maturing themselves throughout the whole world. Assuredly this confederacy ought to be rooted out and execrated. They know one another by secret marks and insignia ... Everywhere also there is mingled among them a certain religion of lust ... they adore the head of an ass, that basest of creatures ... Some say that they worship the genitalia of their priest.

The initiation of young novices is as much to be detested as it is well known. An infant covered over with meal, that it may deceive the unwary, is placed before him who is to be stained with their rites. This infant is slain by the young pupil, who has been urged on as if to harmless blows on the surface of the meal, with dark and secret wounds. Thirstily – O horror! – they lick up its blood; eagerly they divide its limbs. By this victim they are pledged together; with this consciousness of wickedness they are covenanted to mutual silence. Such sacred rites as these are more foul than any sacrilege.[8]

In the wake of such accusations, Emperor Maximinus Thrax decreed on 27 September AD 235, that all Christian bishops and preachers should be seized, their personal wealth confiscated and their churches burned.[9] The captives were sentenced to various forms of punishment and slavery, including penal servitude at the lead mines in Sardinia. On arrival, each captive would have one eye removed and the left foot and right knee damaged to restrict movement. The men were also castrated. If that were not enough, they were chained from their waists to their ankles so they could not stand upright, and the fetters were permanently welded. Not surprisingly, the majority did not live for more than a few months. In those days, being a Christian was in itself dangerous, but to be a known leader was tantamount to signing a personal death warrant.

By the time of Emperor Decius in AD 249, the Christians had become so rebellious that they were proclaimed criminals and their mass persecution began on an official basis. This continued into the reign of Diocletian, who became Emperor in AD 284. During his reign, Christians were required to offer sacrifices to the divine Emperor and they suffered the harshest punishments for disobedience. It was ruled that all Christian meeting-houses be demolished, and disciples who convened alternative assemblies were put to death. All Christian property was confiscated by the magistrates, while all books, testaments and written doctrines of the Faith were publicly burned. Christians of any prominent or notable birthright were barred from public office and Christian slaves were denied any hope of freedom. The protection of Roman law was withdrawn and those who argued with the edicts were slowly roasted alive over fires or otherwise torturously slain. The only possible route to legal representation was for Christians to deny their faith and to offer repentant sacrifice to the Roman gods.[10]

Diocletian attempted to counter the persistent aggression of barbarian invaders by decentralizing control and dividing the Empire into two. From AD 293, the West was managed from Rome, while the East was centred at Byzantium in what is now north-western Turkey. Even so, the assaults continued, notably in the west. These incursions were led by Germanic tribes of Franks and Alamanni, who had previously been held securely across the Rhine. No longer were the Romans an invading power; they were now themselves the constant victims of insurgency from all sides.

One of the most ruthless of the Christians' persecutors under Diocletian was Galerius, governor of the Eastern provinces. He ordered that anyone who did not worship the Emperor above all others would be painfully executed. Just before his death in AD 311, however, Galerius issued a surprising decree of relaxation, giving Christians the right to 'assemble in their conventicles without fear of molestation'.[11] After some two and a half centuries of dread and suppression, the Christians entered a new age of conditional freedom.

The Apostle of Christ

Having been the governor of Britain and Gaul from AD 306, Constantine became Emperor in the West in AD 312, ruling jointly with Licinius in the East. By this time, Christianity had increased its following considerably and was flourishing in Gaul, Portugal, Greece, Spain, Mesopotamia, Germany, Syria, North Africa, Persia, Asia Minor, Britain, and all corners of the Roman domain. Constantine realized that, with his Empire falling apart, there could be some practical merit in harnessing Christianity as a unifying international force that could be used to his own strategic advantage.

Although Constantine had succeeded his father, Constantius Chlorus (AD c250–306), he had a rival for the supreme imperial rank in the person of his brother-in-law, Maxentius. In AD 312, their armies met a little outside Rome at Milvian Bridge, and Constantine was victorious. This victory provided the prime opportunity to declare his personal affiliation with Christianity and he announced that he had seen the vision of a cross in the sky, accompanied by the words 'In this sign conquer'. The Christian leaders were most impressed that a Roman emperor had ridden to victory under their banner.

In the following year, Constantine and Licinius issued the famous Edict of Milan, declaring that the Western and Eastern branches of the Empire would henceforth be neutral with regard to religious worship, thereby officially ending all sanctioned persecution. Licinius later reneged on the Edict and expelled all known Christians from his army before endeavouring to overthrow Constantine in a bid for overall leadership. Constantine then found himself in a position whereby, to uphold the Edict and secure his position, he would need to protect the Christians against possible assaults from the soldiers of Licinius. He therefore summoned the leader of the Christians in Rome, the ageing Bishop Miltiades, and suggested that he, as Emperor, should take charge of the Church in order to ensure its protection.

Among Constantine's first instructions was that the nails from the cross of Jesus should be brought to him – one of which he would have affixed to his crown. His related pronouncement to the bewildered Miltiades was then destined to change the structure of Christianity for all time: 'In the future, We, as the Apostle of Christ, will help choose the Bishop of Rome'.[12] Having declared himself an apostle, Constantine then proclaimed that the magnificent Lateran Palace was to be the future residence of the imperial bishops.

When Miltiades died in AD 314, he was the first Bishop of Rome in a long succession to expire in natural circumstances. Quite suddenly, Christianity had become respectable and was approved as an imperial religion – in fact, as 'the' imperial religion. Following his victory over Licinius at Chrysopolis in AD 324, Constantine became Caesar of all the Roman Empire, thereafter to be known as Constantine the Great.

To replace Miltiades, Constantine (in breach of traditional Christian practice) chose his own associate, Sylvester, to be the first imperial bishop. He was crowned with great pomp and ceremony – a far cry from the shady backroom proceedings of earlier Christian ritual. Gone were the days of fear and persecution, but the price for this freedom was veneration of the Emperor. This was precisely what the Christian forebears had struggled so hard to avoid, but the rank and file had no choice in the matter, and the existing priests were instructed that their Church was now formally attached to the Empire. It was now the Church of Rome and its perceived originator, the first Bishop of Rome, was henceforth deemed to have been St Peter.

In reality, Peter had never been a bishop of anywhere. The first bishop, installed in Rome during Peter's lifetime in AD 58,[13] was Prince Linus of Britain, the son of King Caractacus. This was confirmed in AD 180 by Irenaeus of Lyon who, in writing about Peter and Paul, stated: 'The apostles having founded and built up the Church at Rome, committed the ministry of its supervision to Linus.' In his second epistle to Timothy 4:21, St Paul had written: 'Eubulus greeteth thee, and Pudens and Linus, and Claudia, and all the brethren.' Eubulus (eu-boulos: 'well advised' or 'prudent') was a variation of Aristobulus (aristo-boulos: 'best advised'). Pudens was the Roman senator Rufus Pudens to whom Gladys, the daughter of Caractacus and sister of Linus, was married. She thereby gained the name Claudia Rufina Britannica, as confirmed by the Roman writer, Martial, in AD 68.[14]

Having been installed into high office by the Emperor, Bishop Sylvester was too overwhelmed to perceive the trap into which he was leading the disciples of the Faith. He only saw the route to salvation offered by Constantine, but although this monumental step gained Christians the right to move freely in society, their hierarchy was now to be encased in gold, ermine, jewels and all the trappings that Christ himself had decried. Many were outraged that their leaders had been seduced and corrupted by the very regime that had been the bane of their ancestors. They declared that the new-found status of acceptability was not a victory of conversion, but rather an evil cloud of absolute defeat – a profanation of all the principles they had so long held sacred.

Until this point, the Christian message had been gaining support in all quarters. Those spreading the gospel knew that Constantine and his predecessors were sorely weakened in the face of the Church's growing popularity. It was, after all, one of the reasons why Constantine's father had married the British Christian princess Elaine (Greek: Helen. Roman: Helena). Sylvester and his colleagues in Rome may have considered the new alliance of Church and State to be a politically sound manoeuvre, but Christians saw it for precisely what it was: a strategic buy-out by the enemy. They claimed that the spiritual message of Jesus had been subverted by the idolatry of a self-seeking power striving to prevent its own imperial demise.

Apart from various cult beliefs, the Romans had long worshipped the emperors in their capacity as gods descended from others such as Neptune and Jupiter. Although Constantine had proclaimed his Christianity, he was still intent on retaining his own godly status, and he found the way to do this in AD 314, when a Church synod was convened at Arles in the province of Gaul[15], the purpose of which was to establish forgiveness for those Christians who had denied their faith during the era of the persecutions. In order to retain his traditionally divine status, Constantine introduced the omnipotent God of the Christians as his very own personal sponsor. He then dealt with the anomalies of doctrine by replacing certain aspects of Christian ritual with the familiar pagan traditions of sun worship, together with other teachings of Syrian and Persian origin (*see* page 147). The new religion of the Roman Church was constructed as a hybrid to appease all influential factions. By this means, Constantine looked towards a common and unified international religion with himself at its head.

Helen of the Cross

Providing wealth and trappings for his new Church enterprise was no problem for Constantine, but he was still to obtain the crucifixion nails from the cross of Jesus which he had asked Miltiades to find for him. And so it was that in AD 326 Constantine's 80-year-old mother, Helena, went to Jerusalem to search for them. Tradition relates that she took advice from a divinely inspired resident named Judas, and it was later reported that Helena had excavated an earth mound, miraculously to discover all three of the crosses in accordance with the gospel accounts. Not knowing which was the cross of Jesus, each was carried to the bedside of a woman at the point of death. The first two had no effect but, on touching her with the third, the woman was completely cured, and it was known that the 'true cross' had been found.[16]

If that were not enough of a story to provide the first great myth of the new Church, the account was embellished even further. Helena then carried the cross to the grave of a recently buried man and, on touching his tomb with the relic, he came back to life and arose from the ground. Even more miraculous was the fact that the three nails which had pinned Jesus before he was taken down from the cross were still embedded in the wood. On Helena's return to Rome, one of the nails was affixed to Constantine's helmet, another to his horse's bridle, and the third was used when forging the venerated Iron Crown of Lombardy (the *Corona Ferrea*), which resides today in the Cathedral of Monza.[17] As for the cross, there are supposed fragments and splinters from it in numerous locations around the world.

This is the way the story is told, but there is absolutely no documentary record of the events from the time it was said to have occurred. The first literary mention of Helena's discovery was written more than 20 years later, some time after her death, in the *Catecheses* of St Cyril of Jerusalem. It does not appear in the *Ecclesiastical History* of Eusebius, who had previously compiled the reports of Helena's trip to Jerusalem; nor does it appear in any other authoritative work of the era.

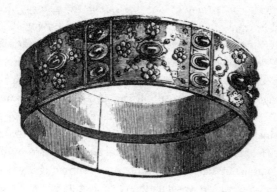

The Iron Crown of Lombardy

Apart from Helena's Jerusalem visit, little else was said about her in the Roman annals until 1622. Prior to that, the key records of her life were kept in England,[18] but then a new Helena myth emerged, instigated by Pope Gregory XV. Just a century earlier, England's Queen Elizabeth I had been excommunicated by Rome when she established the Anglican Protestant Church, thereby separating the realm formally from Catholicism. Pope Gregory decided to cut all historical ties and, in the course of this, invented a new place of origin for Helena. He achieved this by way of his newly established *Congregatio Propaganda Fide* (the College of the Propaganda of Cardinals) whose primary function was to enforce papal dogma wherever it disagreed with customary opinion or documented history.

Although the term 'propaganda' has now moved into general usage, it was first introduced by the Vatican as a specific aspect of dogma. The word originated from Church Latin, akin to the propagation of plants – 'breeding like or cloned specimens from a parent stock'. The objective was to mentally clone the members of Catholicism as obedient, unquestioning servants of their figurative parent, the Pope (*papa* = father). Hence, the Church not only made use of propaganda, it invented the word.[19]

A century or so later, Gregory's revised history of Helena appeared in translation by the English historian Edward Gibbon in his 1776 *History of the Decline and Fall of the Roman Empire*. This was followed by a vindication in 1779, after his spurious accounts of early Christian development were criticized by academic scholars. But Gibbon had converted to Catholicism in 1753 and had felt duty bound to represent Helena in accordance with the then official Church doctrine. According to Pope Gregory (and as repeated by Gibbon), Helena was born into an innkeeping family from the small town of Naissus in the Balkans. Gibbon was subsequently obliged to confess that this notion was a matter of conjecture but, notwithstanding this, his original publication has since been slavishly followed by the subsequent writers of some reference books and encyclopaedias.

All pre-Gibbon records in Britain relate that Princess Elaine (Helena), the daughter of King Coel II, was born and raised at Colchester, and she became renowned for her expertise at political administration. Her husband, Constantius, was proclaimed Emperor at York (Caer Evroc). In AD 290, he enlarged the York archbishopric at Helena's request and, in due course, was buried at York. In recognition of Helena's later pilgrimage to Jerusalem and the resultant legend of her discovery, the church of Helen of the Cross was built at Colchester, where the city's coat-of-arms was established as her cross, with three silver crowns for its arms.

From the time of the Reformation, and especially after the College of Propaganda was instituted, the Vatican undertook a structured programme of disinformation about many aspects of Church history, and this continued with increasing intensity. In practice, however, the revised Roman view of Helena is vague in the extreme, with various Catholic accounts contradicting one another. Many churchmen have put forward the Balkan theory, as repeated by Gibbon; some have located Helena's birthplace near the Bosphorus; a few cite her as a Roman native; and some give her birthplace as Bithynia in Turkey.[20]

Apart from the English records, and perhaps more importantly under the circumstances, the pre-1662 information from Rome also upheld Helena's British heritage, as did other writings in Europe. These included the 16th-century *Epistola* of the German writer, Melancthon, who wrote: 'Helen was undoubtedly a British Princess'. The Jesuit Catholic annals (even the 1905 Jesuit book, *Pilgrim Walks in Rome*)[21] state, when detailing Constantine's own birth in Britain: 'It is one of Catholic England's greatest glories to count St Helena and Constantine among its children, St Helena being the only daughter of King Coilus.'[22]

In all of this, the one person the Church and its more dutiful scribes have chosen to ignore is the most revered of all Rome's ecclesiastical scholars. He was Cardinal Cesare Baronius, the Vatican librarian who, between 1570 and 1601, compiled the 12 folios of the *Annales Ecclesiastici a Christi nato ad annum 1198* (Ecclesiastical Annals from the nativity of Christ to 1198). In this work, when confronted by the propaganda of Pope Gregory, he stated: 'The man must be mad who, in the face of universal antiquity, refuses to believe that Constantine and his mother were Britons, born in Britain'.[23]

It was as a result of this and a series of other such contradictory statements made by Baronius and subsequent truthfully-minded Catholic academics, that the Church felt obliged to introduce one of its most ludicrous items of dogma – the doctrine of Infallibility – pronounced at the First Vatican Council in 1870. This claimed that 'the Pope is incapable of error when defining matters of Church teaching and morality from his throne'.

Feuds and Fragments

The Josephus Dispute

In his 1st-century *Antiquities of the Jews*, Flavius Josephus made two references to Jesus (*see* page 4). On one occasion, he wrote of Albinus, the Procurator (provincial governor) of Judaea:

> Albinus was put upon the road; so he assembled the Sanhedrin of judges, and brought before them the brother of Jesus who was called Christ, whose name was James.[1]

On another occasion, when dealing with the reign of Emperor Tiberius, Josephus stated:

> Now there was about this time Jesus, a wise man, if it be lawful to call him a man; for he was a doer of wonderful works, a teacher of such men as receive the truth with pleasure. He drew over to him both many of the Jews and many of the Gentiles. He was the Christ. And when Pilate, at the suggestion of the principal men amongst us, had condemned him to the cross, those that loved him at the first did not forsake him … And the tribe of Christians, so named from him, are not extinct at this day.[2]

During recent times, it has become fashionable to regard these entries not as documentary evidence of Jesus in history, but as proof that he did not exist. The basic premise is as follows: 'Josephus was a Jew, and he would not therefore have written in such a way about the man whose titular name was applied to Christianity'. As a result it is claimed that the writings of Josephus must have been falsified by way of Christian interpolation. These claims are accompanied by unsubstantiated comments such as: 'Unable to provide any historical evidence for Jesus, later Christians forged the proof that they so badly needed to shore up their literalist interpretation of the gospels'.[3] Beyond the fact that Jesus and his immediate community were also themselves Jewish, statements of this kind have led to much debate over the years and, since it is a matter of some concern to those on either side of the dispute, we should consider the various arguments involved.

In many cases, the main ambition of books which contain such negative assertions is to ridicule and cast doubt upon the ethics and provenance of Christianity, sometimes to stir antagonism against Christians in the same way that anti-Semitic literature is aimed against Jews. Jesus Christ is said not to have existed, hence there were no Christians, and the whole scenario of their early presence is reckoned to be a myth invented by churchmen in later times.

That there were Christians in the 1st century, as described in the Josephus text, is not in doubt. They were mentioned in the *Annals of Imperial Rome* (*see* page 4), and the Romans recorded that the term 'Christian' referred to the followers of Christ – the perceived king (*christos*) of a Nazarene sect of Jews, who had been sentenced to execution by Pontius Pilate.

A Roman barrister named Pliny was the governor for Emperor Trajan (AD 98–117) in Bithynia, Asia Minor. He wrote to Trajan around the turn of the century discussing Christian ceremonies that included recitations about Christ and a communal meal called the Lord's Supper. This letter, one of seven which have been preserved from Pliny, is not without its amusement. The Emperor had instructed him to ensure that the law against the swearing of oaths by clubs and societies was upheld in Bithynia. Pliny discovered, however, that the Christians repeatedly swore an oath at their meetings – but it was an oath not to break the law and not to commit crimes! 'What should I do about that?' Pliny asked the Emperor.[4] In reply Trajan changed the emphasis of the question. He claimed that a greater offence than the Oath was the fact that these people were Christians. He instructed Pliny to challenge them: 'If they are informed against and the charge is proved, they shall be punished … If anyone denies that he is a Christian and proves it by worshipping our gods, he shall be pardoned.'

At about the same time, Ignatius, an early Christian in Antioch, also wrote about the Lord's Supper, and about the ceremony of bread and wine which he called the Eucharist (Greek: *eucharisistia* = thanksgiving).[5] The Roman senator Cornelius Tacitus, who compiled the *Annals of Imperial Rome*, was a colleague of Pliny, but was not so tolerant of the Christians whom he said were 'a class hated for their abominations'. This attitude, which stemmed mainly from Rome rather than the provinces, led to a series of lengthy and scholarly discourses being sent to the emperors in an attempt to explain the merits of the Christian faith. Beginning with Quadratus of Athens writing in about AD 130, through to Eusebius of Caesaria in the early 4th century, these learned Christian men became known as the Apologists.[6]

There is plenty of evidence in the Roman archives of Christians (the *Christiani*) during the time of Flavius Josephus, so the fact that he, as an Israelite Jew, mentioned them in his *Antiquities* is unsurprising, particularly when we discover from his autobiography that he wrote this work when he was living in Rome subsequent to the AD 66–70 Jewish Revolt in Judaea. Having been instrumental in negotiating the surrender of Jerusalem to the Romans when the cause against them was lost, Josephus moved to Rome where he penned a comprehensive history of the Jewish nation. Writing in his native Aramaic, he explained that he was assisted by scribes who translated his text into Greek for the wider market.[7]

In writing his passages about Jesus, Josephus did not claim any personal empathy or affiliation with the Christians; he simply stated that 'the tribe of Christians, so named from him [Jesus Christ], are not extinct at this day'. There has probably never been a Christian who has thought of their faith-inspired movement as a 'tribe'; such terminology is expressly Israelite in concept and certainly does not suggest any Christian interpolation. Neither is there any occasion in the New Testament, nor in any known early Christian literature, where Jesus is referred to as a 'wise man'.[8] According to modern Hebrew academia, the Jews of the era would not have considered Jesus in godly terms, as would the Christians, but (in line with Josephus) they would undoubtedly have perceived him as a wise man with a tribal following.[9]

A primary argument from the anti-Jesus camp is that the quotes from the *Antiquities* of Josephus set out above do not appear in any manuscripts of the work prior to those of the 4th century. This is a thoroughly nonsensical assertion because there are no surviving manuscript copies of the *Antiquities* from before the 4th century.

A further argument is that, if such entries had existed before the time of Eusebius, then he would not have been the first to cite them in his *Demonstratio Evangelica* (AD c320). In this respect, it is maintained that Origen of Alexandria (AD c182–251) would surely have mentioned the *Antiquities* passages. A presumed silence is offered as proof of non-existence, even though (unlike Eusebius in the formative years of the Roman Church) Origen had no particular reason to discuss the Josephus entries. They conveyed nothing that was not already common currency in Christian literature. Furthermore, they were not in any way supportive of Christianity; they simply mentioned Jesus, his brother James, and the existence of Christians at a time when these things were not matters of debate.

The fact is, however, that Origen did indeed cite the *Antiquities* on two occasions. He made the point in his *Commentaries on the Gospel of St Matthew* that it was a 'wonderful thing' that Josephus had made reference to Jesus and his brother James, even 'though he did not accept Jesus as the Christ'.[10] Similarly, in *Contra Celsum* (Against Celsus), Origen referred to Josephus and specifically to the '18th book of his *Antiquities of the Jews*'. In this context, Origen emphasized once again that Josephus had seen fit as a Jew to discuss Jesus in this work, 'although not believing in Jesus as the Christ'.[11]

The debate over the Josephus writings concerning Jesus has become so heated that they have even been identified by their own name: the *Testimonium Flavianum* (the Flavius Testimony). In modern times, the most frequently quoted work on the subject, as upheld by the Jesus dissenters, is a book by Robert Eisler that emerged from Germany in 1929,[12] but the first known historical challenge was offered by an anonymous 5th-century author in an assault against Jews rather than Christians.[13]

Earlier, when St Jerome (AD c340–420) produced a Latin translation of the *Antiquities*, he changed the wording slightly to read 'he [Jesus] was believed to be the Christ', rather than as in the Josephus original, 'he was the Christ'. This was a strange amendment for a Christian leader to make since in effect it lessened the impact of the statement, and it led to criticism from both Christians and Jews. But it was not until the late 16th century that Cardinal Baronius, in his *Annales Ecclesiastici* (*see* page 31), saw fit to stand up for the original wording of Josephus as against that of St Jerome. In 1592, a German Protestant named Lucas Osiander then disagreed with the Catholic viewpoint of Baronius[14] – following which the Jews attacked Osiander, only to be challenged by other Christians.

By the 19th century, with some Jews in opposition to Christians, and Christians arguing among themselves, it became open season for the anti-Semites and anti-Christians, all claiming that the work of Josephus was a conspiratorial forgery. And so the battle still rages, becoming ever more tedious with each new addition to the books written by those who, for reasons best known to themselves, dislike either Christians or Jews, or both.[15]

In the final event, we are left with precisely the same text with which we began – the oldest extant Greek copies of Josephus' work, which state exactly what they have always stated. Do they prove the existence of Jesus? No. What they prove is that Josephus believed in the existence of Jesus, just as did the Christians who wrote the gospels and the Romans who collated the research for the *Imperial Annals* of Tacitus. History is not about proof; it is about documentary evidence and, while the shallow criticisms of the *Antiquities* amount to nothing of any substance, the documentary evidences of Jesus and the early Christians arise from contemporary Jewish, Christian and Roman sources alike.

Gospel Parallels

This debate provides a clear example of the manner in which documents of contemporary record may be challenged in later times by those with motives for having different opinions. Perhaps some of the challenges are justified, while on other occasions they are not. Either way, once a contrasting theory has been published, it becomes possible for subsequent correspondents to claim that the original record has been discredited, when all that has happened is that it has been criticized. The choice, however, remains with each of us: we can accept textually recorded history, we can ignore it or we can reject it, but we cannot delude ourselves into thinking that our personal rejection or criticism will in some way invalidate the original record. The writings of Josephus, Tacitus, Eusebius, or the contents of the *Anglo Saxon Chronicle* for that matter, will not go away just because they do not always suit the philosophies of present-day culture. They are records of their times and places of origin. For a wider insight, they can be compared with other documents from their respective eras – but everything else is just conjecture.

The Jewish writings of Josephus add a great deal of corroboration to the Christian gospels. Beyond his references to Jesus, his work discusses many of the same characters and events while, at the same time, filling in numerous gaps and giving details of rulers, priests, politics and religious factions that would otherwise remain mysterious to modern Bible readers. In fact, the similarities between the gospel of Luke, the Acts of the Apostles and the *Antiquities* text are so striking that it has even been suggested that the author of these New Testament books might have known Josephus in Rome.[16]

These similarities relate to items in Luke and the Acts which are not present in the synoptic gospels of Matthew and Mark. For instance, both Luke and the *Antiquities* state that Jesus was active in the latter reign of Emperor Tiberius (AD 14–37). While Luke actually specifies that Jesus' mission began in AD 29,[17] neither Matthew, Mark nor John make any mention of this. Both Luke and the *Antiquities* discuss the AD 6 census in Judaea conducted by the senator Cyrenius (Quirinius) at the behest of Caesar Augustus.[18] Again, this does not feature in the gospels of Matthew, Mark or John.

The gospels of Matthew and Mark both detail that a daughter of Queen Herodias claimed the head of John the Baptist on a charger, but they do not name this daughter.[19] Josephus does relate, however, that the daughter of Herodius was called Salome,[20] while also confirming that the Baptist was executed by King Herod-Antipas, the son of Herod the Great.[21] Over and above these specifics, Josephus gives us a detailed insight into characters such as the Herodian dynasty of kings and their wives, Pontius Pilate and Joseph Caiaphas the high priest. He also explains the differences between the Jewish sects of the Pharisees, Sadducees and Essenes which all play important, but somewhat ambiguous, roles in the New Testament narrative.

Interestingly, archaeology can now confirm the detail within a significant amount of Josephus' writings with the finding of ancient Israelite coins that were in circulation through to the Jewish Revolt (*see* page 15). On the obverse of one particular coin inscribed *shequel yisroael* (shekel of Israel)[22] were three pomegranates which, like the vine, were symbols of fertility and generation. By way of Mosaic law, the Jews were not permitted to stamp their coins with the heads of kings or priests as the Romans did for their emperors. Such graven images of people were expressly forbidden.[23]

At present, the world's widest ever survey of ancient coins is being undertaken by scholars from Oxford and Valencia Universities, the Bibliothèque Nationale de France and the British Museum. The studies are revealing just how divided were the Eastern and Western parts of the Roman Empire during the centuries before they were amalgamated at the time of Emperor Constantine. Examination of over 30,000 coins from 500 different countries shows how the nations of Spain, Gaul and Britain in the West downgraded or abandoned their cultures and religious traditions in favour of the Roman example. In contrast, the people of

Greece, Asia Minor, the Levant and Egypt emphasized aspects of their heritage on their coins in order to reduce Roman cultural dominion.[24] In these Mediterranean regions of the Jewish homeland and diaspora, the iconography was rich with religious identity – coins displaying everything from Phoenician gods to Noah's Ark. There is a clear picture here of why Christianity became so important to Constantine as a newly developed universal religion that could envelop so many others.[25]

A Secret Gospel

Since the Greek transcript of the *Antiquities* existed long before St Jerome made his Latin translation, there is little point in pursuing the debate over Christian involvement in the original text. We can presume that Josephus was acquainted with Christians in Rome (maybe even with the gospel author of Luke) at the time he compiled the work. As we have seen with the gospel of Mark (*see* page 10), it is evident that the early Christian Fathers were not above doctoring their own inherited literature. A comparatively recent discovery was made by Morton Smith, later professor of Ancient History at Columbia University in New York, concerning the gospel of Mark in relation to a deletion from the original text rather than, this time, to an addition.

In 1941, Smith was studying for a doctorate at the Hebrew University in Jerusalem, when he was invited by the custodian of the Holy Sepulchre to visit the nearby Greek monastery at Mar Saba. Fascinated by the differences between monastic ritual and conventional church worship, Smith returned to Mar Saba in 1958 to continue his research. While cataloguing the library's manuscript collection he ascertained that, following a monastery fire in the 18th century, some individual documents had been bound or glued for convenience into the body of more substantial works, whose titles the books carried on their covers.[26]

One of these books was an edition of the works of St Ignatius of Antioch, but bound into it was a manuscript copy of a letter written in about AD 195 by the pre-Roman Church Father, St Clement of Alexandria. Photographs were taken for subsequent study and stylistic analysis by academics from Jerusalem, Athens, England and America. Of the fourteen scholars involved in the project, only two were unconvinced of the letter's authenticity, but following a majority decision, the details were made known publicly at a congress of the Society of Biblical Literature by a spokesman for the General Theological Seminary in 1960. Twenty years later, after more extensive analysis, the authenticated letter was introduced into the standard register of the works of St Clement in 1980.[27]

Clement's 2nd-century letter was addressed to a colleague named Theodore, and it discussed an unorthodox Alexandrian group called the Carpocrations.[28] Named after their founder, Carpocrates, they were not followers of the Pauline doctrine as later adopted by Rome, but were inspired by the teachings of Mary Magdalene, Martha of Bethany, and their mission colleague Salome.[29] According to Clement, the very concept of female ministry was entirely sinful, and he condemned the Carpocrations, stating:

> Even if they should say something true, one who loves the truth should not, even so, agree with them. For not all true things are the truth; nor should that truth which seems true according to human opinions be preferred to the true truth – that according to the faith ... To them one must never give way; nor, when they put forward their falsifications, should one concede that the secret gospel is by Mark, but should deny it on oath. For not all true things are to be said to all men.[30]

This is a blatant admission from within the Pauline sect that there was a perceived difference between 'the truth' and 'the truth according to the faith'. It is a key example of preferred belief as against documentary evidence – even to the extent that, if the gospel text does not fit the doctrinal belief, then the text must be disregarded.

The 'secret gospel', to which Clement referred, was a section that was henceforth withdrawn from the gospel of Mark, and thus does not appear in the synoptic gospels of Matthew or Luke. Now appearing only in the gospel of John, and in a slightly different form, it is the sequence which features Mary Magdalene and Martha at the time of the events surrounding the raising by Jesus of Lazarus at Bethany.[31]

The story begins when Mary and Martha send word to Jesus that his friend Lazarus was sick, and John explains that the man had died before Jesus arrived at the house in Bethany. John 11:20–29 continues:

> Then Martha, as soon as she heard that Jesus was coming, went and met him: but Mary sat still in the house … [Martha] called Mary her sister secretly, saying, The Master is come, and calleth for thee. As soon as she heard that, she arose quickly and came unto him.

No reason is given for Mary's hesitant behaviour but, apart from that, the passage seems straightforward enough – Martha left the house, but Mary stayed indoors until summoned by Jesus.

The main difference between John and the secret Mark account relates to the behaviour of Mary Magdalene. The portion of Mark suppressed by Clement relates that Mary did indeed come from the house to greet Jesus before receiving his summons, whereupon 'the disciples rebuked her'. The question that arises from both accounts is therefore: Why would it have been acceptable for Martha to step out to meet Jesus, but not acceptable for Mary to do so until she had received his permission?

In the first place, the two women would have been 'sitting shivah' – a seven-day ritual of mourning for the departed Lazarus – in which event it was against Jewish custom for either of the women to leave the house. Martha is not mentioned, however, in the Mark account, whereas in the John version her action goes unquestioned, even though it was strictly unlawful. In both cases, the woman who had to be specifically invited from the house by Jesus was Mary. This was an aspect of bridal practice, a code whereby a woman could emerge from *shivah* in order to greet her husband so long as she had received his express consent and instruction to do so.[32]

The John account leaves Mary in her rightful place in the house without explanation, but the more explicit Mark text was problematic for Clement because it made the marital reality too apparent. In his own words, it exposed the 'truth' rather than conveying the alternative 'truth according to the faith'. The subsequently withheld text of the Mark gospel made it perfectly clear that Jesus and Mary were man and wife.

The Magdalene Papyrus

Following the account of the raising of Lazarus, the gospels of Matthew, Mark and John each relate Mary Magdalene's anointing of Jesus at Bethany. Not only does this constitute an aspect of dynastic bridal ritual – a matter to which we shall return (*see* page 49) – but it was also the means by which Jesus formally became a Messiah (an Anointed One: from the Hebrew verb *maisach* 'to anoint'). In view of this, it is fortunate that the earliest known fragments of a canonical gospel text relate to this very sequence from Matthew 26. (They are aptly the property of Magdalen College at Oxford University.)

The three scraps, just a few square-centimetres each from a codex (book) with Greek writing on papyrus, which had been unearthed at Luxor in Egypt, were donated to the college library by Reverend Charles B Huleatt in 1901. Subsequently known as the Magdalene Fragments, they were thought to originate from the 2nd century, but a re-dating in 1994 revealed them as 1st-century relics, possibly from the AD 60s, making them older than the 2nd-century fragment of John's gospel at the John Rylands Library in Manchester. *The Times* newspaper gave the Magdalene Fragments story front-page coverage on Christmas Eve 1994, following which the worldwide press and media followed suit.[33]

The 8-cm high John fragment, from about AD 125, contains extracts of a few lines from John 18:31–33, and on the reverse from

2nd-century gospel fragment of John and 1st-century fragment of Mark

verses 37–38. Also discovered in Upper Egypt, and also in Greek from a papyrus codex, it relates to the trial of Jesus by Pontius Pilate.[34]

Another tiny papyrus fragment, known as 7Q5, was found at Qumrân by the Dead Sea in Judaea. Dating again from the 1st century, it was thought in the 1960s that it might be an item from the gospel of Mark 6:52–53 (the loaves and fishes story). However, the scrap is smaller than a couple of postage stamps and, since there are only a few legible characters in a broken sequence, it has not been possible for the Mark provenance to be confirmed positively, although the odds appear to be in its favour.[35] Given that all documents from Qumrân date from before AD 68, when the settlement was vacated after being overrun by the 10th Roman Legion during the Judaean Revolt, this would make the Mark fragment much the same age as the Magdalene extract from Matthew. Meanwhile, the oldest known fragment from the gospel of Luke is that known as the Paris Papyrus P4. Dated to the late 1st century, the fragment contains Luke 3:23 and 5:36, and is held at the Bibliothèque Nationale de France.

Marriage of the Messiah

The Enigma of John

Before progressing with the story of the Church of Rome and the bishops' 4th-century gospel selection for the New Testament canon, it is necessary to take a look at the gospel of John. This work differs from the synoptic gospels in content, style and concept. It is clearly influenced by the traditions of a particular community sect and it is far from naive in its account of Jesus. Consequently, the gospel of John has its own adherents who emphasize its distinctive origin from those of Matthew, Mark and Luke. John also includes some major items which do not appear elsewhere – a factor that has led many scholars to conclude that overall it may be a more accurate testimony.

John is the only gospel to carry the story of the raising of Lazarus – with Jesus bringing him alive from the tomb after his death four days earlier. This is reckoned to be one of Jesus' primary miracles, and is stated to have been the reason why the high priest, Joseph Caiaphas, and the Pharisees became so fearful that they 'took counsel together for to put him to death'.[1] Yet, for all its seeming importance as a precursor to Jesus' trial and crucifixion, the story does not appear anywhere else in the canon. Another example of evidence unique to the gospel of John is the wedding feast at Cana, where Jesus is reported to have turned water into wine.[2] Whereas the raising of Lazarus was Jesus' last miracle; the water and wine transformation was his first, and it is similarly confined to the gospel of John.

It is only in John that we learn about the meeting between Jesus and Mary Magdalene in the sepulchre garden after his entombment.[3] Then, subsequent to that event, it is John alone that recounts how Jesus joined the apostles and dined with them after a day's fishing on Lake Tiberius.[4] In some ways, John has similarities with Mark – especially on those occasions where Mark differs from Matthew and Luke. For instance, the Mark and John gospels each begin with John the Baptist and his baptism of Jesus in AD 29. Neither relates anything about Jesus' birth, his infancy, nor any of the pre-ministerial events that have such emphasis applied to them in the gospels of Matthew and Luke.

Luke, the Syrian physician, is generally thought to have been the author of the Luke gospel, whilst the primary candidate for the Mark authorship is considered to have been St Paul's colleague, Johannis Marcus, who is referred to in Acts 12:25 and 15:37 as John Mark.[5]

Whereas the Mark and Luke gospels first appeared in Rome, the gospel of Matthew has a rather more Jewish flavour and appears to have emanated from Judaea. A possible candidate for its authorship is the levitical priest Matthew Annas of Jerusalem.[6] If this were to be the case, then the gospel would be older than the late 1st-century date generally ascribed to it – more in line, in fact, with the AD 60s era of the Magdalene fragment of Matthew (see page 42).

In writing for the Jewish market, the author of Matthew used a number of unique terms, such as his 34 mentions of 'the kingdom of heaven' (the *malkut shamayim*), a phrase which does not appear in any other gospel. Matthew contains 11 specific quotations from the Old Testament (the so-called 'proof texts'),[7] which demonstrate how Jesus fulfilled certain prophecies of the biblical scriptures – for example, 'Now all this was done, that it might be fulfilled which was spoken of the Lord by the prophet'.[8] Matthew also concentrates rather more on lengthy discourses from Jesus, such as at the Sermon on the Mount,[9] in the course of which the *Beatitudes* preached by Jesus are presented almost as the new Commandments.[10]

In considering the gospel of John, we discover that its position as fourth in the canonical listing has nothing to do with it being younger or less influential than the others. The *Catholic Encyclopedia* relates that in many ancient copies of the canon, John was inserted before, or immediately after, the gospel of Matthew.[11] The narrative of John has many peculiarities and intellectual qualities that give it a very distinctive character. It is less dramatic in style than the synoptic gospels, but at the same time more romantically poetic, with Jesus referred to as the 'word of God', the 'light of the world, and the 'true vine'. There is also a personal intimacy with Jesus and a genuineness of style whereby the gospel's message is conveyed with a precision and intensity not evident in the others. John does not dwell on the labours of Jesus in Galilee as do Matthew, Mark and Luke, but instead concentrates on his ministry in Judaea with such detail that the author would seem to have been very close to him during that period. Indeed, when compared to the Dead Sea Scrolls, there is so much of the fourth gospel that is distinctly Nazarene in character that it presents the closest of all representations of what could perhaps be determined as an eyewitness report of Jesus and his community. In these respects, John could very well have been the first written of all the canonical gospels.[12]

Unveiling the Author

The gospel of John is generally associated with the apostle John Boanerges, otherwise known as John the Evangelist or John the Divine. However, unlike the book of The Revelation (*The Apocalypse of St John the Divine*), whose author actually gives his name as John,[13] the gospel is anonymous. Moreover, it was certainly not written by the same hand as The Revelation, nor by the author of the New Testament tract John 1, or the epistles John 2 and John 3.

The main reason for the nominal association is that, towards the end of John we are advised that a personal source of the information contained in the gospel was 'the disciple whom Jesus loved'. This disciple is traditionally considered to have been John although there is no documentary basis for this. In any event, it is not stated that the beloved disciple was the author of the text; the author simply states: 'This is the disciple which testifieth of these things, and wrote these things; and we know that his testimony is true.'[14] The gospel of John is, in fact, the only gospel to make any mention of the 'disciple whom Jesus loved' and, on each occasion, he is referred to in the third person, thereby disassociating him from the gospel's authorship.

Apart from John Boanerges, another contender for the 'beloved' title has long been Mary Magdalene, whom Jesus was said to have loved.[15] However, one of the entries in John describes the crucifixion scene where Jesus appointed the beloved disciple as his mother's guardian. This reference immediately rules out Mary Magdalene since, once again (as with the use of 'his testimony' in the above quotation), the wording specifically denotes a male disciple in this context:

> When Jesus therefore saw his mother, and the disciple standing
> by, whom he loved, he saith unto his mother, 'Madam, behold thy
> son … And from that hour the disciple took her unto his own'.[16]

Apart from the 'beloved disciple', who is cited in John, only Mary Magdalene and Jesus' female relatives are mentioned as being at the cross. This is the case in all the gospels. There is no mention of Peter or any of the apostles at the scene. Prior to the event, Matthew 26:56 and Mark 14:50 both relate that, after Jesus' arrest, the disciples 'deserted him and fled'. Clearly, however, there was one who did not. This might indicate that, as well a being an apostle, he was perhaps also a member of Jesus' family.

The enigmatic disciple subsequently appears in the entombment sequence, which again rules out Mary Magdalene who talks to the beloved character in this scene. It similarly rules out Peter, since he is also separately named:

> Then she [Mary Magdalene] runneth, and cometh to Simon Peter,
> and to the other disciple, whom Jesus loved, and saith unto them,
> They have taken away the Lord out of the sepulchre, and we
> know not where they have laid him.[17]

Subsequently, in a conversation between Peter and Jesus, there are two further references to the 'disciple whom Jesus loved',[18] but his name is not given.

Notwithstanding all this seeming ambiguity, the author of John was not actually remiss concerning the identity of the beloved disciple. John 11:5 states: 'Now Jesus loved Martha, and her sister, and Lazarus'. A little later, in the sequence of Jesus raising his friend Lazarus from the tomb, John 11:36 confirms the relationship yet again: 'Then said the Jews, Behold how he loved him!'

So, if Lazarus was the 'disciple whom Jesus loved', how does this equate with the 'beloved disciple' reference in respect of the Last Supper? It is said in John 13:23: 'Now there was leaning on Jesus' bosom one of his disciples, whom Jesus loved'. Jesus, we are told, was at the supper with his twelve apostles, but Lazarus is not mentioned in any of the New Testament's apostolic listings.

To answer this question, we have only to look at the Matthew and Mark entries relating to when Mary Magdalene anointed Jesus at Bethany. Matthew states that this took place at the house of Simon,[19] and Mark states that it took place at the house of Simon,[20] but the gospel of John does not mention Simon in this regard. In the John account, the anointing takes place at the house of Lazarus, with his sister Martha also present along with Judas and other apostles.[21]

Given that St Clement removed the 'raising of Lazarus' sequence from the gospel of Mark, the synoptic gospels make no reference whatever to Lazarus. But in the gospel of John, the apostle Simon Zelotes is re-named Lazarus by virtue of his entombment. This was clearly an allusion to Lazarus (Eleazar) the Old Testament steward of Abraham since the cave in which Simon was placed was known as Abraham's Bosom.[22] The 'beloved disciple' therefore, as stated in all instances in John, was Simon Zelotes, who became known as Lazarus. There is, however, an interesting parallel in the gospel of Luke, which retains a parable about a certain Lazarus in the bosom of Abraham, with references to rising from the dead.[23]

Returning again to the authorship of John, it seems evident that Simon-Lazarus, the beloved disciple, was a primary source of the gospel's content, but we know that he was not the author. We also know, from various references in John, that the devotional sisters of Simon-Lazarus were Martha and Mary, and that Simon's wife was Jesus' sister Salome. It was she who accompanied Jesus' mother and Mary Magdalene to the foot of the cross,[24] and who subsequently went with them to Jesus' tomb.[25] These are the very same women (Mary Magdalene, Martha and Salome) whose female mission was considered a sinful practice by St Clement in his written assault against the Carpocration followers of their teaching (*see* page 40).

Martha is very much a secondary character in the canonical accounts, and is twice portrayed as serving food in the presence of Jesus and Mary Magdalene.[26] By contrast, Mary is seen as a constant companion of Jesus and was closely allied to his mother. Her importance is strongly emphasized in John by way of her conversation with Jesus after his entombment. John is the only gospel to recount this episode – a private conversation, with recorded dialogue, between Jesus and Mary Magdalene. They were alone together, and yet we are given the details of the intimate words spoken between them. There are therefore only two people who could possibly have written the gospel of John, and it was not written by Jesus. No one else was present to hear them talk in the sepulchre garden, by virtue of which the author of John (whether by her own hand or dictation) can only have been Mary Magdalene.

Bridal Anointing

Since we know that St Clement of Alexandria withdrew the story of Lazarus from its synoptic appearance, it would be reasonable to wonder if perhaps the account of the wedding at Cana was also removed at some pre-canonical stage. Unfortunately, the answer to this is unknown, but it does seem odd that two of Jesus' best-known miracles, his first and last, appear only in the gospel of John. It is worth some closer investigation to see if there might be some connection between the two events.

The 'raising of Lazarus' story in the secret Mark extract (*see* page 41), made it clear that, at that stage in AD 33, Jesus and Mary Magdalene were man and wife. Thus a wedding ceremony, as that at Cana, presents an intriguing possibility, but a difficulty of identification exists because Mary Magdalene is not mentioned by name in the Cana report of John 2:1–11, even though some classical artists have included her alongside Jesus in the wedding table scene (*see* plate 9). We are told only that Jesus and his mother were there, along with some disciples and the ruler of the feast.

There is, however, no mention of any marriage service at Cana, only a wedding feast and the transformation of the water into wine. It would seem that this was not a ceremony of marriage but the wedding meal of a betrothal. The custom was for there to be a formal host (the *architriclinos*: ruler of the feast) who would be in charge of the proceedings. Secondary authority rested only in the bridegroom and his mother, and this is entirely relevant for, when the matter of the communion wine arose, Jesus' mother said to the servants: 'Whatsoever he saith unto you, do it'. No invited guest would have had any such right of command and, as many theologians have commented, Jesus and the bridegroom would appear to have been one and the same.[27]

Intriguing though this might be, it does not confirm any marriage between Jesus and Mary except by way of circumstantial possibility, but it is of particular interest that, when following the chronology of the gospel, the Cana event presents itself as having occurred in the equivalent of the month of June AD 30.[28] In accordance with custom, the first ceremony of a dynastic marriage took place in the month of September (the Jewish month of Atonement) and, in preparation for this, a feast of betrothal was held three months earlier.[29] If the Cana feast was indeed the betrothal of Jesus and Mary Magdalene, we would therefore be looking to find some mention of a marriage ritual in September AD 30.

What we can discover at that time is an account of Jesus at the house of Simon. We learn that, whilst they dined, a woman attended Jesus 'with an alabaster box of ointment'. She 'stood at his feet behind him weeping, and began to wash his feet with tears, and did wipe them with the hairs of her head, and kissed his feet, and anointed them with the ointment'.[30]

Two and a half years later, this same ritual was repeated at the house of Simon-Lazarus, but on this occasion the woman anointed Jesus' head as well as his feet: 'As he sat at meat, there came a woman having an alabaster box of ointment of spikenard, very precious, and she brake the box, and poured it on his head'.[31] The gospel of John relates that on both occasions the anointing was performed by the same woman, and explains that she was Mary, the devotional sister of Martha and Lazarus.[32]

Mary anoints the head of Jesus at the Hieros Gamos in Bethany,
by Julius Schnorr von Carolsfeld (1794–1872)

In biblical terms, our first insight into royal bridal ritual comes from the Old Testament book of the Song of Solomon. These poetic canticles recount the love contest between King Solomon and his brother Adonijah over a Shulamite noblewoman called Abishag – a contest which cost Adonijah his life.[33] In the course of their dialogue, the forlorn Abishag describes her marriage to the king. The similarity between this and the Bethany anointing is so close that in his *Sermon on the Canticles*, St Bernard, the 12th-century Abbot of Clairvaux, alluded to Mary Magdalene as being the Bride of Christ.[34] Long before this in pre-Roman Church times, the early Christian Father, Origen of Alexandria (AD *c*185–254), had also equated Mary Magdalene with the royal bride of the *Canticles* when discussing Mary's anointing of Jesus in his *Commentary on the Song of Songs*.[35]

The Song of Solomon (*Shirath Shiram*) identifies the potion symbolic of royal espousal as the aromatic ointment of spikenard: 'While the king sitteth at his table, my spikenard sendeth forth the smell thereof'.[36] This scene is replicated at Bethany where the office was similarly performed by Mary whilst Jesus sat at the table.[37] It alludes to an ancient rite by which a royal bride sanctified her bridegroom's meal. To perform the nuptial anointing was the express privilege of a messianic bride. Only as the wife of Jesus and a priestess in her own right could Mary have anointed both his head and his feet with the sacred ointment.[38]

Bridal ritual was the only anointing ceremony in which spikenard was used. In all other instances, such as anointing for kingship or priesthood, the office was performed by a high priest, and the holy ointment for such occasions is described in the book of Exodus – a mixture of olive oil, myrrh, cinnamon and calmus.[39] In contrast, the bridal ointment of spikenard was a fragrant oil specially compounded from the nard plant (*Nardostachys jatamansi*). Spikenard was very expensive, growing only in the Himalayan mountains at heights of some 15,000 feet (*c*4,570 m). It was by virtue of the second anointing by Mary in Bethany (anointing his head as well as his feet) that the full rite of consecration (the *māshach*) was achieved. This was a final cementing of their contractual wedlock and the action by which Jesus became a Messiah (Anointed One).[40] In response, Jesus stated: 'Wheresoever this gospel shall be preached throughout the whole world, this also that she hath done shall be spoken of for a memorial of her'.[41]

Subsequent to bridal anointing, it was customary for a dynastic wife to carry a vial of the ointment to be used, eventually, as an unguent in her husband's funerary rites. In such an event, the grieving widow would place a broken vial of the spikenard in her late husband's tomb.[42] Jesus alluded to this burial custom after the anointing,[43] and, as explained in the gospel, it was for this reason that Mary went to the tomb of Jesus with his mother and sisters after his crucifixion.[44]

With regard to Abishag the Shulamite in the Old Testament Canticles, Samuel N Kramer of the Institute of Ancient Near Eastern Studies[45] identified in his commentary on the Song of Solomon that royal spikenard anointing was not a Hebrew prerogative.[46] It was, in fact, a Syrian (northern Canaanite) tradition, and the Shulamites were from the Syrian border town of Sölam.[47] In each of the best-known works concerning *The Life of Mary Magdalene* (by Rabanus Maurus, 8th-century Archbishop of Mayence, and Jacopo de Voragine, 13th-century Archbishop of Genoa), Mary's father, Syrus, is said to have been of Syrian royal stock.[48]

Throughout history, the royal bridal ceremony remained a feature of the Threshing Floor rituals of the King's Week marriage festival of Sölam.[49] This tradition was recorded as being extant as late as 1873.[50] A table was prepared for the king from the threshing planks of the field and, while friends and family paid homage, the bride performed her queenly ritual. In doing this, she sang a wedding-night song that corresponded precisely with canticle sections of the Song of Solomon. The marriage rite was a symbolic bestowing of favour and kingship on the bride's chosen bridegroom[51] at a time when a man could not be a Christ (*christos*: king – equivalent to the Hebrew *malchus*) without a queen, and that queen had to be of a royal bloodline.[52] In terms of being designated for posterity as a Messiah and a Christ, there is no question about Jesus' marital status; he would have to have been married.

The Hebrew verb *maisach* (to anoint), whence comes the term Messiah, derived from the *Messeh* – the sacred crocodile of Egypt. The anointing of kings was performed by the pharaonic brides with the fat of the *Messeh*, and was associated with the sexual prowess of the royal beast.[53] In earlier times, the intrepid monitor dragon of old Mesopotamia was similarly identified as the *Mûs-hûs*.

So often, when the subject of Jesus' marriage to Mary of Bethany comes up for debate, a common Church reaction is that 'the gospels do not state that Jesus was married'. The retaliatory response is generally that 'by the same token, they do not state that he was unmarried'. The fact is, however, that the gospels do indeed state that Jesus and Mary were man and wife, and the anointing ritual of their wedlock could hardly be more explicitly described. A question that remains is: why would there have been two anointings of Jesus by Mary – one in September AD 30 and another in March AD 33? There was a very specific reason for this, as we shall discover when we shall return to the subject in due course (*see* page 96).

The Rule of Four

To conclude our overview of the New Testament gospels, we have seen that there are certain discrepancies between the four canonical texts. Over and above this, there are numerous differences between what the gospels actually state and what people are taught that they relate. Often this is due to the misunderstanding of ancient customs; sometimes to incorrect translations of original Greek and Aramaic words and phrases into English and other modern languages.

In view of the difficulty in analysing the variant and sometimes contradictory material in the gospels, over the years clerics, scholars and teachers have made choices of belief from a set of documents that are very sketchy in places. In consequence, bits and pieces have been extracted from each gospel, to the extent that a whole new pseudo-gospel has been concocted. Students are simply told that 'the Bible says this', or 'the Bible says that'. When being taught about the virgin birth they are directed to Matthew and Luke. When being taught about other aspects they are directed to the gospel or gospels concerned, as if they were all intended to be constituent chapters of the same overall work – which, of course, they were not.

Over many centuries, various speculations about biblical content have become interpretations and these, in turn, have been established by the Church as dogma. The emergent doctrines have been integrated into society as if they were positive facts. Pupils in schools and churches are rarely told that Matthew says Jesus' mother Mary was a virgin, but that Mark does not; or that Luke mentions the manger in which Jesus was placed, whereas the other gospels do not; or that not one gospel makes even the vaguest reference to the stable which has become such an integral part of popular Nativity tradition. Selective teaching of this kind applies to any number of incidents in Jesus' recorded life. Instead, Christians are taught a story that has been altogether smoothed over, or fabricated – a tale that extracts the most entertaining features from each gospel and merges them into a single romantic, but fictitious, tale.

While there is an element of logic in this approach, it also means that the many gospel entries which may be seen as in some way contentious can be totally ignored. The advantage of this was perceived back in the early days when a single amalgamated gospel was produced in Syria before Roman Church times. The author was a theologian named Taitan, and his continuous narrative, called the *Diatessaron*, was published in AD c175. Stemming from the Greek 'according to four', the *Diatessaron* was an amalgam of re-worded extracts from Matthew, Mark, Luke and John.[54]

There is nothing on record to indicate quite why Taitan based his work on these four texts, but his rendition became very much the basis for the way in which the amalgamated gospel story was taught. This was one of the reasons why these gospels were paramount in the bishops' comprehension during the lead-up to the canonical selection. Irenaeus of Lyon (*see* page 19 – a contemporary of Taitan) was clearly of a similar mind, when he denounced two gospels in particular – those of the Hebrews and the Nazarenes – even going on to suggest that the gospel of Matthew was too Jewish to be taken seriously by Christians. Neither was Irenaeus especially keen on the gospel of John because it presented Jesus in terms that were rather too human, referring to him as 'the word of God' who 'was made flesh and dwelt among us' – a man who gave people 'the power to become the sons of God'.[55] While we do not know which two gospels Irenaeus might have preferred to those of Matthew and John, he was convinced, along with Taitan, that four was the optimum number. He wrote: 'It is not possible that the gospels can be either more or fewer than four since there are four zones of the world, four pillars of the universe and four principal winds'![56]

Gospels that we can find listed by the 2nd-century Church Fathers amount to around 50 in total.[57] With some complete and some partial translations of about 30 of these, together with numerous other histories, tractates and epistles, we are fortunate to have a wealth of ancient Christian literature for scrutiny and comparison. In this regard, the New Testament, with its four gospels, selected tractates and some letters becomes little more than a brief introduction to a religion that was extremely diverse in its complexity. Even though there are some noticeable discrepancies between the canonical gospels, we can see from other texts that there were substantial differences in regional and racial Christian perception. The Roman style of Christianity, which ultimately formed the mainstream of belief, is very much a condensed and strategically honed concept when compared with the original broad-based reality of the Faith.

A Conflict of Interests

The First Fathers

Having reported that he had seen a cross in the sky at the battle of Milvian Bridge in AD 313 (*see* page 25), Emperor Constantine doubtless thought that, after 300 years of development, Christianity was pretty much a settled institution. But he soon learnt otherwise: it was actually a minefield of argument and dispute between its various factions. In the Holy Land, Jesus was remembered in much the way that Josephus had described him – as a wise man and a healer with a significant following. His recorded descent in the line of King David, as given in the gospels, was sufficient for many to have recognized him as a legitimate royal heir. In places such as Ephesus and Rome, the memory of Jesus was somewhat more divinely inspired by virtue of the Pauline doctrines, while in North Africa and some other countries Jesus was often portrayed as a supernatural deity in his own right.

Apart from the gospel and epistle scribes, the earliest of influential Christian writers were those known as the Apostolic Fathers. There were some ten of these men, and prominent among them in the late 1st and early 2nd century were three bishops: St Clement of Rome (AD *c*97 – as distinct from the later Clement of Alexandria), St Ignatius of Antioch in Syria (AD *c*114), and St Polycarp of Smyrna in Asia Minor (AD *c*115). Tradition relates that these bishops were disciples of the original apostles of Jesus. Alongside them, were two other 1st-century writers whose names are unknown – one being the Alexandrian pseudo-author of the *Epistle of Barnabas* (AD *c*97), and the other of a treatise called the *Didache* (AD *c*90). Additional works from the 2nd century included a visionary text called *The Shepherd* by Hermas, a former slave in Rome (AD *c*150), and the *Expositions of the Discourses of the Lord* by Papias, the bishop of Hierapolis in Phrygia (AD *c*150).[1]

As the third papal successor to Linus in Rome at the time of Emperor Domitian, Clement was a Christian leader at the height of the persecutions.[2] Among his works is a lengthy epistle addressed personally to Jesus' brother, 'James, the lord bishop of Jerusalem', in which Clement explains his views concerning the duties of those in clerical positions.[3] Ignatius was the third Christian bishop of Antioch when the imperial edict was that all subjects of the Empire must worship the Roman gods. He fell foul of the dictate when Emperor Trajan visited Antioch and accused him of inciting transgressions. Consequently, Ignatius was put in chains and taken to Rome, where he was thrown to the animals in the public arena.[4] Polycarp of Smyrna was reputed for visiting the imperial capital to defend the traditions of his Asiatic movement against the differing Christian customs of Rome – a clear sign of regional disputes even at that early stage. Polycarp was also martyred – stabbed by a Roman guard and burnt at the stake.[5]

Apart from the writings of these men, other texts of the era indicate how the liberal ministry of Jesus was already being restructured to become thoroughly dogmatic and separatist. The *Epistle of Barnabus* is a declaration of how the Christian faithful had been freed from the bonds of Jewish ceremonial law, and were able to practise the virtues of a new faith which would extricate them from sin. Although many of the earliest Christians were of Jewish stock, this epistle claims that 'Judaism is unholy', and that 'circumcision is the work of the devil'. It was, however, included in the 4th-century collection of the *Codex Siniaticus*.[6]

The *Didache* (or Doctrine of the Apostles) was clearly an influential work of its era, and is vehemently opinionated in its interpretations of the codes of life and death. With an emphasis on correct forms of liturgy and ritual, it conveys an adamant mistrust of alternative styles of Christian teaching. Just three decades from the

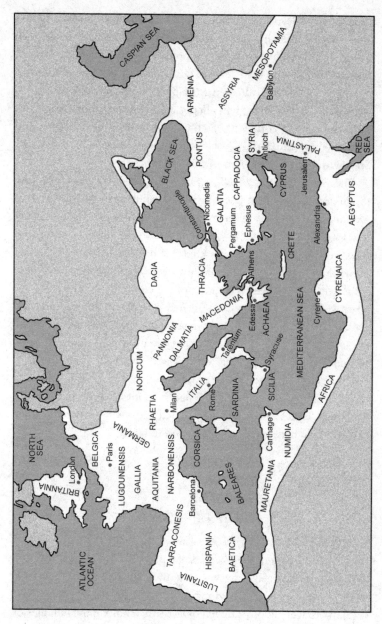

The Roman Empire

crucifixion of Jesus, it provides an example of how animosity was rife within Christian society as the various factions attacked each other in an ongoing struggle for political supremacy. The *Didache* was not included in the eventual Roman canon, but it was accepted by the opposition Church in Ethiopia.[7] Similarly dogmatic in its approach, *The Shepherd* is an allegorical but highly moralistic work detailing how to cope with such evils as lust, filthy thoughts and talkative wives! It did, however, find its way into the *Codex Siniaticus* following the Acts of the Apostles.[8]

The *Expositions of the Discourses of the Lord* discusses both the teachings and the life of Jesus, but it also contains much that is not in the canonical gospels. In the main, its narrative is related to dubious oral traditions as taught by transient presbyters (elderly preachers) who were said to have expounded 'what the disciples of the Lord used to say in old days'. One of these presbyters, a man named John, is thought to have been the author of the New Testament tracts John I and John II.[9] Given that the ancient gospels of Thomas and 'Q' contained such a wealth of Jesus-related material from the middle of the 1st century, it is hard now to imagine why anyone found it necessary to invent new Christine sayings and doctrines a century later. But this was all part of the process whereby individual factions claimed to have some privileged access to information not held by the others. It was also a means by which to draw more positive lines of distinction between Christianity and Judaism.

The Apologists

During the 2nd century, the accusations against Christians were so forceful and frequent that some of the more literate of their number took it upon themselves to write lengthy explanations of their faith to the Senate in Rome. Beginning with Quadratus of Athens (AD c130), there were about a dozen of these men among the notables of the era. The main charge against Christians was that they practised a forbidden religion, and were thus enemies of the State. It seems that the Christians – especially those in Rome – did not actually help their own predicament, and there are many reports of how they kept to their own company whilst making little or no contribution to the affairs of the city's community at large. In addition, despite the religious heritage of Jesus, the Christians outside the Nazarene movement set themselves against conventional Jewish society. As a result, they won few friends from that establishment, and many of the Apologists' letters were directed against Jews as well as against Romans.[10]

A number of the Apologists were bishops in various regions, figures such as Apollinaris of Hierapolis in Phrygia, and Melito of Sardis in Lydia. Some were philosophers such as Aristides of Athens, Justin of Caesarea and Theophilus of Antioch. Others were scholars of one sort or another. While their common cause was that of *Apologia* (the defence of a position against attack), their discourses often came from many differing standpoints. This made it plain to onlookers that there was no cohesion or uniformity in the transregional belief structure of Christianity at that time. In fact, events within the movement were entirely chaotic and wholly uncoordinated. Justin Martyr, in addressing the Jews, even went so far as to insist that Christianity was the true destiny of the Hebrews, and that in not following the true faith, the Jews were godless unbelievers.[11] Tertullian, a lawyer of Carthage, pushed the limits of imperial retaliation by openly inviting the persecution of his fellow Christians, writing to Emperor Lucius Severus in AD 197:

> You think us fools, and we rejoice to suffer for this. We conquer by our death ... We believe this martyrdom to be the remission of all offences, and that he who is condemned before your tribunal is absolved before God.[12]

During this period, there was much internal conflict within Christian society, and its literature evolved in equally clashing styles. The Judaeo-Christians (those of the more Nazarene-style community) regarded Jesus as a human Messiah such as was prophesied in the Old Testament.[13] A primary writer in this regard was Symmachus, who was detested by Tertullian and Irenaeus of Lyon, but seemingly admired by Origen who inherited his work in Ceasarea from a woman named Juliana. Allied to this sect were the Carpocratians (*see* page 40) and a number of other groups in Alexandria and Syria who became classified overall as Gnostics (from the Greek *gnosis*, meaning 'knowledge'). Their key leaders, along with Carpocrates, were Basilides of Alexandria and Valentin of Egypt. It is from this sect that so many important Christian documents of the founding era have survived.[14]

Through a period of some three centuries, numerous Christian leaders pursued their causes against Rome, against the Jews, and against each other. Some, like Tertullian, were brash and antagonistic. Others, like Origen, were modest and discerning. But above all, they were verbose correspondents, and their writings comprise a wonderful library of record. Noticeably lacking in these works, however, is any sense of joy as was apparent in the mainstream of Roman and Greek influenced society. Everything about Christianity was so very serious to the point that the most insignificant details became contentious items of debate and disagreement.

This style of conflict came to a head in the early 3rd century when Hippolytus, a presbyter of the Church of Rome, set himself against Pope Zephyrinus. Their argument was to become the overriding problem of the Church for well over 100 years. It was a fierce dispute about the relationship between God and Jesus: Were these characters separately identifiable, or were they one divinity? Hippolytus was in favour of separate identities for the Son and the Father but, since Zephyrinus would not concede, Hippolytus censured him and had himself proclaimed Pope by his followers. Henceforth there were two competing Bishops of Rome, and Hippolytus subsequently reigned in parallel with three successive popes of the main succession.[15]

When viewing the entire picture, there is little doubt that, although the Nazarene and Gnostic movements would probably have survived, Pauline Christianity would most likely have destroyed itself in the 4th century if Emperor Constantine had not seized it to his own imperial advantage. Necessarily, the first problem that he tackled at the Council of Nicaea in AD 325 was the matter of God the Father and God the Son. By that time, however, there was another complication: Which of them, if either, represented the Holy Spirit (the *Spiritu Sancto*) – or did that constitute a third part of the equation which somehow had to be reconciled?

The Unfathomable Trinity

The Trinity concept of the Father, Son and Holy Spirit is described in Catholic lore as 'the central doctrine of the Christian religion'. It is, however, the strangest of all doctrines, with a basis that is not only incomprehensible, but appears also quite pointless. Its official definition runs as follows:

> In the unity of the Godhead there are Three Persons, the Father, the Son, and the Holy Spirit, these Three Persons being truly distinct one from another. Thus, the Father is God, the Son is God, and the Holy Spirit is God, and yet there are not three Gods but one God.[16]

In attempting to explain what this means, the definition becomes even more complex:

> In this Trinity of Persons the Son is begotten of the Father by an eternal generation, and the Holy Spirit proceeds by an eternal procession from the Father and the Son. Yet, notwithstanding this difference as to origin, the Persons are co-eternal and co-equal: all alike are uncreated and omnipotent. This is the revelation regarding God's nature which the Son of God, came upon earth to deliver to the world.

Catholic scholars admit that there is nothing in any scripture which represents this said Trinity, and that the term first appeared in the writing of a certain Theophilus of Antioch in about AD 180. But his writing is not so complex and is seemingly quite unrelated to the doctrine. Theophilus referred simply to the trinity of 'God, His Word and His Wisdom'. It is therefore maintained that the concept of the Trinity, since it is not referenced in the gospels and since it has no identifiable source of origin, constitutes 'a mysterious and divine revelation'.

Origen of Alexandria had a problem with this theory because it had no logic that he could comprehend. He therefore postulated that, by the very nature of Jesus' earthly origin, he must necessarily be considered subordinate to the Father.[17] Others disagreed, stating that Jesus was eternal and did not have an origin. This position was defended in AD 270 by Gregory of Caesarea, who stated in his *Exposition of the Faith*:

> There is nothing created, nothing subject to another in the Trinity.
> Nor is there anything that has been added as though it once had
> not existed. Therefore the Father has never been without the Son,
> nor the Son without the Spirit: and this same Trinity is immutable
> and unalterable forever.

This conclusion by Gregory, it was stated, 'leaves no room for doubt in the matter'. It clearly confirms 'the distinction between the Persons in the Trinity, and emphasizes the eternity, equality, immortality, and perfection, not only of the Father, but of the Son and of the Holy Spirit'.[18] Not surprisingly, a majority of Christians did not have a clue what Gregory was talking about; there is no Holy Spirit mentioned in connection with God and Jesus anywhere in the New Testament. They asked: was the Holy Spirit perhaps the same as the Holy Ghost? It is written in the gospel of Matthew that 'whosoever speaketh against the Holy Ghost, it shall not be forgiven him, neither in this world, neither in the [world] to come'.[19] Was not Joseph's wife Mary 'found with child of the Holy Ghost',[20] and was not this the child called Jesus? If so, how can he possibly have been his own father? The Trinitarian bishops responded that Jesus had revealed the doctrine in explicit terms, bidding his disciples to 'go and teach all nations, baptizing them in the name of the Father, and of the Son, and of the Holy Ghost'.[21] They concluded:

> The force of this passage is thus decisive, and that the Father and the Son are distinct Persons follows from these terms which are mutually exclusive. The mention of the Holy Ghost thereby denotes that the names are connected by a third Person, which renders them all one and the same God.

So it was all made clear: The Holy Spirit was the same as the Holy Ghost, which was the same as God, which was the same as Jesus – except that they were all different entities and separate persons who, by a process of mutual exclusivity, were somehow one and the same! It might have been clear to the bishops concerned, but it was baffling to the majority – and certainly not in line with Jesus' own teaching. After all, it was argued, Jesus stated (according to the gospel of John), 'My Father is greater than I'.[22] How was this possible? How could he be greater than himself? The answer to this was said to rest in the doctrine of Incarnation, inasmuch as 'the human nature is less than the godly nature; therefore the form of the Son is less than the form of the Father even though they are equal and entirely the same'!

If ever there was a doctrine that was destined to drive a Church into ridicule and ruin, then this was it: a concept that made absolutely no sense and appeared to have nothing whatever to do with the fundamental essence of the mission. It was therefore hardly surprising that, when Constantine convened his first ecumenical Council of Nicaea in AD 325, the Trinity was a primary aspect of debate. The Emperor referred to it as 'an idle dispute about words',[23] but he recognized that, for the sake of peace in his realm, the idea of the Trinity would have to be ruled out altogether – or it would have to become law.

The matter had come to the fore at this time by virtue of an elderly Libyan priest name Arius, who was openly denying the divinity of Jesus. He argued that since God was deemed eternal, whereas Jesus had been physically born from a woman, they could not possibly be the same person. He maintained that Jesus was not himself eternal, but had earned his divine status as the Son by way of adoption, implying that God could equally adopt other sons.[24] Arius had many supporters and, prior to the Council, a friend, the most eminent of all Christian historians, Eusebius of Caesarea, drew up a creed. In this document, every possible term of honour and dignity was attributed to Jesus with the exception of his presumed oneness of substance with God and the Holy Spirit. Those in the opposition ranks determined, however, that this was an extreme heresy, which they dubbed Arianism. (The word 'heresy' derived from the Greek *hairesis*, meaning 'choice'.)

From all corners of the Roman Empire and beyond, there were perhaps some 250 bishops in attendance at Nicaea. At the outset it was known that there were 13 who were in agreement with Arius. They averred that Jesus was the Son and, furthermore, that the Son had been created in the flesh by God, but that he was not himself God. As the debate progressed and more supporters of Arius made themselves known, things became very heated. Then, when Arius rose to speak, Nicholas of Myra punched him in the face and this had a considerable effect in curtailing the enthusiasm of the Arian support group.

In the final event, the notion of the Trinity of God was upheld by a majority vote, following which Arius and his supporters were banished. Some delegates, including Bishop Eusebius, had striven at the last for a form of compromise, but they were compelled to relent fully in favour of the ruling. And so it was that, with God designated as both the Father and the Son, Jesus the man was conveniently bypassed as a figure of any practical significance. The Emperor was now regarded as the messianic godhead – not only from that moment, but as of right through an inheritance deemed reserved for him 'since the beginning of the world'![25]

In AD 330, Constantine declared Byzantium in Turkey the capital of the Eastern (Byzantine) Empire, renaming it Constantinople. Then, in the following year, he convened another Council in that city to ratify the decision of the earlier Council of Nicaea. On this occasion, the doctrine of Arius, which had gained a significant following in the interim, was formally declared blasphemous, but despite this the constant frictions within the Christian movement continued to plague Constantine for the next few years. Even the papal office itself was giving rise to bloodshed as the various candidates for the throne battled physically against each other in the streets.

Eventually, the Emperor's sister Constantia convinced him that he had made a serious error in banishing the Arians, whom she felt were rather more in tune with the real merits of Christianity. Constantine therefore recalled Arius to Constantinople and instructed Bishop Alexander to give him communion in his own church. Soon afterwards Arius died, but the Emperor's subsequent wish during his own last hours in AD 337 was that he should be baptized by Eusebius, the Arian prelate of Nicomedia.[26]

From that time, Arianism began to flourish again with Constantine's son Emperor Constantius, who displayed an open sympathy for its more lucid explanations of the Faith. But the matter would not rest and, in AD 381, the succeeding Emperor Theodosius sought a more permanent end to the debate at a second ecumenical Council of Constantinople. In the interim, the Arian view had been consolidated to teach that the Son (Jesus) had been created by God and that the Holy Spirit had passed from the Father to the Son. This concept was in no way conducive to the Emperor's own presumed right as the imperial godhead, so it had to be crushed and Jesus removed from the reckoning as a separate entity from God. Consequently, it was decreed that the Nicene doctrine of the Trinity must be upheld by all: God was the Father, God was the Son and God was the Holy Spirit. There was to be no more argument.[27]

The greatest single repository of Arian texts, and indeed of all ancient and contemporary documents that were anathema to the imperial regime, was deemed to be the Serepaeum library in

Alexandria. Thus it was that 10 years later, in AD 391, Emperor Theodosius instructed Bishop Theophilus to raze the library to the ground and destroy it altogether.

The city of Alexandria, founded by Alexander the Great in 331 BC, was the most important cultural centre of the ancient world. It was an academic focus for the greatest scholars, scientists, doctors, mathematicians and philosophers, who travelled from far and wide to study the largest collection of arcane documents ever amassed in one arena. Close to the harbour, the majestic library building, with its marble steps, columned halls and magnificent gardens, housed many hundreds of thousands of papyrus and parchment texts, together with fine statues, tapestries and other works of art. The Library attracted Egyptians, Macedonians, Greeks, Anatolians, Italians, Arabians, Persians, Indians and Jews. But the archive was anathema to the newly devised teaching of the Church.

Once inside, Bishop Theophilus and his angry mob smashed everything to pieces and set the texts ablaze – more than half a million irreplaceable documents representing the finest minds of the ancient world. In that one day a vast wisdom of ages was lost for all time, leaving the Church free to make up its own history, to interpret its own science and to establish its own philosophy.

Parting of the Ways

In the midst of all this, there were some who, although prepared to accept the principle of the Triune God, still retained a belief in the separate divinity of Jesus as the biological Son. Since the *Nicene Creed* had been construed in the Eastern Church province of Byzantium, the Western Church (centred on Rome) was pursuing this slightly different and rather more Arian view. This gave rise to yet another creed, which emerged in about AD 390, to become known as the *Apostles' Creed*. It began, 'I believe in God the Father Almighty and in Jesus Christ, his only begotten Son, our Lord'.

Although this reintroduction of Jesus as an individual figure was perceived as a distinct threat to the messianic status of the Emperor, within a few years Rome was sacked by the Goths and the Western Empire fell into decline.

From that point, a new protagonist entered the dispute over the Trinity; he was Nestorius, the Patriarch of Constantinople from AD 428. In accord with the Nazarenes, he maintained that the argument over whether Jesus was God or the Son of God was totally irrelevant, for it was plain to all that Jesus was a man, born quite naturally of a father and mother. From this platform, Nestorius stood against the Eastern ruling, and also against his Catholic colleagues in the West who had brought Jesus' personal divinity back into the picture now that the Empire was failing.

This led to a further debate about the nature of the Holy Spirit. If God and Jesus had separate identities, then the natural connection between them (the conduit for the Holy Spirit) must necessarily have been Jesus' mother Mary. Prior to this notion, the Catholics had referred to Mary as the *Theotokas* (Greek: 'bearer of God') or *Dei Genitrix* (Latin: 'conceiver of God'). But if Jesus was not God, there was clearly something wrong with this definition, and Nestorius raised the matter of the mortality of Mary and Jesus at the Council of Ephesus in AD 431. As a consequence he was condemned by both the Eastern and Western bishops and deprived of his bishopric. Interestingly, though, his supposed heresy did prompt a re-think of the Nicene regulation, and in AD 433 Jesus was newly defined as 'both God and man, a union of two natures'.[28] Mary, for her part was designated as an 'intercessor' between God and the mortal world.

From the middle 5th century, the Church of Rome continued in the West, while the Eastern Orthodox Church emerged from its centres at Constantinople, Alexandria, Antioch and Jerusalem. The unresolved debate over the Trinity had driven a wedge firmly between the factions and each claimed to represent the True Faith. In order to increase its influence, the Church of Rome was reformed under the management of an appointed city administration of cardinals – a title derived from Latin *cardo* (pivot), of whom there were 28 appointees stationed at the Vatican.

While the Church of Rome was being restructured, the Western Empire collapsed – demolished by the Visigoths and Vandals. The last Emperor, Romulus Augustulus, was deposed by the German chieftain Odoacer, who became King of Italy in AD 476. In the absence of an emperor, the prevailing High Bishop Leo gained the title of *Pontifex Maximus* (Chief pontiff or 'bridge builder'). In the East, however, the story was different and the Byzantine Empire was destined to continue for another 1,000 years. Meanwhile, Arianism still flourished, as did the Nazarene Church and the Gnostic movement. Nestorius, having found friends in Egypt and Turkey, established the Nestorian Church at Edessa in AD 489, with missionaries who carried his message into Persia, India and China.[29]

Rome's final split with the Eastern Church occurred in 867, when the latter announced that it maintained the true Apostolic Succession. The Vatican Council disagreed and so Photius, the Patriarch of Constantinople, excommunicated Pope Nicholas I, Bishop of Rome. This sparked a whole new round of argument about the definition of the Trinity. The Catholics of Western Christendom decided to ratify what was called the *Filioque Article*, which had been introduced at the Council of Toledo in 598. This had resulted from attempts to define the role of mother Mary, who had carried the Holy Spirit. The *Article* decreed that the Holy Spirit proceeded 'from the Father *and from* the Son' (Latin: *filioque*). But the Eastern Church disagreed. Its bishops claimed that the Spirit proceeded 'from the Father *through* the Son' (Greek: *dia tou huiou*).[30] Although it was a wholly intangible and quite extraordinary point of theological dispute, it was good enough to split Christianity down the middle. (In reality, it was simply a trivial excuse to contrive a debate over whether the Church should be politically managed from Rome or from Constantinople.) The final result was the formation of two quite distinct Churches from the same original.[31]

As time progressed, the Eastern Church changed relatively little. From its primacy at Constantinople, it continued to adhere strictly to scriptural teachings and its focus of worship became the Eucharist ritual with bread and wine. Catholicism, on the other hand, underwent numerous changes: new doctrines were added and old concepts were amended or further substantiated. From the 12th century, the Seven Sacraments were deemed to embody the Grace of God in a person's physical life (though not all were necessary for individual salvation). They were classified as baptism, holy communion, confirmation, confession and penance, ordination to holy orders, the solemnization of matrimony and the anointing of the seriously ill and dying (the Extreme Unction or Last Rites). It was further decreed that the bread and wine of the Eucharist were transformed, upon consecration, into the physical body and blood of Jesus (the doctrine of Transubstantiation).

Inasmuch as Constantine's Roman Church had commenced as a hybrid, so too was the structure to remain composite. New methods and ideologies were introduced in order to maintain efficient control of congregations from a distance in an expanding Church society. In this way, Roman Catholicism evolved in a strictly regulated fashion and some doctrines that today seem to be traditional are, in reality, recently implemented features. It was not until Victorian times that certain aspects of the Catholic creed (hitherto only implied) were determined as explicit items of the Faith. The doctrine of the Immaculate Conception, for instance, was not formally expressed until 1854, when Pope Pius IX decreed that Mary, the mother of Jesus, was herself conceived free from Original Sin.[32] Mary's non-canonical Assumption into Heaven was not defined until the 1950s by Pope Pius XII, whilst Pope Paul VI did not proclaim her Mother of the Church until as recently as 1964.

Part II

Denouncement of Women and the Papal Succession

Heirs of the Bloodline

The Constant Virgin

Prior to the 19th and 20th-century Articles of Faith concerning Jesus' mother Mary, she had been the subject of dogmatic rulings since the 5th-century *Theotokas* debate. Foremost among these was the doctrine of her perpetual virginity as established at the Council of Trullo in 692. The concept of the Blessed Mary being 'ever virgin' is of particular relevance here since it has a direct bearing on the Church's own perception of the descendant heirs of Jesus.

Mary's virginity had been discussed at the second Council of Constantinople in 553, and was defined by Pope Martin I at the Lateran Palace in 649. Prior to that, the term Virgin Mary had been used in the Nicene creed from AD 381, having had its first known mention in AD 375 in the *Panarion* (Medicine chest) of Epiphanius, the bishop of Salamis in Cyprus (*see* page 100). Then, in AD 383, St Jerome wrote his treatise, *The Perpetual Virginity of Blessed Mary*.[1] In this context, it has long been promoted that 'Mary's personal integrity was miraculously preserved because her body had not been violated'.[2] Her motherhood had been achieved by the 'divine will' of the Holy Ghost.

In terms of scriptural narrative, the notion had been drawn from just two gospel entries: Luke 1:35, when the angel of the Annunciation said to Mary, 'The Holy Ghost shall come upon thee, and the power of the most High shall overshadow thee', and Matthew 1:20, when the angel told Mary's husband Joseph, 'That which is conceived in her, is of the Holy Ghost.' Nowhere is it explained how the intimate details of these two private encounters with an angel would have become known in later times to the authors of these gospels but, that apart, the word 'virgin' does not appear in any of the oldest known gospel texts.

In our familiar New Testament translations, the word 'virgin' appears on just two occasions in respect of Mary. In Luke 1:26–27 it is stated:

> And in the sixth month the angel Gabriel was sent from God unto a city of Galilee, named Nazareth, to a virgin espoused to a man whose name was Joseph, of the house of David; and the virgin's name was Mary.

In explanation of Mary's pregnancy, Matthew 1:22–23 relates:

> Now all this was done, that it might be fulfilled which was spoken of the Lord by the prophet, saying, Behold, a virgin shall be with child, and shall bring forth a son, and they shall call his name Emmanuel.

The prophetic event referred to here, regarding the child Emmanuel rather than Jesus, comes from the Old Testament book of Isaiah 7:13–14. It was given as an indirect pronouncement to King Ahaz of Judah in 735 BC, and reads:

> Hear ye now, O house of David … Behold, a virgin shall conceive, and bear a son, and shall call his name Immanuel.

This foretelling clearly had nothing whatever to do with Jesus more than 700 years later, but it was used by the writer of Matthew to convey the idea that Mary's conception was somehow connected with an ancient prophecy. In contrast to the name Emmanuel as given in this passage, an earlier entry in Matthew 1:20–21 relates more correctly:

> Joseph, thou son of David, fear not to take unto thee Mary thy
> wife: for that which is conceived in her is of the Holy Ghost ...
> And she shall bring forth a son, and thou shalt call his name
> Jesus.

These are the only two occasions in the whole of the New Testament
when Mary is described as being a virgin, and one of the entries
does not concern her in any event. In both cases, however, the translations are incorrect.

The Semitic word which, in these instances, has been translated
to 'virgin' is given in the more original texts of Matthew and Luke
as *almah*. This word meant nothing more than 'young woman', and
the comparative word to denote a physical virgin would have been
bethulah.[3] The strict etymological definition of an *almah* is 'a sexually mature girl' – a damsel, but not necessarily a maiden. In the
plural terminology of Psalm 68:25 the '*almamoth* playing timbrels'
is correctly translated as 'damsels playing timbrels', whereas in
Psalm 45:14 the temple *bethuloth* of Tyre are identified in translation as 'virgins'. In Judges 21:12, the *bethuloth* of Jabesh-gilead are
again properly described as 'virgins who have not known man',
while in Genesis 34:3 the word *almah*, as used in respect of the
defiled Dinah, who was clearly not a virgin, is rightly translated as
'damsel'.

As early as the 3rd century, Origen had written about the Jews
taking issue with the Christians for their misuse of the word *almah*.[4]
He stated that the Jews insisted that the correct word usage might be
found in the Old Testament book of Deuteronomy 22:23. This verse
states that 'If an *almah* that is a *bethulah* be betrothed to an husband
...' which, when correctly translated (as in the King James Version of
the Bible) reads, 'If a damsel that is a virgin be betrothed to an
husband'. Thus, there was a distinct difference in the original
language between the Semitic terms for a young woman (a damsel)
and a virgin.

As a comparison in Latin, Matthew 1:23 in its 4th-century translation by St Jerome, reads, '*ecce virgo in utero habebit et pariet filium et*

vocabunt nomen eius Emmanuhel'. The word in this passage, as translated from *almah*, is *virgo* (ie, 'Behold, a *virgo* shall be with child, and shall bring forth a son, and they shall call his name Emmanuel'). In Latin, *virgo* meant, quite simply, 'young woman' and, to imply the modern connotation of 'virgin', the noun would have to be qualified by the adjective *intacta* (ie, *virgo intacta*), denoting a young woman intact.[5] There is no instance in either the Old Testament prophecy or in the gospels where the early texts cited a virgin or even an unmarried maiden in these respects. In each case, the scriptures simply identified a young woman, a damsel.

How was it, then, that the concept first arose that Mary was a virgin? And why did the 7th-century Lateran proclamation go so far as to determine that 'the Blessed Mother of Jesus Christ was a virgin before, during, and after the conception and birth of her Divine Son'?

According to the records of the Catholic Church, the dogma was based on the Matthew 1:20 entry: 'That which is conceived in her, is of the Holy Ghost'.[6] And since the Holy Ghost was the Holy Spirit (the *Spiritu Sancto*), and the Holy Spirit was deemed to be God (*see* page 65), it was ascertained that Mary conceived by divine intervention – even though, under the Trinity ruling, the Holy Spirit was also Jesus himself!

An item of particular importance in the Luke 1:27 entry is the statement that Mary was 'espoused to a man whose name was Joseph, of the house of David'. In the Matthew 1:20 entry it is further confirmed that Mary was Joseph's 'wife'. Additionally, both Luke 2:5 and Matthew 1:18 refer to Mary as being the espoused wife of Joseph, and the genealogical lists in both gospels denote Jesus as having descended from King David via his father Joseph. There is, therefore, little doubt of Jesus' actual parentage, and we shall return to this matter in due course (page 100). Meanwhile though, there is another pertinent issue to consider.

A Hallowed Distinction

We know from the gospels that Jesus had brothers and sisters, and we have even seen that St Clement of Rome wrote a letter to Jesus' brother James, who was also referenced in the *Antiquities* of Josephus. However, from a doctrinal point of view, irrespective of what the gospels might relate, the Church maintains the view that 'Mary was a virgin before, during, and after the conception and birth of her Divine Son'. The resultant official doctrine, therefore, is: 'The brothers of Jesus are neither the sons of Mary, nor the brothers of Our Lord in the proper sense of the word, but they are his cousins or the more or less near relatives'.[7]

As far as the Church is concerned, Jesus was Mary's only offspring, and she remained a virgin thereafter. Although the point is distinctly and succinctly made in all related Catholic literature, it leads to an intriguing Church admission in respect of the family's subsequent bloodline descent.

During the 1st to the 4th centuries there were references in historical literature to certain dynastic offspring recorded by the chroniclers as being the Heirs of the Lord. This hallowed distinction (in Greek, *Desposyni*) was 'reserved uniquely for the blood relatives of Jesus' and, as noted in the Catholic archive, 'Only those persons in the bloodline with Jesus through his mother qualified as *Desposyni*'.[8]

To historians, the term 'through his mother' would necessarily relate to the descendants of Jesus' brothers and sisters as well as to those of Jesus himself, but the Church insists that Jesus had no brothers or sisters. Hence, according to strict Catholic understanding, the Heirs of the Lord were precisely as described: the descendants of Jesus in the bloodline from his mother.

As we have seen (page 52), the gospels describe that Jesus was married, and now, from both historical and Church archival sources, we learn that he had offspring and descendants.

The Lord's Family

The first officially recognized Church historian was the renowned Eusebius, Bishop of Caesarea (AD c275–329). A prominent figure during the reign of Emperor Constantine, Eusebius is reputed as the Father of Church History and is especially noted for his work, *An Ecclesiastical History to the year 324*. It is in this chronicle that we find references to the *Desposyni* inheritors.

A much earlier writer on the subject of the *Desposyni* had been Hegesippus of Palestine (AD c110–180), a Jewish convert to Christianity and another who wrote about 'James the Just, the brother of the Lord'. *The Church History* of Hegesippus appears in an inventory of books in the Abbey of Corbie in Picardy, founded in the 7th century by the Merovingian dynasty of France. Overall, his work bears the title of *Hypomnenata* (Memoirs). As an upholder of early Judaeo-Christianity, the integrity of Hegesippus was such that he was often quoted by later churchmen when defending their own positions, and he was greatly admired by Eusebius.[9]

Another writer about the *Desposyni* was Julius Africanus of Edessa (AD c160–240). He was a traveller to Alexandria, Greece and Rome, and flourished in the period between Hegesippus and Eusebius, dying in Jerusalem. His works include a world history called *Chronografiai*, and he is known as the Father of Christian Chronography.[10] Africanus made his reputation by translating into Latin a series of works by the 1st-century disciple Abdias, the Nazarene Bishop of Babylon installed by Simon Zelotes and Jesus' brother Jude. The writings of Abdias (Obadiah) amounted to 10 volumes of first-hand gospel-era history entitled *Historia Certaminis Apostolici*. However, like so many other important accounts of the period, his work was rejected for inclusion in the New Testament canon. Abdias is recorded as one of the 72 disciples of Jesus referred to in Luke 9:57–10:1.[11]

The term *Desposyni* did not appear until after the lifetime of Jesus. This makes sense given that it relates directly to the 'heirs of' or those 'belonging to' the Lord. If (as according to the Matthew and

Luke listings) Jesus was the royal heir to the House of David, then the senior dynastic succession would terminate with Jesus unless he had a son. But, in AD 70, when the Roman legions of General Titus finally crushed the four-year Jewish Revolt, it appears that Emperor Vespasian still had a problem with the House of David. This was close to 40 years after the crucifixion of Jesus. In the writings of Hegesippus, we read that Vespasian commanded 'the family of David to be sought, that no one might be left among the Jews who was of the royal stock'.[12] It follows that the family of David was known to be extant at that time in AD 70, but the edict does not refer to every living descendant of David from 1,000 years before – even if it had been possible to tell who they all were. It specifically defines the kingly succession: 'the family' and 'the royal stock', and this narrows the field considerably.

Julius Africanus related that, even before Vespasian, at about the time of Jesus' crucifixion, Herod-Antipas (son of Herod the Great) had ordered the destruction of all aristocratic genealogies. But, Africanus continued: 'A few careful people had private records of their own ... and took a pride in preserving the memory of their aristocratic origin. These include the people ... known as the *Desposyni* because of their relationship to the Saviour's family'.[13]

Succeeding Emperor Vespasian was his son Titus, whose brother Domitian followed in AD 81. Domitian detested the Christians even more than his father had done, and his regime of persecution was as cruel as it had been in the days of Emperor Nero. (According to the Roman annals, a favoured torture of Nero was to tie Christians to stakes in his palace gardens, and to fire them as human torches at night.[14]) It was in Domitian's reign that St John the Divine, author of The Revelation, was sentenced to confinement on the Greek island of Patmos.[15] Hegesippus reported in his *Hypomnenata* that Domitian ordered the execution of all the *Desposyni* heirs of Jesus. Later, Eusebius qualified that although many were seized, some were released and 'on their release they became leaders of the churches, both because they had borne testimony and because they were of the Lord's family'.[16]

During the 1st, 2nd and 3rd centuries, the Judaeo-Christian Church (the Nazarene branch of Christianity for which Jesus' brother James had been the first Bishop of Jerusalem) was dynastically governed by hereditary leaders of the *Desposyni*.[17] By the early 4th century, however, things had changed. Under the new influence of Sylvester's leadership from Rome, Greek bishops had been appointed in Jerusalem, Antioch, Ephesus and Alexandria as part of an imperial strategy to dislodge the *Desposyni* heirs from office. A revised history of Christianity was construed, which ignored Linus as the first bishop in Rome and claimed instead that the office had been held by St Peter. This enabled the new Church leadership to claim a figurative Apostolic Succession for its popes instead of a Desposynic Succession.

There is no record whatever of Peter heading the Church in Rome, but the Apostolic Succession stakes its claim to entitlement on a single gospel entry, that of Matthew 16:18, which states that Jesus said: 'Thou art Peter, and upon this rock I will build my church'. However, the Greek word *petra* (an immovable rock), relating to the Rock of Israel, was conveniently misinterpreted as if it had been *petros* (a stone), and thereby indicative of Peter for which Petros was the Greek nominal equivalent.[18] Originally, the apostle's name was Simon, but Jesus apparently renamed him Cephas (from the Aramaic *kephas*) 'which is by interpretation a stone'.[19] Jesus was actually affirming to Peter (Petros) that his mission was to be founded upon the *Petra* – the Rock of Israel.

This was another reason why the gospel of Thomas was excluded from the New Testamant, since this gospel makes it perfectly clear to whom Jesus bequeathed his personal leadership. When the disciples asked him who would head the mission after his death, Jesus responded quite naturally that his inheritor would be his own eldest brother James: 'Jesus said to them, Wherever you are, you are to go to James the Just'.[20]

In view of the pseudo-apostolic structure introduced for the papal order of Rome, the Nazarene leaders were severely undermined in the provinces. In AD 318, steps were taken in an effort to alleviate this, and Eusebius relates that a *Desposyni* delegation of eight men journeyed to Rome. The Emperor provided their sea passage to the Roman port of Ostia, from where they rode on donkeys to the Lateran Palace to be given audience by Bishop Sylvester.

Through their chief spokesman, Joses, the delegates argued that the Church should rightfully be centred in Jerusalem, not in Rome. They claimed that the Bishop of Jerusalem should be a true hereditary *Desposynos*, while the bishops of other major centres – such as Alexandria, Antioch and Ephesus – should be related.[21] After all, they declared, Bishop Clement of Rome had written that Jesus' brother James was 'the Lord of the Holy Church and the bishop of bishops'. They asserted that their Judaeo-Christian movement was of far higher authority than a contrived Roman offshoot centred upon St Peter, who was a mere apostle of the Lord and not a family member. These blood relatives of Jesus demanded the reintroduction of Jewish customs, which included the keeping of the Sabbath, but Sylvester dismissed their claims. The teachings of Jesus had been superseded, he said, by a doctrine more amenable to imperial requirement, and he informed the men that the power of salvation no longer rested in Jesus, but in Emperor Constantine. Henceforth, Sylvester decreed, the Mother Church was in Rome and he insisted that they accept the appointed bishops of the Empire to lead them.

Jesus the Nazarene

The term 'Nazarene' has been cited many times, and we saw earlier that Irenaeus, in his *Adversus Haereses*, had referred to the Nazarene sect of Judaeo-Christians as Ebionites. This was a transliteration from the Aramaic *ebionaioi*, relating to the 'poor ones' (*see* page 20). He also stated: 'They, like Jesus as well as the Essenes and Zadokites of two centuries before, expound upon the prophetic books of the Old Testament. They reject the Pauline epistles, and they reject the apostle Paul, calling him an apostate of the law'.[22]

The statement, with respect to Paul, is in direct contrast to the New Testament entry in Acts 24:5. This deals with an event when Paul was arrested by the Romans and brought on a charge of religious sedition before the Governor of Caesarea. It states: 'For we have found this man a pestilent fellow, and a mover of sedition among all the Jews throughout the world, and a ringleader of the sect of the Nazarenes'.

Paul (hitherto an ardent Hebrew named Saul) had actually joined the Nazarenes in about AD 40 in Damascus. There was no reason for the Essenes, Zadokites, Ebionites or Nazarenes to have accepted or rejected the Pauline epistles as Irenaeus suggested. These groups were all in existence long before Paul came onto their established scene, and Jesus was obviously a significant figure in their midst a long time before Paul eventually wrote his epistles.

For all practical purposes, the Nazarenes and Ebionites of the Essene community at Qumrân by the Dead Sea were the originators of what became known as Christianity. There was, in fact, nothing derogatory in the Ebionites being regarded as 'poor ones'. They were not poverty-stricken, underprivileged citizens; they were those who had been initiated into the higher echelons of the community and who, on that account, had been obliged to give up their worldly possessions in order to pursue the advanced spiritual course of The Way.[23]

In his *Wars of the Jews*, Josephus explained that the Essenes were very practised in the art of healing and received their therapeutic knowledge from the ancients.[24] Indeed, the term Essene might well refer to this expertise, for the Aramaic word *asayya* meant physician and corresponded to the Greek word *essenoi*. The Jewish philosopher, Philo Judaeus (20 BC–AD 40), added to this, stating that the term was also indicative of the Greek *hosioun*, meaning 'holy'.[25]

Contrary to common belief, the Nazarenes had nothing whatever to do with the settlement at Nazareth. The Essene community of Qumrân was, in general terms, referred to as the *Nazrie ha Brit* (Keepers of the Covenant),[26] and it was from this that the word *Nazarene* derived. The Islâmic Koran refers to Christians as *Nazara*, and a general Arabic expression for them is *Nasrani*.[27] The term Nazarene is adequately described in the gnostic gospel of Philip, which explains:

> Nazara is the Truth. The Nazarene accordingly is the truth. Christ is measured. The Nazarene and Jesus are they who have been measured.[28]

The notion that Jesus was from Nazareth stems from an entry in Matthew 2:23, which relates: 'He came and dwelt in a city called Nazareth; that it might be fulfilled which was spoken by the prophets, he shall be called a Nazarene'. Indeed, there are a number of items in Matthew which attempt to link the story of Jesus with prophetic references in the Old Testament.

It is a point of contention whether the settlement of Nazareth existed at all during Jesus' lifetime. It does not appear on contemporary maps, neither in any books, documents, chronicles or military records of the period, whether of Roman or Jewish compilation.[29] Even St Paul, who discussed many of Jesus' activities in his letters, makes no allusion to Nazareth. The *Jewish Encyclopedia* identifies that Nazareth is not mentioned in the Old Testament, neither in the works of Josephus, nor in the Hebrew *Talmud*. In fact, Nazareth made its first known literary appearance in the AD 60s, around the time of the Jewish Revolt, and became a place of Christian pilgrimage only from the 6th century.[30] Thus, although the author of Matthew would have been familiar with the Nazareth settlement, it was not a place that Jesus would have known – and it was at no time a city as claimed in the gospel translation.

In respect of the Matthew link to the biblical prophecy, there is no mention whatsoever of Nazarenes in the Old Testament. The scripture refers only to Nazarites. What the author of Matthew attempted was to draw yet another Jesus parallel with a story from an even more distant era. From the Old Testament book of Judges comes the tale of the wife of Manoah. It relates:

> And the angel of the Lord appeared unto the woman, and said
> unto her, 'Behold now, thou art barren, and bearest not: but thou
> shalt conceive, and bear a son … and no razor shall come on his
> head: for the child shall be a Nazarite unto God from the womb,
> and he shall begin to deliver Israel out of the hand of the
> Philistines'.[31]

The eventual child of this mysterious conception was the Israelite judge Samson, but there was a direct similarity here between his effort against the Philistines and that of Jesus to help deliver Israel from the hands of the Romans. Hence, unlike the writers of Mark and John, the Matthew scribe introduced his account of the angelic Annunciation. The theme was then progressed in the gospel of Luke, whose writer added that the angel's name was Gabriel, a messenger 'sent from God unto a city of Galilee, named Nazareth'.[32]

In Samson's day (c1100 BC), Nazarites were ascetic individuals bound by strict vows through predetermined periods:

> He shall separate himself from wine and strong drink … All the
> days of the vow of his separation there shall no razor come upon
> his head: until the days be fulfilled, in which he separateth
> himself unto the Lord, he shall be holy, and shall let the locks of
> the hair of his head grow … And this is the law of the Nazarite.[33]

It was by virtue of the treacherous Delilah having the hair cut from Samson's head that he was said ultimately to have lost his holy strength. Since wine, however, was very much a part of later Essene custom, especially in terms of community tables and communion ritual, there were clearly differences between the Old Testament Nazarites and the New Testament Nazarenes. Indeed, it was the bread and wine communion of the Essenes that led eventually to the eucharistic heritage of Jesus.

The *Community Rule* manuscript of the Dead Sea Scrolls was produced by the Essenes some while before the birth of Jesus and it contains a document known as the *Manual of Discipline*. In respect of the bread and wine, it corresponds with the Last Supper of Jesus in detailing the ceremony for a Messianic Banquet. The primary hosts of the banquet were the High Priest and the Messiah of Israel.[34] The people were represented by delegate apostles called the Council of the Community. It states:

> And when they gather for the community table … and mix the wine for drinking, let no man stretch forth his hand on the first of the bread or the wine before the Priest, for it is he who will bless the first fruits of the bread and wine … And afterwards, the Messiah of Israel shall stretch out his hands upon the bread, and afterwards all the congregation of the community will give blessings, each according to his rank.[35]

The Last Supper of Jesus and his apostles (delegates) would necessarily have been an enactment of this ceremonial banquet, and the fact that it coincided with the Passover of AD 33 was entirely coincidental. In detailing his accounts of differences between the various 1st-century Jewish sects, Flavius Josephus wrote in the *Antiquities of the Jews* that the Essenes were precluded from the Jerusalem Temple and did not frequent the capital city.[36] Unlike the Pharisees, Sadducees and others of the Hebrew fraternity, the Essenes did not observe the traditional Jewish festivals in Jerusalem. In earlier times, Philo Judaeus wrote that they 'avoided all cities on account of the habitual lawlessness of those who inhabit them'.[37]

This is doubtless why it was that, when Jesus did eventually ride into Jerusalem prior to his Bethany anointing in March AD 33, he was unrecognized by the citizens. We are told that coats and palm branches were scattered in his path and there was an amount of cheering, 'Hosanna to the son of David'.[38] But we are also informed that this frenetic activity was the work of his disciples.[39] Matthew 21:10 relates: 'When he was come into Jerusalem, all the city was moved, saying, Who is this?' According to Mark 11:11, Jesus entered the Temple, 'and when he had looked round and about upon all things, and now eventide was come, he went out unto Bethany'.

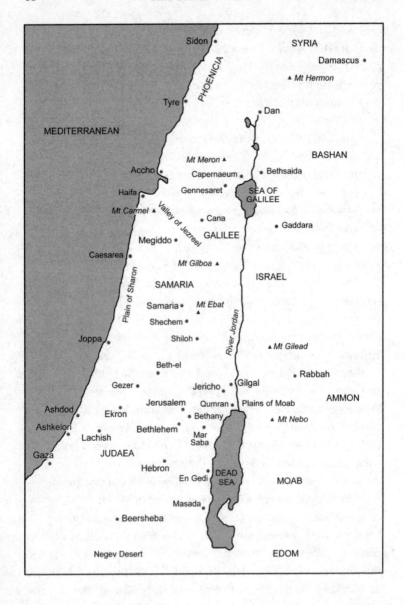

The New Testament Holy Land

Luke 19:40 tells that the Pharisees ordered the disciples to be rebuked for creating a disturbance. Matthew 21:12 adds, 'Jesus went into the temple of God, and cast out all them that sold and bought in the temple, and overthrew the tables of the money changers, and the seats of them that sold doves'. He then returned to Bethany.[40]

Subsequent to this, not one of the gospels mentions Jerusalem as the city location for the Last Supper as is generally supposed to have been the case. They tell only of a house with a large upper room, which was by the Mount of Olives near to a garden in the Valley of Oil (*Gethsemane*). The Mount of Olives location is confirmed in Acts 1:12 and Mark 11:1, which state that it was a short way from Jerusalem, near Bethany.[41]

The Way of the Essenes

The essential difference between the Pharisees, Sadducees and Essenes was that, as Josephus explained, the Essenes 'live the same kind of life as do those whom the Greeks call Pythagoreans'.[42] The community cultures of these three main philosophical groups were distinctly different in many respects, and Josephus described that the Essenes had 'a greater affection for one another than the other sects have'.[43] The Pharisees and Sadducees were strictly regulated in the Hebrew tradition, whereas the Essenes were far more liberal and Westernized. The Pharisees observed ancient Jewish laws, and although the Sadducees had a more modern outlook, they were largely non-spiritual, whereas the Essenes were culturally inspired and inclined towards Hellenic mysticism.

In Matthew 16:1–12 and elsewhere Jesus seems constantly to have challenged the regimes of the Pharisees and Sadducees. His behaviour in all respects was wholly akin to the Essene lifestyle of healing, esoteric philosophy and neighbourly attitude. Josephus, although himself a Pharisee, was nonetheless very complimentary towards the Essenes, and wrote:

> Their course of life is better than that of other men, and they
> entirely addict themselves to husbandry. It also deserves our
> admiration how much they exceed all other men that addict
> themselves to virtue … This is demonstrated by that institution of
> theirs which will not suffer anything to hinder them from having
> all things in common; so that a rich man enjoys no more of his
> own wealth than he who hath nothing at all.[44]

In respect of Jesus, the *Jewish Encyclopedia* makes the point that, although not an overt law-breaker, he was persistently inclined to flout regulations in an attempt to have changes made within the rigid legal structure. It is stated that 'in making these pretensions he was following a tendency which, at the period of his career, was especially marked in the ways of the Essenes'.[45]

Jesus' views on matters such as wealth, marriage and baptism were in no way commensurate with the 1st-century Hebrew culture of the Pharisees and Sadducees, nor even in agreement with the scribes of the Temple law. They all stemmed from Essene tradition as referenced in the Dead Sea Scrolls. Throughout the gospels, Jesus makes his position perfectly clear:

> Woe unto you, scribes and Pharisees; hypocrites! You compass
> sea and land to make one proselyte,[46] and when he is made, you
> make him twofold more the child of hell than yourselves.[47]

Jesus openly criticized the Pharisee rabbis and the Sadducee priests, advising that his own disciples should not follow their examples of preaching one thing and doing another.[48] Inasmuch as the Qumrân scrolls identify the Essene belief system as The Way, St Paul also used this term in explaining his own revised faith when arrested and charged with becoming a Nazarene.[49]

The Ebionite Nazarenes of Jesus' fraternity were thus synonymous with Essenes of Qumrân – the *Nazrie ha Brit* or Keepers of the Covenant who referred to themselves as the *ebionim* (the poor). This related to their eschewing of property and wealth in order to ascend to The Way. It is therefore of particular note that, of all the branches of evolving Christianity, it was the Ebionites whom the Church Fathers accused of being heretics that did not, and would not, concede to the virgin birth dogma or the divinity of Jesus.[50] In this regard, they insisted that Jesus was naturally born of an earthly father and mother, and the ancient gospel of the Ebionites states: 'Jesus was begotten of the seed of a man ... and was called the son of God'.[51]

This Ebionite confirmation that Nazarene Christianity was born out of Essene Judaism is further emphasized by a Qumrân scroll fragment known as the *Aramaic Apocalypse*. This text relates to a prophesied Messiah, who would be 'proclaimed', 'designated' and 'called' the son of God.[52] It was in this regard that John the Baptist sent his disciples to ask Jesus, 'Art thou he that should come, or do we look for another?'[53] It is also the case that teachings of Jesus, such as those of his Sermon on the Mount, were directly based on the Qumrân model. His series of eight *Beatitudes*, each beginning 'Blessed are ...'[54] can be seen to emanate from the sentiments of the *Beatitudes Wisdom Scroll*.[55]

Qumrân falls into the picture again when the events of Jesus' crucifixion are considered. In Matthew, Mark and John, the crucifixion site is named as Golgotha, whereas in Luke it is Calvary. Both names (Hebrew: *Gulgoleth*, Aramaic: *Gulgolta*, Latin: *Calvaria*) derive from words that mean 'skull', and the meaning of Golgotha, as given in the gospels, is a 'place of a skull'.[56]

As the Christian faith evolved from the 4th century, various sites in and around Jerusalem were dubbed with New Testament significance, and a suitable place for the crucifixion was identified on a barren hill that was roughly skull-shaped. But the gospels make no mention of a hill: according to John 19:41, the location was close by a garden which contained an empty sepulchre.

'Places of skulls' are identified in the Dead Sea Scrolls as graveyards and, since it was an act of defilement to walk over the dead, they were marked with the sign of a skull. The New Testament book of Hebrews 13:12–13 adds to this, stating that Jesus suffered 'without the gate' and 'without the camp'. These terms are described in the Old Testament book of Deuteronomy as relating to areas that were ritually unclean,[57] and included places where the bodies of sacrificed animals were burned.

The only real clue as to the actual crucifixion site comes from the book of The Revelation 11:8, which states that Jesus was crucified in 'the great city which spiritually is called Sodom and Egypt'. These were never names attributed to Jerusalem, but they were both applied to Qumrân. The old city of Sodom, as destroyed in the time of Abraham, was by the Dead Sea on the Jordan Valley Fault. It was here that the settlement of Sekhakha, which preceded the renamed Qumrân, was also destroyed by an earthquake in 31 BC.[58] During gospel times, Qumrân was a regional retreat for the healing community of the Egyptian Therapeutate and, when they were in residence, it was dubbed Egypt.[59] It was in Qumrân (Egypt), just seven miles from Jerusalem, that Joseph and Mary had taken sanctuary with the baby Jesus,[60] not the foreign land of Egypt across the Red Sea.

Blemish of the Female

The Judaeo-Christian gospel most frequently mentioned by the early churchmen was the gospel of the Nazarenes. Written in Hebrew and displaying no dependence on anything in the canonical gospels, the earliest date of its composition is reckoned to be the middle of the 1st century when the Jesus traditions were first being collated.[61] As later discussed by Papias, Hegesippus, Clement, Ignatius, Origen, Cyril, Eusebius and Jerome, its primary cause of concern to the early Church Fathers of eventual Catholicism was the Nazarene gospel's express portrayal of the Holy Spirit. It was this original definition, from the very heart of the early movement, that was so fearfully challenged and later dismissed in the Trinity dispute. According to the Nazarene text, the Holy Spirit was a feminine aspect of the divine, known to the Greeks as *Sophia* (Wisdom), and later classified by the Jews as the *Shekhinah* (from the Hebrew abstract verb *sh'kinah*, 'to dwell'). Whilst making no mention of Mary or the birth of Jesus, the Nazarene gospel laid great emphasis on the immersion of Jesus in the River Jordan by his cousin John the Baptist, and it was at this event, not at his birth, that Jesus was said to have been empowered by the Holy Spirit, which he recognized as the Divine Mother.[62]

In his *Discourse on Mary Theotokas* (AD *c*370) Cyril, the Bishop of Jerusalem, took issue with this by stating that the Blessed Mary had paid him a visit and told him personally that it was untrue! Furthermore, he asserted: 'The Hebrews wish for doctrine of this kind greatly, so that they may cast a blemish upon our purity and honour … The Jews cannot be joined unto the doctrine of Christ'.[63]

In making this statement, however, Cyril was entirely wrong. The Nazarenes were indeed Jews, but they were not practising Hebrews of the Eastern tradition like the Pharisees and Sadducees. Although they used the Hebrew and Aramaic languages, their Western philosophies were based on Hellenist thought. Another early text, written originally in Greek, which took the Nazarene stance of the Holy Spirit being female, was the gospel of Philip. It states:

> Some said Mary conceived of the Holy Spirit. They are in error.
> What they are saying they do not know. When did a woman ever
> conceive of a woman?[64]

It was as a result of this that the *Theotokas* and Trinity debates began – essentially to remove Jesus' own Jewish heritage from the newly devised precepts of Roman Christianity and to formulate an approved male definition of the Holy Spirit. There was no room for any consideration of there being a feminine aspect of the divine, and copies of the Ebionite and Nazarene gospels were publicly burned. It was further decreed that, in order to free the Church from any literature that promoted, or even suggested, the notion of female divinity, there would need to be an authorized New Testament canon of carefully selected gospels and texts that were, insofar as was possible, divorced from the original Judaeo-Christian ideal. From that moment, the Nazarenes and Ebionites of the *Desposyni*-led movement were on their own.

The Virgin and the Whore

Prospect of Succession

The connection of Mary, Joseph and Jesus to the Essene community of Qumrân is further cemented by the gospel introduction of the angel Gabriel as the said messenger of the Annunciation. At that time in the 1st century, angels played no part in the rabbinical structure or customs of the Pharisees and Sadducees. In fact, there are no named angels in the Old Testament, and the only character called Gabriel is a man who explains a vision seen by the prophet Daniel.[1] By contrast, the angelic names were very relevant to the Essene community as a feature of their priestly hierarchy. In his exposition on the Essenes in the *Wars of the Jews*, Josephus explains that it was they who 'preserved the names of the angels'.[2] Although not featured in the Hebrew Bible, the angels are listed in the *Book of Enoch* – an Aramaic work discovered at Qumrân and known as Scroll 4Q201.[3] It was written by scribes of the *Hasidim* (Pious Ones), a sect of traditional ascetics who left Jerusalem to build the first settlement at Qumrân in about 130 BC.

Also within the Dead Sea Scrolls collection is a document known as the *War Rule*, which discusses the struggle between the Children of Light (the Essene followers of The Way) and the Sons of Darkness, described as the *Kittim* (Romans).[4] This scroll details the order of angelic ranking, specifically denoting the archangels Michael, Gabriel, Sariel and Raphael.[5] These names were applied to the most senior priests at Qumrân, the two chiefs of which (Michael and Gabriel) also held the Zadok and Abiathar distinctions. From the time of King David, when they became guardians of the Ark of the

Covenant,[6] the line of Zadok retained the primary heritage, while the Abiathar was the second in command.[7] Whatever their personal names, these priests were known respectively to the Essenes, by way of angelic definition, as Michael and Gabriel.[8] In the original Greek, *aggelos* (more usually transliterated as *angelos* – Latin, *angelus*) meant 'messenger'. Modern English derives the word 'angel' from this via Church Latin, but the Anglo-Saxon word *engel* came originally from the old French *angele*. In this respect, the Michael and Gabriel were not just the leaders of the priestly hierarchy, but were also the primary ambassadors of the community.

In the New Testament gospel of Luke, the angelic Gabriel informs the priest Zacharias that a son (the eventual John the Baptist) would be born to his wife Elizabeth.[9] Subsequently, in the same gospel, Gabriel visits Joseph's wife Mary[10] with the announcement that she too will bear a son, to be named Jesus. In Matthew, Gabriel is not named; he is simply called 'the angel of the Lord',[11] and appears to Joseph rather than to Mary.

What we have here is a situation whereby the Abiathar priest, angelically styled Gabriel, performed a dutiful function to advise Zacharias, Mary and Joseph that their sons were each of particular significance. To understand this fully, we can turn again to Flavius Josephus. He advised in the *Wars of the Jews* that the Essenes generally 'neglected wedlock, although they did not absolutely deny the fitness of marriage'.[12] The normal procedure was for the Essenes to take in abandoned or illegitimate children to increase the community fold. In situations where 'the prospect of succession' was important, however, certain of them did marry, although under conditions of a strictly regulated discipline.

The Essenes not only continued the angelic structure within their community, but also preserved the kingly and priestly traditions of dynastic inheritance as applicable to the Zadokite and Davidic successions.[13] In relation to this, the two relevant couples in the early gospel era were Elizabeth and Zacharias (Zadokite) and Mary and Joseph (Davidic). Josephus described that the husbands would 'try their spouses for three years' before the final cementing of wedlock.

This was to ensure 'that they are likely to be fruitful. They then actually marry them'.[14]

The three-year trial period was, as explained by Josephus, to ensure that the wife could conceive, since procreation was the necessary reason for dynastic wedlock. Such marriages, he wrote, were 'not out of regard to pleasure, but for the sake of posterity'.[15] It was therefore a variable trial period, according to individual circumstances, with three years being the maximum duration. If the wife had not conceived during that term then the marital contract would not be fulfilled, and the husband was free to marry another. If there was a conception, then after a further period of three months (in order to guard against a possible miscarriage) the contract could be finalized. Thus, the wife was always three-months pregnant at her contractual wedding.[16]

The reason why the probationary period was as long as three years was that physical relations between the espoused couple were only allowed in the month of *Tebeth* (29 days within December–January). This was to ensure, as effectively as possible, that any resultant dynastic birth would occur in the following *Tishri* (30 days within September–October), the holy month of Atonement (*Yom Kippur*). If the bride did not conceive in the first year, intimate relations were suspended until the next *Tebeth*, and so on.[17]

As set out earlier (*see* page 54), Mary's first bridal anointing of Jesus was in AD 30,[18] and her second anointing was in AD 33.[19] It follows that when Mary Magdalene anointed Jesus on the second occasion in *Nissan* (March–April) AD 33, she was already an expectant mother of three months. It does, however, present an intriguing scenario in respect of the earlier situation concerning Jesus' parents, Joseph and Mary.

We cannot know whether the angelic annunciation (the approval for wedlock) was correctly reported in the gospels, but Joseph's initial reaction does appear strange until the customary details are understood. We are told that Mary's husband 'being a just man, and not willing to make her a public example, was minded to put her away privily' – which is to say, secreted in a monastic environment.

Gabriel's response to this was: 'Fear not to take unto thee Mary thy wife: for that which is conceived in her is of the Holy Ghost'.[20] But why would Joseph have even thought to hide his wife Mary away at such a time? Was there some cause for embarrassment by way of her condition? This would certainly have been the case if Jesus had been conceived at the wrong time of year.

Against the Law

The Jewish calendar is established in a different manner to the familiar Gregorian calendar. It runs through a series of split months, beginning not in January but with the month of *Nissan* (30 days within March–April). The month for dynastic betrothals was that of *Tammuz* (29 days within June–July). Dynastic first marriages were conducted in *Tishri* (September–October), with sexual relations permitted only in the month of *Tebeth* (December–January). The month for contractual marriages (ie, three months after conception) was therefore *Nissan*. *Yom Kippur* (Atonement) occurs on the 10th day of *Tishri* as instituted in the Old Testament book of Leviticus:

> In the seventh month, on the tenth day of the month, you shall afflict your souls, and you shall not do any work ... For on that day shall the priest make an atonement for you to cleanse you from all your sins before the Lord.[21]

The Gregorian solar-based calendar was decreed by Pope Gregory XIII in 1582.[22] It counts days as the basic unit of time, grouping them into years of 365 or 366 (leap year) days. As against this, the Hebrew calendar was lunar in origin, and its 12-monthly year totals 354 days. To make up for the deficiency of 11 days in relation to the solar calendar, it adds a complete calendar month in 7 years of a 19-year cycle.

In contrast to the lunar concept, the Essenes of Qumrân adopted the Romans' Julian calendar in 44 BC. This solar calendar, with its year of 365.25-days, was introduced by Julius Caesar in 46 BC and was based on the tropical year as determined by the length of time that the sun (as viewed from the Earth) takes to return to the same position relative to the equinoxes and solstices.[23] For all practical purposes, therefore, the Essene year adopted the monthly identifications that are applicable today, including March, June, September and December.

In 1992, the results of a remarkable and exhaustive biblical survey were published by Dr Barbara Thiering, a lecturer in Old Testament Hebrew for the School of Divinity at the University of Sydney. A key feature of this 20-year project was the calculation of a sequential New Testament chronology in accordance with the Essene calendar and dating procedure as indicated by the Dead Sea Scrolls.[24]

The Scrolls are now the most useful aids to understanding the Judaean culture of the pre-Gospel era, but they were discovered by pure chance as recently as 1947.[25] A Bedouin shepherd boy, Mohammed ed-Di'b, was searching for a lost goat in the cliff-hill caves of Qumrân, near Jericho, when he found a number of tall earthenware jars. Professional archaeologists were called in and excavations were subsequently undertaken – not only at Qumrân but at nearby Murabba'at and Mird in the Wilderness of Judaea.[26]

During the late 1940s and early 1950s, many more jars were discovered in 11 different caves. Altogether the jars contained around 500 Hebrew and Aramaic manuscripts – among them Old Testament writings and numerous documents of community record, with some of their traditions dating back to about 250 BC. The Scrolls had been hidden during the Jewish Revolt against the Romans (between AD 66 and 70) and were never retrieved. The Old Testament book of Jeremiah (32:14) states prophetically: 'Thus saith the Lord of Hosts ... Take these evidences ... and put them in an earthen vessel, that they may continue many days'.[27]

Dr Thiering's detailed chronology shows that the date of the Annunciation was in June of 8 BC. Without waiting for any 3-month period of confirmation, it appears that Joseph had consulted Gabriel as soon as Mary's pregnancy was suspected at around the time of their betrothal. Then, in the following March of 7 BC (during the reign of Herod the Great), Jesus was born.[28] It appears that the reason for Joseph's concern was that he and Mary had disobeyed the rules of dynastic wedlock by having sexual relations outside the month of December, and even before their first marriage in the preceding September. In strict terms this would have rendered their offspring illegitimate under the law.

Once Mary's unauthorized pregnancy had been confirmed, Joseph would have been granted the option of not going through with the marriage ceremony. To save embarrassment he could have placed Mary in monastic custody ('put her away privily'), where the eventual child would be raised by the priests. But if the child were a boy, he would be Joseph's firstborn descendant in the Davidic succession. It would have made little sense to bring him up as an unidentified orphan. Joseph and Mary's unborn child was plainly a significant prospect and demanded special treatment as an exception to the rule. The angelic Gabriel (the Abiathar priest) would have advised that, since a sacred legacy was at stake, then he would legitimize the conception as being of holy consequence, and that Joseph should go ahead with the marriage ceremony: 'Fear not to take unto thee Mary thy wife' (Matthew 1:20).

Following this dispensation, the normal rules would have been applied once more – the first being that no physical contact was allowed between man and wife until some while after the child had been born: 'Then Joseph being raised from his sleep did as the angel of the Lord had bidden him, and took unto him his wife, and knew her not till she had brought forth her firstborn son, and he called his name Jesus' (Matthew 1:24–25).

At all times from betrothal, through the initiatory marriage and until confirmation of pregnancy, leading to the final marriage, a bride was considered to be an *almah*, even though at the same time regarded as a probationary wife. Only after the marital contract was fulfilled did she lose this identification to be reclassified as a mother.

Hence (although wrongly translated as 'virgin'), the original gospel texts are perfectly accurate in describing that an *almah* had conceived.

The Firstborn Son

The notion of Mary being a constant virgin was first discussed in *The Panarion* of Epiphanius in AD 375 (*see* page 75). In this work he challenged the gospel entries which claimed that Joseph was the father of Jesus – for example, John 6:42, when the residents of Capernaeum asked: 'Is this not Jesus, the son of Joseph, whose father and mother we know?' Dismissing the fact that Matthew 1:25 refers to Jesus as Mary's 'firstborn son', Epiphanius also disputed verses such as Matthew 13:55: 'Is this not the carpenter's son? Is not his mother called Mary and his brethren, James, and Joses, and Simon, and Judas?' Also Luke 2:7 which similarly cites Jesus as Mary's 'firstborn son', along with Matthew 13:56 and Mark 6:3 which both indicate that Jesus also had sisters. According to Epiphanius, these gospel entries were all incorrect and, in his opinion, those who upheld them 'had a grudge against the Virgin and desired to cheapen her reputation'.[29]

What is even more astonishing is the fact that 317 years later the bishops of the Council of Trullo agreed with Epiphanius. This made it perfectly clear that Church dogma was not destined to be based on the gospels, but on the strategic objectives of those who created the doctrines. The situation is no different today: the gospels are cited when they are in line with required Church teaching, but they are equally ignored and dismissed when there are perceived conflicts of doctrinal interest. Turning people to these gospel entries, wrote Epiphanius, 'distracts anyone who wants to track down something about the truth'![30] Once again, just as quoted by Clement of Alexandria two centuries earlier (*see* page 40), there was deemed to be an original 'truth' and a different 'truth according to the Faith'.

In challenging the literal interpretation of the gospels regarding Jesus' brothers and sisters, the Catholic doctrine insists that the Greek words *adelphos* (brother) and *adelpha* (sister), as used in these instances, could equally refer to cousins. Based on that understanding, the words brother and sister could, of course, also refer to people who are quite unrelated, as perhaps in monastic or conventual establishments. But these are not the contexts in which the scriptural words are used.

When the gospels refer to cousins they use a quite different terminology – as for example in Luke 1:36, which refers to Mary's cousin Elizabeth using the term *suggenes*, not *adelpha*. In the Latin translation, *cognata* is used to identify a cousin. The entry in Luke 14:12 draws a good comparison when discussing *fratres* (brothers) and *cognatos* (cousins), while in the Greek rendition it cites *adelphos* (brothers) and *suggenes* (cousins). The gospel words *adelphos* and *adelpha* therefore mean precisely what they denote: brothers and sisters – and indeed more than that: the precise meanings of the words specifically define siblings and offspring of the same parents.[31]

We have seen that St Clement, a 1st-century bishop in Rome, wrote a letter to Jesus' brother James, the lord bishop of Jerusalem (*see* page 58), who was also twice referenced as the brother of Christ in *The Antiquities of the Jews*. Jesus' other brothers are named in Matthew 13:55 as Joses, Simon and Judas. Mark 6:3 also names the brothers as James, Joses, Juda, and Simon. It is also particularly interesting to note that, despite the Catholic concept that Jesus did not have any sisters, 'The Lord and his sisters' are actually mentioned in the Vatican's own *Apostolic Constitutions* as compiled in the 4th century.[32]

The gospel of Philip emphasizes that one of Jesus' sisters was named Mary, the same as her mother.[33] From around AD 150, a work known as the *Protevangelion of James*, gives the names of Jesus' three sisters as being Mary, Salome and Joanna.[34] Then, in his *Panarion* and *Ancoratus*, even Epiphanius lists the very same names.[35] In the New Testament gospels, these sisters appear at the cross and at the tomb of Jesus along with Mary Magdalene and Jesus' mother. Salome appears, for example, in Mark 16:1, while Joanna appears in Luke 24:10, and Mary features in Matthew 28:1.

Jesus' brothers James and Joses, along with their sister Salome, are used strategically in the biblical text to denote the physical state of Jesus during the Passion sequence. Prior to the crucifixion, the Blessed Mary is referred to as 'the mother of Jesus' (for instance, John 2:1). But from the point at which Jesus is placed on the cross, she is defined as 'the mother of James and Joses' (Matthew 27:56 and Mark 15:40), while at the tomb she is given as 'the mother of James and Salome' (Mark 16:1). Subsequently, once Jesus is on the scene again after his entombment, there is a reversion to Mary's previous style as 'the mother of Jesus' (Acts 1:14).

According to the Flesh

Despite the fact that the gospel of John does not detail the Bethlehem nativity, John 7:42 does make an important statement regarding the ancestry of Jesus: 'Hath not the scripture said, that Christ cometh of the seed of David'. This comment is especially intriguing in its reference to 'the scripture'. It denotes that there was a scripture (a sacred writing) concerning Jesus' kingly ancestry even before the gospel itself was written. In addition, St Paul's Epistle to the Romans 1:3–4 refers to 'Jesus Christ our Lord, which was made of the seed of David according to the flesh; and declared to be the Son of God'. Again, in Mark 10:47 and Matthew 22:42 Jesus is called the 'son of David'. In Acts 2:30, Peter (referring to King David) calls Jesus the 'fruit of his loins, according to the flesh'. Even in the earliest sequence of the Annunciation, Gabriel said to Mary that Jesus would inherit 'the throne of his father David' (Luke 1:32). These entries, along with the male-line genealogical lists in Matthew and Luke, make it abundantly clear that Jesus was of direct descent from King David.

It is an intriguing fact that in relating Jesus' lineage, the Matthew (1:6–16) and Luke (3:23–31) listings do not agree on the precise genealogy from King David. Matthew gives the line to Joseph and Jesus as descending from David's son, King Solomon, whereas Luke details a descent from Nathan, another of David's sons.[36] The lists eventually coincide with Prince Zerubbabel in the 6th century BC,[37] but then diverge again. Matthew traces Jesus' descent through a son of Zerubbabel named Abiud, while Luke takes a course through a son called Rhesa. Finally, Jesus' paternal grandfather is called Jacob according to Matthew,[38] but in Luke he is said to have been Heli.[39] Here, however, both versions are correct since Joseph's father, Heli, held the distinction of Jacob in his patriarchal capacity within the Qumrân community.[40]

In discussing the ostensibly variant Solomon and Nathan genealogies down to Jesus, Eusebius of Caesarea referred to a 3rd-century exposition which maintained that a natural father was not necessarily the father in terms of the law. The document claimed that it was all a matter of guardianship and upbringing, but that 'the memory of both was preserved – of the real and nominal fathers'.[41] This explanation does not make complete sense because genealogy is about natural parenthood, even if illegitimate. It is only concerned with matters of law when the inheritance of specific titles is involved. A more honest reason for the biblical discrepancy would be that important females of the bloodline were not included in the lists. This is confirmed in the Old Testament book of Chronicles, which details the patrilineal descent of Zerubbabel from King Solomon (as given in Matthew), whereas Zerubbabel's mother was descended from Nathan, who is cited in Luke.[42]

The fact of Jesus' Davidic paternal descent is laid out in Hebrews 7:14, which relates to his appointment in the high priestly Order of Melchizedek. From the time of Moses and Aaron, only the tribe of Levi had any automatic right to Israelite priesthood. The tribe of Judah, which included David and his dynasty down to Joseph, held the privilege of kingship, but not of priesthood. In writing his epistle to the Hebrews, St Paul clarified the matter of Jesus' new priestly status with the following: 'It is evident that our Lord sprang out of Judah, of which tribe Moses spake nothing concerning priesthood'. Just before this, the point is made that, to accommodate this divergence from custom, there was 'made of necessity a change also of the law'.[43]

When confronted by questions as to whether he was the son of God, Jesus generally avoided the issue. In Matthew, when asked by the High Priest whether he was in truth the son of God, Jesus replied, 'Thou hast said' – implying that the priest had said it, not he.[44] In Luke he answered in virtually identical terms: 'Then said they all, Art thou then the son of God? And he said unto them, Ye say that I am'.[45] On other occasions, Jesus responded to the effect that he was actually the 'son of man'.[46] The perception of Jesus as the physical son of God emanates from things said about him by others.[47] There are 45 entries in the New Testament which state that Jesus was 'declared to be', 'preached as', 'believed to be', 'was called' the son of God. Alternatively, there are 90 mentions of his being the 'son of man', the majority of which references were made by Jesus himself.

When viewed in the context of Jewish, Roman and early Christian record, there is reason enough to acknowledge the person of Jesus Christ (just as did the Nazarenes, Ebionites and Essenes of his own era) without considering him to have been the individual son of God. According to the gospels, Jesus' interrogation by Pontius Pilate centred more precisely on the contentious question of whether or not he was the legitimate King of the Jews.[48] It is therefore entirely possible to believe in the existence of Jesus, and indeed to accept the social and moral aspects of his teachings, without necessarily believing in God at all.

From an historical perspective, the most importantly recorded fact is that Jesus was the reputed heir to the dynasty of King David. From a parallel religious standpoint, it was actually the kingly line of David that was considered to be God's offspring, not Jesus as a lone individual. This premise is laid down in 2 Samuel 7:13–14, where God is said to have announced of King David: 'He shall build an house for my name, and I will establish the throne of his kingdom for ever. I will be his father, and he shall be my son'.

The Greek text of the 1st-century *Didache* (*see* page 57) is particularly expressive in this context. Emanating from shortly after Jesus' own lifetime, this influential work of the original Judaeo-Christians not only references the Davidic 'vine', but cites David and Jesus specifically as the 'servants' of God, not as his sons:

> We thank thee, our Father, for the holy vine of David thy servant, which you madest known to us through Jesus thy servant.[49]

Sins of the Mother

In consideration of Jesus' parentage and the irregular nature of his conception, the Hebrew fraternity of Pharisees and Sadducees refused to accept that he was the legitimate royal heir. But the Hellenist sects of Nazarenes and Ebionites thought otherwise. Mary's pregnancy had been sanctified by the Abiathar-Gabriel and Jesus was therefore legitimate under the law of the Essenes. Joseph and Mary (specifically referred to as the 'parents' of Jesus in Luke 2:27) subsequently presented their son to be legitimized again after his birth by the Gabriel, whose personal name we learn was Simeon.[50] But then seven years later their second son, James, was born within all the rules of dynastic wedlock and there was no disputing his legitimacy. It was James who, according to the rule of Hebrew law, would have held the senior entitlement to the Davidic succession, but subsequent events were destined to circumvent this by way of Zadokite tradition

Through long-prevailing custom, the Davidic kings were allied to the jointly dynastic Zadokite priests and, during the infancy of Jesus, the prevailing Zadok was his maternal kinsman Zacharias. When procreation was embarked upon, a priestly dynast such as the Zadok was suspended temporarily from his ordained role and would pass his religious duties to a deputy. When physical relations with his wife were completed, he would then live apart from her and resume a celibate existence. The story of Zacharias' procreational leave is somewhat veiled in Luke 1:11–23, but we are told that, being concerned about his advancing age, he met with Gabriel and received his paternity sanction. Zacharias was then rendered 'speechless in the Temple', which is to say that he was prevented from preaching in his usual ordained capacity. Having transferred his priestly authority to Simeon the Abiathar, his wife Elizabeth (Mary's cousin) was then permitted to bear a son, who was eventually the Zadokite successor, John the Baptist. As the two sons, John and Jesus, grew to manhood, John became Jesus' ally in the Davidic succession dispute. He baptized him personally in the River Jordan and openly proclaimed him as the legitimate Christ.[51]

The importance of this Zadokite appointment was profound. From the coronation of Britain's King George II in 1727 onwards, George Frideric Handel's anthem *Zadok the Priest* has been sung at each successive coronation in Westminster Abbey, London. The composition alludes directly to the ritualistic installation of King Solomon by Zadok in the 10th century BC as described in the Old Testament book of Kings.[52] As the son of King David, Solomon was the first in a reigning line of the Royal House of Judah that was to prevail for more than 300 years until 586 BC when Jerusalem was destroyed by Prince Nebuchadnezzar of Babylon. This destruction followed an initial assault 20 years earlier when thousands of Israelites were removed into Babylonian captivity. Eventually, the last monarch, King Zedekiah, was also taken hostage along with his sons. The later generations of Israelites did not return to Judah until 536 BC under the leadership of Prince Zerubbabel. He initiated the rebuilding of the Jerusalem Temple, and his descendants progressed (according to both Matthew and Luke) down to Joseph and Jesus.

In terms of the monarchical tradition of Judah, there was only one man who could formally proclaim Jesus (or James if he desired) as the rightful dynast of the Davidic bloodline. This man was the then prevailing Zadok priest, John the Baptist. Regarding his

John the Baptist Proclaims the King,
by Julius Schnorr von Carolsfeld (1794–1872)

performance of this office, the gospels state of Jesus that the Holy Spirit was seen 'descending from heaven like a dove, and it abode on him'.[53] It was this baptismal event to which the gospel of the Nazarenes also referred (*see* page 93), and which the eventual Trinity doctrine sought to deny. All scriptural texts, whether canonical or otherwise, relate that the Holy Spirit descended on Jesus at that moment of his baptism and kingly proclamation. It was not a product of his birth, neither was it associated with his mother Mary; nor was Jesus himself the Holy Spirit. In all previous tradition the Holy Spirit (generally represented by a dove) was considered to be female. In Catholic literature, however, the Holy Spirit is referred to as 'He' and 'Him'.[54]

Since the Holy Spirit was decreed to be one of three male persons comprising the Trinity, Mary's position as Jesus' earthly mother had to be redefined. She was therefore classified not only as a virgin as far as her conception of Jesus was concerned, but as a 'virgin for ever'. There was, however, still the other Mary in Jesus' life to consider: Mary Magdalene – the woman who sponsored him, travelled with him, confided in him, anointed him, married him, and was a loyal companion to his mother and sisters. She was there at the foot of the cross; she went to attend Jesus with spices at the tomb, and was the first to speak with him afterwards in the garden. She is documented in the gospel of Philip as the 'consort' (koinonôs) of Jesus;[55] she has been called the Apostle of the Apostles, the woman whom Jesus often kissed[56] and called his 'blessed one', the 'woman who knew the All',[57] and the woman that Jesus loved.

If Jesus were to be accepted as an aspect of the Holy Spirit, and if the Church was to survive as an institution based on a contrived Apostolic Succession, Mary Magdalene and her offspring had to be removed from the reckoning. Another entry in the gospel of Philip recounts an occasion when the apostles questioned Jesus about his intimacy with Mary Magdalene, asking, 'Why do you love her more than all of us?' In response 'The Saviour answered and said to them, Why do I not love you like her?' Then, pursuing the discussion, he added, 'Great is the mystery of marriage, for without it the world would not have existed. Now the existence of the world depends on man, and the existence of man on marriage'.[58]

Mary Magdalene's presence in various gospels and other texts was such that there was no means by which the Church could deny her relationship with Jesus, but she could certainly be demeaned and scandalized. The method to accomplish this was derived from a sermon given by Pope Gregory I in 591, wherein he classified the Magdalene as a peccatrix – 'a sinner guilty of all the vices'. This was interpreted by the bishops as meaning only one thing: Mary was decidedly unchaste because a female sinner was necessarily a whore – an image which she retained until she was granted forgiveness and canonized just a few decades ago in 1969.[59]

So what was wrong with the idea of a female aspect of the divine? To the early Christians, absolutely nothing, but the Church had a considerable problem with the nature of motherhood. Not only were the two women closest to Jesus sidelined as a virgin and a whore, but a further dilemma arose in consideration of the birth of the Blessed Mary herself. For her to have been so special as to conceive and give birth as a virgin, she must have been somehow unique. She could not have been an ordinary child, and must herself have emanated free of male intervention. Hence, it was construed that her father was not directly responsible, and that Mary was the product of her mother's own immaculate conception.

Not all the early churchmen were in agreement with this philosophy. One who stood against it was Cyril, the Bishop of Jerusalem. His *Discourse on Mary Theotokas* is the first known document to have cited the names of Mary's parents as having been Anna and Joachim, and Cyril was insistent that they were her natural mother and father:

> The mother of the King of Life tasted death like every other human being, because she was flesh and blood. And, moreover, she was begotten by a human father, and brought forth by a human mother … Without flesh and without body, forces would be beings without bodies, and they could not die like mortal men.[60]

His was not the majority Catholic opinion, however, and St John Damascene, the later Patriarch of Jerusalem (c676–754), progressed the concept of Mary's immaculate conception even further. He went so far as to assert that the supernatural influence of God was so comprehensive that even Mary's mother Anna was herself conceived without sexual intervention. The pure generation of the Holy Ghost, he maintained, preserved her line from any evidence of sin.[61]

Although the doctrine of the Immaculate Conception was not formalized until the constitution *Ineffabilis Deus* of Pope Pius IX on 8 December 1854, the dogma was upheld from the early days of the Trinity dispute. Through all the centuries between, the root definition remained the same, and the 1854 pronouncement stated: 'In the first instance of her conception, by a singular privilege and grace granted by God, in view of the merits of Jesus Christ, the Saviour of the human race, was preserved exempt from all stain of original sin'.[62] Precisely the same terminology was used: 'original sin'. Natural motherhood was deemed sinful, and if parental fatherhood was not a feature of the Marian succession, then Jesus could not possibly have been a father.

Nevertheless, there is a contradiction in terms that arises from this. Mary, her mother, and her mother's mother were all deemed to have conceived by the Holy Spirit. But under the Trinity doctrine, Jesus was himself (along with God) reckoned to be the Holy Spirit. Why then could he not have had a wife who was doctrinally regarded to have conceived mysteriously in the family's traditional manner? That was the real nub of the problem. The line had to be seen to end with Jesus. If not, then the whole concept of papal Apostolic Succession would be rendered worthless.

The Myth of Succession

Emulated Passion

Pope Leo XIII stated in his 1896 bull, *Apostolicae Curae*, that the Catholic Church believes the Anglican Church's Protestant consecrations to be 'absolutely invalid and utterly void' because the Church of England does not participate in the Apostolic Succession. The Catholic doctrine asserts:

> Apostilicity is of great importance because it is the surest indication of the true Church ... Since the Church is infallible in its teaching ... we must obey the priests of the Church. If there is but one true Church, and if the Catholic Church is Apostolic, the necessary inference is that no other Church is Apostolic.[1]

Given that Apostolic Succession is reckoned to be so important that all Christian Churches outside that of Rome are in some way inferior, it is useful to look a little more closely at its establishment to ascertain if it truly is so special. It rests primarily on a tradition of St Peter, but also indirectly on St Paul whose own connection with Rome is attested and provides the necessary foundation for the associated Petrine concept.

The underlying principle of apostolicity is contained in the idea of 'succession'. This can be defined in two ways. An offspring might succeed a parent as heir to a title, as in royal dynasties, or anyone might succeed another by way of bequest or appointment without having any personal relationship – as in successive presidents, prime ministers, or indeed any job function. In terms of papal

Apostolic Succession, the Catholic presumption is officially stated to be based on: 1) 'That St Peter came to Rome, and ended there his pontificate', and 2) 'That the Bishops of Rome who came after him held his official position in the Church'.[2]

There is no record of Peter ever holding a pontificate since there was no such office for anyone to hold in his day. The English verb 'to pontificate' is expressly defined as 'being pompously dogmatic and arrogant in the manner of a pontiff'.[3] Stemming from the Latin *pontifex*, the word denotes a 'bridge builder' and, in Christian terms, it relates to the bridge between God and the people. That 'bridge', according to all early understanding, was Jesus, as proclaimed by St Paul himself in a letter from Rome: 'Christ is the head of the church'.[4] In 751, however, this notion was corrupted by Pope Zachary I, who decreed that popes from the time of Sylvester I (as installed by Emperor Constantine – *see* page 26) were the inheritors of a uniquely vicarious licence to represent Jesus as his appointed deputies. The Pontiffs of Rome, he declared, 'were the Vicars of the Son of God' (*Vicarius Filii Dei*).[5]

When Constantine established his Church in AD 314, it was maintained that the bodies of Paul and Peter were buried by the side of roads leading out of the city – St Paul on the Via Ostiana and St Peter on the Via Cornelia. Excavations were undertaken, but no coffins or bodies were found. Consequently, it was suggested that they had probably been moved into the catacombs by Christians who feared they might be desecrated. But as far as could be ascertained, there were no Christians who had any knowledge of this, and it was claimed that the two most prized relics of the Faith in Rome had carelessly been lost. Undaunted, Constantine built churches at the traditional grave locations, which have since become the great basilicas of St Peter and St Paul.

Some years ago, in his Christmas radio broadcast on 23 December 1950, Pope Pius XII made a monumental announcement that the tomb of St Peter had been discovered exactly where it was supposed to be. It had been revealed beneath the high altar of the San Pietro Basilica in the Vatican. 'The tomb of the Prince of the

Apostles has been found,' he exclaimed. There was actually nothing to identify the coffin as being that of St Peter, but it was at least the remnant of a tomb in what was deemed to be the right place, even though it had not existed in that location at the time of Constantine's excavation.

Following requests from pilgrims who also wanted to venerate the tomb of St Paul in the 2000 Millennium celebrations, archaeologists from the Vatican Museum began to excavate beneath the altar of the San Paolo Basilica on the Ostian Way. The *Catholic Herald* subsequently expressed concern that, whereas tourists flocked daily into St Peter's Church, an average weekday afternoon might see only 75 people at St Paul's.[6] But good news was at hand. In February 2005, a marble sarcophagus was unearthed, and in December 2006 it was formally proclaimed to be the tomb of 'Paul Apostle Martyr'. No such tomb was found when Constantine had the site excavated before the original church was built in AD 320. Moreover, the coffin rests on the ground level of the altar as it was in the later reign of Emperor Theodosius. According to the Museum, it was known that Theodosius had lodged a marble sarcophagus at the church in AD 390, and it was this very item that the archaeologists were seeking. This does not, of course, disprove the content to be the remains of St Paul. All that can be said is that the relic is of late 4th-century origin – a time when there was no record of Paul's original coffin ever having been discovered.

✠ ✠ ✠

When the apostles and other disciples first began to travel from their homeland, their Christian missions were established in many countries. One of the earliest was the chapel at Glastonbury in England, built in AD 63 before Peter and Paul were said to have been martyred in Rome. Of primary relevance, however, was the high seat of Jesus' brother James in Jerusalem and, until Constantine's era, there was no seniority between the other churches in Antioch, Carthage, Alexandria, Rome or anywhere else. The primacy of Rome was the result of a 4th-century political decision in which Peter and Paul were granted an assumed seniority over James, and above Simon Zelotes, Thomas, Philip and the apostles who had pursued their missions in other lands.

The first Christian bishop in Rome was Linus (*see* page 26), but there was no way to base an Apostolic Succession on his legacy because Linus had not been an apostle of Jesus. By the same token, although Paul was influential as an early Christian, he had not been an apostle either. Thus, Peter was selected as the apostolic founder of a Roman establishment in which, the popes claimed, that as his 'successors in office', they were the appointed Vicars of Christ. It is for this reason that the Catholic hierarchy refuses to acknowledge Protestant Christian establishments. Those such as the Anglican Church are condemned for insisting that the continuity of Christianity resides in Jesus Christ, whereas Catholicism teaches that continuity of the Church rests in the Apostolic Succession of the popes, who have succeeded by way of a deputized authority from St Peter.[7]

The story of Paul's going to Rome began in AD 57 with the murder of Jonathan Annas, the high priest of Jerusalem. Josephus explains in the *Antiquities of the Jews* that the killing was arranged by Antonius Felix, who had become the Procurator of Judaea (the office once held by Pontius Pilate). Annas had apparently admonished Felix for his bad management of Jewish affairs, and Felix retaliated from Caesarea by sending his assassins to Jerusalem. They arrived at the Temple in the guise of worshippers, but then produced their concealed daggers and slaughtered the high priest along with a number of witnesses.[8]

This led to a good deal of tension and insurgency among the Jews in Jerusalem and other parts of Judaea, in the course of which Governor Felix sent his cavalry into the field and slew many hundreds of rioters.[9] At that time, in AD 58, Paul returned to Jerusalem from Ephesus in Asia Minor, and was immediately protected from the wrath of Felix by King Herod-Agrippa II. Paul had been the young prince's tutor in earlier times, and Agrippa was now the brother-in-law of Antonius Felix who had married Princess

Drusilla. In the light of this personal connection, the Jews then set themselves against Paul, claiming that he was an ally of their enemy. They seized Paul and planned to have him executed, but he was rescued by the Roman tribune, Lysias, who sent him under guard to the court of Governor Felix in Caesarea.[10] A few days later, the succeeding high priest, Ananias, arrived with a Temple orator named Tertullus. They accused Paul of being a seditious leader of

St Paul Rescued by Lysias, by Gustave Doré (1832–1883)

the Nazarenes, and demanded that he must be sent for trial in Jerusalem. Felix ruled against this, and confined Paul to house arrest in Caesarea for nearly two years.[11]

In Rome, the pressure mounted against Felix for his murder of Jonathan Annas the high priest, as a result of which Emperor Nero removed him from office in AD 59. When Porcius Festus was appointed as the new Procurator, he withdrew Paul's protection and arranged to have him sent to face the Jewish Temple elders in Jerusalem. Paul (unwisely, as it transpired) appealed directly to Nero, stating that he would rather stand trial in Rome. Herod-Agrippa II and Queen Berenice then arrived in Caesarea to convene a private hearing. They found no cause for any charges, and Agrippa said that he would have been happy to exonerate Paul there and then, except for the fact that Paul's letter to Nero had caused a problem. As a result of this formal appeal, he must now appear before the Emperor.[12] And so Paul was placed on a ship bound for Rome.

Battling against fearful storms, which led to his ship being wrecked off the coast of Malta, the overall voyage took some months but, once in Rome, Paul lived in the city unhindered until AD 64.[13] Trouble then erupted when the unseated Felix was finally brought to trial. Paul's association with Felix was made known to the Senate, and he was accused of conspiracy in the murder of Jonathan Annas even though he had been in Ephesus at the time. Felix was acquitted, but Paul's further association with Herod-Agrippa II, whom Nero detested, was deemed reason enough to keep him in custody. Shortly afterwards, the city of Rome was set ablaze: the Emperor blamed the Christians, following which he had many of them executed, and it appears that Paul was probably among them.

The whole sequence, from the Annas assassination to the seizure of Paul and his transportation to Rome, is reported in the New Testament Acts 21–28. Subsequent events in his life are detailed in Paul's various epistles to the Romans, Corinthians, Galatians, Ephesians, Phillippians, Colossians, Thessalonians, Hebrews, and to his colleagues Titus, Philemon and Timothy. Overall, this constitutes a total of some 60,000 words of the New Testament, but in all this

Paul's only two mentions of Peter relate to long past events. Galatians 1:18 tells of 15 days that Paul spent with Peter in Jerusalem, and Galatians 2:11–14 relates to a meeting in Antioch long before Paul went to Rome.

In terms of Peter's personal appearances in the New Testament, his last chronological mention is an account of his imprisonment by Herod of Chalcis in AD 44.[14] Following his escape, the item concludes that the guards wondered 'what was become of Peter … Herod had sought for him and found him not'. Shortly afterwards, there is a brief citation concerning Peter's opinions about circumcision – and that is the last we hear of him.

So, did Peter ever go to Rome? Was he there in the early AD 60s at the time of Paul's Roman residence? There is no way of knowing. There is no document that can attest to anything in Peter's life beyond AD 44.[15] If he was in Rome, then Paul never saw fit to mention the fact; neither did any Roman chronicler, nor any other Christian or Jewish writer of the era.

The earliest testimony concerning the death of St Peter comes from Clement of Rome, but he makes no mention of Peter having ever been in the city, neither does he describe the nature of Peter's demise. In a lengthy epistle to the Corinthians, written about AD 96, Clement stated:

> Through zeal and cunning the greatest and most righteous supports have suffered persecution and been warred to death. Let us place before our eyes the good apostle St Peter who, in consequence of unjust zeal, suffered not one or two, but numerous miseries and, having thus given testimony, has entered the merited place of glory.[16]

Given that Clement had written this letter from Rome, it was decided by some early churchmen that Rome was perhaps where Peter had died. Pursuing this theme, the first actual mention of Peter in Rome appears in the *Adversus Haereses* of Irenaeus of Lyon. In this work from AD *c*177, Irenaeus referred to 'the greatest and most ancient church, known by all, founded and organized at Rome by the two most glorious apostles, Peter and Paul'.[17] This was the very same document in which Irenaeus accused Jesus, James and the Nazarenes of Judaea of practising the wrong religion because they did not follow the teachings of St Paul! (*see* page 20).

Then, in the late 2nd century, Quintus Tertullian, an apologist from Carthage in North Africa, stated in his *De Praescriptione* that, in his death, Peter had emulated the passion of Jesus: 'How happy is its church on which apostles poured forth all their doctrine along with their blood, where Peter endured a passion like his Lord's'.[18] From this work it was deduced that 'a passion like his Lord's' must mean that Peter was crucified.

Regarding the said residence and death of Peter in Rome, the Catholic archive, despite the considerable emphasis placed on these things by the Church, states the following:

> We possess no precise information regarding the details of his Roman sojourn … It is widely held that Peter paid a first visit to Rome after he had been miraculously liberated from the prison in Jerusalem [AD 44] … It is not impossible that Peter made a missionary journey to Rome about this time, but such a journey cannot be established with certainty … The task of determining the year of St Peter's death is attended with similar difficulties … Concerning the manner of Peter's death, we possess a tradition, attested to by Tertullian at the end of the 2nd century … that he suffered crucifixion.[19]

But Tertullian did not state that Peter had 'suffered crucifixion'; he merely mentioned 'a passion like his Lord's'. To this day, and based entirely on the interpretation of Tertullian's statement, the dogma remains that Peter was crucified in Rome in a manner that emulated the passion of Jesus. It was adopted by the Church as an item of faith, and enabled the symbol of the cross to be redefined as the cross of St Peter, thereby creating a suitable emblem for the Apostolic Succession. (In some instances, the cross of St Peter is depicted in an inverted fashion – upside down to comply with a philosophy that Peter would have desired to be crucified head downwards as a token of his humility.[20])

Although we have a wealth of information concerning St Paul's reason for going to Rome, plus the accounts of his voyage and his time in the city, there is absolutely nothing to convey even the faintest suggestion that St Peter was there too. What we have is simply a tradition. This does not prove that Peter was not in Rome; there are many traditions with firm foundations in fact – but the problem here is the manner in which this vague tradition has been used as a means of regulatory control. Peter's fabricated pontificate and questionable crucifixion provide the flimsiest of all evidence on which to base the concept of Apostolic Succession. There is simply no evidence, not even circumstantial evidence. His martyrdom stems from the writings of Irenaeus, who openly criticized the teachings of Jesus and James whilst maintaining that 'the greatest and most ancient church' was established by Peter and Paul in Rome. Such writings were sufficient, however, for the bishops of the eventual Roman Church to sideline the missions of apostles in other lands by way of claiming a pseudo-succession from St Peter.

The Apostolic Succession, as contrived in the 4th-century, established the base for papal primacy in a religion that was strategically designed to undermine those who preached the original Nazarene faith of Jesus. The implementation of apostolicity marked the very moment in history when Catholicism became confused with Christianity.

The Denial of Women

Of all the Ante-Nicene writings, the opinions of Tertullian (AD c155–230) were among the most influential in shaping the eventual doctrines of the Church of Rome. This was especially the case in matters concerning the suppression of women. The irony of this is that, in the latter part of his life, Tertullian made a sweeping change of direction and joined a Phrygian group which he had previously considered to consist of superstitious heretics. They were known as the Montanists and two of their leaders, along with Montanus, were Priscilla and Maximilla – women who were professed to be embodiments of the Holy Spirit.

To that point, Tertullian had been one of the most stalwart defenders of Pauline Christianity, but from AD 202 his writings grew ever more bitter against those from whom he parted company. His was one of the most dramatic switches of conscience that occurred in early Christian history. Having recognized the many hypocrisies that existed in his previous undertakings, Tertullian strove to make amends. But although he became perfectly content in the missionary company of women – something he had previously scorned – he could not erase his pronouncements from earlier times, and the reconsidered philosophies of his later life were conveniently ignored.

Tertullian's name is mentioned more than most in terms of how the New Testament eventually was compiled (*see* page 132). A good example of his original style is a treatise entitled *On the Apparel of Women*. In this work, Tertullian wrote of women's lack of grace when compared to the comparative purity of men. He suggested that, when the fallen angels of Genesis came to earth and mated with the daughters of men,[21] they imbued those daughters with lust and carnal desire. They taught them to follow the ways of the serpent, and how to heap ornaments from the devil's head onto their own bodies. Addressing women in general, he continued:

> Do you not know that you are each an Eve? The sentence of God on this sex of yours lives in this age; the guilt must of necessity live too. You are the devil's gateway; you are the unsealer of that forbidden tree; you are the first deserter of the divine law: you are she who persuaded him whom the devil was not valiant enough to attack. You destroyed so easily God's image: man. On account of your desertion even the Son of God had to die.[22]

This was precisely the sort of material on which the early Church thrived in its campaign against women. As a special exception, Jesus' mother Mary was said to be elevated above natural womanhood, while Mary Magdalene was destined to be classified as a whore. But the more general threat posed by mothers was still a thorn in the side of Apostolic Succession. Beyond the control of the Church was the descendant bloodline of the *Desposyni*, the men and women who were running the Nazarene schools and missions, and who continued to marry and procreate. The Catholic bishops could not prevent this, although they could stand apart from it. But what if a pope had offspring? If a pope had an heir, how would that affect the future papacy? Maybe that heir would claim papal inheritance. What then of Apostolic Succession?

A subject that seems never to have been discussed, nor even suggested, was whether Peter might himself have had offspring. We know from the gospels that Peter was married, and in Mark 1:30–31 there is even mention of an incident when Jesus healed Peter's sick mother-in-law. It is also explained that Peter's wife travelled with him, along with Jesus, the apostles and the other wives.[23]

There was only one way to counter all such possibilities, while at the same time denigrating those Christian leaders outside the orthodox movement who perpetuated their leadership through descendant family lines. Women must be vilified across the board; marriage must be scorned and procreation forbidden within the Church. All members of the ecclesiastical establishment must become celibate. Tertullian had written that it was on account of women that 'the Son of God had to die'. This was reason enough to implement restrictive new measures in order to place Apostolic Succession above family succession which, from that time, was considered both inappropriate and ungodly.

But what of the emergent popes and other ecclesiastics – were their own mothers all supposed, in future, to be virgins? Obviously not, but by being celibate themselves they might become divinely superior to the laity, and the sins of their mothers would be forgiven.

Meanwhile, it had to be accepted that everyone, including eventual popes, was born in sin by virtue of having a mother!

Given that many of the clergy were already married when the celibacy discipline was introduced, it was decided that in the interim priests and bishops were allowed to retain their wives so long as they did not live with them. At the Council of Nicaea in AD 325, it was decreed that they might be permitted to live with their mothers, sisters or aunts, but they could not live with female companions, lodgers or wives.[24] This created a very unsatisfactory situation whereby many of the clergy were keen to present an image of celibacy, but led a quite different lifestyle behind the scenes. As a result, the rate of infanticide grew alarmingly, and so priestly contact with women was further restricted. Henceforth, no commerce of any nature was allowed between the sexes. It was decreed that contact with female enterprise was a 'degrading pollutant to the soul'. Then it was impelled that even those clerics with wives could no longer visit them.

Having moved through that generation of churchmen who had been married before the regulations came into force, the absolute rule of perpetual celibacy was enforced from AD 385.[25] In order to make the restriction attractive to the financially ambitious, the proposal was put forward that although sexual abstinence was paramount in order to achieve high status within the Church, the pecuniary rewards were considerable. The prize for obedience would be great glory, riches and power.

From that time, all purposeful contact with women was forbidden and ecclesiastics were prevented from visiting the houses of widows and other single women. In AD 414 it was proclaimed that even unordained deacons of the Church could no longer be married. Every employee had to be single and celibate, living apart from his mother, sisters or any female member of his own family.

In this context, it is quite remarkable that, in later times, so many Christian women, especially the martyrs of those early years, were endowed with posthumous sainthoods. This occurred mainly because, despite the Catholic view of their heresies, these women were already regarded as saints by the Celtic Church, the Nazarene Church, and other establishments outside Vatican control. Mary Magdalene, for instance, was considered a saint from the early 400s by Cassianite and other monastic orders, even becoming Mother Protectress of the Dominican Friars, but she was not accepted for Catholic canonization until 1969. Such now familiar saintly figures were ultimately embraced by the Church of Rome for one reason alone: it was the only way to disguise the fact that the Vatican was not the only church authority with the power to grant sainthoods.

Sex and the Popes

At the Second Council of Arles in AD 443, it was debated that numerous men in Church employment 'preferred sin to ecclesiastical ambition', and that many methods of subterfuge were adopted to avoid detection.[26] At about the same time, Pope Sixtus III was accused of taking undue advantage of nuns in the newly developing convents of women who desired to practise their own regime of chastity within studious environments. Sixtus was charged with sexually accosting a particular nun, but avoided consequences because he, as the Pope, was the designated Vicar of Christ, and therefore his personal actions were sanctified. Not long afterwards the papal fraternity and high-ranking cardinals exempted themselves from the celibacy restrictions, and they were permitted to employ personal mistresses.

This was made possible by way of civil laws compiled by the Roman Emperor Theodosius in the 5th century (the *Codex Theodosianus*) and by the Byzantine Emperor Justinian in the 6th century (the *Codex Justinianus*), thereafter codified in the overall *Corpus Juris Civilis* of 534. This document not only clarified all law in terms of civil jurisdictions, but also influenced the canon law of the Church since it was decreed that '*Ecclesia vivit lege Romana*' – 'The Church exists under Roman law'.[27] Although the Church was entitled to set rules and regulations for its employees, it was also resident as an institution within the precepts of Roman law, wherein prostitution was legal.[28] Thus, although the popes did not marry, their supreme status afforded them the protected privilege of retaining courtesans within the Vatican establishment.

Shortly after the Sixtus affair, Pope Symmachus (AD 498–514) was called before King Theodoric of Italy, charged with unchastity and adultery, but he pleaded his case in a similar manner to his predecessor. Confronting the court, he argued with ultimate success that, since he was the Pope, no human court could possibly judge him.[29] Subsequent to that, the goings-on in Vatican life were constantly interspersed with sexual scandals to the extent that the papal regime was dubbed a 'pornocracy'.

A notorious liaison of later times was that of Pope Sergius III (904–911) and the seductive, teenage Marozia. This led to a departure from the conventional rules of Apostolic Succession when their son eventually became Pope John XI. The Church historian, Cardinal Baronius, wrote that Sergius was 'the slave of every vice and the most wicked of men'.[30] In the interim, Marozia's elder sister Theodora had been the mistress of Pope John X and, by that time, the papal throne had been commonly dubbed 'the groping chair'. After that, Pope John XII (955–964) was accused of establishing a brothel within the Lateran Palace and of using the income to pay off his gambling debts. The laity complained that female pilgrims to the holy places were deterred from visiting Rome because of his 'promiscuous and unbridled lust'.[31] A tribunal convened by Otto, the Holy Roman Emperor, charged John with violating nuns and ravishing two sisters. In response, Pope John had Emperor Otto excommunicated along with all the members of his court. Subsequent to him, Pope John XIII was similarly condemned for defiling his father's mistress and his own niece. Ultimately, he was killed by an enraged citizen who discovered the Pope in adultery with his wife.[32]

By the Renaissance era, the Archbishop of Canterbury in England had become so embarrassed by what he termed 'all manner of shameless and riotous living' that, in 1489, he confronted Pope

Innocent VIII on the matter. Innocent was more concerned, however, with implementing the Spanish Inquisition. He expelled 100,000 Jews from Spain, whilst torturing many others, but in respect of the sexual behaviour of the clergy, he airily dismissed it, stating, 'It is so widespread among the priests and the curia, you will hardly find one without his concubine'.[33] In that era, the *cortigiana* (courtesans) of the papal court were endowed with their own high social status. Many of them used their positions to exercise their own intellectual abilities and display creative attributes that would otherwise be denied to women. Gaspara Stampa (1523–54), Veronica Franco (1546–91) and Tullia d'Aragona (1510–56), for example, each made significant contributions to the poetry of the period. The most renowned mistresses of Rodrigo Borgia, who became Pope Alexander VI (1492–1503), was Vannozza dei Cattanei, who gave him four children including the much maligned Lucrezia Borgia.[34] Vannozza was followed as the Pope's concubine by Giulia Farnese, the 15-year-old granddaughter of Pope Innocent VIII.

Pope Julius II (1503–13), who commissioned Michelangelo to paint the Sistine Chapel ceiling at the Vatican, had three daughters and even issued a papal bull, on 2 July 1510, to establish his own brothel. Like others before him, Julius was notorious for what were called his 'hectic activities amongst prostitutes and boys'.[35] Alessandro, the brother of Guilia Farnesse, became Pope Paul III (1534–49) and was nicknamed Cardinal Petticoat by virtue of his numerous mistresses. One of these was another Lucrezia, who bore him three daughters, along with a professional courtesan named Masina. These women lived in the greatest of papal luxury, with houses, vineyards and all manner of wealth lavished on them. Notwithstanding the celibacy rule that applied within the Church at large, a sexually extravagant lifestyle continued to prevail within the Vatican court.

It was not until the 19th century that things began to change, and this occurred mainly because of a new strategy in the papal election procedure whereby the popes emerged as significantly older men. Competition for the ultimate holy office had, by that time, become strategically organized and the cardinals began a habit of selecting from the oldest among them in order to help secure their own individual prospects for future election. Throughout the preceding era of well over a millennium, however, the difference drawn between close personal relationships with women and intimacy with the papal courtesans was that the latter were paid employees. Thus the women were maintained, but had no automatic or presumed right of claim in terms of inheritance by themselves or their offspring. The Catholic doctrine explains quite clearly that it was not so much the sex, but the heritable aspect of parenthood which caused the greatest concern:

> Among Jews and pagans the priesthood was hereditary. Its functions and powers were transmitted by natural generation. But in the Church of Christ, as an antithesis to this, the priestly character was imparted by the Holy Ghost in the divinely instituted Sacrament of Orders.[36]

This strategy of protecting apostolicity from hereditary intervention was then wrapped in a veil of presumed loyalty to the divine cause:

> Virginity is consequently the special prerogative of the Christian priesthood ... The more holy and exalted we represent the state of marriage to be, the more we justify the married priest in giving the first place in his thoughts to his wife and family and only the second to his work.

Clearly, there are no grounds whatever for this statement. The same could be said of any man doing any job, and there is no evidence that a married man's attention to work is lessened by virtue of his family. In fact, it could equally be said that the responsibility of a family is an inducement to work. Even St Paul wrote in his 1st epistle to Timothy that a bishop should be married to one wife and that he should have children, for a man with responsibility to his own household is better qualified to take care of the Church.[37]

The truth is that the rule of celibacy is not just about marriage or sexual activity; it has far more to do with women in more general terms. It is just as possible for a female priest to remain celibate as it is for a male priest. There were plenty of celibate men and women in the Essene, Nazarene and Celtic Church movements, and celibate men and women have always existed in monastic and conventual establishments. But there are no women priests in the Catholic Church. The rule of celibacy is therefore only one part of the equation. The bigger picture in which the rule resides is about denying women access, by whatever means, to ecclesiastical influence because this would upset the whole tenuous nature of the male Apostolic Succession.

9

The Age of Corruption

Textual Deceit

Famed for his translation into English of the works of Flavius Josephus, which he completed in 1737, was the linguistic scholar William Whiston. A Fellow of Clare College, Cambridge University, and chaplain to the Bishop of Ely, Whiston succeeded his friend Isaac Newton as the Lucasian professor of mathematics, the chair now held at Cambridge by Stephen Hawking.[1]

During the period 1707–10, when Newton was president of the Royal Society in London, Whiston made a particular study of the 4th-century *Apostolic Constitutions*. Although ordained within the Anglican Church, he emerged from this study with a firm conviction that Arianism was the true creed of early Christianity. Subsequently, in 1712, he published his 5-volume work, *Primitive Christianity Revived*, and founded a theological society which met in the coffee houses of London, Bath and Tunbridge Wells to promote the Arian philosophy (*see* page 66). Not only was Whiston confronting the Catholics with his Arian views that disputed the Trinity, but his dismissal of the virgin birth and the divinity of Jesus also angered the Anglican Protestant community. He was consequently proclaimed a heretic, deprived of his professorship and expelled from Cambridge.[2]

Prior to this, Isaac Newton had made his own stand against ecclesiastical dogma. English scientists and natural philosophers were, in those days, expected to take Holy Orders and to be ordained within the Anglican Church, but Newton had always refused to comply, so it was of no concern to him if he was classified as a heretic. He wrote at length about the falseness of the Trinity doctrine and preached that the papists were idolatrous worshippers of relics that had no merit or provenance, and who venerated their pontiff as if he were himself a god.[3]

Isaac Newton, like William Whiston, was also an Arian Christian.[4] In denouncing the concept of the Trinity, he classified it as

The Trinity, by Albrecht Dürer (1471–1528)

'a deliberate, calculated lie, perpetuated through the ages by a series of self interested popes'. He also asserted that the Trinity was wholly illogical: Nowhere in any mathematical method that might be applied did 'three' ever equal 'one'. It was, he stated, 'a pure deceit'. Then, in his intensive study entitled *Observations upon the Prophecies of Daniel and the Apocalypse of St John*, Newton deduced that the beast of The Revelation, that was prophesied to destroy Christianity, had emerged as the Catholic Church itself.[5] It was, he maintained, the Roman institution that had perverted the legacy of Jesus. This refers to Revelation 12:17, which St John had apparently written on the island of Patmos when the imperial edicts were in force to hunt down and exterminate the *Desposyni* inheritors (*see* page 81). The item relates to a woman with the crown of Sophia, who fled with her child from their Judaean homeland to escape the imperial dragon that would 'make war with the remnant of her seed, which keep the commandments of God, and have the testimony of Jesus Christ'.

Newton claimed that the perversion of Christianity reached its peak in the 4th century, when he perceived there was 'a monumental tampering with scripture'. In a letter dated November 1690 to his colleague, the political philosopher John Locke, Newton revealed that there were items in the New Testament that did not conform with the earliest Greek texts. Among his examples, he cited two epistle entries in particular which were used regularly by the Church to uphold the concept of the Trinity: 1 John 5:7–8 and 1 Timothy 3:16. They were corrupted following the Trinity ruling in AD 381.[6] As a result of Newton's comparative analysis, the 1 John entry has since become theologically renowned as one of the foremost examples of textual tampering by the bishops, and is individually characterized as the *Johanneum Clause*.[7] Prior to AD 400, the text read as follows:

> For there are three that bear record: the spirit, and the water, and the blood; and these three agree in one.

Subsequent to the amendment, the additional clause (as *italicized* in the following parenthesis) rendered the whole to read:

For there are three that bear record (*in heaven, the Father, the Word, and the Holy Ghost: and these three are one. And there are three that bear witness in earth*), the spirit, and the water, and the blood; and these three agree in one.

The first work to suggest a motive for the spurious addition was an anonymous 4th-century Latin text called *Liber Apologeticus*.[8] The clause was then incorporated into the revised Latin *Vulgate* Bible in about 800, which was later translated back into Greek to give it an apparent ring of credibility. The oldest extant Greek textual entry in this regard comes from as late as the 10th century.[9] In 1516, the spurious clause was included in a work entitled *Textus Receptus* – the first Greek scripture to be produced on a printing press.[10] A version of this work, from 1550, was partly used for the translation of the King James Version of the Bible, from which the above 1 John verses are quoted.[11] In recent times, the clause has been omitted in some translations since it does not appear in older copies of the epistle and it is not present in the passage as quoted by any of the early Church Fathers.

In all of this, and despite references to scriptural amendment (whether deletions or additions) by the ecclesia in general, there was one man whom Isaac Newton held personally responsible for the encouragement and promotion of the devious practice: he was Athanasius, the 4th-century Patriarch of Alexandria.

The Athanasius Canon

Athanasius (AD c298–373) is revered as a saint by both the Roman Catholic Church and the Eastern Orthodox Church. It was he who, in AD 325, led the opposition against Arius at the 1st Council of Nicaea (*see* page 66). Arius had dared to suggest that there was a time before his birth when Jesus did not exist. But Athanasius asserted that, since God and Jesus were one, then Jesus had always existed before he chose to visit the Earth (a theory that was dubbed *homoöusion* – 'one in substance').[12]

The best known works of Athanasius include a treatise entitled *Against the Gentiles* and three discourses *Against the Arians*. He is on record as being a very violent man who often used physical force to back up his theological views. In Alexandria, he maintained a strong-armed band of henchmen, and used beatings, intimidation, kidnapping, torture and incarceration to silence his opponents.[13] He justified these tactics with the argument that he was 'saving all future Christians from hell'. Eventually he was cited as the inspiration for the brutal Catholic Inquisition instituted by Pope Gregory IX from 1231. The Catholic archive, while ignoring the unprecedented violence of the man, states of Athanasius:

> He was the greatest champion of Catholic belief on the subject of the Incarnation that the Church has ever known, and in his lifetime earned the characteristic title of Father of Orthodoxy, by which he has been distinguished ever since ... From first to last he cared greatly for one thing and one thing only; the integrity of his Catholic creed.[14]

Perhaps, historically, he is best known as the man who prepared the final short-list of texts from which the New Testament selection was made.

From the latter 2nd century, as the different regional and factional belief structures became individually defined, various bishops and churchmen compiled lists of their preferred Christian writings. Some texts that were favourites within certain groups were considered quite unacceptable by others. Through a process of general usage, the amalgamated list was extensive and, after the Council of Nicaea, it fell to Eusebius of Caesarea to draw up a schedule of works that he considered suitable for canonical selection. In the course of this, he set down the Roman Church's opinion of each text, whether deemed fully appropriate, disputed, or regarded as inappropriate.[15]

Within the Eusebian lists were the New Testament books that are familiar today with, for example, the gospel of Matthew in the 'recommended' category, while the book of The Revelation was considered 'unsuitable'. Along with these were many works that did not make it into the canon. They included the gospels of Peter, Thomas, Mary, Judas and Matthias, the Epistle of Barnabas, the Acts of Paul, Peter, John, Andrew and Thomas, gospels attributed to the Hebrews and Egyptians, along with The Shepherd of Hermas, and the Didache. Of these, some were included in certain Bible editions. The Epistle of Barnabus was entered in the Eastern canon and appears in the contemporary Codex Sinaiticus. The 11th-century Greek Jerusalem Codex includes the Didache. Various others, such as The Shepherd of Hermas and the Apocalypse of Peter, appeared in the Bibles of different regions and eras. It was not until the 16th-century Council of Trent that the canon became fixed and rigid in the form we know it today.

In fact, there were dozens to choose from but, apart from creating categories of preference, Eusebius did not presume to dictate a personally identified canon. The man who did that was Athanasius. In his *Epistola Festalis* (Festival Letter) of AD 367,[16] Athanasius established a set of canonical works for his province of Alexandria in North Africa. He also introduced the earliest use of the word *kanōn* (a closed set of rules) in reference to the Christian scriptures.[17] The principle was put forward that while every canonical book was read in public worship, it was not true that every book read in public worship was canonical.

Many early writings (such as the epistles of Clement, the Didache, the epistle of Barnabas and The Shepherd) that were considered by the early Church Fathers to have been divinely inspired, were ruled as heretical by Athanasius. Hence it was that, although Athanasius and his thugs ruled forcibly in Alexandria, the bishops in other regions pursued their own course. At that stage, the Athanasius canon was in no way binding on all churches, whether in the Eastern or Western sectors. But Athanasius managed to impose his will on two other North African sees, with eventual synods held to substantiate his views at Hippo Regius (in Algeria) in

AD 393 and Carthage in AD 397. These were not fully convened ecumenical councils, they were merely local assemblies. But the Synod of Carthage was subsequently deemed to have been generally influential and its selection of New Testament books from the Athanasius canon was accepted in Rome.

The most understated fact in all works concerning the origin of the New Testament is that its content was neither conceived in Rome, nor settled in Rome. It was simply approved in Rome. From the initial selection of books in Alexandria, through a process of debate in Hippo, to the eventual ratification in Carthage, the New Testament emerged as the product of a violently enforced style of Christianity in North Africa.

At the order of Pope Damasus I, St Jerome translated the 27 chosen books into Latin. When incorporated with a Latin rendition of the Jewish Old Testament in the early 5th century, the whole become known as the *Vulgate* – a scriptural compilation that took its name from the phrase *versio vulgata*: 'the common version'. There were no Greek manuscripts before the 9th century which contained the precisely canonical New Testament. In fact, although the Carthage canon became generally recognized, there was no official Church-wide decree in this regard until the Council of Trent was convened in Northern Italy in 1545–63. At this Council, the issue of the canon was hotly debated and was finally decided upon in the 4th session on 8 April, 1546. The agreement was far from unanimous, however, and the Carthage decision was passed by a very split vote of 24 to 15, with 16 abstentions.[18]

There have long been variations in the canons of some branches of the Eastern Orthodox Church in places such as Russia and Syria where certain epistles have traditionally been disputed. As for the Protestant movement, the Anglicans[19] and Calvinists[20] always kept the entire New Testament but, for a time, some Lutheran[21] branches rejected a few epistles and tracts, along with the Apocalypse. The trend of the 17th-century Lutheran theologians was to class all these writings as of doubtful or inferior authority. By 1700, however, the Lutherans had fallen into line with the other Protestant groups.[22]

Rules of Selection

It was determined by the Catholic Church that, in order for a New Testament gospel or other book to be canonical, certain criteria must be fulfilled. This is exemplified by the original Synod of Carthage decision, as ratified more than 1,100 years later at the Council of Trent, to select just 27 books from an original list of dozens.

The first criterion was that a canonical work must be deemed 'apostolic' – ie, that there is a consensus of opinion that it is of legitimate apostolic authorship. Secondly, there must be a recognition that the work was 'divinely inspired'. Thirdly, it must 'relate to the teaching of the Church', or to the 'infallible pronouncements of ecumenical councils'.[23] In the final event, therefore, a work is authentic and canonical if the Church says it is!

Dealing with the first criterion of apostolicity, it is clear that this requirement was ignored from the outset in Carthage, and again in Trent. There are only four gospels in the New Testament: Matthew, Mark, Luke and John. The gospels themselves detail the list of Jesus' apostles, and we know from these that Matthew and John were among the twelve. As for Mark and Luke, they were not apostles; they were later colleagues of St Paul. Apart from that, there is no way of knowing who were the actual authors of any of these gospels; the documents are given simply as being 'according to' each of those named in their titles. Progressing to the Acts of the Apostles, once again we are confronted with an unknown author, but if the work was written by Luke as is generally supposed, then this book is again not of apostolic origin. Following then to the epistles of St Paul, we have a combined set of letters that amount to something approaching 30 per cent of the whole New Testament. But Paul was not an apostle either. Subsequent to that, there are a few short letters of dubious origin, plus The Revelation, seemingly written by St John and the most likely canonical book to be authentically apostolic.

As to whether the books of the New Testament canon were divinely inspired, there is absolutely no way to know the truth of this. Throughout the early Christian era, a number of Church

Fathers and bishops argued their cases, disagreeing with each other in respect of what they each considered to fall under this heading. Even after the Carthage and Trent decisions, the debate continued. We are left, therefore, with the third regulation that the New Testament books are canonical because they are the 'infallible pronouncements of ecumenical councils', and that they were pronounced canonical because they 'relate to the teaching of the Church'. The inference here is that the Church first decided what it wanted to teach, and then picked the literature that best suited the chosen doctrines. The texts were plainly not selected because of their provenance and authenticity; they were selected because they conformed with requirement. On the back of this they were decreed, without any substantiating evidence, to be apostolic and divinely inspired.

This necessarily leaves us to wonder what it was that the Church wanted to teach, and with what doctrinal precepts the 27 canonical texts were deemed compatible, whereas dozens of others were not. More to the point, we should ask what it might have been that the Church did not want to teach. What was in the deselected manuscripts that had to be sidelined and placed under wraps?

There are many references from the Carthage era to the Church's *Apostolic Constitutions*. Indeed, their content was deemed so important that the Ethiopic New Testament even included them as an additional book. William Whiston stated in his *Primitive Christianity Revived* that the *Apostolic Constitutions* were the most essential focus of the New Testament.[24] The work purports to be based on instructions passed down from the apostles of Jesus as promulgated by St Clement of Rome in the late 1st century. The *Constitutions* deal mostly with the duties of bishops, the conduct of the clergy, and matters concerning Christian administration, synods, relations with pagans and Jews, and the various sacraments of the Church. Although clearly not apostolic in origin, the *Constitutions* are generally considered to have emanated from Syria following the Council of Antioch in AD 341, shortly before the Athanasius canon was produced.[25]

Nevertheless, in reality, the essential criterion by which the Gospel selection was made was a wholly sexist regulation which precluded anything that upheld the ministerial status of women or suggested their apostolic involvement.

Certain of the non-canonical gospels and texts have been known for a good length of time; others have only been discovered in comparatively recent years. Since the development of the New Testament, they have all fallen into a category which the Church classifies as 'apocryphal', which means 'hidden things'. This is itself enlightening in that there is no secret made of the fact that, by being non-canonical, the books of the *Apocrypha* have been figuratively 'hidden' beyond the mainstream scriptural environment. A great many of these texts are, however, published and readily available.[26]

Back in the 2nd century, Origen of Alexandria, Clement of Alexandria and Irenaeus of Lyon wrote about some of these works, including the gospels of Truth, of Thomas and of the Egyptians, but these gospel manuscripts, along with numerous others, were not rediscovered until 1945. In December of that year, two peasant brothers, Mohammed and Khalifah Ali, were digging for fertilizer in an old cemetery near the town of Nag Hammadi in Egypt, when they came upon a large sealed jar containing 13 leather-bound books. The books' papyrus leaves contained an assortment of scriptures, written in the tradition that was later to be called 'gnostic' (esoterically insightful). Inherently Christian works, but some with Jewish overtones, they became known as the Nag Hammadi Library.[27]

The books were written in the ancient Coptic language of Upper Egypt during early Christian times, and the Coptic Museum in Cairo ascertained that certain words and general terminology confirmed that they were copies of much older works originally composed in Greek. A few of the texts were discovered to have very early origins, incorporating traditions from before AD 50. Included in the 52 separate tractates are religious texts and a number of hitherto unknown gospels, some of which are revealing with regard to Jesus and Mary Magdalene.

The Magdalene Heresy

In gnostic circles, Mary Magdalene was associated with the wisdom of the immortal Sophia – the epitome of the Holy Spirit. A document which makes this especially clear is the *Pistis Sophia* (Faith Wisdom) acquired by the British Museum, London, in 1785. Purchased from the heirs of a Dr Anthony Askew, it is otherwise known as the *Askew Codex*.[28] This ancient tractate is an amalgam of six works, of which only the second is correctly styled *Pistis Sophia*, although the title is commonly applied to the whole. The more correct title for the entire compilation is *Books of the Saviour*. The bound codex consists of 178 leaves (356 pages) of parchment, and is presented in two columns averaging 32 lines per column. Its Coptic language was a vernacular form of Egyptian which was no longer written in hieroglyphics, but by means of the Greek alphabet supplemented by symbols that represented certain vocal sounds.[29]

In essence, *Pistis Sophia* is a dialogue between Jesus and his apostles, along with his mother, his sister Salome, Mary Magdalene and Martha. The scene is set in AD 44, 11 years after Jesus' sentence of crucifixion. The text begins:

> But it happened that after Jesus had risen from the dead he spent eleven years speaking with his disciples. And he taught them only as far as the places of the first ordinance and as far as the places of the first mystery.[30]

In order to progress his companions' understanding of the higher mysteries of salvation, Jesus brought them together at the Mount of Olives, where they took their turns in a question-and-answer session. Mary Magdalene features prominently in this, with her name mentioned over 150 times as against Peter, for example, who is named only 14 times. Jesus refers to Mary Magdalene as 'Thou pure of the light'. Peter is said to have been annoyed that Mary was hogging the proceedings, and he challenged Jesus, stating, 'My Lord, we are not able to suffer this woman who takes the opportunity from us, and does not allow anyone of us to speak, but she speaks many times'.[31] Jesus rebuked Peter for this but, in her own later response, Mary added, 'I am afraid of Peter, for he threatens me and he hates our race'.[32]

In the ensuing dialogue, Jesus asks each of them in turn to give their interpretation of the mysterious wisdom of Sophia. One by one, they comply, but when Mary Magdalene gives her initial response, Jesus tells her, 'Thou art she whose heart is more directed to the Kingdom of Heaven than all thy brothers'.[33] Mary emerged as the one with the greatest empathy for the immortal Sophia, and was forever after associated with her. It was to Mary Magdalene that St John had referred in Revelation 12:7 when the woman with Sophia's crown of stars fled with her child to preserve the 'remnant of her seed' which had the 'testimony of Jesus Christ'.

The Church of Rome was conceived as the Apostolic Church of St Peter, and yet Peter is portrayed in the *Pistis Sophia* and other non-canonical works as being of no particularly high station in the apostolic ranks. Moreover, he and the others are constantly depicted as being almost incidental in Jesus' eyes when compared to Mary Magdalene. Peter's views are made abundantly clear in the gospel of Thomas, which claims that Peter objected strongly to Mary Magdalene's presence in Jesus' entourage. The text states that, addressing the other apostles: 'Simon Peter said unto them, Let Mary leave us, for women are not worthy of life'.[34]

Another text, the gospel of Mary, discusses events after the resurrection of Jesus. It describes that the apostles exclaimed: 'How can we possibly go to the gentiles and preach the gospel of the kingdom of the Son of Man? If they were ruthless to him, won't they be ruthless to us?' Having already spoken with Jesus at the tomb, Mary Magdalene was able to reply: 'Stop weeping. There is no need for grief. Take courage instead, for his grace will be with you and around you, and will protect you'.

> Peter then said to Mary, 'Sister, we know that the Saviour loved you more than other women. Tell us all that you can remember of

what the Saviour said to you alone – everything that you know of
him but we do not'.[35]

Mary recounted that Jesus had said to her: 'Blessed are you for not
faltering at the sight of me: for where the mind is, there is the treasure'. Then Andrew responded, and said to the brethren, 'Say whatever you like about what has been said. I for one do not believe the
Saviour said that'. Peter, agreeing with Andrew, added:

Would he really have spoken privately to a woman, and not freely
to us? Why should we change our minds and listen to her?

We have already seen how the intimate relationship between Jesus
and Mary is discussed in the gospel of Philip (page 108). First it
relates: 'There were three who always walked with the Lord … his
sister and his mother and his consort were each a Mary'.[36] Then
progressing the Magdalene theme, the gospel explains:

And the consort of Christ is Mary Magdalene. Christ loved her
more than all the disciples, and kissed her often [on the mouth].
They said unto him, Why do you love her more than all of us? The
Saviour answered and said to them, Why do I not love you like
her? … The mystery of marriage is a great one, for the existence of
the world is based on men, but the existence of men on marriage.[37]

Since the 2003 publication of Dan Brown's novel, *The Da Vinci Code*,
there has been much speculation as to whether perhaps the figure
seated next to Jesus in Leonardo's famous mural of *The Last Supper*
might be Mary Magdalene and not the apostle John as generally
supposed. According to Leonardo's own notes and preparatory
sketches, the figure is actually John, but that does not mean that
other artists did not include Mary Magdalene at the Last Supper.
One good example is the portrayal by the Dominican friar, Fra
Angelio, as shown in *The Magdalene Legacy*.[38] In this fresco from 1442,
Mary wears a conventual habit and is depicted in addition to Jesus

and the twelve apostles, not as a possible substitute for one of them. From 1482 is another example from the French artist Godefroy. Mary is shown here crowned and with a sword, as Jesus implements the eucharistic ceremony of the bread and wine (*see* plate 6).[39]

A particularly intriguing painting is *The Last Supper* by the 16th-century Spanish artist, Juan de Juanes (*see* plate 7). In this work, directly below the eucharistic chalice, there is a strategically placed knot in the tablecloth beneath Jesus and the figure he embraces. This character, dressed in red, is far more feminine in appearance than any other John portrayal. But there are only twelve at the table with Jesus, so it is clear in this instance that the figure must be John. Or is it?

Sisters and Deacons

To what extent there is any truth in the non-canonical conversations between Jesus and his followers is just as unknown as any in the canonical gospels. But, notwithstanding this, gospels that limited Peter's status in such a way could not be allowed into the New Testament. On the plus side, however, was the fact that Peter appeared, from such texts, to have a very poor opinion of women, and this suited the Church strategy of creating a male-only Apostolic Succession. They were aided to this end by the writings of Tertullian, who had already set the scene against female involvement in Church matters by stating in his treatise, *On the Veiling of Virgins*:

It is not permitted for a woman to speak in church, nor is it permitted for her to baptise, nor to offer, nor to claim to herself a lot in any manly function, nor to say in any sacred office.[40]

In the gospel of Philip, Mary Magdalene is regarded as being emblematic of divine wisdom, but all such texts were excised by the bishops of the evolving Church because they weakened the dominance of the masculine priesthood. In accordance with St Paul's 1st epistle to Timothy, his teaching was expounded instead:

> Let the woman learn in silence with all subjection. But I suffer not
> a woman to teach, nor to usurp authority over the man, but to be
> in silence.[41]

Such directives, along with other similar pronouncements, are found
in the Vatican's *Apostolic Constitutions*. In their denouncement of
women, the *Constitutions* cite specifically: 'Our Lord, His sisters, also
Mary Magdalene ...' (a reference here to the 'sisters' who are
supposed not to have existed), whilst declaring, 'Our Master and
Lord, Jesus himself, when he sent us the twelve to make disciples of
the people and of the nations, did nowhere send out women to
preach'. Then, quoting St Paul again from his epistle to the
Corinthians,[42] it continues: 'For if the head of the woman is the man,
it is not reasonable that the rest of the body should govern the
head'.[43] The instruction is then given that women should sit in their
houses and not be seen to gad about, for 'these gadders are impu-
dent ... The altar of God does not run and gad about'!

It is plain from the *Constitutions* that, within the Nazarene community of Jesus, women were closely involved in the ministry. As a consequence, the document goes to great lengths in warning against the
practice, claiming that 'there is no small peril to those who undertake
it'.[44] Discussing baptism in particular, the *Apostolic Constitutions* claim
that it is 'wicked and impious' for a woman to perform this or any
other priestly function. In justifying this, it is explained that 'if baptism
were to be administered by women, certainly our Lord would have
been baptised by his own mother, and not by John'. 'These heretical
women,' wrote Tertullian, 'how audacious they are! They have no
modesty. They are bold enough to teach; to engage in argument.'[45]

Many of the women, who led Nazarene-style groups that were
formally pronounced heretical, promoted a teaching based on
instruction from the ascetic community at Qumrân. Such teaching
was inclined to be spiritually based, whereas the Roman form of
Christianity was very materialistic, and mystical teaching was

perceived as an enormous threat. Rome's strategy against the women teachers was that they were to be considered sinners and subordinates on the authority of St Paul, who wrote: 'For Adam was first formed, then Eve. And Adam was not deceived, but the woman being deceived was in the transgression'.[46]

By the 3rd century, a process of segregation had commenced in Christian churches: the men performed the rite, the women worshipped in silence. By the end of the century, even this level of involvement had gone, and women's participation in religious worship was forbidden altogether. Any female known to take part in religious practice was denounced as a strumpet and a sorceress. Over 1,600 years later, nothing much had changed and, in 1977, Pope Paul VI decreed that a woman could not become a priest 'because our Lord was a man'.

In complete contrast, we find that Clement of Alexandria, in his 2nd-century *Commentary on 1 Corinthians*, wrote that the apostles worked in the company of women, who were 'sisters' and 'co-ministers'. Origen of Alexandria, when writing about Paul's assistant, Phebe, stated that women were 'instituted as deacons in the church'. The Roman senator, Pliny the younger, had written in AD 112 about female deacons. A Council of Nicaea transcript discusses the ecclesiastical role of a deaconess, as did Epiphanius of Salamis (AD 315–403), St Basil of Caesarea (AD 329–379) and numerous others.[47]

Among the most famed of ordained women in the 4th century was the wealthy Olympias of Constantinople. She was consecrated as a deaconess by High Bishop Nectarius at the city's principal church, the Hagia Sophia.[48] The well-recorded fact of this particular female ordination has long posed difficulties for the Church. The *Catholic Encyclopedia* states that 'there does not appear to be any formal recognition of consecrated deaconesses in the New Testament', but then admits reluctantly, 'There is indeed the mention of Phebe (Romans 16:1) who is called a *diakonos*'. A further admission is then made about some of the Bible's translatory errors where the word 'widow' has been substituted for what should be 'deaconess'. This error is explained by way of the excuse, 'It is not always possible to draw a clear distinction in the early Church between deaconesses and widows'. Then follows the ultimate confession:

> There can be no question that before the middle of the 4th century women were permitted to exercise certain definite functions in the Church and were known by the special name of *diakonoi* or *diakonissai*.[49]

In the Church's own words, there were female deacons in the Christian ministry prior to the 4th century. Attention is then surprisingly drawn to a 4th-century Syriac manuscript entitled the *Testament of Our Lord* which renders it 'certain that a ritual was in use for the ordination of deaconesses by the laying on of hands'.[50] But for all that, the practice came to a halt from the time of Athanasius, and has since been vehemently denied as if it had never occurred. Instead, from a base reference of the *Apostolic Constitutions*, the supposed dislike of women by Peter and Paul was tactically used to establish a male-dominated Church environment. The quoted statements from these men were, however, chosen selectively and sometimes quite out of context. Despite St Paul's apparent desire for male dominance, his letters made particular mention of his own female helpers: Phebe, for example, whom he called a 'servant (*diakonos*) of the church',[51] along with Julia,[52] and Priscilla the martyr.[53] Also, as we saw in the last chapter (*see* page 126), it was Paul's opinion that a bishop should be 'the husband of one wife'.[54]

We are told in Luke 8:3 that, from the very outset of Jesus' ministry, he had female helpers apart from his mother and sisters. Along with Mary Magdalene and her sister Martha, there were 'Joanna, the wife of Chuza … and Susanna, and many others which ministered to him of their substance'. And St Paul makes it clear enough that there were wives and sisters in the apostolic fold: 'Have we not the power to lead about a sister, a wife, as well as other apostles and as the brethren of our Lord'.[55] In fact, the New Testament (even in its strategically edited form) is alive with women disciples, but the bishops elected to disregard them all so that Jesus' own marital status could be ignored.

Part III

Church Evolution
and the Bloodline Descent

Pagan Origins

Dating the Nativity

When discussing the subject of dynastic marriage (*see* page 99), we learnt that the chronologically plotted birth of Jesus fell in March (*Nissan*) of the year now classified as 7 BC. There are two aspects of this to consider: that of the month, given that the traditional Christmas festival falls in December, and that of the year by virtue of the familiar *Anno Domini* calendar.[1]

The first published sequence of biblical dates relating to Jesus appeared in 526 as calculated by the Scythian monk, Dionysius Exiguus, who was resident at a monastery in Rome. Based on the then current Julian calendar, he ascertained that Jesus was born in the Roman year 754 AUC (*Anno Urbis Conditae* – 'Years after the founding of the City [of Rome]'). Subsequently, in a revised dating structure, this year was designated AD 1 (*Anno Domini* – Year of the Lord).[2]

The first known writer to use the AD dating mechanism was the 7th-century African historian Victor of Tonnenna. Later, in England, the Anglo-Saxon chronicler Bede of Jarrow used the AD format in his *Ecclesiastical History of the English People*, which he completed in 731. In this same work, Bede was the first to use the Before Christ (BC) system,[3] and he established the concept of there being no intervening year 0. Thus the Christian calendar moved from 1 BC to AD 1. In France and the Holy Roman Empire, these definitions were popularized by Emperor Charlemagne, and they became the most common forms of reckoning from around the year 800. They moved gradually into general use throughout Europe and were finally incorporated as an overall standard from the 15th century. These days, by virtue of Jewish and generally cosmopolitan usage, the calendar is often described as relating to CE (the Common Era) and BCE (Before the Common Era) instead of AD and BC. The official Jewish calendar is differently fixed, however, being based on the number of years from the once presumed creation of the world,[4] thereby rendering 2006 as the Jewish year 5767, the year 2007 as 5768, and so forth.

Jesus was reckoned by Dionysius to have been born in the Roman year 754 AUC, but there was an historical problem with this date. The gospel of Matthew 2:1 relates Jesus' birth to the Judaean reign of King Herod the Great, and Herod was not alive in 754 AUC. This became more widely known in the West following the publication in 1737 of William Whiston's translation of the 1st-century works of Flavius Josephus. According to Josephus, Herod had died four years earlier in the April of 750 AUC – the equivalent of 4 BC.[5] Clearly, therefore, Jesus must have been born before that, and the Dionysius calendar was adjusted in Christian literature by the English publisher William Eusebius Andrews (1773–1837) and his New York contemporaries George Pardow and William Denman. From that time it became common practice to add a year or two back from Herod's death, with subsequent biblical chronologies reckoning Jesus' birth to have been in or before 5 BC.[6] According to *The Catholic Encyclopedia*, 'probably the year 7 BC will not be found to be much astray',[7] and this indeed conforms with modern historically based chronological analysis.

The traditional celebration of Jesus' birth is the festival of Christmas – a term that stems from the Old English *Cristes Maesse* (the Mass of Christ) as first recorded in 1038. The Latin equivalent was *Dies Natalis*, whence comes the French *Noël* and the Italian *Il Natale*. Christmas was not a part of early Christian ritual, and receives no mention in the festival dates listed by those such as Irenaeus and Tertullian. The first evidence of any interest in the month of Jesus' birth comes from Egypt where, in about AD 200, Clement of Alexandria wrote about the disputed dates of 28 March, 20 April, or 20 May.[8]

In AD 350, Bishop Cyril of Jerusalem asked Pope Julius to decide on an official date for Jesus' birthday, whereupon (in contrast to all general opinion) Julius assigned the date of 25 December. The unfamiliar concept took a while to spread, but was introduced in Constantinople in AD 380, and seems to have been assimilated into the Church structure, from Antioch in Syria to Cadiz in Spain, by about AD 388. But why did Pope Julius settle on that particular date?

The Emergence of Christmas

The Roman civil calendar of that era displays 25 December as the annual feast of *Natalis Invicti* – the cult of *Sol Invictus*, the unconquered and unconquerable sun. 'O, how wonderfully acted Providence,' it was proclaimed, 'that on that day on which the Sun was born, Christ should also be born'! This was part of a wider strategy to incorporate within Christianity elements that would facilitate a comfortable switch of religious allegiance for the people. December 25th was already a major festival date associated with the winter solstice, and to align the birth of Jesus with the birth of the sun was a relatively simple process.

In many northern hemisphere countries, including Britain and Scandinavia, the solstice origins of Christmas still survive by way of Yuletide celebrations which have become intermixed with the Nativity (from 'native-ity': circumstance of birth).[9] Originating in ancient times with the Yulannu wood lords of Mesopotamia, the midwinter festival of Yule embodies the longest night of the year, either 21 or 22 December. In the pagan tradition, it was the time when the Holly King gave way to the Oak King for the next six months. The Yule log (customarily of oak) was burned in the fire along with ash faggots, while evergreens were lit with candles. Also, puddings of fruit and grain were made to celebrate the fertile richness of the earth. Along with the oak and the ash, the general revelry of food and song included fertility symbols such as holly, ivy, mistletoe and pine cones at a time when the goddess was said to be giving birth again to the sun. At this festival, the Holly King made his final appearance of the year, distributing gifts while the Oak King was reborn for the new season.[10] Eventually, from around 1610, the Holly King was renamed Father Christmas so as to bring his pagan image into line with the Christian festival.

Father Christmas in the English *Holly King* tradition

In order to overshadow the Holly King tradition, the 17th-century Christian establishment introduced a newly concocted story about the origin of Father Christmas. He was associated with Nicholas of Myra, the bishop from Asia Minor who had physically assaulted Arius at the Council of Nicaea in AD 325 (*see* page 66). Apart from his appearance at this Council, very little had been recorded about Nicholas until a fictitious biography was written by the Greek missionary Methodius in the 9th century.[11] As a direct outcome, schoolboys, pawnbrokers, sailors, prostitutes, merchants and apothecaries all claimed the aggressive bishop as their patron saint. Methodius reported that Nicholas had given a bag of gold to each of three girls to save them from prostitution. He was also said to have had the power to calm the seas, while the story which established his traditional link with children claimed that Nicholas successfully restored to life three boys who had been cut into pieces and preserved in brine by their innkeeping parents.

Following these reports, Nicholas became the elected patron saint of Greece, Apulia, Sicily, Lorraine and Russia, and was especially popular with the Eastern Orthodox Church. Then, based upon the 'bags of gold' story, a new tradition grew in and around the Netherlands to the effect that St Nicholas would come each year from Spain to bring gifts for well-behaved children on the eve of his 6 December feast day. This saintly visit has long been acted out annually in places such as Denmark, Holland and Belgium,[12] although an element of confusion prevails because the date does not comply with Christmas Eve when Father Christmas is supposed to arrive.

The 19th-century book entitled *Teutonic Mythology*, by Jacob Grimm (of the Brothers Grimm fame), explains that the European Christmas plays of the 12th century featured the split personality of St Nicholas. On the one hand he was a benevolent saint, but his violent alter ego was a wild satanic figure called Claus.[13] The combination of St Nicholas and the *Satan Claus* evolved in North America, by way of 20th-century anagrammatical corruption to become Santa Claus, while in Europe the red-garbed St Nicholas was similarly renamed Sinterklaas.

The Birth of Jesus

Christmas has evolved as a very strange mix of cults and traditions. Primarily a Christian celebration, it focuses on the nativity of Jesus with its customary image of that starry night in the stable at Bethlehem. Its date of 25 December was arbitrarily selected from the originally Syrian culture of the sun-god, *Sol Invictus*. It was also the said birth date of the Persian cult figure Mithras, who was reckoned to have been born of a virgin. In parallel is the ancient Yuletide festival of the wood lords, which is itself bound up with the ritual of the gift-giving Holly King. This gave rise to the dressing of Christmas by way of decorated trees, presents, rich puddings and general merry-making. Added to this are the separately established characters of Father Christmas, St Nicholas and Santa Claus, merged into a jolly sleigh-riding elf to provide a romantic appeal that is now intrinsic to the whole. Onwards from the 1300s, Christmas carols became a popular addition. Some, like *The Holly and the Ivy*, retain the pagan kingly connotation – 'The holly wears the crown'. Those like *Silent Night* were decidedly Christian inspired, while others such as *The Twelve Days of Christmas* have nothing whatever to do with the nativity of Jesus or with anything that appears remotely relevant.

Even so, it can hardly be denied that the overall combination of the Christmas mix is an enchanting high-point of the Christian festival year. Christmas is, nevertheless, associated with the birth of Jesus by implication only, not because of history or anything written in the scriptures. In historical terms, the 2nd-century Christian concept of Jesus being born in the springtime is still accurate by way of strict chronological calculation.

Although the gospel of Matthew states that Jesus was born during the reign of Herod the Great, there appears to be a distinct anomaly in the gospel of Luke. Since these are the only two gospels to discuss the Nativity, the perceived discrepancy is initially quite disconcerting. Contrary to the Matthew assertion, Luke 2:1–11 relates that Jesus was born in the year of the Judaean census of Emperor Augustus, when Cyrenius was Governor of Syria, and that it was for this very reason that Mary and Joseph travelled to Bethlehem. It was chronicled by Josephus in the *Antiquities of the Jews* that there was a taxing census in Judaea conducted by the Roman senator Cyrenius at the behest of Caesar Augustus.[14] It is the only recorded census for the region, and it took place in the last regnal year of Herod the Great's son, Herod-Archelaus, who was deposed in AD 6.[15]

The New Testament gospels refer to Herod the Great and Herod-Archelaus simply as 'Herod', as if they were the same person. Subsequently, others of the dynasty: Herod-Antipas of Galilee, Herod-Agrippa I of Judaea, Herod-Agrippa II and Herod of Chalcis are each similarly called 'King Herod'. It is therefore essential to put the gospel chronology into perspective so as to understand which Herod is being discussed at any given time.

Regarding the birth of Jesus, we are provided with information that it occurred before 4 BC (Matthew) and in AD 6 (Luke). Since we already know that the best calculated date was 7 BC, we are looking at a considerable time difference. AD 6 (the year of the Cyrenius census) would actually have been the year of Jesus' 12th birthday. It transpires however that, within the Essene community, birth (as with dynastic marriage) was a twofold event. First there was physical birth; then there was birth into the community. The second was a symbolic ritual of rebirth, when the child was ceremonially wrapped in linen cloths (swaddling) and figuratively born into society. This re-enactment is the event which is ambiguously recorded in Luke, whereas Matthew deals with Jesus' earlier physical birth.

These birthing events were 12 years apart for boys.[16] Community birth was the precursor to the *Bar Mitzvah* (Son of the Covenant) tradition which, from the Middle Ages, has signified membership of the Jewish congregation from the onset of age 13. Luke explains that this event took place for Jesus in AD 6 (the year of the census), which provides further confirmation for the accuracy of a 7 BC physical birth date.

The misunderstanding of this 12-year custom led to a subsequent error in the translation of Luke when dealing with Jesus' initiatory raising to manhood. The story is told in Luke 2:41–50 of how Jesus was delayed at the Temple unbeknown to his parents. The event is reported as occurring when Jesus was 'twelve years old', but it should actually relate to the birthday of his designated 'twelfth year'. That is not 12 years after his birth into the world, but 12 years after his birth into the community, at which time he would actually have been 24 – the age of social majority. Instead of accompanying his parents on their homeward journey, he stayed at the Temple to discuss his degree with the elders.[17] The mention of this particular event in Luke is expressly significant because it is stated to have taken place at the time of the Passover, which places it firmly in the month of March (*Nissan*). So, in accordance with the original Christian belief, we know that this was the month of Jesus' birthday.

Reverting to the physical birth of Jesus in 7 BC, there is another perceived anomaly. Matthew 2:11 states that Jesus' birth took place in a house. Referring to the visit of the wise men, the verse relates: 'And when they were come into the house, they saw the young child with Mary his mother, and fell down, and worshipped him'. And yet the common Christmas interpretation of the nativity is that the event occurred in a stable. There is actually no basis whatever for this image. No stable is mentioned in either Matthew or Luke. The confusion arises because of the interpretation of the gospel of Luke, which relates not to Jesus' physical birth but to his community birth. At that time, the events of his actual birth would have been ceremonially played out and, in contrast to the Matthew account with its wise men journeying from Jerusalem, Luke introduces shepherds and an angel – the priestly guardians of the community flock.

The concept of a stable arises from Luke 2:7, which states that Jesus was laid in a manger 'because there was no room for them in the inn'. This translation from the early 1600s is quite dreadful. The word translated to become 'room' was *topos*, which actually meant 'place'. The word that was then translated to become 'inn' was *kataluma*, which actually meant 'room'. What the original Greek text states is that that there was 'no *topos* in the *kataluma*', which denotes that there was 'no *place* (or provision) in the *room*'.[18] Jesus was laid in a manger because there was no cradle provided in the room.

A manger was not a room or a building; it was (and still is) no more than an animal feeding-box.[19] The inference drawn from the Luke mistranslation is that because a manger was used, then the room as described must necessarily have been a stable or some form of animal outhouse. But it was not at all uncommon for mangers to be used as substitute cradles. Coffins, cradles and mangers were all made by the same craftsmen. Quite apart from that, there were no inns in 1st-century Judaea. Actually, there were no stables either; 'stable' is an expressly English word that relates only to horses. Apart from the Roman cavalry, horses were not used in 1st-century Judaea; people rode on mules and donkeys.

In terms of the Christmas nativity, however, the outhouse scene with its manger-crib is very much a part of the customary portrayal, complete with its familiar cast of attentive animals. Especially featured are the ox and the ass, neither of which is mentioned in any gospel account. The *Catholic Encyclopedia* makes the point that the crib and its embracing scene, as generally perceived, were derived from an ideal of St Francis of Assisi, whereas the ox and the ass evolved from a convenient misapplication of the Old Testament book of Isaiah 1:3, which states philosophically concerning ignorance among the people, 'The ox knoweth his owner, and the ass his master's crib'.[20]

When St Francis visited Rome in 1223, he made known to Pope Honorius III his plans for a scenic representation of the Bethlehem nativity. After receiving papal sanction, St Francis left Rome for Greccio where, for Christmas Eve display, he constructed a crib and grouped around it figures of Mary and Joseph, the ass, the ox, and the shepherds who came to adore the new-born Saviour.[21] It was the first known presentation of the now familiar Christmas scene. A fresco depiction of St Francis and *The Institution of the Crib at Greccio*, by Giotto di Bondone (*c*1298), is in the Church of San Francesco in Assisi (*see* plate 17).

The Origin of Easter

The principal feast of the ecclesiastical year is Easter. In Christian terms (from Good Friday to Easter Sunday), it reflects upon the crucifixion and resurrection of Jesus. Easter is said to be 'the cornerstone on which the Faith is built'. It is also reckoned to be 'the oldest feast of the Christian Church – as old as Christianity itself'.[22] Hence it is perhaps surprising that the first ever mention of this feast day comes from no earlier than the 4th century. Eusebius, in his *Ecclesiastical History*, made a reference back to the year AD 190, stating that there had been a great controversy over the dating of the Lord's suffering. The word Easter was not used in this account, but the debate had been about whether Christian remembrance of Jesus' crucifixion should fall in line with the Jewish Passover on the 14th day of *Nissan* (whatever day of the week that might occur), or whether the 'third day' of his resurrection should always be remembered as a Sunday. Pope Victor decided that celebration of the Lord's resurrection should always fall on a Sunday.[23] The fact that Easter was not stated by name, neither had it received any mention by any of the Church Fathers, is given in the Catholic archive to have been 'purely accidental'.[24] Somehow, all the bishops and chroniclers had forgotten, through 300 years, to make any mention of the said 'cornerstone on which the Faith is built'!

The next known reference to the subject occurred at the Council of Nicaea in AD 325. The debate on this occasion was again about dates because different regions were following different procedures. In Antioch, the 'Pascha of Jesus' was still associated (as in the gospels) with the Jewish Passover, while in Alexandria and Rome the Sunday principle had been adopted, but there was no agreement as to which Sunday in particular. Should it fall before or after the spring equinox?

It was decided that, for the date always to fall on a Sunday, the feast day would have to become a movable event. The Jewish Passover, as ruled in the Old Testament book of Leviticus, falls on the 14th day of *Nissan* (March–April), being the first full moon after the equinox.[25] It was therefore agreed to hold the Christian feast on the first Sunday after the first full moon which occurs after the vernal equinox. Thus, the annual dates would vary between 22 March and 25 April. It was called the Lord's Day, the Pascha of Jesus and even Christ's Passover – but there was still no mention of the word Easter.

It was close to a further 300 years before the next round in what was termed the Paschal Debate. During this period it had become even more imperative, in the minds of the bishops, to disassociate the Christian festival from the Jewish Passover. In the Old Testament book of Exodus, God had instructed Moses to take an unblemished male lamb and keep it until the 14th day of the month, and then sacrifice it in the evening. The lamb should be roasted and eaten with herbs and unleavened bread.[26] The lamb of this annual thanksgiving event was called the Paschal Lamb – from the Aramaic *pasca*, which related to the Hebrew *pesah*: Passover. The Christian bishops decided that since Jesus was the designated Lamb of God,[27] then he constituted personally the Jewish sacrifice at the time of his Passover crucifixion. They somehow figured that what the Jews were celebrating was the suffering of Jesus, and they sought the means to confront this abominable heresy!

Soon after the installation of Pope Gregory I (590–604), his missionaries brought word from Britain that the people were ignoring the Roman directive concerning the Pascha of Jesus. They were holding an alternative feast in accordance with Jewish dating and, moreover, they were calling the annual event 'Easter'. In practice, what the Britons were celebrating had nothing to do with Jesus and, at that time, the Roman Church had no real influence in the land. Christianity had, nevertheless, prevailed in Britain from the earliest times and in AD 330, when recounting the early apostolic missions, Eusebius had written in his *Demonstratione Evangelii* that 'the apostles passed beyond the ocean to the isles called the British Isles'.[28]

In 597 Gregory sent his colleague Augustine to England in order to investigate the situation, and specifically to establish Catholicism more firmly in that country. His arrival was deliberately timed to follow the death that year of St Columba, the prominent Father of the Celtic kindred. Augustine and his team began their work in the South East where King Aethelbert of Kent had married the Catholic princess, Bertha of Paris. Four years later, having acquired a suitable property, Augustine proclaimed himself the first Archbishop of Canterbury, and then attempted to become Primate of the Celtic Church as well. However, such an endeavour was destined to fail and the Celtic Christians remained far more Nazarene than Roman. During subsequent decades Catholicism gained some popularity in eastern and southern England, but acquired no significant foothold in the north or the west, nor indeed in Scotland, Wales or Ireland.

More than half a century later, as reported by the venerable Bede, a synod was held in 664 at the Abbey of Whitby in Yorkshire.[29] The purpose was for the Roman Church to overwhelm Britain's Celtic community with regard to Easter. The main protagonists were King Oswiu of Northumbria fronting the Celtic tradition, and Saint Wilfrid of York representing Rome. As it transpired, the Roman faction won the day in enforcing its judgement regarding the date of the Pascha of Jesus. At least, that is how the story is told. What actually occurred was that the Roman bishops simply adopted Britain's traditional name of Easter and applied it to their own Pascha festival, thereby usurping the Celtic tradition by way of a nominal takeover. Nothing actually changed thereafter within the Celtic kindred; operations continued just as before. It was, however, regarded as a milestone event in Catholic terms because their alignment of Easter with Jesus' resurrection tended to suppress the true origin of the festival as time progressed.

In terms of customary British lore, Easter – or more correctly Eostre – was the goddess of spring, and her festival occurred at the vernal equinox, a little before the Jewish Passover. It is the time when day and night are of equal length – the time when the Holly King was said to be reborn, and when Eostre appeared in the vines to present the Eostre egg of her spring fertility.[30] Her personal emblem was a young rabbit, the Eostre bunny, and she was portrayed with an abundance of spring flowers. Coloured eggs, charged as talismans, were given as presents; curative fires were lit at dawn; seeds were planted for new grains; homes were spring-cleaned; buns with solar crosses were baked, and baskets woven just as the birds had made their nests.

The result in real terms has been that, although Easter is indeed now a recognized Christian festival, the Roman strategy was not entirely successful, and many popular symbols of the original celebrations persist more than 1,300 years after the Synod of Whitby. Just as with the mistletoe, holly and fir trees of Christmas, there is no Jesus tradition that connects in any way with Easter eggs, bunnies, chicks, or hot-cross buns; these are all remnants of the original Celtic goddess symbolism.

The Domesday Secret

As Eusebius confirmed in the 4th century, Christianity in Britain traces back to the very earliest days of apostolic activity. At the time of Emperor Nero in AD 64 (the same year that St Paul was seemingly martyred in Rome) a wattle-built chapel at Glastonbury became the first known above-ground Christian mission in the world.[31]

Among the apostles credited with visiting Britain in the 1st century was Simon Zelotes. The Byzantine historian Nicephorus (758–829), Patriarch of Constantinople, wrote:

> St Simon, surnamed Zelotes … travelled through Egypt and Africa, then through Mauritania and all Libya, preaching the Gospel. And the same doctrine he taught to the peoples of the Occidental Sea and the islands called Britannia.

Around five centuries earlier (shortly before Eusebius had referred to apostolic missions in Britain), Bishop Dorotheus of Tyre in Phoenicia had written in his *Synopsis de Apostole* that 'Simon Zelotes preached Christ through all Mauritania and Afric the less; at length he was crucified in Britannia, slain, and buried'. The 1601 *Annales Ecclesiasticae* of the Vatican librarian, Cardinal Baronius, also confirm Simon's martyrdom in Britain. He was executed by the Romans under Catus Decianus at Caistor in Lincolnshire.

A noted Christian convert of the 1st century was Aristobulus, the exiled brother of King Herod-Agrippa I.[32] He was referred to in Britain as Aristobulus the Old (Arwystli Hen), and the Welsh town of Arwystli in Powys was named after him. The writings of the Roman churchman Hippolytus (AD c180–230) list Aristobulus as a Bishop of the Britons. The Benedictine monk Cressy, who lived shortly after the Reformation, maintained that Aristobulus was a bishop in Britain ordained by St Paul himself.

The Greek *Church Martyrology* (a calendar of the lives of the saints) claims that Aristobulus was martyred in Britain 'after he had built churches and ordained deacons and priests for the island'. This was further confirmed by St Ado, Archbishop of Vienne (800–874), in the *Adonis Martyrologia*. Much earlier, in AD 303, St Dorotheus of Tyre wrote that Aristobulus was in Britain when St Paul sent greetings to his household in Rome – as related in Romans 16:10: 'Salute them which are of Aristobulus' household'. And the Jesuit *Regia Fides* additionally states: 'It is perfectly certain that before St Paul reached Rome, Aristobulus was away in Britain'. He was executed by the Romans at Verulamium (St Albans) in AD 59.[33]

It is on record that three British clerics had attended Emperor Constantine's very first Council of Arles in AD 314; they were Eborius of York, Restitutus of London and Adelfius of Caerleon. It is clear, therefore, that despite all Church propaganda to the effect that St Augustine brought Christianity into Britain from Rome in the early 600s, what he actually brought was Catholicism. The Celtic Christian movement, based on the Nazarene tradition of the Ebionites of Qumrân, was flourishing for nearly six centuries before Augustine made his appearance and, moreover, had a far more legitimate apostolic claim than the Roman foundation. The monk Gildas III Badonicus (born 516), wrote in his *De Excidio Britanniae* that Christian Britons were traceable back to 'the latter part of the reign

of Tiberius Caesar' who died in AD 37, just four years after the crucifixion of Jesus.[34]

In final confirmation of the Glastonbury heritage, we have the
words of St Augustine himself. After taking stock of the situation in
England, he sent in his report to Pope Gregory in the year 600.
Known as the *Epistolae ad Gregorium Papam*, it states:

> In the western confines of Britain there is a certain royal island
> of large extent, surrounded by water, abounding in all the beau-
> ties of nature and necessaries. In it the first neophytes,[35] God
> beforehand acquainting them, found a church constructed by no
> human art, but by the hands of Christ himself for the salvation of
> his people.[36]

Plainly, the chapel of Glastonbury was not built by the hands of
Christ himself, but Augustine was sufficiently impressed, and there
was indeed a tradition that Jesus had been to the place in AD 64 and
consecrated it to his mother. How then did the Catholic churchman
Augustine of Rome go along with this presumption when it was
known that the chapel was built and consecrated three decades after
the crucifixion of Jesus? And why would the famous *Domesday Book*
of 1086 refer to an aspect of the Glastonbury chapel as the *Secretum
Domini* – the Secret of the Lord?[37]

11

The Crystal Isle

Chapel of the Stone

The *Domesday Book* was commissioned in 1085 by King William I, the Norman conqueror of England, in order to record details of some 13,418 towns, villages and settlements within 40 of the nation's counties and shires. The book is currently housed in a specially made chest at London's Public Record Office in Kew. With regard to Glastonbury in the western shire of Somerset, the chronicle states that this *Dominus Dei* (Home of God) 'possesses in its own villa twelve hides of land which have never paid tax'.[1] (A hide was an area of land reckoned agriculturally to support one family for one year with one plough – equal in Somerset to 120 acres or *c*48.5 hectares.)

The wattle and daub chapel (the *vetusta ecclesia*, made from flexible sticks and mud) was said to have been founded at Glastonbury by Joseph of Arimathea. It was restored by the monks Fagan and Dyfan in the 2nd century, and was later encased in boards with a leaded roof to preserve it. In time, a church and monastery were added, and Saxon incomers rebuilt the complex in the early 8th century. In the course of this, some of the old cladding was removed, but a charter of King Ine of Wessex confirmed in 725 that the encased wattle structure remained. A later charter of King Edgar relating to Benedictine houses in 972 listed Glastonbury as 'the first church in the kingdom, built by the disciples of Christ'.[2] Then, in 1032, a deed of King Cnut (Canute) also cited the *lignea basilica* (wooden church) of Glastonbury. In the interim, a stone casing had been erected around the chapel to keep its remains intact.[3] In 1184 a disastrous fire destroyed the buildings, and King Henry II of England granted a Charter of Renovation for 'the mother and burying place of the saints, founded by the disciples of our Lord themselves'. The new buildings grew to become a vast Benedictine abbey, second in size and importance only to Westminster Abbey in London.

Some years before the 12th-century fire, the history of Glastonbury had been written by the chronicler William of Malmesbury, who died in about 1143.[4] This work, *De Antiquitate Glastoniensis Ecclesiae*, was a commission from the monks of Glastonia, and includes information from library editions that were subsequently lost in the blaze. In his 1140 work, *De Gestis Regum Angolorum* (The Acts of the Kings of England) William referred to these as being 'documents of no small credit'.[5] Fortunately, a good many manuscripts were salvaged, but many of them met their end in 1539 when King Henry VIII Tudor destroyed the Abbey in his Dissolution of the Monasteries. Henry's ambition was to separate the English Church from the papal lordship of Rome in his bid for a divorce from Catherine of Aragon. But, in the course of this, his ruthless destruction of monasteries nationwide caused one of the greatest archival and architectural losses in British history. Abbot Whiting of Glastonbury had objected to the royal divorce, as a result of which he was strapped to a hurdle and dragged to be slung on a gallows at the top of Glastonbury Tor. His head was then stuck above the Abbey gateway, and his body quartered and sent as warnings to neighbouring monastic centres.[6] Today, along with other wrecked institutions of the Middle Ages, Glastonbury Abbey exists only as a desecrated ruin.

One of the more intact sections of the Glastonbury ruin is the building known as the Lady Chapel. Dedicated to St Mary, this had replaced the stone casing that was built over the original *vetusta ecclesia*.[7] It is this building that contains the oldest record of the *Secretum Domini* – the Secret of the Lord as referred to in the *Domesday Book*. In the outside south wall of the chapel is a stone inscribed with the words 'Jesus Maria'.[8] As one of the most venerated relics of Glastonbury, this stone was a prayer station for pilgrims in medieval times, and it relates to the consecration of the original chapel by Jesus in memory of his mother (*see* page 161). However, the *vetusta ecclesia* was not built until AD 63, and was dedicated in the following year – three decades after the crucifixion of Jesus. This, according to John Capgrave, William of Malmesbury and John of Glastonbury, was 15 years after the death of Jesus' mother.[9] What then was the nature of the 'secret' held within the words of the 'Jesus Maria' stone?

The first Abbot of Glastonbury in the 5th century was St Patrick. In AD 488 his Irish disciple, St Bridget of Kildare, visited Glastonbury. Standing then in wet marshy country, the site was called *Yneswitherim*, alternatively *Ynys Witrin* (Crystal Isle). On returning home to Eire, Bridget wrote about the lake island in Glastonia, and documented that she had been to 'an oratory consecrated in honour of St Mary Magdalene'. She named the place *Becc Eriu* (Beckery), meaning Little Ireland.[10] A later Glastonbury legend related that, when staying with a group of nuns at Wearyall Hill,

The *Jesus Maria* stone at Glastonbury

King Arthur had a dream that he should arise and go to the Chapel of Mary Magdalene at Glastonbury. There he envisioned a Mass of a holy mother and child, and Mary presented him with a crystal cross to mark the event.[11] The Abbey Gatehouse and main entrance to the abbot's hall, is now preserved as a museum in the aptly named Magdalene Street. The question that arises, therefore, is: Why the consecration to Mary Magdalene? The answer is to be found in the Benedictine archive.

One of the great abbeys whose fabric was left intact after the Dissolution – although looted by Henry VIII – was the Abbey Church of St Albans in Hertfordshire. This Benedictine establishment was founded by the Saxon King Offa in 793. It was substantially expanded by the Norman kings in the 11th and 12th centuries, with further additions in later times, to become eventually the largest cruciform church in the realm. Many ancient records of the St Albans library were chronologically documented by Abbot John de Celia in the 12th century. His colleague, the Benedictine monk Matthew Paris, collated and continued the work in his richly illustrated 7-volume *Chronica Majora*.[12] Now held at Corpus Christi College, Cambridge, it explains that AD 63, the year when William of Malmesbury states that Joseph's chapel was built at Glastonbury,[13] was the very year in which Mary Magdalene died in Aix-en-Provence.[14]

Who then was the son who had dedicated the foundation to his mother Mary in AD 64 as claimed in the ancient records? Everything points to the fact that he was the offspring of Jesus and Mary Magdalene, a son who also bore the name Jesus. Although there are no indications in any archive which suggest that Jesus Christ ever came to Britain, there are a number of instances where a younger Jesus is recorded in England's West Country, to where he was said to have travelled with his uncle, Joseph of Arimathea.[15] These were the traditions that gave rise to William Blake's famous 18th-century poem, *Jerusalem*. It was set to music by Sir Charles Parry and performed at London's Albert Hall Jubilee celebration of King George V in 1935.

And did those feet in ancient time
Walk upon England's mountains green?
And was the holy Lamb of God
On England's pleasant pastures seen?

Annals of Glastonia

Notwithstanding the accounts of Peter and Paul in Rome, it is unde-
niable that the most numerous records of apostolic and Holy Family
missions in the post-crucifixion era relate to Britain and Gaul
(France). Throughout the centuries, historical writers and Church
chroniclers were unanimous on this subject and, in many cases, the
accounts were geographically connected. Freculphus, for example, a
9th-century Bishop of Lisieux, wrote that the apostle St Philip of
Galilee (*Philippus Galilias*) sent the mission from Gaul to England
'to bring thither the good news of the world of life and to preach
the incarnation of Jesus Christ'.[16] William of Malmesbury later
confirmed this from the annals of Glastonbury.[17] Much earlier, the
5th-century monk Gildas I Albanius had described Philip as the
inspiration behind Joseph's mission in Glastonia. And in his *Nova
Legenda Angliae*, the Augustinian friar John Capgrave (*c*1418) stated
that 'Joseph came to Philip the apostle among the Gauls'. He cited
this from a manuscript that had been discovered by Emperor
Theodosius (AD 379–395) at the Pretorium in Jerusalem.[18] Even as far
back as the early 2nd-century times of the Church Fathers, Tertullian
had written about those 'places of the Britons unreached by the
Romans, but subject to Christ'.[19]

The various accounts of Mary Magdalene and Joseph are historically entwined at all stages. In respect of Glastonbury, it will help to
look first at the story of Joseph, the man reputed to have been 'of
Arimathea'.

In 1502, a scholar named Polidoro Virgilio, from Urbino in Italy,[20]
was sent to England as a tax-gatherer for Pope Alexander VI. He

remained in the country for many years, becoming a deacon of the Somerset diocese of Bath & Wells, which included Glastonbury. It was during the reign of King Henry VII (father of the Dissolution monarch) that Polidoro wrote:

> So as not to make bad use of my leisure, at the request of that most excellent King Henry, I have been writing the achievements of that people and reducing them to the style of a history.

Polidoro was fascinated by the colourful history of Britain – especially that of the early Britons. His studies in Italy had suggested only a tribal nation of barbarians and sorcerers but, once in England, he discovered an ancient land of great learning and rich kingdoms. By 1534, the results of his research were 26 books entitled *Anglicae Historicae*. Tracing back to the early days of Roman occupation, he wrote in his section concerning the reign of Emperor Nero (AD 54–68):

> Arviragus was the principal chief in Britain during the principate of Nero ... At this time Joseph of Arimathea, who according to Matthew the evangelist gave burial to Christ's body, either by happenstance or in accordance with God's will, came into Britain with no small company of followers, where both he and his companions earnestly preached the gospel and the teaching of Christ. By this, many men were converted to true piety, filled with this wholesome fruit, and were baptized. Those men were assuredly full of the Holy Spirit. They received as a King's gift a small plot of land about four miles from the town of Wells, where they laid the first foundations of the new religion, and where today there is a magnificent church and a Benedictine monastery. The name of the place is Glastonbury. These first beginnings of Christian piety existed in Britain.[21]

These were not words that the Catholic hierarchy of the Church of St Peter in Rome wanted to hear: that the 'first beginnings of Christian piety existed in Britain'. As Gildas III Badonicus had written 1,000 years earlier in his *De Excidio Britannaie*, Christianity was prevalent in Britain from AD 37, just four years after the crucifixion of Jesus and 27 years before Paul was said to have been martyred in Rome. St Augustine had mentioned the *Ealde Chirch* (Old Church) of Glastonbury long before in his letter to Pope Gregory (*see* page 161), but the matter had conveniently been forgotten. Now, as a result of Polidoro's text, a new round of study began within the Vatican archive.

In 1570, Cardinal Cesare Baronius, the most learned Vatican librarian of his era, embarked on a 30-year project – an in-depth study of Church history which emerged in 1601 entitled *Annales Ecclesiastistice*. In this work, he went even further than Gildas or Polidoro. From manuscripts in the Vatican collection, Baronius maintained that the Britons had embraced Christianity as early as AD 35. Furthermore, he told of how Joseph of Arimathea, Mary Magdalene, Martha, Lazarus, Philip and others had later sailed to Marseilles, and that Joseph and his company had progressed their voyage onwards to Britain.

Just as Freculphus, William of Malmesbury and others had stated, Western Britain and Provence in Gaul became the new homes of the Holy Family in the years following the crucifixion of Jesus. It now becomes clear why the Church of Rome was limited to nothing more than a contrived Apostolic Succession. The key *Desposyni* inheritors had moved to the Gallic and Celtic realms.

The Holy Families

King Arviragus, as recalled by Polidoro, was the ruler of Siluria, which embraced Glastonia. He was the brother of Caractacus, Pendragon of the Isle (*Pen Draco Insularis*), whose son Linus was the first appointed Bishop of Rome (*see* page 26). St Irenaeus of Lyon confirmed this in AD 180: 'The Apostles having founded and built up the Church at Rome, committed the ministry of its super-vision to Linus'. But why would such a commitment of control have been granted to a foreign prince? The reason was that by AD 58, marital links were already being forged between the British royalty and the Holy Family. When the leadership of the Church was passed to Linus, the intention appears to have been for an institution with its leadership roots embedded in the messianic line.

Gladys Claudia, the sister of Linus, was married to the Roman senator Rufus Pudens.[22] It was to these three that St Paul referred in his second epistle to Timothy: 'Eubulus greeteth thee, and Pudens and Linus and Claudia' (2 Timothy 4:21). Outside of Glastonbury their hospice for pilgrims and martyrs in Rome, although not a chapel, was the only other above-ground Christian foundation of the era.[23] In AD 66, however, Senator Pudens was himself martyred under Emperor Nero for running the hospice and disobeying the rule of Rome against Christian establishments.

Soon after the death of Linus, Emperor Vespasian issued his edict of persecution against the *Desposyni* (*see* page 81)[24] – an edict perpetuated by his successors Titus and Domitian. A primary motive of this was to prevent any further involvement of the Holy Family in the affairs of Rome. Ultimately, as we have seen, the British-born Emperor Constantine took charge of the Church himself on the basis that, via his mother St Helen of Colchester, he was personally a descendant of the Holy Family – a right of inheritance which he claimed was reserved for him 'since the beginning of the world'! But the imperial leadership was not destined to last, and in little more than a century the Western Empire of Rome collapsed. Henceforth, the Church was fully incorporated into the Apostolic Succession of the popes.

The 2nd-century Roman poet, Decimus Juvenal, wrote that 'no name had trembled the lips of Rome more greatly than that of King Arviragus of the Silurian Britons'.[25] Despite the extent of Roman incursion into Britain, the Silurian lands of Arviragus were never fully penetrated, and were recorded as 'territory inaccessible to the

Romans, where Christ is taught'. It was Arviragus who granted the 12 hides of Glastonbury land to Joseph of Arimathea and his adherents. The land grant was deemed so sacred and auspicious that even in feudal Norman times, over 1,000 years later, the *Domesday Book* recorded that this land was not a taxable estate.

Arviragus and Caractacus were the sons of Cymbeline (Cunobelinus) of Camulod, who reigned as Pendragon (King of Kings) in AD 10–17 during the lifetime of Jesus Christ. They were of a line from Beli Mawr (Billi the Great), Sovereign Lord of the Britons 132–72 BC, whose sons were Llud and Casswallan. From those early times, Billingsgate and Ludgate, two of the principal gates to the city of London were named after the kingly figures of Billi and Llud. The city was then known as Caer Lud (City of Llud), later corrupted to Caer Lundein, and then to Londinium by the Romans.

Camulod, from where Cymbeline governed the Belgic tribes of the Catuvellauni and Trinovantes, was the most impressive Iron Age fort in the land. Romanized as Camulodunum, it became eventually the city of Colchester in the East of England. The name Camulod stemmed from the Celtic *camu-lôt* meaning 'curved light'. Later, its royal court became the model for the similarly named Court of Camelot in Arthurian romance.[26]

North of Cymbeline's domain, in Norfolk, the people known as the Iceni were ruled by King Prasutagus, whose wife was Boudicca (or Boadicea). She led the great, but unsuccessful, tribal revolt against Roman domination from AD 60, yelling her famous war-cry *Y Gwir erbyn y Byd* (The Truth against the World). It was immediately after this that Joseph of Arimathea came from Gaul to set up his Glastonbury church in the face of Roman imperialism.

King Tenantius (the son of Llud) was the father of Cymbeline. King Llyr (the son of Casswallan) was the father of Brân the Blessed, Archdruid of Siluria.[27] Cymbeline's cousin Brân was married to Anna, the daughter of Joseph of Arimathea. The Harleian MS collection at the British Library confirms that their son Beli founded the Royal House of Wales.[28] Their daughter Penardun (a protegée of Queen Boudicca) married King Marius of Siluria (AD 74–125), the son of Arviragus. In these dynastic lines from Brân the Blessed (Brân Vendigaid) and Joseph's daughter Anna, the Holy Families of Britain were born.[29]

Divine Highness

The accounts of Joseph of Arimathea and young Jesus in south-western Britain focus on three separate occasions. The first relates to a time when Joseph and Jesus voyaged to Marazion in Cornwall. The second recounts a time when they were at the Mendip village of Priddy in Somerset. Thirdly is the account of young Jesus dedicating the *Ealde Chirch* of Glastonbury to his mother in AD 64. Clearly, this could not have related to Jesus Christ and his mother Mary, but more likely to a younger Jesus and his mother, Mary Magdalene, as referred to by St Bridget.

Along with these traditions, another family member also makes his appearance in the annals – a foster-son of Joseph by the name of Josephes. He appears in an interpolation of William of Malmesbury's *De Antiquitate*, which states that Josephes came to Britain with the noble knight Joseph of Arimathea.[30] He also occurs in the *Cronica sive Antiquitates Glastoniensis Ecclesiae* by the monk John of Glastonbury, *c*1343.[31] This work expands the role of young Josephes, explaining that he had been baptized by St Philip in Gaul, and that he became the chief of the Arimathea disciples in Glastonia.[32]

To whatever extent these traditions might be true, they set a scene for two possible nephews of Joseph of Arimathea, the elder named Jesus and the younger named Josephes. The inference is that they were the sons of Jesus Christ and Mary Magdalene. What we need to ascertain, however, is who precisely was Joseph of Arimathea.

Joseph makes his first and only New Testament appearance at the time of Jesus' crucifixion. He negotiated with the Roman governor, Pontius Pilate, to have Jesus' body removed from the cross before the Sabbath and placed in his own garden sepulchre. He is described in the gospels as an 'honourable counsellor' who 'waited for the kingdom of God' (Mark 15:43). He was also said to be 'a disciple of Jesus, but secretly, for fear of the Jews' (John 19:38). But Joseph's allegiance to Jesus came as no surprise to Pontius Pilate, who readily accepted the man's involvement in Jesus' affairs. That same involvement was no surprise either to Jesus' mother Mary, or to his consort Mary Magdalene, nor to his sisters Mary, Salome and Joanna. They all went along quite happily with Joseph's arrangements, accepting his authority without question. By virtue of this, the view has long been held that Joseph was a relative of Jesus, and it is commonly assumed that he was an uncle of Jesus' mother Mary.

That Joseph was a member of the Holy Family is not in doubt. Jesus was sentenced to execution by the Roman Governor with approval from the Jewish elders. Crucified felons were thrown after death into mass graves, but both Roman and Jewish law had provision for the nearest relatives personally to take charge of the bodies if they so wished.[33]

Crucifixion was a torturous ordeal which protracted dying over many days – sometimes a week or more. To prolong the agony, chest pressure was relieved by fixing the victim's feet to the upright post. After a while, in order to free up the crosses, the executioners would sometimes break the legs of the victims so as to increase the hanging weight and compress the lungs to accelerate death. When Joseph of Arimathea approached Pilate, however, Jesus had only been hanging for a few hours on that Friday. Pilate was amazed that Jesus should have died in so short a time: 'And Pilate marvelled if he were already dead' (Mark 15:44).

To expedite matters, Joseph would likely have cited a Jewish rule based on the Mosaic law of Deuteronomy: 'If a man have committed a sin worthy of death, and he be put to death, and thou hang him on a tree, his body shall not remain all night upon the tree, but thou shalt in any wise bury him that day'.[34] Pilate therefore sanctioned the change of procedure from hanging (as manifest in crucifixion), and allowed Joseph to take Jesus for burial. (It is perhaps significant that in Acts 5:30, 10:39 and 13:29, the references to Jesus' execution all relate to his being 'hanged on a tree'.) The Jewish equivalent to Roman crucifixion was burial alive.

Nowhere in the gospels or in any other account is it stated that Joseph was Mary's uncle. This concept did not arise until the Byzantine Church introduced the notion in the 9th century. In any event, the chronology does not hold up.

If Jesus' mother Mary was born in about 26 BC, as is generally reckoned, she would have been aged 19, or thereabouts, when Jesus was born. By the time of the crucifixion she would have been in her middle 50s. If Joseph had been her uncle, then he would have been, say, 20 years older than Mary – putting him somewhere in his middle 70s at that point in time in AD 33. But then, 30 years later (at over 100 years of age) he is reputed to have built the wattle church at Glastonbury. Furthermore, Cressy's Benedictine *Church History* (which incorporates records from Glastonbury Abbey) asserts that Joseph of Arimathea died nearly two decades later on 27 July AD 82.[35] Clearly, none of this makes any sense, as a result of which two possibilities arise. Either Joseph of Arimathea was a much younger man than is generally supposed at the time of the crucifixion – a man of Jesus' own generation – or maybe the 'Arimathea' distinction was titular and hereditary, giving rise to successive holders of the title.

Given that there never was such a place as Arimathea, reference books generally suggest, very unsatisfactorily, that Joseph of Arimathea perhaps came from Ramleh or Ramathaim in the north of Judaea.[36] It transpires that Arimathea was in fact a descriptive title like many others in the New Testament. It represented a particularly high status. Just as the apostle Matthew held the priestly distinction 'Levi of Alphaeus' (Levi of the Succession), so Joseph was 'of Arimathea'. But (as with Matthew's titular style of Levi), Joseph was not his true baptismal name and 'Arimathea' derived from a combination of Hebrew and Greek elements. Its component parts were the Hebrew: *ha rama* (of the height) and the Greek: *Theo* (relating to God) – together meaning 'of the Highest of God' (*ha Rama Theo*) and, as a personal distinction, Divine Highness.[37]

As confirmed many times in the gospels, Jesus was the heir to the throne of King David. Thus, he was 'the David', just as John the Baptist had been 'the Zadok'. In the kingly line, the patriarchal title of Joseph was applied to the next in succession.[38] In the same way, Jesus' paternal grandfather is called Heli (his baptismal name) in Luke 3:23, but is called Jacob (his patriarchal name) in Matthew 1:16. When a dynastic son of the House of Judah (by whatever personal name) succeeded to become the 'David' (the King), his eldest son (effectively the Crown Prince) became the 'Joseph'. But if there was no son at the time of a Davidic accession (or if the son was in his minority), then the eldest brother of the David would hold the Joseph distinction. It would be relinquished to the senior line if and when a son was of age. In this respect, James (the eldest of Jesus' four younger brothers – born AD 1) was the designated Joseph (Hebrew: *Yosef*, meaning 'He shall add').[39] Hence, he was the Joseph *ha Rama Theo*, which became linguistically corrupted to Joseph of Arimathea.

Joseph of Arimathea emerges, then, as Jesus' own brother James. Consequently, it comes as no surprise that Jesus was entombed in a sepulchre that belonged to his own family. Neither is it surprising that Pilate should allow Jesus' brother to take charge of the proceedings at Golgotha; nor that the women of Jesus' family should accept the arrangements made by Joseph (James) without question. As a result, if the characters of Jesus junior and Josephes, from the Glastonbury annals, were his nephews and foster-sons in the post-crucifixion era, it may be inferred that they were indeed the sons of his elder brother, Jesus Christ. At a later stage (*see* page 221) we shall consider these sons from a different perspective of documentary investigation.

The Lord's Vineyard

Among the visits Joseph made to Britain, two were of great significance to the Church and were later cited by a number of clerics
and religious correspondents. The first of these visits (as described
by Cardinal Baronius) followed Joseph's initial seizure by the
Sanhedrin elders after the crucifixion. The visit in AD 35 ties in
precisely with an account of Jesus' brother, James the Just, in Europe.
This is hardly surprising since Joseph of Arimathea and St James
were one and the same. The Rev Lionel S Lewis (Vicar of
Glastonbury in the 1920s) also confirmed from his annals that St
James the Just was at Glastonbury in AD 35.[40]

The other important visit to Britain by Joseph followed the AD 62
stoning and banishment of James from Jerusalem as recounted by
Flavius Josephus.[41] This condemnation of James by the Jewish elders
resulted from the assassination of the Annas high priest by
Governor Festus, and the fact that James's colleague, St Paul, was
implicated in the murder (see page 114). It has been considered by
some Church writers that this stoning was an execution of James,
but stoning was a punishment not necessarily a form of execution.
James was hounded out of the city, following which it was documented that he lived for many years afterwards.[42]

Regarding the earlier incident, Cressy, the 17th-century
Benedictine chaplain to Catherine of Braganza (wife of King Charles
II), wrote:

> In the one-and-fortieth year of Christ [that is AD 35], St James,
> returning out of Spain, visited Gaul, Brittany and the towns of the
> Venetians, where he preached the gospel, and so came back to
> Jerusalem to consult the Blessed Virgin and St Peter about
> matters of great weight and importance.

These weighty matters concerned the necessity for a decision on
whether to receive uncircumcised Gentiles into the Nazarene
Church. As Jerusalem's first bishop, and as discussed in the New

Testament Acts of the Apostles, Jesus' brother James presided at the meeting which handled the debate.[43]

A number of old traditions relate to St James in Sardinia and Spain, but they are often attributed to the wrong St James. Apart from James the Just (James Justus), two apostles also carried the same name: James Boanerges and James of Alphaeus (James being a Western variation of the name Jacob). An attempt to forge a Spanish apostolic link was made in 820, when it was announced that the remains of St James Boanerges had been unearthed at Compostela. In 899, the resultant shrine of Sant Iago (St James) became a great cathedral, later to be destroyed by the Moors in 997 and rebuilt in 1078. But it was common knowledge from the New Testament that James Boanerges (the brother of John the Evangelist) was executed in Jerusalem by Herod of Chalcis in AD 44 (Acts 12:2). It is possible that the relics of Santiago di Compostela might be those of James of Alphaeus, but there is no record of his death as occurring in Spain.

Misunderstandings, caused by the apparent anomalies and duplicated entries concerning Joseph of Arimathea and James the Just, provoked some argument between the bishops at the Council of Basle in 1434. As a result, individual countries decided to follow their different traditions. It is St Joseph who is most remembered in connection with Church history in Britain, whereas it is as St James that he is revered in Spain. Even so, the English authorities compromised when linking him with the nation's monarchy, and the Royal Court in London became the Palace of St James. This primary residence of England's royalty was built in 1531–36 on the site of a hospital for leprous women (as established by the 12th-century Glastonbury benefactor King Henry II), which had also been dedicated to St James.[44] The feasts observed at the foundation were those of St James and of St Dunstan, Abbot of Glastonbury, 940–46.

The bishops' debate had begun at the Council of Pisa in 1409 with a dispute over the seniority by age of national Churches in Europe. The main contenders were England, France and Spain. The case was ruled in favour of England because the church at Glastonbury was founded by Joseph/James *statim post passionem Christi* (shortly after the passion of Christ).[45] Henceforth, the monarch of France was entitled His Most Christian Majesty, while in Spain the appellation was His Most Catholic Majesty. The bitterly contested title of His Most Sacred Majesty was, however, reserved for the King of England.[46] The debate continued at the Council of Constance in 1417, and records of this *Disputatio Super Dignitatem Angliae et Galliae in Concilio Constantiano* state that England won her case because the saint was not only granted land in the West Country by King Arviragus, but was actually buried at Glastonbury.[47] The possibility that another Saint James (whether Boanerges or Alphaeus) might have visited Spain at some stage was not relevant to the debate.

The Royal House of David was considered to be the 'Lord's cherished plant' (*see* page 15), with Jesus himself stating, 'I am the true vine'. In this context, it is therefore significant that, about two centuries after the Council of Constance, Archbishop Ussher of Armagh (the 17th-century compiler of Bible chronology) commented on the Council records of Constance. From these he quoted: 'Immediately after the passion of Christ, Joseph of Arimathea, the noble decurio, proceeded to cultivate the Lord's vineyard, that is to say, England'.[48]

The Holy Relic

Misconceptions

It is significant that Archbishop Ussher used the term 'noble decurio' in relation to Joseph of Arimathea. The same had been said of him by the Benedictine scholar, Rabanus Maurus (776–856), Archbishop of Mayence and Abbé of Fulda in the days of Emperor Charlemagne. Gildas Albanius had also used the expression in the 5th century. The term 'decurio' relates to an overseer of fortified mining estates,[1] and originated in Spain where Jewish metalworkers had been operative in the celebrated foundries of Toledo since the 6th century BC. It was not, however, a loose definition of Joseph's occupation; it was taken directly from the earliest Latin text of the New Testament, as translated from the Greek by St Jerome in about AD 382. This Bible, known as the *Vulgate* (*see* page 134), refers twice to Joseph of Arimathea in this manner. The first mention in Mark 15:43 cites him as a *noblis decurio*, and the second in Luke 23:50 as a *decurio*.

These are the verses that veil the reality of Joseph in the English translations which do not refer to him as a 'noble decurio', but as an

---

42 ET CUM IAM SERO ESSET FACTUM QUIA ERAT PARASCEVE
QUOD EST ANTE SABBATUM
43 VENIT IOSEPH AB ARIMATHIA <u>NOBILIS DECURIO</u> QUI ET IPSE
ERAT EXPECTANS REGNUM DEI ET AUDACTER INTROIIT AD
PILATUM ET PETIIT CORPUS IESU
44 PILATUS AUTEM MIRABATUR SI IAM OBISSET ET ACCERSITO
CENTURIONE INTERROGAVIT EUM SI IAM MORTUUS ESSET
45 ET CUM COGNOVISSET A CENTURIONE DONAVIT CORPUS
IOSEPH

Latin transcript of Mark 15:43 from the 4th-century *Vulgate* Bible

'honourable counsellor'. This definition has often been misconstrued as if the term used was 'councillor' (relating to a council
member) – but the term 'counsellor' (an advisor) is quite meaning-
less in an undefined context. Joseph was clearly involved in the
world of metals – a long-standing tradition that is confirmed in the
gospels and exists in the histories of both Britain and Gaul.[2]

As early as 445 BC, the Greek historian Herodotus referred to
Britain as the 'tin islands'. In about 350 BC, the Greek geographer
Pytheus circumnavigated Britain, calculating its shoreline distance
to within 2.5 per cent of modern estimates. In writing of the country,
he made specific mention of the prevalent tin trade. In about 160 BC,
the Greek historian Polybius commented about the same British
mining industry in his work *The Histories*. And in *c*30 BC, the Greek
historian Diodorus Siculus wrote: 'The tin ore is transported from
Britain into Gaul, the merchants carrying it on horseback through
the heart of Celtica to Marseilles and the city called Narbo[nne]'.[3]

The heartland of the British tin industry (in those times and
forever after) was in Cornwall. Diodorus wrote that the Cornish tin
was mined, beaten into squares and carried across the low-tide
causeway to the island of Ictis, as the later named Mont St Michael,
off Marazion, was called. Indeed, the very name Marazion (Market
Zion) was directly related to Jerusalem. From Ictis, the tin was taken
over the Channel to Morlaix in Brittany and transported across
France on packhorses to the port of Marseilles. From there it was
shipped to Phoenicia and other Mediterranean destinations.[4] Tin
was essential in those days to the production of bronze. Thus, in
accordance with ancient writings from the BC years, the connection
between Marazion and Marseilles is explained – the very two places
as described in the accounts of Joseph of Arimathea's travels in
connection with young Jesus and Mary Magdalene.

Along with the Cornish tin trade, the region most famed for its
silver-bearing lead mines was that of the Mendip Hills[5] – a cave-
riddled limestone ridge that extends to the marshy Somerset Levels
and the nearby towns of Glastonbury and Wells. Again, this is
precisely the region frequented by Joseph, including his visits with

young Jesus and Josephes. The British Museum contains two splen-
did examples of lead from the Mendip mines near Glastonbury,
dated AD 49 and AD 60 respectively. In Latin, one bears the name
of 'Britannicus, son of the Emperor Claudius', and the other is
inscribed, 'British lead: property of the Emperor Nero'.

While on the subject of Jesus' family and metals, it is also worth
considering the descriptions of Jesus and his father in the gospels.
With regard to Jesus, Mark 6:3 states, in its English translation, that
the people of the synagogue asked, 'Is not this the carpenter, the son
of Mary ...?' Similarly, Matthew 13:55 relates, 'Is this not the carpenter's son; is not his mother called Mary?' Once again, as occurred
with 'decurio', the translation is incorrect. The earliest Greek texts of
the Codex Vaticanus do not use any terminology that relates to Jesus
or his father being carpenters. The term that is used is tekton.[6] As
pointed out by the Semitic scholar and Scrolls translator Dr Geza
Vermes, this description did not identify Joseph or Jesus as wood-
workers.[7] More precisely, it defined them as men with skills – scholars and masters of their occupation. A more correct translation of a
tekton would be 'master craftsman'. This might refer to learned men
of a particular trade or profession, and could equally be used for
those highly skilled in stonework or metallurgy.[8] It described in
particular one who employed the art of cunning (from kenning: inge-
nious knowledge), as for example Hiram, the artificer of metals at
King Solomon's Temple, who was 'filled with wisdom, and understanding and cunning' (1 Kings 7:14).

² καὶ γενομένου σαββάτου ἤρξατο διδάσκειν ἐν τῇ
συναγωγῇ· καὶ πολλοὶ ἀκούοντες ἐξεπλήσσοντο λέγοντες,
Πόθεν τούτῳ ταῦτα, καὶ τίς ἡ σοφία ἡ δοθεῖσα τούτῳ καὶ
αἱ δυνάμεις τοιαῦται διὰ τῶν χειρῶν αὐτοῦ γινόμεναι;
³ οὐχ οὗτός ἐστιν ὁ τέκτων, ὁ υἱὸς τῆς Μαρίας καὶ
ἀδελφὸς Ἰακώβου καὶ Ἰωσῆτος καὶ Ἰούδα καὶ Σίμωνος;
καὶ οὐκ εἰσὶν αἱ ἀδελφαὶ αὐτοῦ ὧδε πρὸς ἡμᾶς; καὶ
ἐσκανδαλίζοντο ἐν αὐτῷ.

Greek transcript of Mark 6:3 from the 4th-century Codex Vaticanus

The Vessel of Life

John Capgrave's *Nova Legenda Angliae* tells of how Joseph was imprisoned by the Jewish elders of the Sanhedrin Council after the crucifixion of Jesus. This event, although not mentioned in the New Testament, is also described in the *Acts of Pilate* and was incorporated into the 3rd-century *Evangelium Nicodemi*.[9] It was further related by Gregory, Bishop of Tours, in his 6th-century *History of the Franks* – a scholarly account of the Merovingian dynasty of Gaul. Gregory wrote:

> Joseph, who had embalmed Christ's body with spices and hidden it in his own tomb, was arrested and shut in a prison cell. He was guarded by the high priests themselves for, as is related in the accounts sent by Pilate to Emperor Tiberius, the hatred which they bore him was fiercer than that which they felt for the Lord himself.[10]

The reason given for Joseph's arrest was that, with consent from Pontius Pilate, he had entombed the body of Jesus in accordance with Jewish executional custom, but had then treated him with herbs and medicines, and allowed him to go free. The story concludes nevertheless with an account of Joseph's own escape from confinement. In later times, the theme was taken up and expanded in the 12th-century romance *Le Conte del Graal* by Chrétien de Troyes. This work explains that, following his imprisonment, Joseph was exiled from the Holy Land with the golden Grail that contained the blood of Jesus. It continues:

> Joseph and his company prepared their fleet ... and did not end their voyage until they reached the land which God had promised to Joseph. The name of the country was White Isle [Albion] ... One part belongs to England, which is enclosed and locked by the sea.[11]

Joseph's escape with the Holy Grail was recounted yet again in the poem *Joseph d'Arimathie* by the 12th-century Burgundian chronicler, Sire Robert de Boron. This work tells of how the Grail was a chalice of divine blood presented to Joseph by Christ himself, who appointed Joseph as its guardian.[12] These European Grail legends concerning Joseph are mysterious and symbolic, as against the straightforward accounts of his voyages to Gaul and Britain, but there are esoteric similarities. In the Marseilles and Glastonbury versions, Joseph travelled with Mary Magdalene, while in the Chrétien and De Boron versions Joseph travelled with the Holy Grail. In this regard we can return to the Vessel and Vine concept as introduced in chapter 1 (*see* page 15). This is alluded to in the transcript from the Council of Constance (*see* page 177), which maintained that Joseph 'cultivated the Lord's vineyard', while the sacrament of the Eucharist (called the Grail Mass by Chrétien) relates to the eternal blood of the Messiah.

The medieval *Litany of Loretto*, a prayer of exaltation to the Blessed Mary, describes Jesus' mother as the *vas spirituale* (spiritual vessel). In esoteric lore, the womb was identified as the 'vessel of life' and was represented by a cup or chalice. Prehistoric shrines dating from 3500 BC associate the emblem of a cup with the womb of the Mother Goddess.[13] If, therefore, a dynastic bloodline had emanated from Jesus, as would appear to be the case, then Mary Magdalene might also be construed as the *vas spirituale* whose womb (the *vas uterus*) conveyed the blood of Christ.

During the 13th century a widespread enthusiasm for Vessel and Vine symbolism occurred among disciples of the Magdalene tradition in Provence. Throughout the Middle Ages, Provence was the international hub of the paper trade and the world's first ever watermarks were produced there from 1282. Although Grail-related imagery was regarded as heretical by the Church, watermarks provided a secret means of portrayal; variously designed and royally adorned grape chalices have now been discovered in the pages of French Bibles of the era.[14]

The Catholic Inquisition was then in full swing, having been formally implemented against heretics in 1231, but the content of these Bibles went unseen by the Inquisitors. On the surface, they were like any others produced at the time, but hidden within was the heretical watermarked legacy of Mary Magdalene and the Holy Grail. The troubadours of Provence referred to Mary as the Grail of the World.[15]

In 1959, a controversial tract concerning Jesus and Mary Magdalene was issued by the Dominican friar Antoine Dondaine.[16] Entitled *Durand de Huesca et la polémique anti-cathare* (Durando d'Osca and the anti-Cathar polemic) the report was compiled for the journal *Archivum Fratrum Praedicatorun* – the annual review of the Dominican Historical Institute in Rome.[17] In discussing the archival records of Provence, Dondaine related that it was believed there in the Middle Ages that 'Mary Magdalene was in reality the wife of Christ'.[18]

In the *Cronica sive Antiquitates Glastoniensis Ecclesiae*, John of Glastonbury refers to the *Sanctum Graal* (Holy Grail) and to a family descent. Details are given of a nephew of Josephes called Alain (Helains),[19] who also appears in De Boron's *Joseph d'Arimathie* and was said to have inherited the Lordship of the Grail.

12th-century Provençal watermark tracing of the *Sangréal*

From around 1220, and written by Cistercian monks, is the book *Estoire del Saint Graal*, which forms part of the *Vulgate Cycle* of Grail tradition. This work maintains that, on the death of Alain, the Lordship of the Grail passed to his brother Josue. There are some variations in different accounts of this transference of heritage. John of Glastonbury cites Josue as Alain's son rather than his brother, whereas other texts give them as cousins. In Glastonbury lore, the anchorites (devotees) of Joseph of Arimathea were later called the 'Brethren of Alain', which explains the reference to Josue being Alain's brother. The *High History of the Holy Grail* states: 'This Alain had eleven brethren, right good knights, like as he was himself'.[20] Also it is given by De Boron that Alain was celibate[21] which, if correct, rules out the possibility of a son. Hence, Josue was more likely Alain's cousin. The picture beginning to emerge is that Alain was perhaps the son of Jesus II (also called Gais or Gésu), while Josue was the son of Josephes – each of them being first cousins, whilst also grandsons of Jesus Christ and Mary Magdalene.

As we have seen, John of Glastonbury referred to a family descent of the *Sanctum Graal* (often abbreviated to *Sangraal*). The earliest ascribed account of the *Sangraal* comes from the year 717, when a British hermit called Waleran of Albion was reputed to have envisioned Jesus and the Grail. His resultant manuscript, as related in the *Grand Saint Graal*, was said to have been passed down through the centuries, and was probably the earliest to use the term *le Seynt Graal* (the Holy Grail).[22] Waleran's record was later referenced by Helinand, a French monk of the Abbey of Fromund in around 1200; also by John of Glastonbury and by the Dominican friar, Vincent de Beauvais, in his *Speculum Historiale*, *c*1250. Each of these texts relates how Jesus placed a book in Waleran's hands. It began:

> Here is the Book of thy Descent.
> Here begins the Book of the Sangréal.

As distinct from *Sangraal* and *Seynt Graal*, the word *Sangréal* relates more specifically to 'blood royal' (*sang réal*), thereby enforcing the eucharistic interpretation of the holy relic, while also attaching its significance to a family descent – a desposynic line who became known as the Fisher Kings.

Knights of the Grail

Significant within the Grail romances is the influence of the Knights Templars: the Poor Knights of Christ and the Temple of Solomon, as constituted in the early 12th century under the Cistercian patronage of Abbot St Bernard de Clairvaux. Although intermixed with Arthurian knightly characters such as Gawain, Perceval, Lancelot and Galahad from a different era, the Templars were said to be the guardians of Grail heritage. The Knights feature particularly in the *High History of the Holy Grail* (also called the *Perlesvaus*) – a Franco-Belgian work dating from about 1200. It is specific about the importance of Grail lineage, asserting that the Grail is a repository of royal heritage, thereby reiterating the dynastic principle of Waleran's *Sangréal*. On the Island of the Ageless, Perceval is met in a glass hall by two Masters. One acknowledges his familiarity with Perceval's royal descent. Then, clapping their hands, the Masters summon 33 other men who are 'clad in white garments', each bearing 'a red cross in the midst of his breast'.

In a similar Templar vein, we have seen that the *Vulgate Cycle* (incorporating the *Estoire del Graal*, the *Queste del Saint Graal* and the *Livres de Lancelot*) was written by monks of St Bernard's Cistercian Order. The Grail romance of *Parzival*, by the Bavarian knight Wolfram von Eschenbach, *c*1220, also includes Templar references and its story was said to have been obtained from a Templar attaché called Kyôt le Provençal.[23] From the outset of the genre with Chrétien de Troyes' *Le Conte del Graal* (The Story of the Grail), the Templar influence was evident. This work was sponsored and encouraged by Countess Marie and the Court of Champagne, and was dedicated to Philippe d'Alsace, Comte de Flandres. The Counts of Alsace, Champagne, Léon and Flanders all had affiliations with the Order.

Countess Marie's mother, Eleanor of Aquitaine (following the annulment of her marriage to Marie's father, King Louis VII of France) was married to King Henry II of England. In 1155, the Jersey-based writer Robert Wace composed an epic work called *Roman de Brut* (the Story of Brutus), which introduced King Arthur, Guinevere and the Knights of the Grail. He dedicated this book to Queen Eleanor and presented it to her as a gift. She then gave it to Marie, who passed it on to Chrétien as a reference for his work in 1170.

Wace's lengthy poem was itself based on an earlier work called *Historia Regum Britanniae* (History of the Kings of Britain) by Geoffrey of Monmouth, Bishop of St Asaph,[24] which had been written in about 1140. In turn, this was partly based on the 9th-century *Historia Brittonum* by the Welsh monk Nennius. Thus, although the Grail legends of the Middle Ages came out of Western Europe, their roots were firmly set in a rather more ancient British tradition – hence the inclusion of characters from Joseph of Arimathea to King Arthur.

Pursuing the Templar connection with the Grail, we find an interestingly related item in the Benedictine *Chronica Majora* of Matthew Paris. Within the entries for October 1247 is an account of how the Templar masters presented a crystal jar that was said to contain some of Jesus' blood (the *Sang Réal*) to King Henry III of England. Having received this on the Feast of St Edward at St Paul's Cathedral in London, the King carried the container on foot to Westminster Abbey, where a great gathering of bishops, abbots, archbishops and other prelates were assembled. He then lodged it within the Abbey for safekeeping.[25] The authenticity of the relic was never questioned since it came with the testimony of a good many seals, including that of the Patriarch of Jerusalem. Whether deemed real or symbolic at the time, the occasion was nevertheless regarded as particularly significant to the Grail legacy of England, and the auspicious event was portrayed by illustration in the *Chronica* (*see* plate 23).

A Play on Words

Although generally classified as romantic adventures, the Grail stories are not actually romances; they are spiritual fables that reside on different levels of interpretation. Things are not always what they seem and, for those with empathy for the writings, their inner meanings will always transcend the veil of the superficial accounts. The problem with inner meanings, especially if moralistic in approach, is that they are often boring, even patronizing, when directly conveyed. They are best left for the mind of the beholder to discover within the wrap of an entertaining story, and Grail legends work in precisely this way. This was well exampled in 1220 when Cesarius of Heisterbach addressed a chapter of Cistercian monks, exclaiming that he had something wonderful to tell them about King Arthur. But instead of giving them the adventure, he gave them the moral explanations, and the story is that a majority of his audience fell asleep.[26]

Many facets of Grail lore are veiled behind names and descriptions that are of greater significance than are perhaps initially apparent. In both the *Estoire* and the *Queste* for example, Grail Castle is denoted by the name *Corbenic*. This play on words derives from *Cors benicon*, a corruption of *Corpus benedictum*: the 'Body blessed' of Jesus Christ. In parallel, the *Sangréal* represents the perpetual blood of Jesus. Together, as the body (bread) and blood (wine) they constitute the Eucharist – the Grail Mass of the Fisher Kings, whose own style also derives from gospel terminology.

Baptismal priests of the gospel era were called 'fishers' because their proselyte candidates were brought forth from the water into boats for baptism. It was in this respect that Jesus promised his apostles to make them 'fishers of men' within his own liberal ministry (Mark 1:17).[27] In the New Testament book of Hebrews 5, it is explained how, following the crucifixion event, Jesus was himself admitted to the formal priesthood even though he was born into the kingly line of David, which did not support a priestly heritage. Thereby, Jesus became a Priest King (a Fisher King) and the symbolism is progressed into his line of senior succession within the Grail accounts of the Fisher Kings of the family of the Body Blessed (*le Corbenic*).

Embedded then within the legacy of the *Sangréal* is the story of the trials and tribulations of the *Desposyni* inheritors of the Grail bloodline, while the quest for the Grail is emblematic of a will to reinstate that heritage. John 20:34 claims that Jesus was pronounced dead by virtue of the centurion whose spear pierced him on the cross – a wound from which his dignity was never seen to recover. Thus, as given in the *High History of the Holy Grail*, the key to the reinstatement of messianic heritage lies in the notion that the barren wasteland will only return to fertility when the lance-wound of the Fisher King is healed.

The Line of the King

An intriguing feature of the Grail stories is the way in which Jewish names or names of Jewish extraction pervade the texts – names such as Josephes, Lot, Elinant, Galahad, Bron, Urien, Hebron, Pelles, Joseus, Jonas and Ban. In addition, there are many references to Joseph of Arimathea, King David and King Solomon. Even the priestly Judas Maccabaeus of the 2nd century BC is featured.[28] Over the years, many have thought it strange that this well-born Hasmonaean hero of Judaea is treated with such high esteem in a seemingly Christian story.

When the majority of Grail romances were written in the Middle Ages, there was little love for the Jews in Europe. Dispersed from Palestine, many had settled in the West but, owning no land to cultivate, they turned to trade and banking. This was not welcomed by the Christians and so money-lending was prohibited by the Church of Rome. In the light of this, King Edward I had all Jews expelled from England in 1209, except for skilled physicians. In such an atmosphere, writers (whether in Britain or continental Europe) would not have found it natural or politically correct to use a string of Jewish-sounding names for local heroes, knights and kings. Yet the names persist, from those of the early protagonists such as Josephes, to that of the later Galahad, a son of the Fisher King's daughter who, in the *Queste del Saint Graal* is identified as being descended from the high lineage of King David.[29]

In the early Grail stories, Galahad was identified by the Hebrew name Gilead. The original Gilead was a son of Michael, the great-great-grandson of Nahor, brother of Abraham.[30] Gilead means 'a heap of testimony'. In Genesis, the mountain called Gilead was the Mount of Witness[31] and Galeed was Jacob's cairn, the Heap of the Witness.[32] Christian writers would not have exalted men of Jewish heritage to high positions in a chivalric environment unless their names were already known and well established. As one example, the 12th-century Lincolnshire Abbot, Gilbert de Hoyland, equated the Arthurian Galahad directly with the family of Jesus in the Cistercian *Sermons on the Canticles*.[33]

The Third Day

As might be inferred from the *Secretum Domini* of Glastonbury tradition, and the wound-healing objective of Grail romance, Jesus did not die on the cross. We have further deduced (*see* page 96) that his marriage took place in Bethany just one week before his crucifixion, at which time Mary Magdalene would have been three months pregnant.

As we saw earlier, the mystical resurrection sequence was added to the gospel account in the 4th century, and those of the original Nazarene faith never subscribed to the concept (*see* page 11). What Joseph of Arimathea had negotiated with Pontius Pilate was not the removal of Jesus' corpse from the cross, but a change of procedure from Roman execution (crucifixion) to the Jewish equivalent (burial alive). The oldest Greek text relates that, after just a few hours of hanging, Joseph requested that he might take down Jesus' *soma*, meaning 'live body'. Based on advice from the centurion, however,

Pilate granted his permission for the removal of Jesus' *ptoma*, which presumes a 'dead body'.[34] There was a distinct difference between a *soma* (live body) and a *ptoma* (corpse).

Mark 15:43

ἐλθὼν Ἰωσὴφ ὁ ἀπὸ Ἁριμαθαίας εὐσχήμων βουλευτής, ὃς καὶ αὐτὸς ἦν προσδεχόμενος τὴν βασιλείαν τοῦ θεοῦ, τολμήσας εἰσῆλθεν πρὸς τὸν Πιλᾶτον καὶ ᾐτήσατο τὸ σῶμα [*swma*] τοῦ Ἰησοῦ.

King James Version

Joseph of Arimathea, an honourable counsellor, which also waited for the kingdom of God, came, and went boldly unto Pilate, and craved the body of Jesus.

Mark 15:45

καὶ γνοὺς ἀπὸ τοῦ κεντυρίωνος ἐδωρήσατο τὸ πτῶμα [*ptwma*] τῷ Ἰωσήφ.

King James Version

And when he knew it of the centurion, he gave the body to Joseph.

Greek gospel text denoting *soma* and *ptoma*

There are a number of gospel references in the pre-crucifixion accounts specifying that Jesus would be raised on the 'third day'. This is from Matthew 20:18–19:

> Behold, we go up to Jerusalem; and the Son of man shall be betrayed unto the chief priests and unto the scribes, and they shall condemn him to death, and shall deliver him to the Gentiles to mock, and to scourge, and to crucify him: and the third day he shall rise again.[35]

This same terminology relating to a precise number of days also occurs in the story of Lazarus, who was similarly raised from the dead. The record of this event was removed from the gospel of Mark, and resultantly it appears only as an edited version in the gospel of John. The section removed from its synoptic position reveals that Lazarus was not actually dead before his resurrection.

The story in John 11:1–44 relates that Jesus was summoned to Bethany by Mary Magdalene and Martha, whose messenger informed him that their brother Lazarus was 'sick'. Jesus then proclaimed, 'This sickness is not unto death', following which he waited around for two days and then announced, 'Lazarus is dead'. On his arrival in Bethany a day later, we are informed that Lazarus had 'lain in the grave four days', and Martha exclaimed that 'he hath been dead four days'.

The anomalies here are: 1) Jesus contradicts himself regarding the nature of Lazarus' condition; 2) Just one day after his death, Lazarus is said to have been dead four days. What we glean from this is that after three days of sickness, Lazarus died on the fourth day, but was then said to have been dead throughout. It is then claimed that Jesus rolled back the stone, called Lazarus out from the tomb, 'and he that was dead came forth'.

In contrast, the version withdrawn from Mark in AD 195 states that when Jesus approached the tomb, 'a great cry was heard from the tomb; and going near, Jesus rolled away the stone'. With that done, Lazarus emerged and was thereby raised from the dead even though he was not dead and had previously called out to Jesus.[36] The significance of this story rests on two aspects: firstly, the precise nature of the designated 'death', and, secondly, the importance of the 'third day' after which the retrospective death of Lazarus took place. What we are looking at here is a priestly custom which might be better understood as spiritual death, rather than physical death.[37]

Having committed some grievous offence, Lazarus appears to have been cast out by the Temple elders and sentenced to death by burial alive. After placing such a victim in a cave tomb, the first three days were classified as days of 'sickness'. But on the fourth day of such a sentence, 'death' was proclaimed as a retrospective decree whether he remained alive or not, and he would be left to his fate. It was the custom nevertheless that, in such a circumstance of civic sentence, the victim could be reprieved and released on the third day by the authority of the high priest. This style of death (as also later experienced by Jesus in his sepulchre) is referenced by the Scrolls translator Dr Robert Eisenman from an entry in the Qumrân *Damascus Document*. It was, in effect, a curse of excommunication that rendered the victim non-existent under the law.[38]

Jesus held no priestly status at the time of Lazarus' entombment, but decided to presume a priestly function and perform the raising in any event. In flouting the law, he went so far as to purposely ignore the third day rule, arriving in Bethany on the fourth day when the law was fully implemented and Lazarus was legally dead. The fact that Jesus did this, and seemed to get away with it, was regarded by the community as a miracle. But in performing the unauthorized act, Jesus signed his own death warrant and, as a direct result (as given in John 11:47–53), High Priest Caiaphas and the Pharisees 'took counsel together for to put him to death'.

Soon afterwards, Jesus found himself in a worse position than Lazarus. Sentenced by Roman law, and not by Jewish law, he was sent for crucifixion. It then took his brother James (Joseph of Arimathea) to negotiate a change of procedure with Pontius Pilate, and the sentence was switched to burial alive in accordance with the rule of the Qumrân *Temple Scroll*.[39] This provided the opportunity for yet another flouting of the law: Jesus, now entombed on the first day of his sentence, could be nursed thereafter, and resurrected on the third day. We learn that Joseph of Arimathea and Nicodemus tended his wounds with myrrh and aloes (John 19:39–40), subsequent to which Jesus was figuratively raised from the dead. This was the offence for which the *Acts of Pilate* explain that Joseph of Arimathea was arrested and imprisoned. Just as Jesus had achieved with Lazarus, Joseph/James had master-minded and performed a 'third day' raising without any priestly authority or entitlement.

The net result of all this was that Jesus could reappear as the long-awaited Messiah who would redeem the nation from oppression. But, to achieve such recognition, a series of strategically arranged events had been necessary to set the appropriate scene. These things had been prophesied in the Old Testament book of Zechariah. First it had been said: 'Rejoice greatly, O daughter of Zion … behold, thy King cometh unto thee: he is just, and having salvation; lowly, and riding upon an ass' (Zechariah 9:9). In accordance with the scripture, Jesus had done precisely this, and his riding into Jerusalem on an ass was seen to relate to the prophecy. Matthew 21:4 states, 'All this was done that it might be fulfilled which was spoken by the prophet'.

It was then necessary for Jesus to comply with other foretellings in Zechariah 12:10 and 13:6. These required that he must be pierced and mourned in death, and that he would be wounded in the hands. Crucifixion would certainly qualify, so long as he could be removed quickly enough from the cross to avoid physical death. Once again, in the wake of this event, John 19:36 confirms the strategy that was employed for the crucifixion and resurrection sequence. Referring once more to Zechariah, it is stated: 'These things were done, that the scripture should be fulfilled'.

13

Conquest and Concession

Captives in Rome

Some while before the first edict against the *Desposyni* was declared by Vespasian in AD 70, a pre-emptive strike was made by Emperor Claudius against those whom he called the 'Christus Jews'.[1] His decree was especially directed towards the Island Britons, whom he proclaimed to the Senate were the ringleaders of a menacing enterprise. Claudius asserted that the Druids and Nazarenes had become inextricably linked, and he classified the membership of either sect to be a capital offence even though Britain was beyond his jurisdiction and not then a province of the Empire.[2] Contrary to the rule of Rome, the druidic colleges in Britain were teaching law, science, astronomy and religion. They had to be crushed. According to Gildas I, there were 40 seats of druidic learning in Britain,[3] the most influential of which was on the Isle of Mona (later Anglesey).

At that time, the Roman culture was wholly pagan, and the emperors had never expressed any particular concern about the equally pagan Druids in Britain or Gaul. The term 'Christians' had not moved into general use, but the Arimatheac mission in Siluria was perceived as a threat that might pervade the imperial stage if it were allowed to expand beyond the shores of Britain. Anna, the daughter of Joseph of Arimathea who led the Christus Jews, had married the Archdruid Brân the Blessed, and the international metals trade was becoming increasingly dominated by the alliance. For military and other purposes, the strength of Rome relied heavily on metals, but the Romans were not inclined to purchase their supplies; they wanted to own the resources. To expedite this, it was necessary to widen the imperial boundaries, and Britain became a primary target. Placed in charge of the Claudian invasion force that swept into Britain via Gaul in AD 43 was Aulus Plautius.

Around a century earlier, Julius Caesar had made two Roman incursions into Britain in 55 and 54 BC. The first, as reported by the political commentator Marcus Cicero (106–43 BC), was an exploratory visit in search of gold, silver and tin, but Caesar was not well received and returned to Britain in the following year with 800 ships and an invasion force. This did not lead to any form of conquest although Casswallan, the son of Beli Mawr, was defeated north of the River Thames when attempting to halt plundering by the Romans. Thereafter, he continued to harry the legions by the use of chariot-led guerrilla assaults and sharpened stakes, clad with iron, to scuttle Caesar's ships.[4] The 'wallan' aspect of Casswallan's name denoted a wood lord. It was a variation of the Kassite tribal term Yulannu from whose ancient culture the winter solstice Yuletide festival derived (see page 149).[5] His tribe was that of the Cassi (later called Catuvellauni). A cassi was a 'place of wood' – a sacred mound-dwelling of the king within his fortress enclosure. In Casswallan's case, this was a formidable earthwork called Devil's Dyke at Wheathampstead near St Albans.

Although Julius Caesar's armies did not manage to penetrate Britain, Senator Tacitus later confirmed in his Life of Agricola, AD c98, that Caesar did succeed in mapping the lie of the land.[6] Ultimately, his records of hill-fort locations such as Camulod and Devil's Dyke were of great assistance to the Claudian invasion by Aulus Plautius. He landed in AD 43 with four legions of 20,000 men, and an equivalent number of auxiliary troops. Initially, though, even this massive strength was not sufficient to push inland beyond the south-eastern coastal areas until Emperor Claudius arrived with war elephants, catapults and other heavy weapons. The result in the east of Britain was the Roman defeat of Caractacus the Pendragon and the seizure of Camulod.

As the legions moved westward under Ostorius Scapula, they were confronted by the Silurian troops of Arviragus and his brother

Guiderius, who was slain in the conflict. A period of truce was then declared in AD 45, at which point Emperor Claudius decided on a change of plan. To facilitate a diplomatic treaty, he brought his daughter Genuissa from Rome and gave her as a wife to Arviragus.[7]

The object of the marriage was to create an alliance between the houses that would ease the pressure of war in Siluria whilst gaining a foothold in British government for Rome. The city of Caer Gloyw (Gloucester) was founded to mark the event and Claudius returned home. But the war did not abate for long and, despite the Emperor's lessened enthusiasm for battle, General Vespasian arrived to renew hostilities by blockading the south-western fortified settlement of Caer Penhuelgoit (later Exeter).

In AD 51, King Caractacus (Caradoc), who then commanded the Welsh and Dumnonian Silures, was seized and taken captive to Rome along with his wife, brothers, sons and daughters. Even though a hostage of war, Caractacus retained his kingly pride, and his address from the dais is documented in the *Annals of Imperial Rome*. In justifying his campaign of retaliation against the Romans in Britain, he challenged his captors with a question: 'If you want to rule the world, does it follow that everyone else welcomes enslavement?'[8]

So powerful and convincing was his speech to the tribunal and the crowded Senate that Claudius released the Pendragon and his family from their chains, granting them an immediate pardon. Empress Agrippina arose from her throne to embrace Caractacus as the most noble of all adversaries, and the only restriction imposed on the royal family was that Caractacus should remain in Rome for a period of seven years. The rest of the family were free to travel as they wished. His sons Cynon and Cyllinus returned to Britain along with their sister Eurgen. The remainder took up residence at the *Palatium Britannicum* (the British Palace) that was built for them on Viminalis Hill.

Gladys, a daughter of Caractacus, was adopted into the imperial court and given the name Claudia Rufina Britannia. She was married at the age of 17 in AD 53 to Senator Rufus Pudens (*see* page

26), whom she had first met in Britain when he was stationed at Chichester.[9] Of her, the contemporary Roman poet Martial (AD 40–102) wrote, 'Our Claudia, named Rufina, sprung we know from blue-eyed Britons; yet behold, she vies in grace with all that Greece or Rome can show'. Euergen, the second daughter of Caractacus, became in time the very first British female saint, noted for her work in Caer Salog (Salisbury) and at the Cor Eurgain mission at Llan Illid in Wales.[10]

The son of Caractacus most famed in Christian history was Linus (Lleyn), who was appointed in AD 58 to be the first bishop of the Christians in Rome. The third bishop, St Clement of Rome, referred to his predecessor as '*Sanctissimus Linus, frater Claudiae*' (St Linus, brother of Claudia).[11] Thus it is clear that Christianity was prevalent in Rome before St Paul first went there in AD 60, and that neither he nor St Peter founded the mission in that city as is erroneously claimed. St Paul was actually under guard in Caesarea, following the Festus murder charges, at the time of the Linus appointment. The Church in Rome was plainly active during the earlier captivity of the Caractacus household, and it was they whom St Paul later met and sent them greetings in his letter to Timothy: 'Eubulus greeteth thee, and Pudens and Linus, and Claudia, and all the brethren'.[12]

The chances are that, had Claudius not died in AD 54, the Roman penetration into Britain might have been limited or handled more diplomatically. But despite his own change of heart towards Caractacus, Arviragus and the British establishment, Claudius was succeeded by the unstable Emperor Nero whose hatred for Britons and Christians was unrelenting. Fierce new campaigns were launched into the Silurian West under the Roman governors Veranius and Paulinus. Then, in AD 60, the legions were moved eastwards to confront Queen Boudicca and her two daughters, who led the warriors of the Iceni and Trinovante tribes. Boudicca regained Camulod (Colchester), Verlamion (St Albans) and Caer Lundein (London) from the Romans, but was eventually vanquished and died of a fever. Some 80,000 Britons fell in these encounters, but the Senate was so impressed by the Queen that her initial battle address,

Early Britain in the Dark Ages

after she and her daughters had been flogged and raped, was recorded in *The Annals of Imperial Rome*. It began:

> I am descended from mighty men, but I am not fighting for my kingdom and wealth. I am fighting as an ordinary person for my lost freedom, my bruised body, and my outraged daughters … That is what I, a woman, plan to do. Let the men live in slavery if they will.[13]

The battles in Siluria continued until AD 76 when the increasing might of Rome finally prevailed outside Wales and the West. Vespasian had succeeded as Emperor, and his legions marched northwards to take Caer Loit-coit (Lincoln) and Caer Evroc (York). The Romans' newly appointed governor in Britain was Gnaeus Julius Agricola, who subjugated most of the remaining tribal confederacies and by AD 81 had reached the border of Caledonia (later Scotland). The Roman occupation of what subsequently became known as England was sufficiently complete. It was now a dominion of the Western Empire, but the price to be paid by Rome was the significant rise of Christianity. Just as the papal emissary Polidoro Virgilio had eventually stated: 'These first beginnings of Christian piety existed in Britain'. Emperor Claudius had known this and had launched his AD 43 campaign in an attempt to prevent a spread of the Faith within the Empire. But in doing so, he opened the very door that allowed it to happen in his own capital by bringing the popular British Pendragon and his family to Rome.

A Strategy of Compromise

It was during the AD 69–81 period of the Roman conquest of Britain that the Emperors Vespasian, Titus and Domitian issued their brutal dictates against the *Desposyni* Heirs of the Lord (*see* page 81). In the light of this, it is useful to re-examine the 4th-century Emperor

Constantine who, in spite of all this hatred, claimed to have a personal messianic descent. Although there is no record of his lineage from Jesus, it does appear that he had a desposynic heritage in a British royal line from Brân the Blessed and Anna, the daughter of James (Joseph of Arimathea).

Constantine's mother was Princess Elaine (St Helena), the daughter of King Coel II of the Britons at a time when the houses of Siluria and Camelod were conjoined. Coel was the grandson of King Lucius who, via his father Coel I, was the grandson of King Marius of Siluria (son of Arviragus) and Penardun (the daughter of Anna and Brân). Hence, Constantine was an 8th generational descendant from the brother of Jesus.

There are four younger brothers of Jesus listed in the New Testament gospels, of whom James (the Joseph *ha Rama Theo*) was the eldest. In confirmation of Jesus' seniority, both Matthew 1:25 and Luke 2:27 explain that Jesus was Mary's 'firstborn' son. His brothers are named in Matthew 13:55 and Mark 6:3 as being James, Joses, Simon and Jude. In the New Testament Epistles, St Paul specifically refers to his meeting in Jerusalem with 'James, the Lord's brother',[14] and the 1st-century chronicles of Flavius Josephus also relate to 'James, the brother of Jesus, who was called Christ'.[15]

In addition to Jesus' brothers, Matthew 13:56 and Mark 6:3 both state that he also had sisters. They are named in the *Panarion* and *Ancoratus* of Epiphanius[16] as being Mary, Salome and Joanna. Jesus' sister Mary is also mentioned in the gospel of Philip[17] and, in reference to Jesus' regular entourage, the Church's own *Apostolic Constitutions* likewise identify 'Our Lord and his sisters'.[18] In the New Testament gospels, these sisters appear at the cross and at the tomb of Jesus, along with Mary Magdalene. The sisters Mary and Salome appear, for example, in Mark 15:47, while Joanna and Mary appear in Luke 24:10, and Mary features again in Matthew 28:1.

Following the destruction of London by Queen Boudicca, the more northern city of Caer Evroc became the key centre for Roman rule in Britain. Subsequently named York, it was here that in AD 305 Constantius Chlorus, an adopted son of Emperor Maximianus, was proclaimed Emperor in the West. Prior to that, he had married Princess Elaine of Camulod. This gained her the titular style of Flavia Helena Augusta, in which name her coins were struck.[19] The 4th-century ecclesiastical writer Sulpicius Severus wrote that, following the death of Constantius in AD 306, Helena reigned as Empress in Britain jointly with her son Constantine. Then, in AD 312, Constantine took the reins of the Western Empire, at which time he was called to Rome to confront Marcus Maxentius.[20] He was the natural son of the earlier Emperor Maximianus, and had previously lost out to Constantine's father in the imperial selection process.

The armies of Constantine and Maxentius met at Milvian Bridge, a little outside Rome, and Constantine was victorious. It was after this battle that he announced he had seen a vision of a cross in the sky, accompanied by the words 'In this sign conquer' (*In hoc signo vinces*). It led, in the following year, to the famous Edict of Milan, which declared that the Western and Eastern branches of the Empire would henceforth be neutral with regard to religious worship, thereby officially ending all previously sanctioned persecution of Christians. Subsequently, in AD 324, Constantine also gained the Eastern imperial title, becoming Emperor overall and acquiring his historically familiar style as Constantine the Great.

With this knowledge of Constantine's background, it is understandable that he adopted Christianity as the State religion of Rome. He was born in Britain and raised by a Christian mother, whose religion was perfectly natural to him as against the pagan environment that he encountered in Rome. Constantine was fully conversant with Christianity when he became Emperor. What he discovered, however, was that it was a widespread and very diverse form of religion. Britain and Gaul might have been the earliest seats of the Faith in Western terms, but other branches had evolved over 300 years in places such as Syria, Egypt, Greece, Mesopotamia and Turkey. Their belief structures were all different to greater or lesser degrees, and the regional Church Fathers and bishops were severely at odds with each other in many respects.

It is simple to criticize Constantine for what might be perceived today as corrupting the Christian faith when formulating his Catholic Church, but in reality his attempt appears to have been quite the opposite. What he saw was a highly competitive religion which had fiercely opposing groups within its geographically spread ranks – all operating within the Empire that he was supposed to control. Christianity had already become severely corrupted to the point that it was far from recognizable as a cohesive whole. The best that Constantine could hope to achieve was a series of compromise doctrines based on mutual discussion and a system of gaining majority votes at each stage. To this end, he settled on the idea of debating forums to which delegates would be invited and, following initial synods in Rome and Arles, he began this strategy with the First Council of Nicaea in AD 325.

Alongside this, the Emperor's additional problem was how to introduce Christianity into Rome itself. Such a feat would mean a complete about-turn from the policies of his predecessors who had hounded and persecuted Christians for three centuries. Somehow, Constantine had to create a hybrid religion that was, as far as he could manage, acceptable to all. The result might not have been the same as the Nazarene based teachings that he grew up with in Britain, but he was faced with little other choice and the best weapon that he perceived within his own armoury was his own desposynic family descent. This was something to which no other Emperor before him could have aspired.

For all practical purposes it becomes clear that, apart from Constantine's imperial predecessors, the greatest destroyers of Christianity in any form that Jesus and James might have recognized were the bigoted Church Fathers such as Tertullian and Clement of Alexandria. Worst of all was the dreadful Athanasius, whose violently self-seeking methods led to the sidelining of so much valuable literature in the years after Constantine's death. What we know, however, is that despite the various Council rulings during Constantine's lifetime, it was the so-called heretical views of Arius which he found more comfortable to proclaim on his death-bed (*see* page 67). This probably indicates that the Arian perspective was the closest to the style of Christianity that Constantine had encountered in Britain – a belief system that had evolved, without Church Father interference, from the original teachings of James/Joseph in Silurian Glastonia.

The Pauline Mythology

The main culprit, whose writings might be blamed for the corruption of Jesus' legacy in the Mediterranean regions, appears to have been St Paul. But, having said that, it may be that he can be excused in many respects. Some of the writings attributed to Paul are spurious fabrications. Apart from that, the peculiar nature of his original undertaking outside his homeland involved him in a competitive world of religious extremes that would have been entirely unfamiliar to him.

Paul makes his first New Testament appearance as one Saul of Tarsus in The Acts of the Apostles during the years following the crucifixion of Jesus. He is first encountered in Jerusalem consenting to the stoning of a disciple called Stephen, who had prophesied that Jesus would destroy the Temple.[21] Thereafter, Saul approached the High Priest and received a commission to pursue and arrest the disciples of Jesus in Damascus, and to bring them bound to Jerusalem.[22] The biblical story of Paul (Saul) begins therefore with him being an enemy of Jesus' apostles and an emissary of the Temple elders. His Hebrew name was Saul, whilst his given Roman cognomen was Paul,[23] by which name we shall now refer to him. The details that he was originally from Tarsus and trained as a Pharisee are given in Acts 22:3 and 26:5.

The year AD 37 had been one of administrative change throughout the Roman Empire, and especially in the Holy Land. Emperor Tiberius had died and the new Emperor, Gaius Caligula, dismissed Pontius Pilate and installed Antonius Felix as Governor of Judaea in his stead. In Jerusalem, Joseph Caiaphas had been replaced as the High Priest by Theophilus, and a whole new administration was in place – more answerable to Rome than ever before.

As Jesus had long maintained, the Jews could never overthrow Roman occupation while divided from the Gentiles. Paul, on the other hand, was equally sure that association with Gentiles represented a weakness that left the Jews vulnerable and exposed. The account in The Acts suggests that, in AD 40 (seven years after the crucifixion of Jesus), Paul went to confront the Nazarenes at a conference in Damascus, Syria, with a mandate from the High Priest in Jerusalem. This cannot have been the case: the Jewish Sanhedrin Council of elders had no jurisdiction whatever in Syria.[24] It is likely that Paul, a supporter of the House of Herod, was operating for the King's administration in an attempt to suppress the Nazarenes.[25] However, before he had a chance to make his presence felt, he was confronted by the voice of Jesus, asking, 'Saul, Saul, why persecutest thou me?' (Acts 9:4–5).

Jesus subsequently instructed the disciple Ananias to enlighten Paul in the Nazarene philosophy, but Ananias hesitated, knowing that Saul was an enemy agent: 'Lord, I have heard by many of this man, how much evil he hath done to thy saints at Jerusalem'.[26] Nonetheless, the disciple obeyed, saying, 'Brother Saul, the Lord, even Jesus, that appeared unto thee in the way as thou camest, hath sent me, that thou mightest receive thy sight'.[27] The use in this passage of the words 'sight' and 'the way' are cryptic in a common New Testament style; Paul had been blinded by sectarian dogma and was to be introduced to the community doctrine of The Way (*see* page 14). Those who were uneducated in the philosophy were considered 'blind to the light'.[28] After a course of instruction, he was initiated so that he could see the path to salvation offered by Jewish unity with the Gentiles: 'There fell from his eyes as it had been scales: and he received sight forthwith, and arose, and was baptized' (Acts 9:18).[29]

From this experience, Paul forsook his Hebrew sympathies and emerged as a fully-fledged Hellenist. At once, he began preaching in Damascus – but there was a problem, for the people could not

1. *The Arrest of Christ* – Betrayal at Gethsemane
Guiseppe Cesari, *c*1590

2. *Myrrophore* – Mary Magdalene, the Myrrh Bearer
Syrian, AD *c*240

3. *Triumph of the Faith* – Martyrs in the time of Nero
Eugene Thirion (1839–1910)

4. *St Anne Conceiving Her Daughter Mary* – The Immaculate Conception
Jean Bellegambe (1467–1535)

5. *In the House of Simon* – Mary Magdalene and Jesus
Peter Paul Rubens, 1620

6. *The Last Supper* – with crowned Mary Magdalene
Godefroy, 1482

7. *The Last Supper*
Juan de Juanes (1510–79)

8. *Jesus and Mary Magdalene*
Window at Kilmore Church, Dervaig

9. *The Wedding Feast at Cana* (detail) – with Mary Magdalene next to Jesus
Gerard David, 1503

10. *The Supper at Emmaus* – after the Resurrection
Michelangelo Caravaggio, 1601

11. *St Helena of the Cross* – Mother of Emperor Constantine
Cima da Conegliano, 1495

12. *Triumphant Entry of Constantine into Rome*
Peter Paul Rubens, 1622

13. *Queen Boudicca of the Icene*
Gordon Frederick Browne (1858–1932)

14. *Joseph of Arimathea and the Britons*
William Blake, 1794

15. *Mary Magdalene and the Queen of Marseilles*
Pera Matas, 1526

16. *The Flight of Gradlon Mawr*
Evariste Vital Luminais, *c*1884

17. *The Institution of the Crib at Greccio* – St Francis and the first Nativity display
Giotto di Bondone, 1298

18. *Fontaine de Fortune* – The Golden Cup of the Stone
René d'Anjou (1408–80)

19. *Parsifal in Quest of the Holy Grail*
Ferdinand Leeke, 1912

20. *Lazarus, Bishop of Marseilles, with Mary Magdalene and Martha*
Master of Perea, *c*1490

21. *Galahad's Achievement of the Holy Grail*
Sir Edward Burne-Jones and William Morris (tapestry), 1894

22. *The Battle of Tolbiac,* AD *496* – King Clovis the Merovingian
Ary Scheffer, 1837

23. *King Henry III at Westminster with the Sang Réal in 1247*
Matthew Paris (1200–59)

24. *Nascien and the Fish*
French, 14th century

25. *The Round Table and the Holy Grail*
French, 1470

26. *Queen Eleanor of Aquitaine*
Anthony Frederick Sandys, 1858

27. *The Death of Arthur*
John Mulcaster Carrick, 1862

28. *The Last Sleep of Arthur in Avalon* (detail)
Sir Edward Burne-Jones, *c*1889

29. *The Grail Mass of Josephes*
French Cistercian, *c*1351

believe that the man who had come hotfoot to challenge the Messiah was now promoting him instead. The Nazarenes were confused, distrustful and angry to the extent that Paul's life was threatened and the disciples had to spirit him out of the city. By AD 43, however, Paul was a fervent evangelist, but his conversion had been so traumatic, his change of heart so far-reaching, that he regarded Jesus not just as an earthly Messiah with an inspiring social message, but as the manifest son of God, a heavenly power-lord.

Paul's missionary journeys took him to Anatolia (Asia Minor) and the Greek-speaking areas of the eastern Mediterranean. But his dramatically revised version of the gospel was that an awesome Saviour would soon establish a worldwide regime of perfect righteousness – and in this he was aided by ambiguous Old Testament writings such as from the book of Daniel:

> I saw in the night visions, and, behold, one like the son of man came with the clouds of heaven … And there was given him dominion, and glory, and a kingdom, that all people, nations, and languages, should serve him.[30]

When written in the 2nd century BC, these texts had nothing whatever to do with Jesus, but they were stimulating enough for Paul and provided the necessary inspiration for his fiery invective.[31] In his excitement, he proclaimed the Wrath of the Lord with all the zeal of an Old Testament prophet, making outrageous claims that gained him unprecedented attention:

> For the Lord himself shall descend from heaven with a shout, with the voice of the archangel, and with the trump of God: and the dead in Christ shall rise first. Then we which are alive and remain shall be caught up together with them in the clouds, to meet the Lord in the air: and so shall we ever be with the Lord.[32]

Through Paul's imaginative teaching, a whole new concept of Jesus arose. No longer was he simply the long-awaited Messiah who would reinstate the Davidic line and free the Jews from Roman oppression. He was now the heavenly saviour of the whole world.

While James and the apostles were preaching their less fanciful messages, Paul had strayed into a realm of pure fantasy. In his unbridled enthusiasm, he invented an inexplicable myth and uttered a string of self-styled prophecies that were never fulfilled. Yet for all that, it is Paul who dominates the bulk of the New Testament beyond the gospels. Such was the power of Paul's teaching that Jesus was transformed into an aspect of Almighty God, while Jesus the dynastic Christ of the House of Judah was lost to religious history altogether.

Paul's allotted task was to further Hellenic-Jewish instruction among the Gentiles of the Mediterranean coastal lands, and to take Jesus' message to those Jews who lived outside their homeland in the Diaspora. Instead, he ignored the root objective and (as was perhaps inevitable) contrived his own cult following. For Paul, the veneration and outright worship of Jesus was sufficient to ensure redemption and entry into the Kingdom of Heaven. All the social values professed and urged by Jesus were cast aside in Paul's attempt to compete with a variety of pagan beliefs.

Throughout the ancient Mediterranean world, there were many religions whose gods and prophets were supposedly born of virgins and defied death in one way or another. They were all of supernatural origin and had astounding powers over ordinary mortals. To be fair to Paul, he certainly encountered problems that Jesus had never faced in his native environment. Paul's route to success against such odds was to present Jesus in a way that would transcend these paranormal idols. In the event he created an image of Jesus so far removed from reality that Jewish society regarded him as a fraud. Notwithstanding, it was the transcendent Jesus of Paul's invention who later became the Jesus of orthodox Christianity.[33]

The Lost Testaments

Inasmuch as St Paul exaggerated the image of Jesus for the benefit of his pagan audience, there is no doubt that the later Church Fathers manipulated Paul's writings to suit their personal endeavours just as St Clement brazenly corrupted the gospel of Mark. Even during his own lifetime, Paul had occasion to warn people about fictitious letters purporting to be from him,[34] and it was not uncommon for epistles to be fabricated for propagandist purposes.[35]

Paul's letters to Timothy, Titus and Philemon have been the subjects of particular linguistic scrutiny, and it is doubtful that they represent authentic missives from his own hand.[36] These individually addressed correspondences (known as the Pastoral Letters) are very different in language, style and vocabulary from the sermon-like epistles addressed to community congregations such as the Corinthians, Galatians and Thessalonians. There are numerous elements of these personally addressed letters which relate to doctrinal writings of the 2nd century that would have been unknown to Paul,[37] and many scholars now believe they were written some considerable time after Paul's death.

Paul emerges from all this as both the culprit and the victim. The founding doctrines of the Church of Rome were based upon the opinions of the pre-Roman Church Fathers. Their primary works of inspiration are said to have been the epistles of St Paul and, in many respects, Church dogma rests entirely on these Pauline teachings. They constitute some 30 per cent of the New Testament, and yet not one fragment of any such letter exists in Paul's own hand. Similarly, there are no original 1st-century documents for any of the works selected by Athanasius and the 4th-century bishops for New Testament inclusion – and yet the world's libraries and museums are bursting with tens of thousands of documents from much older times. Of the original 27 New Testament scriptural texts, not one is known to have survived, although numerous other gospels and tractates which the Church does not acknowledge, have been unearthed in the past century or so, including dozens of Dead Sea Scrolls texts, along with the extensive Nag Hammadi collection of pre-New Testament Christian manuscripts.

Currently, the oldest known items from the New Testament are those few tiny scraps, the Magdalene Fragments (*see* page 42). It seems inconceivable that no discovery has yet been made of manuscripts that would transform the New Testament into an historically documented reality. If the Church Fathers of the 2nd and 3rd centuries had such documents in their possession, then one might justifiably wonder what happened to them. Were such important documents on which a major world religion was founded truly lost by the very men who established that religion? One possibility is that perhaps such items do exist, but that they were so substantially altered in transcript that the purpose of the clergy is best served by keeping them hidden. It is also possible that they might have been purposely destroyed for the very same reason. Either way, it remains the case that the best attested gospel with the most authentic and original provenance is probably the gospel of Thomas, but this early record of the sayings of Jesus was dismissed by the Church because it dared to suggest that the spirit of Jesus was everywhere, and not a prerogative of the ecclesiastical establishment: 'Split a piece of wood, and I am there. Lift up a stone, and you will find me'.[38]

Even more of a thorn in the side of the Church is Item 12 in the Thomas gospel: The disciples said to Jesus, 'We know that you will depart from us. Who will be our leader?' In responding to this, Jesus did not mention St Peter as the bishops would have preferred. If he had, it is a fair guess that the gospel of Thomas would be embraced within the body of approved Christian literature. In fact, Jesus did not name any of his apostles; he had no vision whatever of an apostolic succession. Instead, he proclaimed that the leadership of his mission should rest firmly with his own brother, and he answered: 'No matter where you are, you are to go to James the Just'.[39]

14

A Royal Family

Druids and Christians

Although a form of early Christianity entered Britain in the middle 1st century, it is evident that this did not constitute a wide-scale conversion to a new faith. Despite the fact that Linus and his sister Gladys were embraced by the Christian fraternity in Rome, there is no record to suggest that Cymbeline, Arviragus or Boudicca became Christians. Their way of life was built on druidic principles and the Britons maintained their old beliefs for another few centuries while Christianity evolved alongside. While Polidoro, Baronius and other writers might have attributed the beginnings of Christian piety to Britain, they were using a terminology of their own later era. According to the Roman biographer Suetonius (AD c100), Emperor Claudius had not used the term Christian in his AD 43 edict against the Britons; he cited only Druidism and the Jews of Christus.[1] The term Christian appears to have first been used a year later at Antioch in Syria.[2]

The style of Christianity that came into Britain with Joseph of Arimathea, and into Gaul with Philip and Mary Magdalene, was a Nazarene concept that seems to have been, in some ways, compatible with the druidic culture. Brân the Blessed (the son-in-law of Joseph/James) was not a Christian; he was the archdruid of the Silurian kingdoms. In reference to the year AD 57, Tacitus wrote in the *Annals of Imperial Rome* of a certain Pomponia. She was the daughter of the Roman consul Gaius Pomponius Graecinus, and had married Aulus Plautius, the Claudian invader of Britain. It is not made clear whether Pomponia had been in Britain with her husband but, when Plautius returned to Rome, his wife was charged with embracing a 'foreign superstition'.[3] This is generally thought to refer to Christianity but, whatever the case, Pomponia was acquitted.

Whereas St Paul was experiencing difficulty in conveying his eccentric version of Judaeo-Christianity in the Mediterranean world, the tenets of Jesus and James were more easily assimilated into the Celtic environment. Even in the 1st century BC, the Druids had been described by the Greek geographer Strabo as 'students of nature and moral philosophy'.[4] He continued:

> They are believed to be the most just of men, and are there-fore entrusted with judgements in decisions that affect both individuals and the public at large. In former times they arbitrated in war, able to bring to a standstill opponents on the point of drawing up in line of battle; murder cases have very frequently been entrusted to their adjudication.

The Sicilian-born Diodorus Siculus, another writer of the time, described the Druids as great 'philosophers and theologians, who are treated with special honour'. The Druids were additionally said to have been both exceptional statesmen and divine seers.[5] One ancient text relates:

> The Druids are men of science ... enjoying direct intercourse with the deities and able to speak in their name. They can also influence fate by making those who consult them observe positive rules or ritual taboos, or by determining the days to be chosen or avoided for any action that is contemplated.

As Nazarene Christianity gained a foothold alongside Druidism in the West, the emergent culture gave rise in the 6th century to an amalgam that became known to later historians as the Celtic Church. By that time, the Church of Rome was firmly established and the bishops looked for the slightest excuse to denounce the Druid priests and Celtic monks, finding the mark of sin even in their hairstyles. They wore long hair flowing from the back of their heads, with the fronts of their heads shaved across from the temples. The alternative Roman tonsure, as introduced by Pope Gregory I and brought to England by St Augustine in 597, was a circlet of short hair around an otherwise clean-shaven head, supposedly representative of a holy crown. According to Rome, the Celtic hairstyle was the heretical symbol of the Magians, and they condemned it as 'the tonsure of Simon Magus'.[6]

It was the Roman philosopher Pliny, a colleague of Emperor Vespasian in the 1st century, who had made the initial comparison between the Druids and the Magians, and the term *magus* was indeed equivalent to the Irish *druí* from which *druídecht* (druidism) derives. Both words relate to 'magical wisdom' although the Irish word also identifies the strength of the oak-tree.[7] Simon Magus, to whom the Celtic tonsure was credited, is perhaps better known as the apostle Simon Zelotes, whom various writers have described as a companion of Joseph and Philip in Britain and Gaul (*see* page 159).

Simon was head of the West Manasseh Magi, a priestly caste of Samaritan philosophers who supported the legitimacy of Jesus' birth against the Hebrew dissenters.[8] They were founded by Menahem the Essene in 44 BC. According to Acts 8:9–13, the Magians believed that Simon represented the 'great power of God', and he was said to have travelled extensively with the apostle Philip. The text further relates, however, that Simon and Peter were severely at odds in matters of Christian interpretation. By virtue of this, Roman Church writers were always quick to disparage Simon's name.[9] In the magical realm, he was reckoned to have been a master show-man, and manuscripts of his life deal with matters of cosmology, natural magnetism, levitation and psychokinesis.[10] He was a confirmed advocate of war with Rome and, accordingly, was known as Simon the *kananites* (Greek: 'fanatic'). This was later mistranslated in a couple of gospel entries as Simon the Canaanite.[11]

When Diodorus wrote of the Britons in the 1st century BC, he referred to the works of the Greek historian Hecataeus from three centuries before, and called them Hyperboreans (people from beyond the North Wind). He told how the god Apollo visited a Hyperborean temple 'every nineteen years – the period over which the return of the stars to the same place in the heavens is accomplished'. This 19-year astronomical cycle was used by the Druids for calendar calculation, as confirmed by the old Calendar of Coligny found in the French Department of Ain, north of Lyon, in 1897.[12] The calendar (a fragmented bronze tablet) dates from the 1st century and is the longest ancient document to be unearthed in Gaul. It gives a table of 62 consecutive months (about five solar years), each month having either 29 or 30 days. Also intercalated is the alternative lunar calendar of 13 months per year. The days of each month are related to each other, with inherent dark and light periods, and are annotated as auspicious and inauspicious days. The Coligny Calendar indicates a significant druidic competence in astronomical science, and they were said to 'have much knowledge of the stars and their motions, of the size of the world and of the earth, and of natural philosophy'.

According to Plutarch, a 2nd-century Greek priest of Apollo at Delphi, 'the Druids celebrate the feast of Saturn once every thirty years because they contend that Saturn takes thirty years to complete its orbit around the sun'. They not only knew that the Earth and planets were in orbit around the Sun, but they calculated Saturn's orbital time to within six months of correctness. This was some 1,500 years before the Polish astronomer Nicolas Copernicus announced his related heliocentric principle to an astonished academic establishment. On presenting his theory, Copernicus suffered an onslaught of abuse from the Catholic Church, which insisted that the Earth was the centre of the universe, and his work was not published until his death in 1543. To the earlier Druids, with their advanced knowledge of heavenly bodies, the very idea of an Earth-centred universe would have been unthinkable. In common with the Samaritan Magi, the Druids were practitioners of advanced numerology and healing, and likewise the Essenes of Jesus' community at Qumrân were especially interested in the mathematics which governed the order of the cosmos.

Hostility or Harmony

An essential difference between Druidism and Christianity was that the druidic order was not a religion. Rather more akin to the Essene community, the Druids maintained their own government, courts of law, educational colleges and surgeons. The members of the order were its statesmen, legislators, priests, physicians, lawyers, teachers and poets.[13] Diogenes Laërtius, a 3rd-century chronicler of philosophies, wrote that the three main druidic tenets were 'to worship the gods, to do no evil, and to practice manly virtue'.[14]

It can be seen from the plurality of 'gods' that the Druid and Nazarene religious beliefs were distinctly different.[15] Key figures in the druidic pantheon of deities were Taranis (god of storms),[16] Teutas (god of commerce), Esus (god of war), Belenus (sun god), Ardena (goddess of the forest) and Belisarna (queen of the heavens). The Roman poet Lucan (AD 39–65) provides the earliest known writing concerning Taranis (meaning 'thunderer') in his poem *Bellum civile*, better known as the *Pharsalia*.[17] A similarity between Druidism and Christianity, which has led many to presume a closer connection than truly existed at the time, was that both used the symbolism of a 'cross'. The emblem of Taranis was a cross within a circle,[18] and it may be that this evolved to become the Celtic cross of later generations. It was also a Druid custom to strip an oak tree leaving two principal branches to form a cross with the trunk on which they would carve the name of *Taranis*, with *Belenus* and *Esus* on the left and right cross-arms and *Teutas* on the stem above.[19]

In the Gallic and Celtic realms, where it is known that Christianity flourished from 1st-century times, the main factor which allowed this to happen so naturally appears to have been the jointly held Pythagorean beliefs of the Druids and the Nazarenes. Both expressed the doctrine of the immortality of the soul; they believed equally in an afterlife and in a heavenly Otherworld.[20] Immortality of the soul (rather than of the body) was around as a concept long before Jesus' time. In the ancient Greek world it was promoted by the followers of the Athenian philosopher Socrates

The Celtic god Taranis

(c469–399 BC), and Pythagoras had expounded the doctrine a century earlier.

The Essenes of Qumrân, to whom the Nazarenes were attached, were notable advocates of the Greek philosopher Pythagoras (c570–500 BC) who, in his study of arithmetical ratios, searched for meaning both in the physical and metaphysical worlds through mathematical proportions. Flavius Josephus wrote of the Essenes: 'These men live the same kind of life as do those whom the Greeks call Pythagoreans'.[21]

Along with the jointly accepted belief in the immortality of the soul, the Nazarenes and Druids also expressed a common aptitude for astronomy and the healing arts. If we add to these things the fact that the lands of the Druids were a primary mining resource for the Jewish and Judaeo-Christian miners and metal traders, there is sufficient reason to understand how it was that the two cultures became so easily entwined. Meanwhile, in the Mediterranean world, Christianity was being arrogantly promoted as an alternative religion against the requirements of those in various pagan countries, and this gave rise to hostility instead of harmony.

It was not until 597 that Christian hostility had any effect in Britain, but this was not a matter of Christianity challenging an alternative religion. It was a case of Roman Catholicism challenging six centuries of Celtic Church evolution. The moment chosen by Pope Gregory to send St Augustine to England from Rome was strategically timed to follow immediately the death of St Columba. It was presumed that the Celtic Church would be temporarily weakened by this event, and the plan was to demolish the Christian movement in Britain, which the Vatican authorities had declared more or less heretical. But, having proclaimed himself the first Archbishop of Canterbury in 601, Augustine's effort to overawe the Celtic Church was doomed to failure at that stage. The days of Roman imperialism were over, and no army that the Roman Church could muster would have defeated the fierce troops of the British kings. It is against the background of this struggle (Christian against Christian) that the histories of King Arthur and the Grail are set – in essence a contest between the Roman establishment and the kingdoms of the *Desposyni* inheritors.

A Child is Born

In parallel with Joseph's establishment of what was to become the Celtic Church among the Britons, Mary Magdalene and her colleagues had established their own mission among the Gauls of Provence from AD 44. This was precisely the year in which the ancient Askew Codex of the *Pistis Sophia* was set (*see* page 138). It was 11 years after the crucifixion of Jesus, when he gathered his disciples for a conference at the Mount of Olives.

Jesus' resurrection from spiritual death by way of his brother James's intervention, with help from Nicodemus and Simon, is referred to in an early Coptic tractate called *The Second Treatise of the Great Seth*, discovered among the books of Nag Hammadi. It explains that Jesus did not die on the cross, and that he said after the event: 'For my death, which they think happened, happened to them in their error and blindness'.[22] In about AD 120, the philosopher Basilides wrote in his Alexandrian treatise, *A Gospel Commentary*, that the events of the crucifixion were being misinterpreted in church teaching. Around a century later, the prophet Mani (in defiance of Clement, Tertullian and others) was still making precisely the same assertion – as detailed in the *Codex Manichaicus Coloniensis*,[23] discovered near Luxor in 1969.

In fact, the gospels themselves do not state that Jesus died. They explain only that, after being given some vinegar, he 'gave up the ghost'.[24] This is an abbreviated version of Genesis terminology which, in respect of Abraham, Ishmael and Isaac, states that they each 'gave up the ghost and died'.[25] The difference in Jesus' case, as against these other three instances, is that the words 'and died' are not included. To 'give up the ghost' simply means to relinquish the spirit (not the body), and Jesus emphasised this with his statement, 'Father, into thy hands I commend my spirit',[26] thereby placing himself at the mercy of circumstance. The soldiers then thought he was dead, which came as a great surprise to Pontius Pilate, who allowed Joseph of Arimathea to remove Jesus into a private sepulchre from where he was raised on the third day.

Not only were the prophecies of Zechariah fulfilled by this sequence of events (*see* page 193), but the vinegar (wine soured with gall) was a direct reference to the same potion in the lament of Psalm 69:21. Jesus is even cited as calling from the cross the exact words from the opening of Psalm 22:1, 'My God, my God, why hast thou forsaken me'?[27] In explaining the proceedings at the cross, the gospels make no secret of the fact that 'These things were done, that the scripture should be fulfilled'.[28] Never before that moment, not in all his ministry, had Jesus ever appeared more like the Saviour who had been prophesied – not a deceased Messiah, but one who conformed to all that was expected, and had just begun to reign.[29]

✠ ✠ ✠

Mary Magdalene anointed Jesus at their marriage in Bethany in March (*Nissan*) AD 33, a week before the crucifixion. At that time Mary was three months pregnant (*see* page 96). In AD 44, 11 years after this, Jesus was alive and well at the time when Mary voyaged to Provence and when, according to the monastic references, she appears to have two sons. When the New Testament book of The Acts of the Apostles (a chronological continuation of the gospels) is read with this sequence of events in mind, its content comes across rather differently from the way it is portrayed in Church teaching.

Beginning the post-resurrection story at the end of the gospel of Luke, there is an account of Jesus dining at Emmaus with Cleopas and another disciple.[30] Subsequently, he joined the apostles in Jerusalem and they thought he was a spirit but, on touching him, they discovered him to be physically real. This event is repeated in John when Thomas questioned the reality of Jesus' presence, but on placing his finger on Jesus' wound he was convinced of a flesh and blood Saviour.[31] After that, Jesus joined the apostles for a fishing trip on Lake Tiberius.[32] Items such as these were expressed in particular to make the point that Jesus' appearances after the crucifixion were in no way visionary: he had undoubtedly survived the experience and was back among his supporters.

Slipped into the midst of this sequence, however, it is stated that after the fishing trip, Jesus had gone with the apostles to Bethany, where he 'parted from them and was carried up into heaven' (Luke 24: 50–51). At the opening of The Acts, this same event is repeated, with the precise location given as the Mount of Olives,[33] near Bethany, to the east of Jerusalem.

Bethany was the home of Mary, Martha and Lazarus – the place where Lazarus was raised from the tomb and where Mary anointed Jesus. Also significant to Jesus being 'carried up to heaven' is the date of the incident. It was September AD 33, six months after the second anointing of Jesus and the very month in which Mary Magdalene would have expected her first child.[34] Such an event would have been a milestone in messianic history, while at the same time being strategically veiled in the authorized books of the New Testament. It is perhaps significant that the magnificent Russian Church of St Mary Magdalene stands at precisely this location on the Mount of Olives. This church is noted for its painting of Mary holding (in the style of the goddess Eostre) the red egg of fertility.[35] The legend surrounding this portrayal is that she showed the red egg to Emperor Tiberius in order to convince him that Jesus was alive and his seed eternal.[36]

Considering St Paul's epistle to the Hebrews, which relates also to the Ascension event in AD 33, we find it rather differently explained. Instead of discussing a heavenly ascent, it describes a priestly ordination. It states that, even though Jesus was descended in the kingly line of Judah which held no priestly status, Jesus did in fact gain entry into the priesthood in the Order of Melchizedek. Paul emphasized that, although priesthood was reserved for the succession of Levi, a change was made in the law to accommodate Jesus.[37]

Jesus being 'carried to heaven' is a clerical misrepresentation of what the scripture actually imparts. Before his departure, it is stated that Jesus announced to his apostles:

> Ye shall be witnesses unto me both in Jerusalem and in all Judaea, and in Samaria. And when he had spoken these things, while they beheld, he was taken up, and a cloud received him out of their sight (Acts 1:8–9).

It is then described:

> Two men stood by them, in white apparel, which also said, Ye men of Galilee, why stand ye gazing up into heaven? This same Jesus which is taken up … shall so come in like manner as ye have seen him go (Acts 1:10–11).

Linking this with St Paul's explanation, it emerges that the 'two men in white' were Essene priests. Josephus makes it clear in *The Wars of the Jews* that the Essene apparel was white,[38] as against the coloured garb of the Hebrew priests. Heaven in this ritualistic context, we learn from Dead Sea Scrolls interpretation, was the name given to the angelic platform of the Essene high monastery where the priests would worship and communicate with God.[39] As for the 'cloud' that conveyed Jesus into the heavenly state (the priesthood), this was a community style applied to the designated Leader of the Pilgrims. It was a cloud that had led the ancient Israelites into the Promised Land,[40] and the appearance of God to Moses on Mount Sinai had been accompanied by a cloud.[41] Thus, along with preserving the names of the angels (*see* page 94), the Cloud distinction was retained as a symbolic designation within the Essene community. At the time in question, the titular Cloud was the head of the Nazarenes, the crown prince of the messianic line and the patriarchal Joseph of the community. The Cloud who conveyed Jesus into the monastic kingdom of heaven was his own brother James.[42]

In the way that this brief episode is presented, it would have been perfectly straightforward to those of the era when written. It was eminently suited, however, to supernatural interpretation by the later Church Fathers and New Testament promoters. Jesus had been crucified and had been raised from spiritual death; hence it could be claimed by the bishops that he had died for the sake of people's sins. But he had not died, he was still around, eating and fishing with his friends; the scriptures are clear about this. Although not termed as such in The Acts, Jesus' entry into the priestly kingdom of heaven was therefore given a new name, the 'Ascension', and it was claimed that he was actually borne up by a vaporous cloud into an astral abode. But that was not the end of the biblical story. The Acts entry continues by stating that 'This same Jesus which is taken up ... shall so come in like manner as ye have seen him go'.[43] And indeed he did return, making appearances throughout The Acts that have been conveniently explained by classifying them as supernatural visions.

Looking overall at the timing of the Ascension, its occurrence on the Mount of Olives at Bethany, and the confinement of Mary Magdalene, a picture emerges of the true significance of the event. Within the regulations of dynastic wedlock it was the case that a husband and wife would be separated for predetermined periods following the births of their children. When a son was born, no further physical contact between the parents was permitted for six years. Alternatively, if the child was a daughter the ensuing period of celibacy was limited to three years.[44] Such periods would culminate at the 'times of restitution' – their returns to the married state. It is stated in The Acts:

> And he shall send Jesus Christ, which before was preached unto
> you; whom the heaven must receive until the times of restitution
> of all things.[45]

The priests had said that Jesus would return in due course, and Jesus had said himself that he would be seen again throughout Judaea and Samaria. Seven years later, in AD 40, Jesus was even in Syria with the disciple Ananias who instructed St Paul. In AD 44 he was back at Bethany and the Mount of Olives with his apostles.

The fact that Jesus is mentioned in connection with the 'times of restitution' indicates that he had become a father and was, therefore, obliged to lead a monastic existence for a predetermined time. There is no suggestion in the text that this child was a son, and Jesus did not return to the scene for another three years, which means that the child born to Mary Magdalene in AD 33 was a daughter. She appears to have been named Tamar – assimilated in Greek to Damaris.[46] This is a revelation in itself, but it does not help to confirm the Glastonbury references or the messianic succession accounts of Gaulish origin about the sons, Jesus junior and Josephes.

Discovering the Sons

In weighing the Essene writings of Qumrân found in the Dead Sea Scrolls against the Christian scriptures, Dr Barbara Thiering (*see* page 98) discovered a series of scribal techniques that were rigidly applied throughout. Their application made it imperative for the old texts to be translated verbatim, with no room for interpretation or deviation from the linguistic terms actually used. It became clear that words, names and titles which have a specific or cryptic meaning are used with that same meaning throughout. Not only do they have the same meaning every time they are used, but they are used every time that same meaning is required.

In some cases, individual representations of names or titles might be complex or obscure, but more often they are straightforward, though not always immediately obvious. On many occasions our attention is drawn to specific textual passages by the words, 'He that hath ears to hear, let him hear' – as for instance in Mark 4:9 – the phrase being an inevitable precursor to a passage with a hidden meaning. The original gospels were compiled so as not to arouse the suspicions of the Roman overlords when politically contentious matters were discussed. They were designed for a specific audience, and much of their content was esoterically phrased for those who would understand what was written between the lines. Similar methods of conveying veiled messages in an allegorical form have been used throughout the centuries in literature, art and music. Modern examples of the technique in recent times are found in the work of the dissident Russian composer Dmitry Shostakovich (1906–75). Constrained by the restrictions of the oppressive Soviet regime, he confided that the notational structure of his music embodied politically sensitive information that was 'camouflaged for those who had ears to listen'.[47]

In gospel terms, the governing rules of the scribal techniques were necessarily fixed and the symbolism remains constant. From the outset of the gospel of John, Jesus is personally defined as the *Logos*: the 'Word of God':

> In the beginning was the Word, and the Word was with God …
> And the Word was made flesh, and dwelt among us, and we
> beheld his glory (John 1:1, 14).

Thereafter, whenever the phrase 'the Word of God' is used (with or
without a capital W, according to different translations), it means
that Jesus either was present or is the subject of the narrative. The
terminology was used, for example, in Luke 5:1 when the word of
God 'stood by the lake'. The phrase is also used in The Acts to identify Jesus' whereabouts after the Ascension. So when we read that
'the apostles which were at Jerusalem heard that Samaria had
received the word of God' (Acts 8:14), we may immediately understand that Jesus was in Samaria, just as he had previously said he
would be after his marital restitution.

It follows, therefore, that when we read in Acts 6:7 that 'the
word of God increased', we should recognize at once that Jesus
'increased'.[48] Scribal references of this type are generally set up
beforehand by some other entry which determines the scriptural use
of the term in accordance with a premise as explained by Jesus to the
disciples:

> Unto you it is given to know the mystery of the kingdom of God:
> but unto them that are without, all these things are done in
> parables: That seeing they may see, and not perceive; and hearing
> they may hear, and not understand.[49]

The parables are therefore not just moralistic stories as they appear
on the surface; they also provide linguistic guidelines for the reader.
In the parable of the Sower and the Seed, it is stated: 'And other
[seed] fell on good ground, and did yield fruit that sprang up and
increased'.[50] Thus, the Acts reference denotes that 'Jesus [yielded
fruit and] increased' – that is to say, he had a son. The gospel of
Philip relates,

> There is the Son of man and there is the Son of the Son of man.
> The Lord is the Son of man, and the Son of the Son of man is he
> who is created through the Son of man. The Son of man received
> from God the power to create. He has the ability to beget.[51]

As required by the messianic regulations, the birth took place in AD 37 – the year after Jesus returned to his married state at the 'time of restitution'. Following the birth of a son, however, Jesus was destined for six more years of monastic celibacy. In the course of this, we know that he was at the Damascus monastery for the Nazarene conference in AD 40 when he met with Paul – so we should look at three years or so after this event. Sure enough, there is a second entry relating to the year AD 44, with Acts 12:24 stating once again, 'The word of God grew and multiplied'. A second son had been born.[52]

The first son of Jesus and Mary Magdalene, whose story is told in the book of The Revelation (a chronological continuation of The Acts) was named Jesus. On reaching his dynastic majority in Corinth, he was granted the style of Justus as previously applied to his uncle James the Just, and is referred to by St Paul as Jesus Justus in Colossians 4:11.[53] On the eventual death of his father, Jesus Christ, he became head of the family, stating, 'I am thy fellow servant, and of thy brethren that have the testimony of Jesus ... And his name is called The Word of God'.[54]

At the time of the Davidic accession, the younger brother would have gained the Justus distinction as the new Joseph *ha Rama Theo*. This is the only name by which the second son is known. Hence, the brothers were Jesus (Joshua in Hebrew) and Joseph respectively, in complete accord with the Glastonbury references to Jesus the younger (Gais) and Josephes.

15

Legacy of the Bride

The Last Council

The relevance of the period leading to AD 44, when Jesus held council at the Mount of Olives and Mary Magdalene's party sailed to Gaul, is that opinions had begun to differ within the ranks of Jesus' supporters. Peter and Andrew were at odds with Matthew and Philip over matters of female involvement, while others were in dispute over aspects of Jewish law. Some asserted that male Gentile converts to Judaism should be circumcised; others did not agree. Hence it was that during the middle AD 40s the apostles began to go their separate ways. Peter and his team favoured Syria, and began to work in Antioch; James and his Nazarenes remained operative in Judaea, and Simon Zelotes had previously established a new base in Cyprus.[1] Origen recorded that Andrew pursued his mission in Scythia, and some early chroniclers maintained that Thomas ended his days in India. The main reason for the group's disbanding appears, however, to have been the AD 44 assassination of King Herod-Agrippa I in which some of the apostles were thought to have been implicated.

To that point, Peter had been Jesus' right-hand man but, although Peter was married, he had a low opinion of women and was not on the best of terms with Mary Magdalene. This is made especially clear in the *Pistis Sophia*, which states that Peter was annoyed by her involvement on the Mount of Olives (*see* page 138).[2] He challenged Jesus about Mary's right to be vocal in apostolic company, and was duly rebuked for his comments.[3] This document from the *Askew Codex* is wholly in line with the gospels of Philip, Thomas and Mary, which all cite occasions when Peter objected angrily to Mary's presence and participation in Jesus' affairs.[4]

Alongside the elevation of Mary's status in these non-canonical texts, the *Dialogue of the Saviour* – an early tractate based on the 1st-century gospel of 'Q' (*see* page 13) – also refers to Mary Magdalene as an insightful visionary. She was said to be the apostle who excels above the others, and the 'woman who knew the All'.[5] In his *Commentary on the Canticles*, Hippolytus, a 2nd-century presbyter of the early Christians in Rome, associated Mary directly with the royal bride in the Old Testament *Song of Songs*. He referred to her as the Apostle of the Apostles (*Apostola Apostolorum*), and she was revered as the Bride of Christ.[6]

Mary Magdalene's great significance to the Nazarene movement is portrayed in early artwork. Apart from the underground drawings in the catacombs of Rome, Christian art did not evolve publicly until after the Edict of Milan in AD 313, but the earliest known Magdalene portrayal comes from about AD 240. Discovered in 1929 at Dura-Europos on the River Euphrates in Syria, and entitled *Myrrophore* (Myrrh bearer), it was a wall-painting of Mary's arrival at the tomb of Jesus, as in John 20:1 (*see* plate 2). The painting was removed from its chapel house in the 1930s and is now at the Yale University Art Gallery in New Haven.[7]

In the early AD 40s, James the Just and his followers had become an increasing threat to Roman authority in Jerusalem. As a direct result, the apostle James Boanerges was seized and executed by the King's brother, Herod of Chalcis (Acts 12:1–2). The royal advisers had decreed that the newly dubbed Christian movement was subversive and would lead to the overthrow of secular and Temple authority, and so Peter was also arrested and thrown into prison. Soon afterwards, King Herod-Agrippa I was poisoned, and the blame for the assassination was laid on Simon Zelotes and the remaining apostles.[8] Simon managed to elude his pursuers, but Thaddaeus was not so fortunate; he was caught attempting to cross the River Jordan, and was executed. Peter then managed to escape from his cell,[9] and the others made due preparation to flee from Judaea.

Having fulfilled his dynastic obligation to father two sons, Jesus had been released from his marital restrictions and was able to lead a normal life once more. Everything points to the fact that Jesus and Mary Magdalene had agreed on a formal separation from that time. Paul wrote in his letter to the Corinthians that Jesus was exempt from the rules governing marital curtailment.[10]

It was this event that caused Mary to become so closely associated with the forsaken bride in the *Song of Solomon*. Throughout the four years of Jesus' early ministry from AD 29, she had been constantly at his side from the time of her first appearance with Joanna and Susanna.[11] But from the moment of Jesus' second anointing in AD 33, they had spent nine of their eleven married years apart. From the birth of their second son in AD 44, Jesus should have been destined for another six years of monastic separation. The alternative, in order to gain his freedom to work in the field, was a release from the constraints of his wedlock. Another option was to ignore the dynastic regulations as his own parents had done when they resorted to a normal manner of Jewish family life after the birth of James. Unlike his father, who had no interest in princely pursuits, it appears that Jesus elected for a marital annulment. Alternatively, it might have been the case that Mary instigated this, deciding to leave her husband's dangerous environment for the sake of her children.[12]

Either way, as Origen of Alexandria (AD *c*185–254) stated in his *Commentary on the Song of Songs*, Mary had attended Jesus with her spikenard, thereby giving him the odour of her faith, and had received in return the fragrance of Christ for herself.[13] As with Abishag and Solomon, wrote Origen, the king was anointed and the bride was fulfilled. The same theme was taken up by Hippolytus, St Bernard de Clairvaux and others.[14] Thus, Jesus and Mary were perceived as being equally imbued with the Holy Spirit and each was seen as independently complete, with no further need for reliance on the other.

There is no mention in any known text or tradition of Jesus and Mary ever meeting again after the Bethany council at the Mount of Olives in AD 44. Jesus separated not only from Mary but from many

Mary Magdalene Instructs the Apostles, (12th century)

of his immediate followers, and his mission was now destined to be spread far and wide as they embarked on their individual travels. Jesus had told the apostles that the new head of the Nazarenes was his own brother James.[15] Additionally, he had nominated his wife over and above Peter as a leader of the gospel mission, stating, 'Thou art she whose heart is more directed to the Kingdom of Heaven than all thy brethren'.[16]

With a daughter and two young sons to consider, one newly born, Mary Magdalene was placed in a precarious situation when the arrests and persecutions began after the Agrippa assassination. Herod of Chalcis knew that she was a close friend of Simon Zelotes and his wife Salome, but Mary also had other good friends, especially in James (Joseph) and Philip. She also appears to have been on good enough terms with Paul, who (as Saul of Tarsus) had been a tutor to the late king's son.[17] At the age of just 17, the young prince was soon to become Herod-Agrippa II.

The Herod kings sprang from an Idumaean Arab called Antipater, who was installed as Governor of Judaea by Julius Caesar. His son, Herod I (the Great), became King of Judaea by way of Roman appointment in 37 BC, and from him the reigning dynasty had descended to young Herod-Agrippa II in the third successive generation. It is recorded in the *Wars of the Jews* that the Herods were granted lands in Gaul, to where Herod-Archelaus (brother of Herod-Antipas of Galilee) had been exiled in AD 6. The Herodian estate was at Vienne, near Lyon, to the north of Marseilles in Provence. Flavius Josephus explained that Archelaus had been retired to this place by Emperor Augustus because of his bad management in Judaea.[18]

By way of Paul's connection with the late King's son, arrangements were made to give Mary Magdalene and her companions safe passage to the Provençal region in Gaul.[19] It was from that moment in AD 44 that the histories of Mary, Martha, Simon/Lazarus, Joseph and Philip, along with Jesus' sisters Mary Jacob, Salome and others moved into the chronicles of the West. Jesus embarked on a mission to Galatia, in central Asia Minor, with the chief proselyte[20] John Mark and, apart from Joseph/James, there is no indication that any of the others ever visited the Holy Land again. Their names all disappear from the New Testament, which settles thereafter on the ensuing activities of Paul, Luke, Barnabus and Mark. But even they were long gone from Judaea when the Jewish Revolt against the Romans began in AD 66. This led to the utter destruction of Jerusalem in AD 70, subsequent to which Emperor Vespasian issued his edict for the hunt and seizure of the *Desposyni*.

Annals of Provence

The oldest recorded testimony of Mary Magdalene's life in Provence comes from the 2nd-century writings of Hegesippus as referenced in a 9th-century manuscript entitled *Vita emeritica beatae Mariae Magdalenae*.[21] Other aspects of her story date from the early 400s, and a hymn from the 600s was republished in the records of the *Acta Sanctorum* by the Jesuit, Jean Bolland, in the 17th century.[22] The most treasured of early works, however, is *The Life of St Mary Magdalene* by the Benedictine scholar, Rabanus Maurus (776–856). He was renowned as the most learned sage of his era, and it was said that, 'in matters of scriptural knowledge, canon law and liturgy, he had no equal'.[23] Composed as 50 chapters, and bound into 6 volumes of richly illuminated manuscript, his work incorporated much that was held on record about Mary back in the 4th century when the Church of Rome was founded by Emperor Constantine.

In the early 1400s, a monastic copy of the Rabanus manuscript was discovered in England at Oxford University. It tells of how Mary, Martha, Simon-Lazarus and their companions boarded a ship and left the shore of their homeland:

> Favoured by an easterly wind they went round about, down the Tyrrhenian Sea between Europe and Africa, leaving the city of Rome and all the land of Italy to the right. Then, happily changing course to the right, they came near to the city of Marseilles in the Gaulish province of Vienne.[24]

Their point of disembarkation in Provence was Ratis, which later became known as Les Saintes Maries de la Mer.[25]

Another writer on the subject was Jacopo di Voragine,[26] a 13th-century Archbishop of Genoa, who included the *Légende de Sainte Marie Madeleine* within his greater compilation, the famous *Légenda Aurea* (Golden Legend). Two centuries after Jacopo's death, this was one of the earliest books printed at Westminster, London, by William Caxton in 1483. Previously published in French and Latin, Caxton was persuaded by William, Earl of Arundel, to produce an English version translated from the European manuscripts.[27]

Although independently written in two different countries, and by no means identical in content, the most surprising aspect of the extensive works by Rabanus and Jacopo is that both authors obtained their source material from Roman Church records. On the one hand, the priests and bishops were vilifying Mary Magdalene's legacy, while on the other hand, the accounts of her life and mission in Provence were given public readings on a regular basis in medieval monasteries and some churches.

In earlier imperial times, the heritage of Mary Magdalene and the *Desposyni* heirs had posed enormous problems for the Roman overlords. Attempting to suppress the Nazarene believers, Emperor Septimius Severus had concentrated his assaults specifically on Lyon and Vienne. In AD 208, he had 19,000 Christians put to death as martyrs in the region where numerous shrines were later established to the memory of Ste Marie de Madeleine. These included her burial site at St Maximus la Sainte-Baume.[28] The place was named after the Holy Balm (*la Sainte Baume*) with which Mary had anointed Jesus at Bethany, and her sepulchre and alabaster tomb were subsequently guarded, day and night, by Cassianite monks.

The Cassianite Order was founded by John Cassian in about AD 410, and was the earliest monastic foundation to maintain independence from the episcopal Church. In commenting on the Church of Rome, Cassian denounced the taking of Holy Orders as 'a dangerous practice' and declared that his monks should 'at all costs avoid bishops'. Initially an ascetic hermit in Bethlehem, John Cassian established two conventual schools at Marseilles – one for men and another for women.[29]

For more than 1,000 years from AD 411, the Cassianites guarded the sacred relics of La Sainte-Baume.[30] They referred to the rock-spring of their hermitage as the 'fountain of living waters' in reference to an entry in the Old Testament *Song of Solomon* with which Mary Magdalene had become so closely associated.[31] Aix-en-Provence, where Mary Magdalene died in AD 63, was the old town of Acquae Sextiae.[32] It was the hot springs at Aix (Acqs) which gave the town its name – *acqs* being a medieval derivative of the old Latin word *aquae* (waters). In the Languedoc tradition of Provence, Mary was known as *la Dompna del Aquae*, the Mistress of the Waters.

Both Rabanus Maurus and Jacopo di Voragine give insight into Mary's parentage. As we saw earlier, her father Syrus was of Syrian royal stock, a fact which gave rise to the particular style of marriage ceremony conducted between Mary and Jesus in Bethany (*see* page 52). Jacopo further explained that Mary's mother, Eucharia, was also of royal kindred: 'She was born of right noble lineage and parents which were descended of the lineage of kings.' In his earlier manuscript, Rabanus gave a little more detail, explaining that Eucharia was a descendant of the Royal House of Israel.[33] That was not Jesus' own Davidic House of Judah, but the priest-kingly house of the Hasmonaean Maccabees who reigned in Jerusalem from 166 BC until the Roman occupation in 63 BC under General Pompeii.[34]

Jacopo's text also indicates the derivation of Mary's name, linking it with the 'castle of Bethany' – the tower or *migdal* of her inheritance. It denoted a high community station of community guardianship, as in Micah 4:8, the *Magdal-eder* (Watchtower of the flock), and it is to this social status that the 'Magdalene' distinction refers.[35] Thus it is significant that, at Mary's biblical introduction in Luke 8:2, she is described as 'Mary, called Magdalene' – that is 'Mary, called the Watchtower'.

These and other accounts all give the leader of the Provençal mission as Simon Zelotes, who became known as Lazarus the Great One (Maximus). He established his principal seat at Marseilles, where his statue was erected at St Victor's Church by the harbour. The church records at Lyon state that Lazarus was in Gaul with Mary Magdalene and Martha, where he became the first Bishop of Marseilles.[36] In AD 303, Bishop Dorotheus of Tyre wrote in his *Synopsis de Apostole* that Simon-Lazarus was eventually killed in Britain, and this is confirmed in the 1601 *Annales Ecclesiasticae* of the Vatican librarian Cardinal Baronius. At the saint's own request, however, his remains were later placed with those of Mary Magdalene in Provence.

Martha's remains lie buried in a church dedicated to her at Tarascon in Vienne. Built in the form of an inverted boat, the church pillars simulate masts, and artwork portraying the Magdalene voyage adorns the nave. Also, there is an inset wall tablet commemorating a visit to the site's earlier chapel by the Merovingian King Clovis in the year 500.[37] According to the will of St Caesarius of Arles (AD 470–542),[38] the Collegiate Church of St Martha was originally called *Sancta Mariae de Ratis* and, relating to Mary even today, the vespers of the church include the words, '*Veni, Sponsa Christi, accipe coronam, quam tibi Dominus præparavit in æternum*' (Come, thou bride of Christ, receive the crown which the Lord hath prepared for thee for ever). In respect of Martha, it is added in the lesson:

> This is one of those wise virgins, whom the Lord found watching, for when she took her lamp, she took oil with her ... And at midnight there was a cry made, Behold, the Bridegroom cometh, go ye out to meet him. And when the Lord came, she went in with him to the marriage.[39]

The relics of Jesus' sisters, Mary Jacob and Mary Salome (constituting, with Mary Magdalene, the 'Three Maries' of Provence) are to be found in the Chapel of the Holy Marys at the church of Les Saintes Maries in the Camargue. In a chapel beneath are the remains of their companion Sarah.[40]

Relics of the Magdalene

Another prominent literary work concerning Mary Magdalene in Provence is *Sainte Marie Madeleine* by the Dominican friar, Père Jean-Baptiste-Henri Dominique Lacordaire (1802–61).[41] He is described in *The Catholic Encyclopedia* as 'the greatest pulpit orator of the 19th century'.[42] Before becoming a Dominican friar, he was trained as a lawyer and practised as a successful Bar advocate for a number of years. Subsequently ordained by the Archbishop of Paris, he became a noted champion of religious freedoms and a free press. It was said that no one, whether layman or cleric, royalist or liberal, was safe from his assailing pen or his critical lectures.

Lacordaire was greatly revered and, in 1835, was offered the cathedral pulpit of Notre Dame de Paris, where he hosted a series of astonishingly controversial conferences. Forsaking prayers, hymns and scriptural readings, he spoke on subjects never before heard in the confines of a church, and he was especially concerned with matters of religious history that were not generally discussed. He followed these with similar conferences at Metz and Toulouse, and his open style of oratory became renowned. In the course of this, he entered the Dominican Order of the Friars Preachers, and was invited into the foremost literary arena of the Académie Française. For a while, after the 1848 revolution of the Second Republic, he was editor of the New Era journal *L'Ere Nouvelle*, but spent most of his latter years writing a series of works based on unfamiliar aspects of Church record. Among these was his book *Sainte Marie Madeleine*, wherein he recounted the 13th-century excavation of Mary's tomb at St Maximus la Sainte-Baume.

Beginning his story in the early 8th century, Lacordaire explained that Arabs and Berbers from north-west Africa had made extensive incursions into Provence and Northern Spain. The Spanish called them Moors, while in France they were known as Saracens.[43] These Muslims of the Baghdad Caliphate soon took control of the whole Iberian peninsula, and were dominant for around 300 years.[44] With the Saracen capital at Narbonne (along the coast from Marseilles) and a strong foothold at Nimes in Languedoc, the Cassianite monks at La Sainte-Baume became apprehensive. Consequently, they moved Mary's remains from her alabaster tomb to another coffer in the same crypt: the marble sepulchre of St Sidonia, Bishop of Aix. As a precautionary measure, they also placed a written notice of what they had done in the tomb. Meanwhile, the monks continued their vigil, but when word was leaked in the 11th century that Mary's tomb was empty, a provocative rumour was initiated. It was said that Gerard de Roussillon, Governor of Provence, had taken Mary's bones to a new home at the Abbey of Vézelay, where they were kept hidden in the chancel beneath the high altar.

The diocesan bishop of Autun and Vézelay became worried that false story might cause his beloved 9th-century abbey to become an unwarranted tourist attraction. He therefore applied to the Holy See in Rome for an edict to prevent this. Much to his surprise, Pope Paschal II became personally enthused by the prospect of a new pilgrimage centre. He even arranged for the old abbey-church to be transformed into a magnificent basilica from 1096. Then, in 1103, he issued a papal bull to proclaim the new site, inviting all Catholics to congregate at Vézelay.[45] The place acquired such a reputation that King Louis VII, Queen Eleanor and St Bernard de Clairvaux went there in 1147 to preach the Second Crusade, with the French and Flemish nobility and around 100,000 people in attendance. This event was particularly relevant to St Bernard who, as patron and protector of the Order of the Temple of Jerusalem, had required from the Templars their 'Obedience of Bethany – the castle of Mary and Martha'.[46] From that date, the veneration of Mary Magdalene was intimately allied to the crusaders' campaign, and, in 1189, Philippe Augustus and Richard Coeur de Lion of England announced their Third Crusade at Vézelay, where it met with similar enthusiasm.

It was not until 1254 that King Louis IX began to wonder what proof there was of Mary's relics being at Vézelay. After all, the Bishop of Autun (who was in charge at the time) had strongly denied that such a transfer had ever taken place. Louis discovered that there was no truth in the rumour and, along with the Sire de Joinville, he set out

at once for St Maximus la Sainte-Baume, where the monks were still
in residence. The Lord of Joinville wrote in his memoir:

> We came to the city of Aix in Provence to honour the Blessed
> Magdalene who lay about a day's journey away. We went to the
> place called Baume, on a very steep and craggy rock, in which it
> was said that the Holy Magdalene long resided at a hermitage.

King Louis was outraged that his royal predecessors and St Bernard,
Abbot of Clairvaux, should have been so unwittingly deluded. The
Dominican records tell how Louis decided to set matters straight,
even at that late stage. He embarked on an enterprise with his
nephew Charles, Prince of Salerno and Count of Provence, who later
became King Charles II of Naples and Count of Anjou. Of the initial
investigation by Charles, it is related:

> He accordingly came to St Maximus without any parade,
> accompanied by a few gentlemen of his suite, and after having
> interrogated the monks and old men, he had a trench opened in
> the old basilica of Cassian, the 9th December 1279.[47]

It was subsequently recorded that, on advice from the monks,
Charles entered the tomb of St Sidonia nine days later on 18
December. In the presence of King Louis, the bishops of Arles and
Aix, together with several prelates and others, the prince broke the
seals of the sarcophagus and opened it. In front of all the attesting
witnesses, he removed a roll of fragmenting cork, from which he
produced the parchment that was placed in the tomb so long before
by the Cassianites. He read the document:

> The year of our Lord 710, the 6th day of the month of December,
> in the reign of Eudes the most pious of France.[48] When the
> Saracens ravaged that nation, the body of our very dear and
> venerable Mary Magdalene was very secretly, and during the
> night, removed from its own alabaster tomb and placed in this

one, which is of marble, whence the body of St Sidonia had been previously taken, in order that the relics of our holy saint should be more secure against the sacrilegious outrage of the perfidious mussulmen.

An authorized copy of the document and its discovery was drawn up by Prince Charles and signed by the archbishops and bishops present. On 5 May in the following year, an assembly was held of prelates, counts, barons, knights and magistrates from Provence and the neighbouring areas. The details of the Vézelay hoax were made known at this convention and, on 12 May 1280, the delegates were taken to see the Magdalene relics at La Sainte-Baume. It was reported that 'the head of the saint was perfect, while the other parts of the body were only a few bones', and a deputation from the Tribunal of the Cassation of Aix (including the President, the Solicitor General and two councillors) signed a statement of witness.

Prince Charles then separated Mary's bones into three shares. He had her skull encased in a magnificent gold bust, with a moulded glass covering for the face.[49] His father, Charles I of Anjou, sent his own crown from Naples so that its gold and jewels might be used in the holy enterprise. Mary's other bones were laid to rest in a silver casket, and in later times her upper arm bone, the humerus, was placed in a reliquary of silver gilt upon a pedestal supported by four lions.

It was then determined that, since the Church of Rome had been responsible for perpetuating the Vézelay myth, the prevailing Pope should consecrate the relics to set the record straight. At that stage, however, Charles was called to other duties following the death of his father, and it was nearly five years before he gained his audience with Boniface VIII in the chair of St Peter. Prior to this, the sworn declarations of all the noble and ecclesiastical Sainte-Baume witnesses were presented to the Pope, along with the original parchment of the 8th-century Cassianite monks.

On 6 April 1295, Pope Boniface issued a bull declaring the relics to be the true and authentic remains of St Mary Magdalene. He authorized Charles (then King of Naples and Count of Provence) to transfer the monastery of St Maximus to the recently constituted Dominican Order of the Friars Preachers. Funding was made available to build a great basilica on the site of the old Cassianite oratory where the relics would be displayed.

It took far longer than Charles's lifetime to design and construct the majestic Gothic edifice, and the work was not fully completed for nearly 200 years.[50] Meanwhile, there was the question of what to do with the gold and silver-encased treasures. At that time, the Capetian King of France was Philippe IV (1285–1314), and he duly staked his royal claim. Pope Boniface, however, was no friend of this wayward monarch, who was levying illegal taxes against the clergy. This led to Boniface's papal bull *Clerics laicos* on 24 February 1296, in which he forbade the clergy to give up ecclesiastical revenues or property without permission from the Apostolic See; also that princes imposing such levies – essentially King Philippe – were declared excommunicated.

Royal Lineage

From 1295, one of the primary objectives of the Dominican Friars Preachers was the basilica project at St Maximus la Sainte-Baume as instigated by Pope Boniface VIII. Mary Magdalene was designated as the patron saint and Mother Protectress of the Order, which was also responsible for the convent of the Sisters of Saint Magdalen in Germany.[51]

Along with the Dominicans, a key player in the affairs of the Magdalene relics was King René d'Anjou, Count of Provence (1408–1480). His sister Maria was married to King Charles VII of France, and his daughter Margaret was the wife of King Henry VI of England. Along with his queen-consort, Jehanne de Laval, René arranged Magdalene pilgrimages and had Mary Magdalene's right arm-bone set into the silver-gilt casing in which it is still displayed[52] along with the skull reliquary designed by Prince Charles. René designed and made this casing in 1473 before the new basilica of St Maximus la Sainte-Baume was opened. He also designed and built the ship-like collegiate church for St Martha's remains at Tarascon, while at Reculée, near Angers, he founded the hermitage-shrine of *La Madeleine de St Baumette*.[53] Above all others, King René became the principal benefactor of the Magdalene tradition in Provence; he arranged the popular Bethany festivals at Marseilles, Tarascon and Aix, and was president of the Feast celebrations of *Les Saintes Maries*.

The Dominican annals tell of many notable people who made pilgrimages to La Sainte-Baume. The French King Louis XI (1461–83) was insistent about Mary Magdalene's dynastic position in the royal lineage, and claimed her as 'a daughter of France belonging to the monarchy'.[54] His successors, Charles VIII and Louis XII, followed his example. Anne of Brittany (successively the wife of both monarchs) had a small gold figurine of herself set within the shrine. François I (1515–47) made extensive additions to the Sainte-Baume Hospital for Strangers, and his successor Charles IX made further bequests to the foundation. In 1622, Louis XIII paid his respects at the holy site and, on 4 February 1660, Louis XIV arrived with his mother, Anne of Austria. They presided over the placement of Mary's silver casket of small relics into a porphyry crystal urn, which had been specially made and sent from Rome by the General of the Friars Preachers. Never before had a saintly shrine attracted so much auspicious attention. In one single day during the basilica's construction, five kings arrived from different parts of Europe,[55] and in the course of just a century no less than eight popes were recorded at the site.[56]

A certain amount of damage was done at La Sainte-Baume during the French Revolution (1789–99) when unruly citizens were intent to demolish everything previously held sacred in their land. But the key relics were preserved in safe custody, except for the crystal urn that was lost. By the Monday of Pentecost 1822, the necessary repairs had been accomplished and some 40,000 people congregated to watch the Archbishop of Aix return Mary's gold and silver-clad relics to their rightful home.

Soon afterwards, in 1842, the imposing church of *La Madeleine* was completed near the River Seine in Paris. Overlooking the Place de la Concorde, where *Madame la Guillotine* had done her work in the Revolution, this Napoleonic monument, commissioned by Lucien Bonaparte, reflected the Magdalene fever that was sweeping through the nation. Built in the style of a classical Athenian temple, the church facade mirrors the National Assembly building opposite, across the square beyond the Luxor obelisk. Within this church is one small Magdalene relic – a piece of bone removed from the porphyry urn at the request of Louis XVI in 1785. It was originally a gift to the Duke of Parma but in view of the subsequent loss of the urn and Louis' execution in the Revolution, it was passed to the Archbishop of Paris in 1810.

Mother Protectress

The great anomaly in all this is that, despite Mary's considerable importance to the early Christians, her official image had been changed within the Roman Church establishment when, based on no evidence, biblical or otherwise, Pope Gregory I accused her in 591 of having been a dreadful sinner (*see* page 108). By the 12th century she had become thoroughly defamed by a Church that did everything in its power to suppress her influence within orthodox Christianity. In his vindictive *Commentary on the Feast at Cana*, the German theologian Honorius Augustodunensis wrote that Mary was 'a filthy and common prostitute who, regardless of her birth and of her own free will, founded a brothel of sin, a temple of demons'![57]

Outwardly, there was a persistent denigration of Mary Magdalene in the public domain, while at the same time it is clear that her legacy was actually prized and venerated by those who moved in the highest circles. For centuries, popes, cardinals, bishops, abbots and kings visited her shrine, and much was made of Mary's matriarchal standing in terms of the desposynic royal lineage of France. Her maternal status was also acknowledged by virtue of being joint Mother Protectress of the Dominicans along with Jesus' own mother.

In 1969, Mary was formally sainted by the Catholic Church (feast day 22 July), but it is of interest to note that in the 17th century a request for this, made by the Dominicans at La Sainte-Baume, had been rejected.[58] This move on the part of the French Dominicans was instigated by Fra Michaelis of Provence, an active reformer at the time of his election as Prior of St Maximus la Sainte-Baume. Previously, in 1691, the historian Thomas Souéges, who composed the saintly details for each day in *The Dominican Year*, wrote in his entry for 22 July: 'Mary Magdalene, the Mother Protectress of the Order of Preachers'. He then added, as a personal aside to Mary: 'You were kind enough to do us the honour of treating us as children and brothers ... It pleased you that you wished the precious remains of your body to be guarded, and the place of your penance honoured'.

The first Dominican prior, Guillaume de Tonneins, had taken possession of the Sainte-Baume shrine from the Cassianites on 20 June 1295 and, apart from a short lapse during the French Revolution, the monks remained in residence until 1957. The monastery was then handed over to nuns who had established their convent there in 1872. Subsequent to the work at St Maximus la Sainte-Baume by King Charles II of Naples, Sicily and Provence, along with his Dominican adviser and confessor Pierre de Lamanon, Mary Magdalene's feast day was first celebrated throughout the Dominican Order in 1297 as recommended by the General Chapter of Bologna.[59] Fra Mortier, author of *The Dominican Liturgy*, wrote: 'The body of the Magdalene is guarded by the Preachers; the Order of Preachers is guarded by the Magdalene'.[60]

A conclusion that might be drawn from all this is that, despite the staunchly promoted dogma of the Church's own Apostolic Succession, it was understood by the governing fraternity, and particularly by the monastic institutions outside the episcopal movement, that there was indeed another succession to consider, and that Jesus' own chosen *koinonôs* (consort)[61] could not be ignored.

Part IV

Grail Heritage
and the Arthurian Tradition

16

The Greater Quest

Various Lines

James the Just (Joseph *ha Rama Theo*) is the first in a recorded descent of *Desposyni* heirs in Britain. His wife was said to have been a daughter of a King of Logres – the Celtic name for southern Britain before it became known as England (Angle-land).[1] If this were to have been the case, the marriage would need to have taken place in about AD 37 in order to comply with the Nazarene regulation for dynastic wedlock. It was the rule that Davidic heirs should father a first child in or about the year of their 40th birthday (this being the Judaic royal generation standard).[2] Hence, as was the case with Jesus, the dynasts tended to marry onwards from their 36th birthday, and James was born in AD 1. We also know from the Vatican librarian, Cardinal Baronius, that James first visited Siluria in AD 35 (*see* page 168). Given the date in question, his wife would appear to have been a daughter of King Cymbeline (Cunobelinus), and therefore a sister of Caractacus and Arviragus. Her name appears in the *Grand Saint Graal* as Enygeus, which is remarkably similar to an historically known daughter of Cymbeline called Innogen.[3] Such a marital link would certainly explain the Glastonbury land grant to James/Joseph by Arviragus, as well as justifying the subsequent marriage between Arviragus' son, Marius, and the *Rama Theo's* granddaughter.

Additionally, we know of three offspring from Jesus and Mary Magdalene. All were born by AD 44. By the reign of Emperor Vespasian from AD 69, Tamar would have been the eldest at age 36, with Jesus Justus aged 32, and Josephes the youngest at age 25.

Along with any children they might have had by that date, and in company with Jesus' other brothers, sisters and their offspring, they would have constituted the extent of the *Desposyni* heirs against whom Vespasian issued his edict of persecution.

Despite clear documentary evidence, some churchmen and theologians assert that Jesus was the only offspring born to Mary. Although this is contrary to what the gospels state, and does not equate with the biblical entries that Jesus was Mary's 'firstborn son',[4] it is deemed a necessary aspect of Catholic doctrine in order to preserve the official image that Mary was forever a virgin. By virtue of this, it is maintained that Jesus' brothers and sisters were actually his cousins, or that they were the offspring of Joseph, but not of Mary. When it comes to the *Desposyni*, however, this argument presents a considerable problem for the Church since the Vatican archive relates that 'only those persons in the bloodline with Jesus through his mother qualified as *Desposyni*'.[5] By insisting that Jesus was Mary's only son, it is therefore implied that the *Desposyni* inheritors were explicitly the descendants of Jesus himself. Thus it is plainly acknowledged in Church record that Jesus had offspring.

For our purposes, it is better to view the wider picture in accordance with the gospels, rather than apply the notion of Mary's perpetual virginity which limits the *Desposyni* to Jesus' own personal bloodline. For its own part, since the official doctrine is that the *Desposyni* are confined to being the descendants of Mary, the Church has to decide which is more important as an item of faith: a virginal mother or a celibate son. By virtue of the *Desposyni*, it is impossible to have both.

✠ ✠ ✠

The disciple Cleopas was mentioned earlier in respect of the supper at Emmaus following Jesus' resurrection (*see* page 217). The gospel of John relates that Cleopas was the husband of Jesus' sister Mary,[6] and Hegesippus recorded that they had a son called Symeon.[7] The Rabanus manuscript details that Mary Jacob Cleopas was in the Magdalene party that voyaged to Gaul, but there is no mention of her son. Eusebius wrote that he remained in Judaea, where he became a bishop in Jerusalem and was martyred under Emperor Trajan (AD 98–117).[8]

Hegesippus also wrote in the 2nd century that Jesus' brother Jude had a son called Zoker and a grandson named Jacob (James).[9] Additionally, he reported that Emperor Domitian interrogated three other grandsons of Jude.[10] The *Desposyni* spokesman, Joses, who met with Bishop Sylvester in Rome in AD 318, was said to have been a descendant in this same line, although there is no known record of the generations in between. Our main concern rests, however, with the descents from Jesus and James whose records are more complete. In tracing these two lines, it would be especially interesting to discover any marital alliances between them, thereby creating a dually desposynic heritage.

Descent in Britain

An item worth discussing in respect of James (Joseph of Arimathea), before moving further into his successive family, is the matter of his place of burial. The *Iolo Manuscript* (as transcribed from a text attributed to Maelgwyn of Llandaff, AD c450),[11] states that Joseph was buried south of the altar in the old chapel of Glastonbury.[12] But in apparent contrast, the Cistercian *Estoire del Saint Graal* claims that he was buried at the Abbey of Glais in Scotland. This is not as contradictory as it seems, for at the time of Joseph's death the Scots had not yet settled in the Western Highlands. They were a tribal population of Northern Ireland (Ulster) who had infiltrated the south-west of mainland Britain. The West Country areas of Siluria, when settled by the early Scots, were often referred to as Scotland (land of the Scots) when the far North of Britain was still called Caledonia. The word *glais* comes from the Irish Goidelic, and means 'stream' or 'rivulet'. The name Douglas, for example, derives from *dubh glais* (dark stream).[13] Glastonbury was set amid steams and watery marshland,

and was called the Isle of Glais. Thus, Joseph's burial place at the Abbey of Glais actually referred to the Abbey of Glastonbury, sometimes given as the Isle of Glass (*Ynys Witrin*: Crystal Isle).

Joseph's daughter, Anna (the wife of Brân), is listed in a number of ancient pedigrees, including the Harleian and Jesus College manuscript collections which classify her as a '*consobrina*' of Jesus' mother Mary. The Harleian pedigree of Gwynedd, for example, defines Anna as a '*consobrina Mariæ uirginis matris*'.[14] A consobrina was a junior kinswoman – a younger cousin, niece or granddaughter. Anna appears as such in the genealogies of the Holy Families of Britain, which credit her with a son called Beli, the father of Avallach, father of Euguein.[15]

In his *Roman de l'estoire du Graal*, Robert de Boron describes Anna and Brân as the parents of all 12 of the Arimathea disciples,[16] but this relates to their matriarchal and patriarchal status rather than to natural parentage.

Beli and Avallach, the son and grandson of Anna and Brân, are given in numerous genealogical listings as founders of the Royal House of Gwynedd via Avallach's son Euguein. From his other son, Oudoleum, came the northern rulers of the kingdom of Rheged in Cumbria. More important in the present case is the descent from their daughter Penardun and her husband, King Marius of Siluria. It was their grandson, King Lucius, who became most famed as the instigator of Celtic Christianity in Britain. The venerable Bede wrote in his *Ecclesiastical History* that Lucius had entered into correspondence with a certain Eleutherius, who was at that time the leader of the persecuted Christians in Rome.[17] Consequently, the later Catholic Church was unable to ignore Eleutherius, and he was listed in the *Liber Pontificalis* as a saint with a feast day on 26 May.

Increasing the Light

Marius and Lucius are Romanized names by way of records written in Latin. Their actual Silurian names were Meuric and Lles.[18] In the *Historia Regum Britanniae*, Geoffrey of Monmouth related that Gildas had written at length about the deeds of Lucius,[19] but there is no mention of him in the well-known *De Excidio Britanniae* by Gildas.

The name of Gildas is used with some abandon in modern literature, but there were actually three monks of that name whose works are often confused. Gildas I (known as Gildas *Albanius*), was a Welsh monk at Glastonbury, who lived AD c425–512. Gildas II (known as Gildas *Sapiens*: the Wise) was Pictish and lived AD c497–570. Gildas III (known as *Badonicus*), the writer of *De Excidio Britanniae* (On the Destruction of Britain), was Irish and lived 516–572. Even the descriptive styles of Albanius, Sapiens and Badonicus have been tossed around willy-nilly since the 19th century, as if they all apply to the same man. Gildas I and II were both Celtic Church monks, whilst the writings of Gildas III are antagonistic towards the Celtic movement in Britain.[20]

The Anglo-Saxon Chronicle refers to 'Lucius, King of the Britons' in its entries for the year AD 167. It states that he sent a deputation to meet with Bishop Eleutherius in Rome,[21] which confirms the similar entry in the Vatican's *Liber Pontificalis*.[22] The Augustinian friar John Capgrave (1393–1464), and Archbishop Ussher of Armagh in his 17th-century *De Brittanicarum Ecclesiarum Primordiis*, both recounted that the missionaries sent to Rome by Lucius were named Medway and Elfan.

Although Christianity was substantially intermixed with Druidism in Britain at that time, Lucius had elected to proclaim his Christianity at the court of Caer Guent (Winchester) in AD 156.[23] He then sought a royal attachment to the Roman fraternity that was previously headed by his grandfather's cousin Prince Linus. Geoffrey of Monmouth reported that two representatives, namely Faganus and Duvianus (Fagan and Dyfan in the Welsh annals), were sent from Rome in response to Lucius. It was they who were reputed to have instigated the first restoration of the wattle chapel at Glastonbury (*see* page 162). They baptized Lucius at the mission's Holy Well (now called Chalice Well), and have since been credited with the second foundation of Christianity in Britain.

In his letter of approach to Eleutherius, Lucius asked for advice as to how he should operate a Christian kingdom, and details of the bishop's letter in reply are documented in the *Sacrorum Conciliorum Collectio* in Rome. He advised that the people of the realm should be treated as if they were sons of the king.[24] Subsequently, in AD 179, Lucius founded the first Christian archbishopric in Britain, which he settled in London at the place where St Peter's Church stands in Cornhill.[25] It was from there, in the early 7th century, that the Catholic St Augustine eventually transferred England's primary seat of the Church to Canterbury, at that time called Dorobernia.[26]

During his lifetime, the reputation of Lucius was said to have spread far and wide. He built the first Glastonbury tower on St Michael's Tor in AD 167, and the church at Llandaff was dedicated to him as Lleurwgg the Great. It is here that Dante Gabriel Rossetti's famous Pre-Raphaelite *Seed of David* altarpiece can be seen today. Lucius was said to have 'increased the light of the first missionaries' and, accordingly, became known as *Lleiffer Mawr* (the Great Luminary). He died on 3 December 201, and was buried at St Mary le Lode in Gloucester. Subsequently, his remains were moved to St Peter's Church in London.[27]

On the death of King Lucius, Emperor Severus sent his legions into Britain in order to quell the Christian insurgency against Roman law at a time when Lucius had no immediate male successor. His son Keriber had predeceased him, and his grandson Llyr was too young. But Keriber did have an older sister named Gladys, whose son succeeded to the crown as King Coel II. Thereafter, the battles continued for many years, to the point that Coel entered into a peace treaty with the Roman governor, Constantius. They agreed that, although Britain would pay tribute to Rome, the nation would retain its own sovereignty and its own monarchy. As part of the arrangement, Coel's daughter Elaine (Elen Luedbog) was later married to

Constantius who, after Coel's death, declared himself King Consort of the Camulod Britons.[28] Their son was Constantine, who eventually became Emperor and proclaimed Christianity as the State religion of Rome.

Princess Elaine's younger brother Kenau (Cunedd) was not in a position to confront the kingly claim of Constantius, and he settled for being Lord of Gloucester.[29] In time his descendants became rulers in the northern region of Strathclyde, ultimately to marry into the Scots Kings of Dalriada in the 6th century. Meanwhile, the primary kingship in Britain fell to a 7th generational descendant of Anna and Brân in the Silurian West. He was Caradawc Vreichvras (Strongarm) – a grandson of Lucius' son Llyr, who was the ruler of Gwent and Archenfield in Wales.[30]

Veiling the Truth

For a significant period following Constantine's reign, the emperors remained at the head of the Church. But after the fall of the Empire, the popes onwards from Leo I (AD 440–61) were left to contend with a particular dilemma: the Empire had collapsed – so where did that put Roman Christianity? Jesus had been very much in second place in relation to the emperors who had been the godheads, and it was necessary to bring him back into prominence in order to save the Church. There was, however, the edict against the *Desposyni* heirs to consider, and it was deemed appropriate to sideline this for a time. It could be revisited with a new emphasis (as indeed it was) in the future but, in the interim, a better plan was to align the past emperors more firmly with Jesus, and to pretend that they had been upholders of the Faith from the outset long before Constantine. With this strategy in mind, a number of new stories were concocted – one of the best known being that of Veronica's veil.

Within an early text called the *Acts of Pilate* was a brief account of a woman who had accompanied Jesus to Calvary and had wiped his face with a cloth. This was perfectly suited to a new interpretation, and it was maintained that upon this cloth was imprinted the image of Jesus' face, the *vera icon* (true image).[31] Hence, in the 5th century, the woman was said to have been named Veronica.[32] It was given in a document called the *Cura Sanitatis Tiberii* that this vernicule (veil of the true image) had miraculous healing powers, by virtue of which the 1st-century Emperor Tiberius had converted to Christianity on being cured of some malady. In later times, the *Vindicta Salvatoris* went so far as to maintain that the AD 70 destruction of Jerusalem by General Titus (the son and imperial successor of Emperor Vespasian) was actually a Roman revenge against the Jews for crucifying the Lord. Moreover, it was claimed that Titus was himself cured of leprosy by the magical veil. Thus it was that both emperors, Vespasian and Titus, the two initiators of the edict against the *Desposyni*, were newly portrayed as having themselves been upholders of the Christian faith!

Over the Water

Before the time of Emperor Vespasian, Mary Magdalene was in Provence. It does not appear that either her daughter Tamar or eldest son Jesus Justus were with her on the voyage, only her new-born son Josephes. He was the 'man-child' of The Revelation, the seed of Jesus with whom the dragon of Rome was set to make war.[33] The story of his elder brother is told chronologically in The Revelation, and is the Jesus of the Apocalypse.[34] In AD 73, at the age of 36, he was married in Ephesus, following which his son was born in AD 77.

Given that so many texts were excluded from the New Testament when the selection was made at the Council of Carthage in AD 397, it is remarkable that St John's *Apocalypse* escaped close scrutiny at that time. It was greatly disputed, however, and seems only to have passed the selection process because Eusebius claimed it was an authoritative work and, although he considered it in some ways unsuitable, he refused to condemn its apostolic provenance. Even so, the Church has since done its best to divert people from this book by portraying it as a sinister prophecy of foreboding and doom. By way of propaganda from the 1622 Congregation for the Propagation of the Faith (the *Congregatio Propaganda Fide*), even the very word 'apocalypse' has become emblematic of disaster. But the fact is that John's writing (esoteric as it is in some respects) amounts to precisely what its title conveys. The Greek word *apocalypse* translates quite simply to 'revelation' and relates more precisely to the 'revealing of hidden truths'.[35]

In the early days from Mary Magdalene's departure to Gaul, her daughter Tamar (Damaris) seems to have been placed in the guardianship of St Paul, to whom it is biblically implied she might have been married at the age of 20 in AD 53.[36] It has recently been suggested in novelistic terms that she was the female named Sarah who was with the three Marys in Provence, and was born there to Mary Magdalene.[37] This is wholly incorrect. Sara is independently listed as one of the women who was on the original voyage as Martha's companion. She was a black-garbed Nazarite priestess and is the subject of her own personal cult in Provence. Sarah came to be revered as the patron saint of the gypsies, who call her *Sarah-la-Kali* (Sarah the Black). Even now, from 24 May each year, the Romany gypsies attend in pilgrimage from all over the world to carry her reliquary in a procession to the sea at Les Saintes Maries de la Mer.[38]

There are traditions that St Paul visited Spain, Gaul and even Britain during his travels before going to Rome. In fact, he wrote of a planned trip to Spain in his epistle to the Romans 15:24. In 1780, Charles Sonnini of the Paris Society of Agriculture was commissioned by the French Government to undertake research in Asia Minor and the Middle East. While in Constantinople, he discovered an ancient Greek extension to The Acts of the Apostles in the archive of Sultan Abdoul Achmet. Now known as the *Sonnini Manuscript*, the document relates that Paul preached on the Hill of Lud, as was called Ludgate Hill where St Paul's Cathedral was eventually built in London.[39] There is no other known record of this event, but

Bishop Clement of Rome did write in the 1st century that St Paul had 'been to the extremity of the West' and, in AD 425, the Syrian bishop Theodoretus of Cyrus confirmed that this said extremity was Britain.[40] If it were the case that Paul travelled further West than is generally supposed, then it is possible that Tamar might have accompanied him to Gaul. We do know that Jesus Justus accompanied his uncle Joseph/James to Britain on at least two occasions, and later dedicated the Glastonbury chapel to his mother in AD 64. As far as the family in Provence is concerned, we are left primarily with young Joseph to consider – the son born in AD 44 and generally referred to as Josephes so as to distinguish him in literature from his uncle and paternal guardian.

Ark of the Grail

A foremost work in the medieval cycle of Grail legends is that known as the *Grand Saint Graal*, which is attributed to Walter Map, Archdeacon of Oxford and Chancellor to King Henry II of England (1154–1189).[41] Walter was also a colleague of Count Henri I of Champagne.[42] The *Roman de Brut*, by Robert Wace, reached the hands of Chrétien de Troyes by way of Marie de Champagne, the daughter of Louis VII of France and Eleanor of Aquitaine (*see* page 186). Following an annulment at Louis' instigation, Eleanor was married in 1152 to Henry II of England, after which event the *Grand Saint Graal* emerged. It subsequently became the model for the later Burgundian writings of Robert de Boron, who cited it as *'le grant livre'* in his *Roman de l'estoire du Graal*.[43] Indeed, separate prose works entitled *Lancelot* and *Tristan* are collaboratively ascribed to Map and De Boron.

Walter Map (1140–1209) is also thought to be the author of the two-part *Lancelot* epic, which includes *The Quest of the Holy Graal* and *The Death of Arthur*. The great volume of Grail and Arthurian literature emanating from Map has caused some writers to claim that he could not possibly have written so much within such an otherwise busy life.[44] However, an extant French printing of the era carries the assignment of 'Maistres Gualtiers Map', and is described as being 'written by him for the love of his lord, King Henry, who caused it to be translated from Latin into French'.[45] Given the full extent of the works, it is probable that Map did not pen the manuscripts himself, but, at Queen Eleanor's behest, he was undoubtedly the instigator with the clerks of the Royal Household under his personal jurisdiction.

The foremost precept of the *Grand Saint Graal* is that it contains 'the greatest secret of the world'. It also maintains that the Grail keepers of the succession, beginning with Josephes, have a claim of dignity superior to that of any priesthood or apostolic succession.[46] Furthermore, this dignity lies within the mystery of the Eucharist itself – the eternal body and perpetual blood of Christ, which constitute the secret of the Grail as defined by the lineage of Josephes.

The picture which emerges is that the Lordship of the Grail was first inherited by Alain from Gais (or Gésu) who represents Jesus II Justus (Joshua) in Grail lore. The name Alain is a Breton form of Galain.[47] Thus, for ease of understanding, Alain is synonymous with Jesus III, and the *High History of the Holy Grail* does indeed state that Alain was the son of Gais.[48]

When Jesus Justus was married in AD 73, his bride was said in the Bible to have been 'arrayed in fine linen, clean and white' (Revelation 19:8). Subsequently, on the death of Jesus Christ, his son announced, 'I am thy fellow servant, and of thy brethren that have the testimony of Jesus … And his name is called The Word of God' (Revelation 19:10–13).

Jesus III, born in AD 77, was to become the *Alpha* and *Omega* (Revelation 21:16). This was a Sadducee priestly distinction of the House of Herod, which was transferred to the House of David in AD 102 when the Herodian establishment terminated.[49] In acknowledgement of his inheritance, Jesus III (Alain) pronounced, 'I am the root and the offspring of David, the bright and morning star' (Revelation 22:16).

Alain joined the followers of his grand-uncle's mission in Siluria and became the head of them (*see* page 184). Accounts differ as to his marital status, but there are no records of any offspring. Some texts maintain that he was celibate, although this would not have been in line with dynastic practice. We have seen that it was the rule for Davidic dynasts to father a first child in or about the year of their 40th birthday. In accordance with this custom, Alain's father had married at age 36, as had his grandfather Jesus Christ. It is possible that Alain died before marrying but, whatever the case, the *Grand Saint Graal* confirms that on the death of Alain the Lordship of the Grail passed to Josue, the son of Josephes.[50] Josue was reputed to have been married to the daughter of a King Calaphas, and it was just 10 days after this event that both Alain and Calaphas were said to have died.[51]

It is said in the *Grand Saint Graal* that Josephes' legacy was steeped in 'a mystery that never was on land or sea', and that his was the sacred Vessel of the Graal into which 'the *Sang Réal* was poured therein'.[52] The Grail Mass of Josephes features in this work and in the Cistercian *Queste del Saint Graal*, which states that the very image of Christ himself was seen by the knights within the Holy Vessel (*see* plate 29).[53]

These works also identify that, by the time of Mary Magdalene's death in AD 63, her son Josephes had become the Bishop of Sarras. In Sir Thomas Malory's *Morte d'Arthur*, Sarras features as the realm of King Evelake, and is mentioned in the story of *Galahad and the Grail*.[54] The name Evelake is a corrupted form of Avallach who was the grandson of Anna and Brân in descent from Joseph of Arimathea (*see* page 246). In practice, Avallach was not so much a name as a title emanating from the Greco-Egyptian *Alabarch* – a procurator or regulus. Evelake and Avallach are shown as being synonymous in the Middle English pedigrees of Celtic saints and princes.[55] Moreover, the *Grand Saint Graal* identifies that the baptismal name of Avallach was Mordrains.[56]

In the *Cronica sive Antiquitates Glastoniensis Ecclesiae*, John of Glastonbury denotes that Alain (given in Latin as Helains) was the nephew of Josephes. Thus the lines from Jesus Christ and Joseph/James are separately defined before the continuing succession is detailed from Josephes. This begins with his son Josue, precisely as listed in the descendant lineage of the *Grand Saint Graal*. It is then given that the son of Josue was Aminadab.[57]

The name Aminadab is an Old Testament derivative from the time of Moses and Aaron.[58] In Grail terms, it relates directly to the Song of Solomon 6:11–12, wherein the king searches for his lost bride. Likening her hair to the flocks of Galaad (whence derives Galahad),[59] he wonders how the Vine will flourish without her, and pursues his quest 'like the chariots of Aminadab'.[60]

It is in connection with Aminadab that Eleanor d'Aquitaine, the mother of Marie de Champagne, appears again. Born in 1122, Eleanor was the daughter of William X, Duke of Aquitaine. Her grandfather was famed as Guilhelm the Troubadour, and she was raised at the most cultured court in Europe. Her distant ancestor, William I, had established the academy of St Guilhelm-le-Désert in 800 – a long-standing Magdalene seat that flourished during medieval times.[61] Eleanor's upbringing was steeped in the Grail lore of Provence and in the feminine ethos of *Amour Courtois* (Courtly Love), which gave rise to the Age of Chivalry.

When Eleanor was married in 1137 to Louis de France at the Cathedral of Saint-André in Bordeaux, she was accompanied by the Benedictine Abbot Suger, who was the first minister to the crown when her husband became King Louis VII.[62] Suger was a colleague of the Cistercian Abbot, St Bernard of Clairvaux, who had formally constituted the Knights of the Temple a few years earlier, and Suger's own abbey was at St Denis to the north of Paris. It had been founded in 630 by the Merovingian King Dagobert, and in 653 was proclaimed wholly exempt from any episcopal jurisdiction.[63] Consequently, in 1140, when Suger undertook to rebuild his abbey as a great cathedral, there were no limitations on decoration, and Eleanor (the most powerful woman in Europe even before she married the King) was consulted. Eventually, in 1144, Abbot Suger escorted Queen Eleanor and her mother-in-law, the dowager Queen

Adelaide, to the cathedral's consecration. Also in attendance were St Bernard de Clairvaux and Theobald, Count of Champagne.[64]

The Basilica of St Denis was the first great cathedral of France upon which Chartres and others were partially modelled. As had been the abbey from the death of Dagobert, the basilica became the primary burial place of the French monarchs, and it is here that we find the medallion window of Aminadab. Contrived in a uniquely surrealistic manner for its era, Aminadab (the great-grandson of Jesus and Mary Magdalene) is portrayed supporting the crucifixion cross of his ancestry. The cross rests in a four-wheeled cart (*quadrige*), which is denoted as pertaining to the Ark of the Covenant, and the window carries the legend 'Quadrige Aminadab'.

The Aminadab Window at St Denis

Because of this attribution, the German theologian Honorius Augustodunensis (1080–1156)[65] classified the cart as being the *quadriga* of the Song of Solomon. But there is no such single *quadriga* related to Aminadab in the Song of Solomon; the reference is plural, as in the *Vulgate* Latin: '*nescivi anima mea conturbavit me propter quadrigas Aminadab*'. In any event, a *quadriga* is expressly a two-wheeled chariot pulled by four horses in line.[66] In contrast, the window's four-wheeled cart is adequately described as being the cart that conveyed the Ark of the Covenant (*Federis ex Arca*),[67] and it is explained in the window below that 'From the Ark of the Covenant is established the Altar of Christ'. Honorius also stated in his *Commentary on the Song of Songs* that 'Aminadab standing in the cart represents the crucifixion, and that the four horses are the four evangelists'.[68] But Aminadab is not standing in the cart, he is standing behind it. And there are no horses, only an ox, lion, man and eagle – the 'four living creatures' from the Old Testament book of Ezekiel 1:10.

Honorius was a vehement opposer of Mary Magdalene's apostolic position (*see* page 239) , and he condemned her in his literature as a 'filthy and common prostitute'. In his various commentaries he seized every malicious opportunity to revile her legacy. But his near contemporary, the Portuguese friar St Antony of Padua (1195–1231), had other thoughts concerning the window in his *Sermones Dominicales*. He applied the term *quadriga* (*quadri* relating to 'four') not to any non-existent chariot or horses, but to the four living creatures who were biblically said to protect the divine throne. This throne was stated in Numbers 7:89 to be the Ark of the Covenant. Thus, the initially perceived image of the medallion window is of Aminadab supporting his crucified ancestor upon the throne of his birthright. The intriguing fact, however, is that in this particular instance, the throne (the Ark) is missing; only the cart remains.

This seemingly anomalous imagery is described in the story of Lancelot, entitled *Le Chevalier de la Charrette* (The Knight of the Cart), by Chrétien de Troyes and dedicated to Countess Marie. An item from the *Grand Saint Graal*, explains that Josephes built 'an Ark like that of the Old Covenant for the reception of the Holy Grail'.[69] It was called the Ark of the Graal. The only man he allowed to look inside the Ark was King Mordrains the Avallach, who 'saw the holy dish and the chalice' of the eucharistic Grail Mass.[70]

In *Le Chevalier de la Charrette*, Chrétien revealed that portrayals of the cart alone were representative of persecution and humiliation. He described that every town had a cart in which those who were deprived of civil and legal rights (as was Jesus) were paraded through the streets, 'never afterwards to be heard, honoured or welcomed in any court'. Thus, the Aminadab window depicts Jesus' crucifixion in precisely this manner with him and his cross in the cart, indicating that the Grail was humiliated and its legacy deprived.

Returning to the Magdalene connection, it is stated in the *High History of the Holy Grail* that the damsel who bore the Grail was called the Damsel of the Cart,[71] and that she was 'bald without hair'.[72] The Cistercian Abbot, Gilbert de Hoyland (died 1172) drew a comparison in his 23rd *Sermon on the Canticles*, relating this figurative baldness to the 'flocks of Galaad' reference in the Song of Solomon. The loss of the bride's hair was indicative, he said, of the baldness of the Church, whose tresses fall when its flock becomes separated from the truth.[73] The Grail bearer of Corbenic was always emblematic of Mary Magdalene, and Gilbert's colleague St Bernard de Clairvaux had already stated the Cistercian view in his own *Sermon on the Canticles*. He alluded to Mary as the Bride of Christ, whilst also equating her with the lost bride in the Song of Solomon.[74] The combined imagery is therefore apparent in both Grail lore and the Aminadab window: The legacy of Jesus (the Fisher King) and Mary Magdalene (the Grail Bearer) has been lost to the Christian flock, and the dignity of their heirs confined to the humiliation of the cart.

The Fisher Kings

In some Grail texts, such as those from Chrétien de Troyes and Wolfram von Eschenbach, there are *post hoc* insertions suggesting that the Fisher Kings must have enjoyed fishing! Only Robert de Boron's *Roman de l'Estoire du Graal* undertakes to give any original reason for the descriptive style of the Fisher King which, as we have seen (page 187) denotes a Priest King. De Boron additionally states that Bron provided a fish that became the mystic meal of the Grail in which the unworthy could not partake. The fish was associated with Christ, with the Greek word *ichthys* (fish) being an acronym formed from the initial letters of *Iesus Christos Theou [H]Yios Soter* (Jesus Christ, God's Son, is Saviour).[75]

Jesus' great-grandson, the Fisher King Aminadab, as listed in the annals of Glastonbury, called Eminadap in the *Grand Saint Graal*, is said to have married a daughter of the King of the Britons.[76] The British king at that time was Coel I (a grandson of Anna and Brân). His son was to become King Lucius, and the marriage of Lucius' sister Eurgen to Aminadab forged an early dynastic link between the lines from Jesus and James. Subsequently, their descendants were dually desposynic (*see* chart: Origins of the Desposyni).

Both sets of record agree on the generations thereafter, although using sources that provided different spellings, as with Aminadab (Eminadap). In the *Cronica sive Antiquitates Glastoniensis Ecclesiae*, the successive sons are given as Castellors and Manael, later followed by Lambord[77] – whereas the *Grand Saint Graal* names them as Carceloys, Manuiel and Lambor. In a descendant line from Josephes, Josue and Aminadab, these characters are each stated to have been Fisher Kings of the succession.[78]

In the *High History of the Holy Grail*, the Fisher King is called the King Fisherman, and is said to have had a brother named Pelles, who was known as King Hermit. In the *Prose Lancelot*, the Grail bearer is called Elaine, and is said to be the daughter of Pelles. Chrétien de Troyes does not name the Fisher King in his *Le Conte del Graal*, but states that he was the father of the Rich Fisher. Robert de

ORIGINS OF THE DESPOSYNI

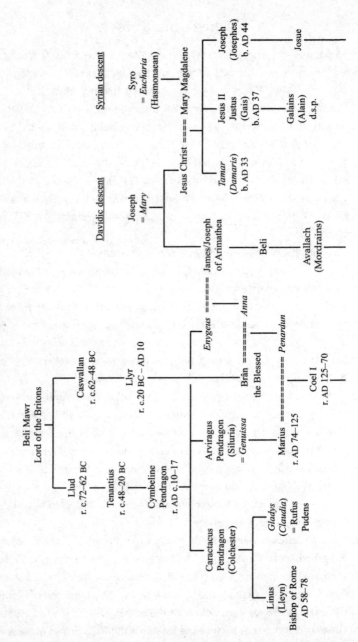

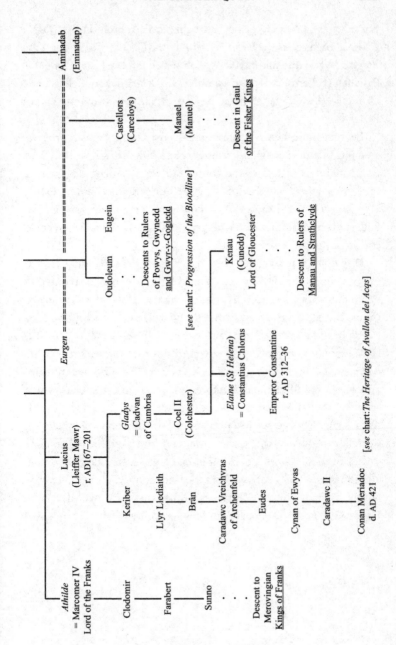

Boron cites the Rich Fisher as being called Bron in his *Joseph d'Arimathie*, as does the *Didot Perceval*. In the *Quest of Galahad* and the *Vulgate Merlin*, the maimed king – although not the Fisher King – is Pellehan (Pellam), the son of Lambord and a kinsman of Pelles.[79] The *Queste del Saint Graal* clarifies, however, that Pelles was the son of Pellehan.

Beyond those items which remain consistent, there is a progressive muddle of names and relationships within these works. They occur mainly because of the contracted time-frame of the stories, with 6th-century knights of King Arthur's Round Table existing alongside 1st and 2nd century characters – even to the extent that Pelles, the grandfather of the knight Galahad is said to have been a cousin of Joseph of Arimathea.[80]

Discrepancies have also occurred because, in expanding certain themes within the Grail cycle, the successive writers endeavoured to make the stories increasingly more romantic. This led ultimately to the colourful knightly adventures of Sir Thomas Malory's *Morte d'Arthur* in the 15th century. Confronted by these elements of confusion, there are only two places to turn in order to begin to get the desposynic lineage into perspective. They are the Silurian chronicles and the *Grand Saint Graal*, the foremost work on the subject which specifies by name some of the designated Fisher Kings in descent from Jesus. They were Joseph (Josephes), Aminadab (Eminadap), Castellors (Carceloys), Manael (Manuel) and Lambord (Lambor). The *Grand Saint Graal* was inspired by Queen Eleanor of Aquitaine, and the names were derived from the troubadour culture of her own family heritage. In the *Queste* and other literature, we also have Fisher King Pellehan (Pellam) and his son Pelles.

Descent of the Grail

Extending the Line

There is an entry in the Silurian archive which is intriguing in that, beyond the figure of Lambord, the line of Fisher Kings descends to a woman called Ygerna.[1] She also appears in an ancestral genealogy prepared for King James I of England (James VI of Scots) in 1604. This chart agrees with those previously cited, detailing Ygerna's ancestors as being Lambord and his predecessors, 'Manael, son of Sisarklos [Castellors], in descent from Eurga [Eurgen, the wife of Aminadab]'.[2]

Ygerna (Igraine) features in Robert de Boron's *Merlin*, the *Prose Lancelot*, Thomas Malory's *Morte d'Arthur* and the *Vulgate Merlin*, as well as in the *Historia Regum Britanniae*.[3] In historical and most Grail literature she is given as being the mother of King Arthur, but there is an element of confusion in Wolfram's *Parzival*, which records her name as Arnive. This is thought by some to be an anagram of a Gemanic form of Ygerna,[4] but some of Wolfram's character names differ from those in the French and English texts, and are often difficult to equate.

In consideration of Ygerna's grandfather Lambord, the *Grand Saint Graal*, the *Estoire del Saint Graal* and the *Queste del Saint Graal* tell of how Lambord (also called Labran) was slain by the sea-borne invader, King Urlain (Varlan). When being chased to his ship, Urlain turned upon Lambord and split him in two with his sword.[5] It is said that this event took place in Logres (England), and the hill-fort remains of Dun Urlain can still be seen on Great Blasket Island, off the west coast of Ireland. There is, however, a genealogical gap of

some generations to fill between the earlier Fisher King Manael and
Lambord, but the relevant names are not immediately apparent in
British literature. The name of Ygerna's father is also missing from
the lists, and the Latin record from the *Glastonbury Chronicle* simply
states: '*Lambord genuit filium qui genuit Ygerna*' (Lambord begat a son
who begat Ygerna).

To discover the names of some other Fisher Kings, we must turn
to the Bavarian knight Wolfram von Eschenbach and his story of
Parzival from the early 1200s. Unlike the previous French and British
romances, Wolfram's is a rather more brooding account with a
deeper psychological aspect which has been discussed at length by a
number of writers.[6] In Wolfram's text, Grail Castle is located on the
Mount of Salvation (Munsalvaesche) which has long been associated
with the mountain fortress of Montségur in the Languedoc region of
southern France. This geographical association actually stems from
another work begun by Wolfram and completed after his death
by Albrecht von Scharffenberg. Entitled *Die Jüngere Titurel* (The
Younger Titurel), the text locates Grail Castle specifically in the
Pyrenees.

Built in the early 1200s, the Cathar fortress of Montségur was
demolished after its capture by papal troops in 1244, but *Die Jüngere
Titurel* was not completed until 1280. The hill-top castle whose ruin
provides a tourist attraction today was not built until the 1600s.[7]
Interestingly, however, the current ruin is classified as Montségur III,
and it is archaeologically accepted that there was a castle at the site
long prior to the Cathar fortress which is now referenced as
Montségur II.

At a mid-point in his story, Wolfram diverts to explain that his
version of the Grail legend was obtained from a certain Kyôt le
Provençal, who had translated an Arabic manuscript found in
Toledo. The original was said to have been composed by the learned
Flegetanis, a scholar from an old Israelite family in Spain.[8] It has
been suggested that Kyôt le Provençal might perhaps have been the
troubadour Giot de Provins, but this is unlikely since Giot was from
Provins in Champagne, not from Provence.

In many ways, *Parzival* differs from other Grail Quest accounts in that it owes very little to the Arthurian tradition. Beyond the realm of Grail Castle, there are references to the separate Court of King Arthur and the Round Table to which Parzival is attached. The key protagonists are the familiar knights Gawan (Gawain) and Parzival (Perceval) himself – but that is the extent of any Arthurian connection. There is no Merlin, no Lancelot, no Galahad, nor any of the other regular players. Moreover, Wolfram locates King Arthur's Court at Nantes in Brittany, although he does mention the Countess of Edinburgh (Tenabroc) as being in the Grail Queen's retinue.

As with the *Perlesvaus* (*The High History of the Holy Grail*), Wolfram's *Parzival* lays great stress on the importance of Grail lineage and the succession of the Grail Family. Unlike in all other accounts, however, Wolfram's Grail is not a vessel of any kind. The Grail of *Parzival* is a magical stone,[9] but it is not always perceived as such. The Grail princess is called Repanse de Joie, and when she appears with the Grail, it is said to be 'the perfection of earthly paradise, both roots and branches'.[10] Thus, the concept of the Vine is inherent in Wolfram's portrayal even though the more familiar Chalice is not.

Wolfram explained that the register of the Grail Keepers was held by the House of Anjou, and that Parzival was himself of Angevin blood. This is an interesting aside because Geoffrey Plantagenet, Count of Anjou, was the father of King Henry II of England to whom Eleanor of Aquitaine was married. The House of Anjou was thereby linked to Eleanor's own troubadour culture of Provence a few decades before Wolfram wrote his story. In this regard, the connection of Parzival with Anjou places aspects of Wolfram's account in a later era than other Grail literature since the county of Anjou was not founded until 898, long after Arthurian times.

Unlike Robert de Boron and other writers who had amalgamated 6th-century Arthurian romance with Joseph, Brân and figures of the 1st century, Wolfram elected to move Parzival, Gawan and the Arthurian Court forwards in time. He even included the Knights

Templars of his own era. In making this adjustment, his Grail Kings are seen to be of a later date than those of other texts, and he gave their names in succession as Titurel, Frimutel and Anfortas in accordance with the Anjou register.[11]

Anfortas is the wounded king of *Parzival*, and his name appears to be a Wolframic variation of the Latin *In fortis*, meaning 'In strength'.[12] Wolfram was well known for his anagrams and other styles of word play (as perhaps with Ygerna and Arnive), and it is possible that the names Titurel and Frimutel might have been similarly contrived. Their 'el' suffixes, as in all such names, relate to El (God), and the name Manael (or Manuel) in the other Grail King lists is an abbreviated Western European corruption of the Hebrew name Emmanuel, meaning 'God is with us'. Titurel and Frimutel may have similarly derived connotations. The name Anfortas appears to equate with the Hebrew name Boaz, which similarly means 'In strength'. Boaz was the great-grandfather of King David in whose line Jesus descended.

The Forbidden Cross

An intriguing character in Wolfram's *Parzival* is the enigmatic Grail messenger. She is a wild-haired sorceress named Cundrie, who seduces knights into the Holy Quest and provides nourishment from the Grail. Her revised nominal role as Kundry is expanded somewhat in Richard Wagner's 19th-century grand opera *Parsifal*, wherein she is transformed by the magician Klingsor (Wolfram's Clinschor) from a loathly hag into a beautiful maiden. At the castle she becomes the bearer of the Grail, thus duplicating Wolfram's Repanse de Joie. In the course of her activities, Kundry's connection with Mary Magdalene is made evident. At first she appears with a flask of balsam for the wounded king. Then later, when Parsifal is himself to be anointed as a Lord of the Grail, Kundry washes his feet and wipes them with her hair.

The biblical scene of Mary Magdalene washing Jesus' feet and wiping them with her hair[13] was long held to be heretical by the Catholic Church. It represented the first stage of their wedlock and was considered to be a sinful portrayal. This is no better exampled than in the British history of the Forbidden Cross of Ruthwell.

Even though Mary Magdalene had been vilified by Pope Gregory I in 591, it is clear that she was venerated not only in Gaul but also in Britain thereafter. One of the oldest and most prized Christian monuments of old Angle-land is the 7th-century Ruthwell Cross. At over 17 feet in height (5.2 m), the stone cross stood at Ruthwell in the Northumbrian Scottish border region of Bernicia. It was unearthed in three pieces in the late 18th century from the floor of the old parish church. Subsequently, it was repaired in 1823 and erected at the entrance of the manse. In 1871 it was further restored and moved into the church, where it remains protected by the Ancient Monuments Act.

How the cross came to be cut into three and buried is a fascinating story. In 1640, the Assembly of Presbyterian Covenanters proclaimed it to be 'an idolatrous monument that should be cast down and destroyed'. The Ruthwell church minister, Rev Gavin Young, had no option but to obey, so he had it taken down and sectioned with chisels, but not beyond repair. Instead of destroying the cross, he set the pieces into a specially dug trench, where they remained until it became necessary to lay a new floor more than a century later.

The reason why the Covenanters perceived the cross as idolatrous was that its main panel depicted Mary Magdalene kneeling at the feet of Jesus. The panel's surrounding text states in Latin from Luke 7:37–38, 'She began to wet his feet with her tears, and wiped them with the hair of her head'. Above this panel is a portrayal of Mary Magdalene and Martha, which describes them as 'meritorious ladies'.[14] Even worse, as far as the Church authorities were concerned, was that the two lengths of the side faces of the cross were carved with the Grail imagery of running vines.

The historical significance of the Ruthwell Cross is that in 664 it was decreed at the Synod of Whitby in Yorkshire that the Celtic

Magdalene panel of the Ruthwell Cross

Church must submit in all respects to the Catholic Rule which forbade any Magdalene cult representation. Plainly, however, the monks of the then Ruthwell monastery decided not to comply as far as the cross was concerned. Contrary to the dictate, the cross remained in situ, unmolested for 1,000 years until the puritanical Covenanters of the Kirk took exception to the heresy of its Magdalene and Vine reliefs.

North of Ruthwell, on the Isle of Mull, there is an intriguingly intimate portrayal of Jesus and Mary Magdalene in a stained-glass window at Kilmore Church, Dervaig (*see* plate 8). Designed by Stephen Adam, the foremost northern glass artist of Victorian times, the window was installed along with others that depict Jesus holding the bread and wine of the Eucharist, together with the legend 'I am the True Vine'.

Outside of medieval France, the people of England were equally enthused by the desposynic legacy of Mary Magdalene. She was especially venerated in the South West as exampled by the early Beckery Chapel at Glastonbury (*see* page 164). Disregarding Roman Church directives, a sanctuary was dedicated to her at Barnstaple in the 11th century, and King Athelstan (924–939) was said to have lodged a Magdalene finger-bone at Exeter Church (the site of the later cathedral). It is unlikely that this was an authentic relic, but it was nevertheless greatly prized among the establishment's treasures, appearing at the head of the listing:

> First, a finger of Mary Magdalene, who living washed our Lord's feet with her tears, whom our Lord truly loved and honoured.[15]

House of the Lion

We have seen how the romantic Grail culture came into England in the 12th century with Queen Eleanor of Aquitaine. But how did the Arthurian tradition, which became attached to it, first move into

France? Why would Wolfram have located king Arthur's Court in Brittany when it had otherwise been portrayed at the variously designated *Camu-lôt* sites in Britain?

There are two relevant facts for consideration in this regard. The first is that Arthur's mother, Ygerna (Igraine), was born in 6th-century Burgundy as a descendant of the Fisher Kings. Associated with her side of the family was the Breton knight Lancelot du Lac, the son of King Ban le Benoic (from the Latin *ille Benedictum*: 'the Blessed'). The second aspect is that the French region known as Brittany (Little Britain) had been settled from the 5th century by Dumnonian (Devonshire) princes in the Arimatheac succession. Prior to that, the region had been called Armorica ([country] facing the sea).[16] Consequently, Brittany features prominently in Arthurian romance. At Paimpont, about 30 miles (48 km) from Rennes, is the enchanted Forest of Brocéliande. From there stretches the Valley of No Return – the place where Arthur's sister Morganna was said to have confined her lovers. Also to be found is the magic Spring of Barenton, although most of the stories of Brocéliande were actually transposed from earlier accounts of the historical Merlin in the Caledonian Forest of Scotland known as *Coed Celyddon*.[17]

Barenton was a centre of druidic learning where the college ran a 20-year course of instruction. The ultimate prize was a cloak of feathers and the distinction of a bardic chair. It was here that Merlin was said to have held his Breton court, and the court's flat-stone threshold, called the *Perron de Merlin*, is still signposted today. Standing by the magic spring known as *La Fontaine de Fortune*, a cup for travellers was said to have been chained to the stone in bygone days. An upright interpretation of this stone was featured as an illustration in the *Livre du Cueur d'Amours Espris*, a story of the Knight of Love produced by King René d'Anjou in 1457 (*see* plate 18). It was said that a downpour of rain would be induced if water from the cup was poured onto the stone, and it was at this place that the *Vulgate Cycle* and the *Morte d'Arthur* relate that Viviane (Vivien), the Lady of the Lake, enchanted Merlin into loving her while he slept.[18]

Viviane and Merlin at Barenton, by John Moyr Smith, 1875

Breton Domnonée, which sits due south across the English Channel from Dumnonia, was recognized as a kingdom from the early 5th century. A line of kings emerged from the leaders of the British settlement, but they were not actually Kings of Brittany; they were Kings of the immigrant Bretons. The region was a Gallo-Roman department of the Western Empire that subsequently became a Frankish province of the Merovingian kings after the Roman Empire collapsed. From that time in the middle 400s, the local Breton kings (princes of royal houses in Britain) were made subordinate to Merovingian authority. In overall charge were appointed non-royal Counts styled the *Comites non regis*.[19] The supreme Lord of Brittany

540–544 was Chonomore, a native of the Frankish state, whose commission was to oversee the development of Brittany by the settlers.[20]

The pedigrees of Brittany show that a primary noble house from the latter 500s was that of the Counts of Léon d'Acqs, founded by Ywayn (Eógain) the son of King Urbgen.[21] The later arms of Léon bore the black Davidic lion on a gold shield (in heraldic terms, 'Or, a lion rampant, sable'). The Léon province, in which Morlaix resides, was so named because *léon* was Provençal for 'lion', thereby indicating a dynastic heritage from Provence. The English spelling of 'lion' appeared in the 12th century as a variant of the Anglo-French *liun* but, until the 14th century, the Scots Lord Lyon, King of Arms, was still called the *Léon Héraud*.

The British annals refer to Ywayn (Owain) of the Armorican Tract as being the son of King Urien of Rheged in the northern region of Cumbria.[22] British and Breton records agree that Ywayn married Alienor (Eleanor), the sister of King Hoel I of the Bretons, and that his father Urbgen (Urien) was married to Morgaine, the daughter of Ygerna del Acqs. This same Morgaine is listed in a 9th-century Royal Academy text as 'Muirgein, daughter of Aedàn in Belach Gabráin'[23] – a matter to which we shall return (page 303). Meanwhile, we have it that Ygerna was the mother of Morgaine, who in turn was the mother of Ywayn de Léon d'Acqs. Morgaine is known in Arthurian lore as Morganna or Morgan le Fay. Her husband, King Urbgen of Rheghed and Gowrie in the north of England, is usually called Urien of Gorre,[24] and the appointed bard to King Urien and his son Ywayn was the Welsh poet Taliesin.[25]

Given the later heraldry of Léon d'Acqs, Chrétien de Troyes focused on Ywayn (Ywain) in his work *Yvain, le Chevalier au Lion* (the Knight with the Lion).[26] In Arthurian literature, Ywain appears as a foremost knight of the Camelot court, and features prominently in the Cistercian *Vulgate Cycle* and Malory's *Morte d'Arthur*. He was succeeded in Brittany by his son Withur de Léon d'Acqs, from whom the early Counts of Léon descended.[27]

Living Waters

In the *Livres de Lancelot*, Viviane is called the Lady of the Lake (*la Dame du Lac*) – the same description that applied to Ygerna del Acqs (of the Waters). Viviane was said to have raised Lancelot du Lac, and Ygerna's grandson was Ywayn d'Acqs. The Welsh version of Viviane's story (based on Chrétien's *Chevalier au Lion*) calls her the Lady of the Fountain, and in the French works she is associated with the magic Spring of Barenton. At all times Viviane and Ygerna are connected with water, and the *du Lac* or *del Acqs* family style traces back to the original Mistress of the Waters, *la Dompna del Aquae*, Mary Magdalene (*see* page 231). Just as the male generations of senior descent were called Fisher Kings, so the aquatic theme persisted in the female and princely lines with a heritage from what the Cassianite guardians of La Sainte-Baume called the 'fountain of living waters'.

Returning to Lambord in the Fisher King lists, wherein the name of Ygerna's parents are missing, the family's nominal style of Acqs, along with the Arthurian chronology, indicates that Ygerna's mother was Viviane del Acqs, a Queen of Avallon (a little south of Troyes) in Burgundy. It is here that Arthur's sword, *Caliburn*, was said to have been forged,[28] while in the *Post-Vulgate Cycle* and the *Morte d'Arthur*, it is confirmed that Arthur received the prized sword of Avallon from the Lady of the Lake.[29]

In the *Prose Merlin*, Viviane is again called the Lady of the Fountain. She is also called Repeire de Joye, ostensibly linking her with Wolfram's later named Grail bearer Repanse de Joie, the sister of Anfortas. Intriguing as this might be, this does not render Viviane as synonymous with Repanse; it serves only to help qualify her lineal descent.

Although Viviane's daughter Ygerna was correctly named in the *Historia Regum Britanniae*, a subsequent written Welsh version of the *Perlesvaus* entitled *Y Seint Greal* rendered her name as Eigyr in the 13th century. Among numerous name changes made for the revised Welsh setting of the Grail story,[30] Viviane became Nimue,[31]

Alain became Evrawg, and Perceval became Peredur.[32] Most significantly, Lambord's name was given as Amlawdd. He was portrayed
as a son of Cynwal in a Welsh royal line, and was said to be a *wledig*
(military commander) of Dumnonia. Amlawdd was subsequently
mentioned in the Welsh legend of *Culhwych and Olwen*, and his wife
(a daughter of the northern regulus, Cunedda Wledig of Manau)
was called Gwen.

The Hermit King

Irrespective of Titurel, Frimutel and Anfortas, all records show that
Ygerna's grandfather was Lambord (Amlawdd) in the succession of
the Fisher Kings. The literary character who forges a link in the
earlier genealogical chain is Nascien, the Hermit King who appears
firstly in the *Queste del Saint Graal*, and later in Malory's *Morte
d'Arthur*. In reference to the 'fountain of living waters', along with
the general relevance of Acqs and the water mythos, Nascien gives
one of the best and most explicit descriptions of the *Sangréal*:

> The fountain is of such a kind that one cannot exhaust it, for
> never will one be able to take enough of it away. It is the Holy
> Grail.[33]

There are actually two Nascien characters in Grail lore. The first is
otherwise known as Seraphe and appears as a 2nd-century brother-
in-law of Mordrains the Avallach. The second, with whom we are
more concerned, appears later in the story. This Nascien is described
as a great king who became a hermit and was the recipient of the
secrets of the Grail.[34]

In John Capgrave's *Nova Legenda Angliae*, and a related treatise
entitled *Joseph Aramathy*, Nascien II (sometimes called Nacion,
Natian or Naciam) is described as being a Duke of the Medor.[35] This
related to the Midi, a stretch of southern France bordering the

Spanish frontier that became known as Septimania. Established by King Pepin of the Franks in 768, and including centres at Béziers and Carcassone, the Midi (or Medor) corresponded roughly to the later Cathar region of Languedoc, although classified as a department of Burgundy.

Septimania was a Jewish princedom with its capital at Narbonne, and was ruled by recognized descendants of the House of David.[36] More than 300 years later, the Davidic succession was still extant in the Midi, although the princedom had ceased to function by that time. In 1144 the English monk Theobald of Cambridge stated:

> The chief men and rabbis of the Jews who dwell in Spain assemble together at Narbonne, where the Royal Seed resides, and where they are held in the highest esteem.

Nascien's era was clearly much earlier than the foundation of Septimania, but as a Prince of the Midi in the early 5th century, he would have been related to the original Sires of Toulouse, Aquitaine and Burgundy in which Avallon resides. These early dynastic lines all descended from Faramund,[37] who was elected King of the West Franks in AD 419. Faramund married Argotta, the daughter of his predecessor Genebaud, Lord of the Franks, and she has since been called the Mother of all the Kings of France. It was with Meroveus, the grandson of Faramund and Argotta, that the Merovingian dynasty of the Franks began in about AD 445.[38] The Merovingian line descended in the first instance from Faramund's son Clodio (the father of Meroveus), whereas from Clodio's brother Fredemund (AD c400) came the line of Nascien, as referenced in the *Prose Lancelot* (*see* chart: Progression of the Bloodline).

✠ ✠ ✠

In the *Estoire del Saint Graal*, Galahad is said to have been a descendant of Nascien. The *Prose Lancelot* explains that Galahad was the son of Lancelot du Lac (the son of Ban le Benoic), and that his mother was Elaine le Corbenic (the daughter of King Pelles).

Lancelot's own mother was also called Elaine, but he was raised by the Lady of the Lake, who is said (during Elaine's lifetime) to have been Lancelot's foster-mother. Viviane del Acqs is referred to as the Lady of the Lake, but it is explained that her title did not denote an actual lake; her court was like that of any other queen – 'a palace with a great park around it'.[39] Since both Lancelot and Viviane's great-grandson, Ywain, carried the same family name, they were undoubtedly cousins, with Elaine being a junior kinswoman of Ygerna. The heritage of Acqs (whether *del Acqs*, *du Lac* or *d'Acqs*) traced through Nascien, the Keeper of the Grail, and the *Prose Lancelot* makes this clear when Lancelot has a vision of his ancestors, Nascien and Celidoine.[40]

Duplicated Names

There are certain anomalies in the Grail texts in that the writings do not always differentiate clearly between family members with the same names. Not only were there two Nasciens, but also two Alains. Additionally, there were two Vivianes, three Elaines and two Lancelots spanning five generations.

Ygerna was the daughter of Viviane I, but Ygerna's sister Elaine del Acqs had a daughter who was also called Viviane. As Viviane II and the succeeding Lady of the Lake, she was the mother of Ban le Benoic and the grandmother of Lancelot. Ban's wife was also called Elaine. Hence it was that, when Ban was killed and his widow was distraught, it was Ban's mother Viviane II (not the earlier Viviane) who took her grandson Lancelot into her care.

We also learn from the *Prose Lancelot* that Nascien's line descends to King Ban via a Alain le Gros, and that Ban was the son of an earlier Lancelot who was the son of a king by the name of Jonas.[41] Ban therefore named his son after his own father. Thus we discover that Ban's son (the Arthurian knight) was in fact Lancelot II du Lac, whose mother, Elaine, was also said to be of the *Radix Jesse* (the Root of Jesse).[42] It is from the legacy of Jesse, the Old Testament father of King David, that the concept of 'roots and branches' (as in *Parzival*) entered into Grail lore. The book of Isaiah 11:1 states, 'There shall come forth a rod out of the stem of Jesse, and a branch shall grow out of his roots'.

The *High History of the Holy Grail* explains that Alain le Gros (the second Alain in Grail history) was married to Yglais, and that they were the parents of Perceval and his sister Dindrane.[43] In practice, Alain II must have been Perceval's rather more distant ancestor since King Jonas (the grandfather of Ban le Benoic) was also said to have been descended from Alain a couple of generations earlier. The *Morte d'Arthur* and other works iron out this discrepancy when moving Perceval forwards into a later time-frame.[44] His parents are then given as being Pellinore and Yglais. Meanwhile, in this same descent from Nascien via Lambord (an ancestor of King Jonas) came Pellehan, followed by Pelles and his daughter Elaine le Corbenic, who bore Lancelot II's son Galahad.

✠ ✠ ✠

As we have seen above from the *Grand Saint Graal*, the *Estoire del Saint Graal* and the *Queste del Saint Graal*, Lambord was killed by his enemy Urlain, whose mighty sword 'cleaved him in twain'. In the *Queste*, Lambord's story is closely followed by another incident in which King Pellehan (sometimes Parlan) was lanced after boarding a ship.[45] This wounding with a lance was said to be indicative of the spear wound that Jesus received on the cross.[46] The wound given to Jesus by the Roman soldier was, at all times in Grail lore, symbolic of the Roman persecution of the bloodline inheritance. The act of the wounding was called the *Dolorous Stroke*,[47] and the enduring wound was the individually received mark of the maimed Fisher Kings in succession. The *Suite du Merlin* emphasizes that this persistently repeated wounding was responsible for creating the barren Wasteland, which could only become fertile again when the wound was healed.[48]

The Fish and the Flood

Alain II le Gros (Greallán) is better known historically as Gradlon or Gralon Mawr (Gralon the Great), King of the Bretons in the middle 400s.[49] He was said to have been beguiled by a water fay (fairy), a great queen called Malgven, just as Merlin was later enchanted by Viviane of the Lake. One of Gralon's legends concerns a marvellous golden fish that he shared daily with a hermit in the Forest of Menez-Hom. Each day they were sustained by the fish, which was always miraculously whole again afterwards. This is in keeping with the later stories of the Grail as a vessel of endless provision for the Fisher Kings. It is also reminiscent of Nascien, the hermit king, who was stranded on the mysterious Turning Island in the *Estoire del Saint Graal* (*see* plate 24). But, as with many old legends, the magical story of Gralon and the fish became Catholicized to the extent that the hermit was redefined and said to have been the Breton bishop St Corentin. Today, the statue of Gralon, crowned and on horseback, commands the city of Quimper from between the great spires of the 13th-century Cathedral of St Corentin in Finistère.

The reason for the amending of Gralon's records was largely because they included Grail traditions that were problematic as far as the Church was concerned. Not least was the claim that it was Gralon who 'brought the Vine into Brittany'. This claim was indicative of his marriage to Malgven, the daughter of Nascien II in the line of the Fisher Kings. Their descendants prevailed as Kings of the Bretons, ultimately progressing to Viviane I del Acqs. In later times, the esoteric concept of the Vine was corrupted as if it had referred to Gralon having introduced wine into the region! Once the Cathedral of St Corentin was built, an annual custom was instituted whereby a chorister would climb to a high platform in front of Gralon's statue, symbolically to offer a cup of wine to the king.[50]

The situation in Brittany during Gralon's 5th-century era, as indeed before and thereafter, demonstrates that the style of Celtic Christianity brought in from Britain was different to that of the orthodox Roman movement in Gaul. Even as late as 590, Bishop

Regalis of Vannes complained about the invading religious culture, while earlier bishops had asserted in 520 that the immigrant Bretons should be made to conform to the Latin Rule.[51]

Gralon's realm was Breton Cornouaille in the south-west of Brittany, and his original capital was thought to have been at Caer Ys in the Bay of Douarnenez near Quimper. It was a low-lying settlement with a large dyke to keep back the sea. Eventually it was vacated because of flooding. Consequently, Gralon moved his base to Quimper. Whether or not Caer Ys actually existed is unknown, but its legacy gave rise to yet another story in the attempt to make Gralon's desposynic posterity acceptable to the Church.

The tale recalls an event when Dahut (Dahud-Ahé), the daughter of Gralon and Malgven, was enticed by her lover to open the sluice-gates of Caer Ys so that the sea poured in. Gralon leaped to his horse, pulling Dahut up behind him, and raced to higher ground where they met St Gwénolé. Knowing that Dahut was responsible for the flood, the saint caused Gralon's horse to rear, so that his daughter fell into the sea, and immediately the waters subsided (*see* plate 16). Through the literary introduction of St Gwénolé (just as happened with St Corentin and the fish), the story was contrived so as to focus on his saintly powers whilst diminishing the maternal heritage of Gralon's daughter.[52] The original legend of Caer Ys was based rather more on the premise that Dahut carried the water tradition of Acqs in the Nascien line.

Gralon's father was the Welsh-born Conan Meriadoc, Lord of the Armorican Tract and first King of the Bretons until AD 421. Conan was a 9th-generational descendant of King Lucius in the desposynic succession via Caradawc Vreichvras. He firstly married Ursula, a daughter of Donaut of Domnonée, and his second wife (the mother of Gralon) was Darerca, a grand-niece of St Martin of Tours.[53] Two predominant lines emerged from Gralon (Alain) via his sons Salomon and Guitol. We are primarily concerned with the latter, whose grandson was Riatham the Great (or Riothamus, meaning Greatest leader). He reigned in Domnonée a couple of generations before Jonas.[54] Riatham (identified as Riotimus) is recorded in the work entitled *Gothic History* by the 6th-century writer Jordanes, which relates to his fierce battle against King Euric of the Visigoths.[55] In the aftermath of this event in AD 470, Riatham died en route to Avallon in Burgundy.

By virtue of his prominence and the Avallon connection, it has been speculated that Riatham might have been the king known as Arthur.[56] But, apart from the fact that Riatham lived some while before Arthur was recorded, the main problem with this is that Riatham of Brittany's name was not Arthur. In any event (*see* page 324), King Arthur is positively recorded by name in a number of British records. Nevertheless, a family connection is apparent, and Viviane I del Acqs emerges as a daughter of Riatham – the heiress of a great leader who had no sons.

Following the two lines of succession from Gralon, we see that the descent from Salomon progressed to King Hoel I (d *c*545), whose sister Alienor married Ywain de Léon d'Acqs (the great-grandson of Viviane I in the succession from Guitol). Also in the descent from Guitol we find Jonas (as featured in the Grail accounts) in the same generation as Viviane's daughters. Jonas was a succeeding King of the Bretons, although he was not actually the son of Alain, being historically five generations removed. It was with Jonas that the Frankish Count Chonomore seized his opportunity for power in Brittany by murdering him in 540 while his youngest son Judwal was still a child.[57] The Breton annals relate that Judwal's mother escaped with him to the Merovingian court of King Childebert in Paris, where he was raised. Eventually, Judwal took up arms against Chonomore who was defeated and fled from the country.

From the generational chronology of these various characters, we learn that Nascien II's line certainly did descend to Lancelot II via Alain II as given in the *Prose Lancelot*. This suggests that a son of Nascien's descendant, Lambord, married into the line of Riatham. We are now back to where we began this chapter – with the *Glastonbury Chronicle*, which states, '*Lambord genuit filium qui genuit Ygerna*' (Lambord begat a son who begat Ygerna). So who was this son of Lambord who fathered the daughters of Viviane I del Acqs?

The Missing Father

There were two men who were closely associated with Viviane's life in the Grail romances. They were Merlin whom she was said to have charmed, and Taliesin who was the bard to Urien and Ywain. The earliest documented reference to Taliesin comes from the 9th-century writings of the Welsh monk Nennius in his *Historia Brittonum*. He listed the five most famed poets of the 6th century, including Taliesin, but there is no mention in his work of Merlin.[58]

A difficulty of identification is caused by the fact that neither Taliesin nor Merlin were proper names; they were descriptive styles. Taliesin means 'radiant brow', as applied to the shaved frontal tonsure of the Druids (*see* page 211). The Merlins were appointed seers to the kings, akin to the far-seeing merlin falcons. However, it is intriguing to read in the *Ystoria Taliesin* (much of which was previously attributed to Merlin)[59] that the poet wrote: 'The prophet Johannes called me Merlin, but now all kings know me as Taliesin'.[60] There is an implication here that these two characters were perhaps one and the same.

The two central texts of Taliesin's work are the *Llyfr Taliesin*[61] and the *Ystoria Taliesin*.[62] The *Llyfr Taliesin* is a 14th-century manuscript compilation of 60 poems, 12 of which are ascribed to the 6th-century Taliesin, and 15 to a later poet also called Taliesin. The *Ystoria Taliesin* is a 16th-century collection of ancient Welsh prose and poetry, some of which is again attributed to the original Taliesin.[63]

Given that Taliesin's life was so heavily veiled, a good deal of mythology emerged concerning his boyhood as a certain Gwion Bach (the son of Gwreang of Llanfair) who was employed to stir the cauldron of the sorceress Ceridwen. That apart, Taliesin's poetry is a maze of riddles and conundrums. When investigating his work in the 1940s, the scholar Robert Graves concluded that Taliesin was 'hiding an ancient religious mystery – a blasphemous one from the Church's point of view'.[64]

At that time, Graves was researching the ancient goddess culture and its impact on early Christianity. In the course of this, he cited

numerous of Taliesin's poetic lines which contained hidden traditions. Among these were: 'I have been in the firmament with Mary
Magdalene',[65] and another which relates that he met 'creatures of
distinguished lineage among the fish'.[66] The latter might well be
indicative of the Fisher Kings.

Robert Graves entered more deeply into the story of Mary
Magdalene in his 1946 novel *King Jesus*. Setting the scene at a druidic
altar known as the Heel Stone, he described the wedding ritual of
Jesus and Mary Magdalene, incorporating Mary's enthroned crown-
ing and a Grail ceremony of the bread and wine.[67]

In due course (*see* page 311) we shall consider the figure of
Merlin, but whether or not Merlin and Taliesin were synonymous,
there is nothing to suggest that either of them was a father to any
kings in Brittany. In fact, when historical chronology is applied, it
becomes clear that it was Viviane II, Lady of the Lake, who charmed
Merlin, not her grandmother Viviane I.

Although Amlawdd (Lambord) is recorded as Arthur's maternal
grandfather in the Welsh texts of *Culhwych and Olwen* and *Y Seint
Greal*, it is of relevance that he is otherwise identified in the Breton
history of St Illtud as Anblaud, a ruler in British Dumnonia.[68] A
Welsh genealogical tract cites his forebears as being Cynwal
(Kynwal) son of Ffrwdur, son of Gwrvawr – tracing back, via Conan,
to Caradawc Vreichvras and beyond. Thus, he is attributed with the
same ancient ancestry as that of Gralon.[69] Whereas Gralon was the
son of Conan and Darerca of Tours, Amlawdd was a descendant
of Conan and his first wife, Ursula of Domnonée. An anomaly
is presented, however, by the fact that the Welsh texts classify
Amlawdd as the maternal grandfather of Arthur, but other records
(including the *Glastonbury Chronicle*) maintain that he was Arthur's
maternal great-grandfather.

If Viviane I was the inheritor in Domnonée following the death of
her father, Riatham, then her likely husband would have been the
king who succeeded Riatham, thereby gaining his sovereign entitlement in the region by way of that marriage. If so, then we should
expect to find that this man was also the historical father of King

Jonas, from whom Lancelot II was descended, as given in the *Prose Lancelot*.

The man who appears on cue, and who reigned in Breton Domnonée until *c*520, is Riwal (Rivallous). He was a Prince of Archenfield in south-eastern Wales, who arrived with a large migratory fleet in the Bay of St Brieuc.[70] Subsequently, he was said to have been a ruler on both sides of the English Channel.[71] As a son of Lambord, he is the only contender in the quest for Viviane I's husband – and his own son and successor was indeed King Jonas of the Bretons. Moreover, the 13th-century records of the Saints of Brittany relate that Riwal was an ancestral kinsman of King Arthur.[72] In complete accord with the *Prose Lancelot*, the elder son of Jonas was Lancelot I, who married Viviane II to become the father of King Ban.

Since Perceval, the brother of Elaine le Corbenic, is reckoned to have descended in the Grail line from Alan the Great (Gralon), the route of his descent also appears to have been via Lambord. Unfortunately, neither his grandfather Pellehan nor his uncle Pelles can be found in historical record. Based on available material, however, it seems that Pellehan (by whatever name in reality) was a brother or close kinsman of Riwal. Aiding this identification is the fact that the *High History of the Holy Grail* details that Ban le Benoic was Perceval's uncle,[73] and we know from the *Grand Saint Graal* that Ban was the grandson of King Jonas, the son of Riwal.[74]

Readers of *Bloodline of the Holy Grail* will notice a number of amendments, additions and modifications in the foregoing genealogical structure from Nascien to Ygerna. During the past 10 years certain hitherto inaccessible texts have become available, and these records now make it possible to construct the family lines more accurately, while at the same time introducing some characters who were previously missing from the generational lists. The overall picture is now shown in the revised chart, The Heritage of Avallon del Acqs (*see* pages 332–3).

18

The New Kingdoms

The French Connection

In Robert de Boron's *Joseph d'Arimathie*, it is held that Joseph carried the blood of Jesus in a chalice to the West. The *Grand Saint Graal* further relates that this chalice was the sacred vessel into which 'the *Sang Réal* [Blood Royal] was poured therein'.[1] In addition we have the long-standing chalice representation of the *vas uterus* (the womb), in which regard Mary Magdalene was said to have carried the blood of Jesus Christ. Emblematic of this tradition is a window at the 13th-century Cathedral of Bourges, which depicts Mary Magdalene with her chalice, collecting Jesus' blood from his *Dolorous Stroke* wound at the cross.

As with the Aminadab portrayal at St Denis, it might be wondered what such non-biblically themed windows are doing in Catholic establishments. In fact, there are many similar examples from the High Gothic era that do not conform to Roman Church doctrine. One of the main reasons is that these cathedrals were largely funded by the Knights Templars, who were instrumental in their design and influential with regard to their content. The Kings of France were financially reliant on the Templars who ran the banking network during the 12th and 13th centuries, and this afforded a degree of esoteric compromise in the realm of church decoration.

We have seen that to whatever extent the *Desposyni* inheritance had been sidelined by the Church, its legacy was preserved in many ways – from the simplicity of secret watermarks, through genealogical listing, and onwards to the romantic lore of the Holy Grail. A commonly held view is that the Merovingian dynasty of France was

The Magdalene and Chalice window at Bourges

associated with the messianic bloodline[2], but no Merovingians appear in a generational list that runs in parallel with Nascien II's line for about 350 years. Even so, Nascien was clearly a Grail dynast, and his grandfather, Faramund, was also the grandfather of Meroveus via a fraternal strain (*see* chart: Progression of the Bloodline).

From the time of Nascien in the early AD 400s, the Fisher Kings progressed in a sequence of Franco-British relationship. The same had applied from the outset when Aminadab of Gaul married Eurgen, the daughter of King Coel I of the Britons. But this consolidation of the separate lines from Jesus and his brother James in the latter 2nd century does not explain Nascien's position in the Grail Family because we do not know his ancestral line of descent, nor has it been ascertained whether his inheritance was from Josephes (the Jesus line) or from Avallach (the Arimatheac line). What we do know, from the *Grand Saint Graal*, is that the titular Avallach of Siluria was called Mordrains, and that he was the only man allowed by Josephes to look into the Ark of the Grail (*see* page 258). This is plain evidence that the lines were allied across the water and in communication from the start.

Precisely the same uncertainty applies in respect of Nascien's kinsman and contemporary Meroveus, the founder of the Merovingian dynasty. Their mutual forebear was Faramund, King of the West Franks, from whose culture France (previously Gaul) eventually took its name. It is therefore to Faramund's ancestors that we must look in order to discover the heritage of both Nascien and Meroveus. The family of Faramund can be traced back into the BC years, as can that of his wife Argotta. This provides a chance of finding a marital link with at least one of the desposynic houses.

Fortunately, a connection is not difficult to discover since it appears in the French and British royal genealogies. The connection occurs in the ancestry of both Faramund and Argotta, whose individual lines emerged from a king called Dagobert in about AD 300. His son Genebaud was the 6th generational ancestor of Faramund, while the family of Genebaud's brother Clodomir descended to Argotta. Prior to Dagobert, the single-line ancestry traces back to Francio, from whom the Franks were named in around 11 BC. Before that, the Franks were known as Sicambrians – a tribe from the Black Sea region of Scythia.[3] Nominally styled after the weapon for which they were most famed, the names Francio and Frank derive from *frankon*, meaning 'lance'.[4]

The Bibliothèque Nationale in Paris contains a facsimile of the reputed *Fredegar's Chronicle* – an exhaustive 7th-century historical work of which the original took 35 years to compile. A special edition of Fredegar's manuscript was presented to the illustrious Nibelungen Court and was recognized by the State authorities as a comprehensive official history. Fredegar (who died in 660) was a Burgundian scribe, and his *Chronicle* covered the period from the earliest days of the Hebrew patriarchs to the era of the Merovingian kings. It cited numerous sources of information and cross-reference, including the writings of St Jerome (translator of the Greek Bible into the Latin *Vulgate*), Archbishop Isidore of Seville (compiler of the *Encyclopedia of Knowledge*), and Bishop Gregory of Tours (author of *The History of the Franks*).

Fredegar's Prologue asserts that his own researches were even more painstaking than those of the writers that he cited. Fredegar wrote,

> I have judged it necessary to be more thorough in my determination to achieve accuracy … and so I have included … (as if source material for a future work) all the reigns of the kings and their chronology.[5]

To achieve such accuracy, Fredegar, who was of high standing with Burgundian royalty, made use of his privileged access to a variety of Church records and State annals. He wrote that in the late 4th century the Franks were in the Rhineland, to where they had moved from Pannonia (west of the Danube) in AD 388 under their chiefs, Genebaud, Marcomer and Sunno. Settling into the region of Germania, they established their seat at Cologne. Over the next century, their armies invaded Roman Gaul and overran the area that is now Belgium and northern France. It was at this stage that Genebaud's daughter Argotta married Faramund, who reigned AD 419–430 and is regarded as the founder of the French monarchy.

Some generations before Faramund and Argotta, at the time of Lucius and Aminadab (the grandson of Josephes), it is stated that Marcomer IV of the Franks married Princess Athilde (Athildis), a daughter of King Coel I of the Britons.[6] The year was AD 129 – before the marriage of Aminadab and Eurgen, the younger sister of Athilde (*see* chart: Origins of the Desposyni). Coel was the son of Marius of Siluria and Penardun, the daughter of Anna and Brân. He was the cousin of Mordrains the Avallach, and the great-grandson of James (the Joseph *ha Rama Theo*) as well as being the father of King Lucius, Athilde and Eurgen. Thus we have a desposynic line that progressed to Faramund and Argotta, whose offspring descended within two

PROGRESSION OF THE BLOODLINE

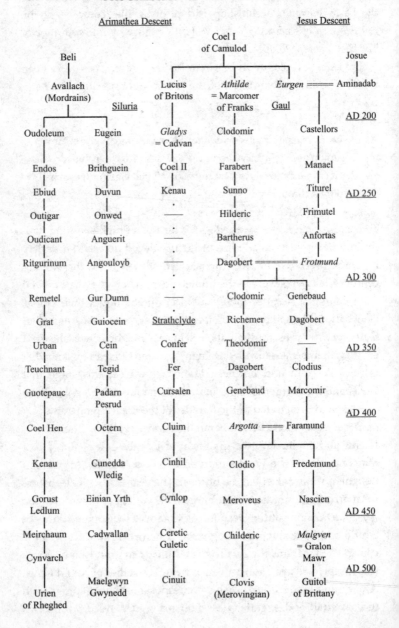

Arimathea Descent   Jesus Descent

			Coel I of Camulod			Josue

Beli — Avallach (Mordrains)

Siluria

Lucius of Britons — *Athilde* = Marcomer of Franks — *Eurgen* ===== Aminadab

Gaul

Gladys = Cadvan — Clodomir — Castellors

AD 200

Oudoleum — Eugein
Endos — Brithguein — Coel II — Farabert — Manael
Ebiud — Duvun — Kenau — Sunno — Titurel — AD 250
Outigar — Onwed — . — Hilderic — Frimutel
Oudicant — Anguerit — . — Bartherus — Anfortas
Ritgurinum — Angouloyb — . — Dagobert ======= *Frotmund*

AD 300

Remetel — Gur Dumn — . — Clodomir — Genebaud
Grat — Guiocein — Strathclyde — Richemer — Dagobert
Urban — Cein — Confer — Theodomir — AD 350
Teuchnant — Tegid — Fer — Dagobert — Clodius
Guotepauc — Padarn Pesrud — Cursalen — Genebaud — Marcomir

AD 400

Coel Hen — Octern — Cluim — *Argotta* ===== Faramund
Kenau — Cunedda Wledig — Cinhil — Clodio — Fredemund
Gorust Ledlum — Einian Yrth — Cynlop — Meroveus — Nascien — AD 450
Meirchaum — Cadwallan — Ceretic Guletic — Childeric — *Malgven* = Gralon Mawr
Cynvarch — — — — AD 500
Urien of Rheghed — Maelgwyn Gwynedd — Cinuit — Clovis (Merovingian) — Guitol of Brittany

generations to Meroveus. There is, therefore, no doubt that the Merovingian kings could claim a bloodline inheritance from the *Desposyni* heirs.

A Double Inheritance

Although ultimately renowned for their centuries of reign in France, the Merovingian culture was largely Germanic following their ancestors' time in the Rhineland. It was from a German perspective that the Bavarian knight Wolfram von Eschenbach wrote his later account of *Parzival* – the very reason why this particular Grail legend (as against the French versions) was of interest to the German composer, Richard Wagner, for his opera *Parsifal*. In fact, Wolfram's *Parzival* is referred to within the Grail tradition as the German Cycle.[7]

We have it from the *Morte d'Arthur* and other works that Perceval's father was Pellinore. In the *High History of the Holy Grail* and elsewhere, Perceval's mother is Yglais. And yet, disregarding other writers and records of the French and British cycles, Wolfram refers to Perceval's parents in *Parzival* as Gahmuret and Herzeloyde. The Grail bearer is generally Elaine le Corbenic, but to Wolfram she is Repanse de Joie. Gawain's mother is known throughout Grail tradition as Morgause, but in *Parzival*, although still a half-sister of Arthur, she is called Sangive. The wise hermit of *Parzival* is not called Nascien, but Trevrizent. It is he who explains the wounding of the Fisher King and the secrets of the Grail, whereas in the *Queste del Saint Graal* and elsewhere Nascien is the custodian of the secrets.

In no instance is there any similarity between the names used by Wolfram and those which are familiar and consistent in other texts. We are left, therefore, with the mysterious figures of Wolfram's Fisher Kings: Titurel, Frimutel and Anfortas, who appear by those names in no other literature. Our only clue to their identity lies in the fact that Trevrizent is said to have been related to Anfortas. Thus, if Trevrizent is synonymous with (or representative of) Nascien, then Anfortas similarly falls into the dynastic line of Faramund (variantly known as Pharamond).

In the chivalric and heraldic records of France are the details of coat of arms devised in the 15th century for numerous royal and noble houses during an era of jousting and tournaments. The foremost patron and master of tournaments at that time was King René d'Anjou, who wrote *The Manual for the Perfect Organization of Tournaments*, along with *Battles and the Order of Knighthood*. The first of these works was produced in 1460, and onwards from that year (published in sections between 1460 and 1475) came *La forme quon tenoit des tourneys et assemblees au temps du roy Uterpendragon et du roy Artus* by the Vicomte de Carlot. Wolfram von Eschenbach wrote that the register of the Grail Keepers was held by the House of Anjou (*see* page 265), and this heraldic work details the form of the tournaments and assemblies at the time of Uther Pendragon and King Arthur. Of particular interest in these illustrated manuscripts of the tourneys is the fact that Faramund is listed as a member of the Pendragon Court that became known as the Order of the Round Table.[8] He also appears as King Pharamond (the guardian of young Tristan) in the French Arthurian work known as the *Prose Tristan* from about 1230, a greatly expanded version of the legend of *Tristan and Iseult*.[9]

King Louis XI of France, who reigned in that same era (1461–83) was a close colleague of René d'Anjou. Louis was insistent about Mary Magdalene's dynastic position in the royal lineage, and claimed her as 'a daughter of France belonging to the monarchy' (*see* page 238).[10] Louis was referring to the ancient heritage of the first monarchy of his realm – the Merovingian kings. Despite the strange names used by Wolfram, his Fisher Kings were clearly related to the dynasty of Faramund and, for whatever names they were used in substitution, Titurel, Frimutel and Anfortas appear as ancestors of Meroveus in a descent from Aminadab, Castellors and Manael. It is in this succession that we find Frotmund, the wife of Dagobert (*see* chart: Progression of the Bloodline). By virtue of her marriage into

Medieval Gaul and Brittany

the Arimatheac line from Athilde and Marcomer, both Argotta and Faramund emerge as being dually desposynic.

This might well account for the mystery that surrounds the Merovingian ancestry. Although the generational Franks are fully recorded, their legend (as recounted by the 5th-century historian Priscus of Thrace) was that the House of Meroveus was sired by an arcane sea creature called the *Bestea Neptunis*.[11] Once again, this brings the sea mythos and a fish creature into play. These are constant features of Grail lore that perhaps relate to the poetry of Taliesin, who wrote during the Merovingian era that he met beneath the sea 'creatures of distinguished lineage among the fish'.[12]

Regarding the confusion of names experienced in *Parzival*, a considerable problem is caused because many of the kings became known by names attributed to them in later life, not necessarily by their birth or family names. Moreover, even those names have been corrupted at various stages of history. The Merovingian king Clovis, for example, should be rendered as Chlodo-wech, meaning 'battle glory'.[13] Similarly, the Frankish king Chlot-hari ('war celebrated') became better known as Lothar.[14] The names of Wolfram's Fisher Kings doubtless fall into this type of category, or they might even be birth names before the application of distinctive styles based on their kingly performance.

Rivalry

A story of some early conflict between the Frankish strains is told in the *High History of the Holy Grail* and the *Prose Lancelot*. As the descendants of Faramund ousted the Roman governors and rose to power in Gaul, the Breton kings of the Dumnonian succession were brought under the supervision of *Comites non regis* appointed by the Franks (*see* page 271). In the main, relationships between the Breton and Frankish houses were good, but there was a branch of the East Franks whose members created problems for the alliance. They were the descendants of Faramund's ancestral strain from Genebaud, as against that of Argotta's strain from Clodomir who were called the West Franks. Although Faramund was an East Frank by birth, Argotta's line was regarded as the senior in rank because it descended from the elder of the sons of Dagobert and Frotmund. Upon his marriage Faramund became King of the West Franks, gaining overall control while his original family were made dukes in their subordinate realms. The successors of Faramund and Argotta became the Merovingian kings, and this sidelined the East Franks, who made regular warlike incursions into the Merovingian provinces. Not the least of these was Brittany.

At the time of Queen Viviane II, a sub-kingdom of the Breton region was said in Arthurian literature to have been governed by her son Ban le Benoic, with neighbouring territory under his brother Bors de Gannes (probably the district of Vannes). Ban was married to Elaine, the sister of Pelles and Yglais, whose other sister Eviane was the wife of Bors. Historically at that time, a duke of the East Franks named Clodius led a number of assaults into Brittany, becoming an enemy of both the West Franks and the Breton kings. He appears in the *High History of the Holy Grail* and the *Prose Lancelot* as King Claudas, and is featured again by that name in the *Morte d'Arthur*.[15] Claudus became a significant enemy of Ban and Bors, who both died in their battles against him. Ultimately, it is recounted that Claudin, the son of Claudus, remained to become a friend of the cousins, Lancelot (son of Ban) and Bors II (the son of Bors). In the interim, following the death of Ban and his wife Elaine's resultant anguish, the young Lancelot was placed in the care of his grand-mother, Viviane II del Acqs.

The House of Meroveus

The Franks were known as the people of the *Newmage* (New Covenant)[16] in much the same way that the Essenes of Qumrân were referred to as the *Nazrie ha Brit* (Keepers of the Covenant). Contrary to the style of the day, the Merovingians grew their hair long, and this was reckoned to afford them magical properties,[17] much as the biblical judge Samson's strength was related to his long hair. It was even decreed that if any Merovingian allowed his hair to be cut, he would lose his kingship.[18] In the manner of the Nazarites, and not dissimilar to the Druids, the Merovingians were greatly revered as teachers, judges, priests and healers. They were priest-kings of a traditional style, and their revered model was King Solomon, the son of David. Their disciplines were largely based on Old Testament scripture but, in spite of this, the Roman Church proclaimed them irreligious. The 6th-century Catholic bishop, Gregory of Tours, maintained that the Franks were 'followers of idolatrous practices',[19] and they were called the long-haired Sorcerer Kings.

The Merovingians did not own or rule the land, nor were they politically active. Like the Kings of the Bretons in Brittany, the Merovingians were Kings of the Franks, not Kings of France.[20] Their governmental functions were performed by appointed Mayors of the Palace (chief ministers), while the kings were more concerned with military and social matters. Among their primary interests were education, agriculture and maritime trade. They reigned not by coronation or created appointment, but by an accepted tradition that corresponded to an accepted right of past generations.[21]

Not only were the Merovingians akin to the early Nazarites, but they retained other customs from biblical times. According to Essene tradition, boys were 'reborn' at the age of 12 when, wrapped in a simple linen robe, they would undergo a ritual re-enactment of birth (*see* page 153). A boy would thus symbolically be born again and installed into his community position. Merovingian royalty followed a similar practice whereby princes were granted an hereditary right to dynastic kingship by initiation on their 12th birthday. There was no need for later coronation. The dynasty was not one of 'created' kings but a succession of natural kings, whose entitlement was automatic by virtue of hallowed appointment. It was said that Merovingian blood could not be enobled by any match, and that the *raison d'être* of their kingship rested in the ultimate nobility of their bloodline.[22]

Beginning with Meroveus, who was proclaimed Guardian at Tournai in the middle 400s, the Merovingian dynasty took shape as a monarchical house under his grandson King Clovis in the latter 5th century. Gaining the throne at the age of 15, Clovis took advantage of the Roman imperial decline, leading his armies through northern Gaul in a five-year campaign to assume overall control. By AD 490, his realm included centres at Reims, Troyes and Soissons, so that by his early twenties Clovis was destined to become the most influential figure in the West. At that time, the Roman Church greatly feared the increasing popularity of Arianism in Gaul, while Catholicism was dangerously close to being overrun in Western Europe.[23] Clovis was neither Catholic nor Arian, and it occurred to the Vatican hierarchy that his rise to power could be used to their own strategic advantage if they could get him on side.

The Roman ambition to align Clovis with the Church was greatly aided when he married Clotilde, the daughter of King Chilperic of Burgundy. Although the Burgundians were traditionally Arian in their beliefs, Clotilde was a Catholic and she made it her business to evangelize her version of the Faith. For a time she had no success in promoting the doctrine to her husband, but her luck changed in AD 496. King Clovis and his army were locked in battle against the invading Alamanni tribe at Tolbiac near Cologne and, for once in his illustrious military career, the Merovingian was losing. In a moment of desperation he yelled 'Jesus Christ!' at much the same instant that the Alaman king was slain. At the loss of their leader, the Alamanni faltered and fell into retreat, whereupon Clotilde wasted no time in claiming that Jesus had caused the Merovingian victory. Clovis was not particularly convinced of this on the basis of his wild exclamation, but his wife sent immediately for St Remy, Bishop of Reims, and arranged for Clovis to be baptized.[24]

In due allegiance to their leader, around half of the Merovingian warriors followed Clovis to the font. Word soon spread that the high potentate of the West had become a Catholic, and this was of enormous value to Bishop Anastasius in Rome. A great wave of conversions followed and the Roman Church was saved from almost inevitable collapse. Were it not for the baptism of King Clovis, the ultimate Christian religion of Western Europe might now be Arian rather than Catholic. Nevertheless, the royal compliance was not a one-way bargain; in return for the king's agreement to be baptized, the Roman authorities pledged allegiance to him and his descendants. They promised that a new Holy Empire would be established under the Merovingians. Clovis had no reason to doubt the sincerity

King Clovis the Merovingian at *Notre Dame* de Paris

of the Roman alliance, but unwittingly he became the instrument of a bishops' conspiracy against the desposynic bloodline. With the blessing of the Church, Clovis was empowered to move his troops into

Burgundy and Aquitaine. It was calculated that the Arians would be obliged to accept Catholicism, but the bishops also had a longer-term strategy in mind – a plan to manoeuvre the Merovingians out of the picture, leaving the Bishop of Rome supreme in Gaul.

Following a succession of military conquests, King Clovis was succeeded by his sons Theuderic, Chlodomir, Childebert and Lothar. By 511 the Merovingian domain was divided into separate kingdoms. Theuderic succeeded in Austrasia (from Cologne to Basle), based at Metz. From Orléans in Burgundy, Chlodomir supervized the Loire Valley and the west of Aquitaine around Toulouse and Bordeaux. Childebert succeeded in the region from the Seine across Neustria to Armorica (Brittany), with his capital at Paris; and Lothar inherited the kingdom between the Scheldt and the Somme, with his centre at Soissons. Their decades of combined rule were tempestuous. Conflicts persisted against the Gothic tribes, and eventually afforded Merovingian penetration into eastern Aquitaine, with Burgundy being fully absorbed into the realm.[25]

A Monastic Age

The Merovingian era, as well as corresponding with the Arthurian period, had begun during an age of saints in Britain and Gaul. These characters emerged from the monastic movement – a scholarly sect that evolved on the druidic fringe of Christianity. It was based on a solemn, regulated existence such as the Essene community had established at Qumrân. A strictly austere type of religious discipline was essential to the monastic regime and, whether applied to secluded communities or to ascetic hermits, it was entirely appropriate to a life of study and contemplation. These saintly figures of the Celtic persuasion are known to have denied the episcopacy of the Roman Church but, in contrast to this, Church history has subsequently incorporated them as if they were a part of its structure from the outset.

The monastic pioneer in France was St Martin of Tours (AD *c*316–397), who is perhaps best remembered for dividing his cloak to share it with a naked beggar. Originally from Pannonia, west of the Danube, Martin was a successful soldier in the Imperial Army before he settled in Poitiers and established Gaul's first great monastery at Marmoutier. From about AD 371 he was said to have been appointed as a bishop at Tours, but continued his monastic existence regardless. Later he was to become a patron saint of France.[26]

An early monastic missionary from France was St Germannus d'Auxerre, who visited Britain in AD 429 and was the teacher of St Patrick. The son of a Celtic Church deacon, Patrick had been captured as a boy by pirates and carried to Ireland.[27] After some time in slavery, Patrick escaped to Gaul, where he was trained as a missionary at the monasteries of Lérins and Auxerre. Then, in AD 432, he returned to Ireland and began his own mission. Patrick's teachings were different in many respects from those of Rome, and they indicate a distinct tendency towards the Arian and Nestorian traditions. He was not at all popular with the Catholic Church, whose governors stated definitively that he was unsuited to the priesthood. Much the same could have been said about monastic types in general. As John Cassian had declared: 'Monks should at all costs avoid bishops'.

During Merovingian times, a prominent religious figure in Brittany was St Samson of Dol, who died in 565. A grandson of King Buidic I of the Bretons, and the son of Prince Amon Ddu, Samson was born in Wales and entrusted to the care of St Iltudd. Eventually, he built a Breton monastery at Dol, where King Childebert (a son of Clovis) is claimed to have nominated him as the bishop. Of interest however, with regard to Martin, Samson and others, is that the bishoprics to which they were appointed did not actually exist during the lifetimes of these men. They were written into accounts of their lives later in order to bring their history into the orthodox Christian arena. Church scribes, particularly those of the 11th and 12th centuries, made a habit of dedicating the origins of extant bishoprics to long-dead saints and martyrs.[28] Even the *Catholic Encyclopedia* makes the point that, although Samson was said to have become the Bishop of Dol in the middle 500s, there was no such bishopric until the 9th century.[29]

The foremost saint of the era was St Columba, the founder of the Sacred Kindred of the Celtic Church. He was expressly relevant to Arthurian history, and established the most ancient royal and ecclesiastical seat of the early Kings of Scots at Dull, near Aberfeldy in Perthshire. Born of Irish royal stock in 521, Columba was eligible to be a king in Ireland, but he abandoned his legacy to become a monk at Moville, County Down. He founded monasteries in Derry and around, but his greatest work was destined to be in the Western Highlands and Isles of Scots Dalriada. He was banished from Ireland in 563 having mustered an army against the unjust King of Sligo, following which he was imprisoned at Tara and then exiled at the age of 42. With 12 disciples, he sailed north to the island of Iona and established the Columban monastery there. Further north in mainland Caledonia, Columba's royal heritage was well received by King Bruide of the Picts, and he attained prominence as a political statesman at the druidic court. With a fleet of ships at his disposal, Columba subsequently visited the Isle of Man and Iceland, setting up schools and churches wherever he went – not only in Caledonia and the islands but also in English Northumbria (Saxonia).[30]

The Birth of England

At much the same time that the Germanic Franks had infiltrated Gaul, the 5th century also saw a persistent incursion into Britain by other Germanic tribes. According to the venerable Bede, they were known as Saxons, Angles and Jutes. Bede explained that from the country known as Old Saxony (the north of modern Germany around Bremen and Hamburg) came the East Saxons, the South Saxons and the West Saxons. From a land called

Angulus, north of Old Saxony came the Angles, and from the Jutland peninsula of Denmark (to the north of Angulus) came the Jutes.[31] These realms had been beyond the boundary of the Roman Empire and, once the Roman defences of the Rhine collapsed in AD 407, a northward migration into Saxon territory encouraged the Saxons and others to move westward across the sea to the fertile lowlands of Britain. Although there is little documentary evidence of this episode outside of Bede's writings (c730) and the *Anglo Saxon Chronicle*, archaeological discoveries on Britain's eastern seaboard confirm their account of the waves of incomers.[32] A district of Schleswig on the German-Danish border is still called Angeln, and the remnants of a timber village at the mouth of the River Weser in Old Saxony indicate that the place was abandoned in about AD 450.

Meanwhile, following the Romans' withdrawal from Britain in AD 410, regional leadership had reverted to tribal chieftains. One of these was Vortigern of Powys in Wales, whose wife, Rowena, was the daughter of the previous Roman governor, Magnus Maximus. Having assumed full control of Powys by AD 418, Vortigern was elected Pendragon of the Isle in AD 425.[33]

By that time, kingly branches had emerged in the Arimatheac lines from Anna and Brân the Blessed. Among the most prominent of these local kings was Cunedda (AD c400), the northern ruler of Manau by the Firth of Forth. In a parallel family branch was Cunedda's father-in-law, the wise Coel Hen (Coel the Old), who led the Men of the North (the *Gwyr-y-Gogledd*).[34] Fondly remembered in nursery-rhyme as Old King Cole, he governed the regions of Rheged from his fortress at Carlisle. Five generations later, in the line from Coel Hen, came Urien of Rheghed and Gowrie (the brother-in-law of Arthur), who died in about 579.

Another noted leader was Ceretic, a descendant of King Lucius. From his base at Dumbarton, he governed the more northerly regions of Clydesdale in around AD 450. Together with Vortigern, the three kings, Coel, Cunedda and Ceretic, were the most powerful overlords in 5th-century Britain. Theirs were the families who also

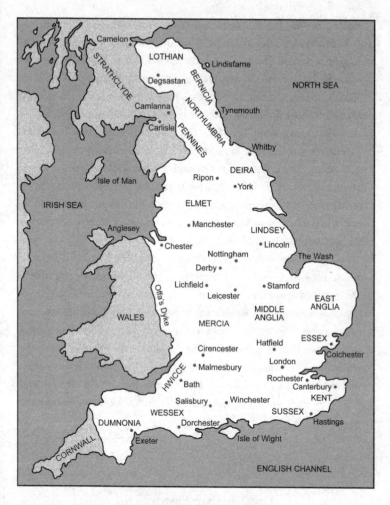

Britain in Anglo-Saxon Times

bore the most famous Celtic saints such as St Cadoc, St David and St Carannog, and were accordingly known as the Holy Families of Britain.[35] They were all descended from 1st-century Silurian-Arimatheac stock, and these branches of the same original family governed Wales and all the western and northern lands up to the Caledonian border.

In the middle AD 400s, Cunedda and his sons led their armies into North Wales to expel unwanted Irish settlers at the request of Vortigern.[36] In so doing, Cunedda founded the Royal House of Gwynedd in the Welsh coastal region west of Powys. The Picts of Caledonia in the far north then took advantage of Cunedda's absence and began a series of Border raids across Hadrian's Wall. An army of Jute mercenaries, led by Hengist and Horsa, was imported by Vortigern to repel the invaders but, having succeeded, they then sought to acquire territory for themselves and took up arms against Vortigern. Horsa was killed in this battle, but Hengist then turned his attention to the South East and seized the kingdom of Kent. It was in the wake of this that other Saxon and Angle warriors invaded from northern Germany.[37]

The Anglo-Saxon onslaught was such that the Britons (who had lost much of their military strength when the Romans departed) could not hold out against them. The Saxons took the south of Britain, developing the kingdoms of Wessex, Essex, Middlesex and Sussex, while the Angles occupied the rest of the land (excluding Wales)[38] from the Severn estuary up to Hadrian's Wall, comprising Northumbria, Mercia and East Anglia. In the latter 5th century, new kingdoms emerged under the Saxon kings Aelle, Cerdic and Cynric, and in time the combined domain became known as Angle-land.

The Terrible Pendragon

In terms of character identification before the time of Arthur, we are currently left with the mystery of the man called Celidoine. He appears by name in the *Prose Lancelot* when Lancelot has a vision of his ancestors, Nascien and Celidoine.[39] Originally connected with Mordrains the Avallach, Celidoine is said to have been a son of Nascien I and his wife Flegentyne.[40] Celidoine is initially cast in the *Grand Saint Graal* and in the *Estoire del Saint Graal* as a 2nd-century figure, but later in the story he emerges more realistically as a king in 6th-century Britain who fought against the invading Saxons.[41]

Although the first Celidoine is not apparent in historical record, the second is easy enough to find. The name Celidoine (along with its variants, Celydone, Kelyddon and Celyddon) constitutes an early identification of Caledonia in the far north of Britain. The king known as Celyddon was otherwise King Maelchon (Máelchu) of Caledonia, who reigned in the middle 500s and was the father of King Bruide I of the Picts. He fought to prevent the Saxons penetrating his realm, and his son Bruide was the king who welcomed St Columba into Caledonia.[42]

Of particular relevance is the fact that Celyddon's daughter, Domlech (the sister of Bruide), was married to a King of Scots Dalriada called Aedàn mac Gabràn, who reigned 574–606. Earlier (see page 272), we learnt that Arthur's sister Morgaine, the youngest daughter of Ygerna del Acqs, was recorded in the 9th-century as 'Muirgein, daughter of Aedàn in Belach Gabráin'.[43] We also know that Ygerna was otherwise married when she conceived Arthur. Domlech was the second of the two queens of Arthur's father, and the identification of King Aedàn as Ygerna's lover before they were married is crucial to understanding Arthur's own kingly inheritance. Aedàn was the overall King of British Kings, and was called the *Uthir Pen Draco* – the Terrible Pendragon.

19

The Church and the Quest

Pagans and Wizards

By the 6th century Christianity of the Roman style had made little impact in Britain, and throughout the 500s the Celtic Church prevailed. In 574, Britain's first kingly installation by way of a Celtic Christian rite was performed when St Columba of Iona anointed King Aedàn mac Gabràn of Dalriada.[1] It was not until 597 that St Augustine arrived from Rome, and not until 664 that the Catholic bishops enforced some of their doctrines at the Synod of Whitby. The Vatican maintains that King Oswiu of Northumbria conceded at this Synod to the papal authority of St Peter in order to gain admission to the Kingdom of Heaven.[2] But, when the presumed papal supremacy was tested on the stalwarts of the British Church, they asserted that they recognized no such authority. They reiterated the words of Dianothus, Abbot of Bangor. At a conference with Augustine in 607, Dianothus had stated that he and his colleagues were prepared to acknowledge the Church of God, 'but as for other obedience, we know of none that he whom you term the Pope, or Bishop of Bishops, can demand'.[3]

The introduction of Roman Christianity into Britain was largely facilitated by the Saxon King Aethelbert of Kent, great-grandson of the Jute invader Hengist. Aethelbert's wife was the Frankish princess Bertha who, like Clotilde of Burgundy, swayed her husband to the Roman faith. When Augustine arrived in 597, Aethelbert gave him a palace in Canterbury as a centre for the new Church in Angle-land.[4] Ultimately, since Aethelbert was the senior king of the Saxon realm, other kings followed him to the font. The native Britons were then confronted by two threats: their kingdoms had been usurped by Germanic invaders, and now their ancient Celtic religion was being subsumed. As the land filled from its eastern shore with Angles and Saxons, the Britons were forced westwards across the island to the far reaches of Wales and Cornwall, and northwards into the regions of Cumbria, Northumbria and Strathclyde.

Some time after Augustine's arrangement with King Aethelbert, a tablet was placed above the vestry fireplace at the London church of St Peter's in Cornhill, explaining:

> In the year of our Lord 179, Lucius, the first Christian king of this island now called Britain, founded the first church in London, well known as the Church of St Peter in Cornhill; and founded there the archiepiscopal seat, and made it the metropolitan church and the primary church of his kingdom. So it remained for the space of four hundred years until the coming of St Augustine … Then, indeed, the seat and pallium of the archbishopric was translated from the said church of St Peter in Cornhill to Dorobernia, which is now called Canterbury.[5]

The greatest of all travesties is that, as Roman Christianity overran Celtic Christianity, the literature of the latter was systematically destroyed, to be replaced with strategically designed forgeries. Not a scrap survives of any Gaelic writing by St Columba, and yet much of his liturgy is supposedly extant. During medieval times, many ancient Celtic manuscripts from before 600, including the works of Columba, were re-written in Latin and presented as original documents. *The Cathach* of St Columba, who died in 597, provides a good example of this subterfuge. The 58-folio work, held by the Royal Irish Academy from shortly after its discovery in 1813, is reckoned to be the oldest Irish illuminated manuscript in existence.[6] It is said to have been a copy made by Columba himself from manuscripts given to him by St Finian prior to 561. Palaeographic evidence proves, however, that the document was written long after Columba's death and, moreover, it is mostly in Latin – a language that was unknown in Ireland during the saint's lifetime and which was never used by the Gaels. With its inclusion of Bible sections from the Latin *Vulgate*, the *Cathach* was either a pure fabrication or a substantial corruption of Columba's original work since the text is wholly Romanized to comply with post-Augustinian teaching after the Synod of Whitby.[7] Other such works followed, including the 7th-century *Book of Durrow* and the 9th-century *Book of Kells*. Historically, they are all important, and they are individually wonderful in artistic terms, but they are all Roman Church fabrications, produced to subvert the Old Faith of Britain and Ireland.

It was not as if the Celtic churchmen were unaware of the impending threat posed by Pope Gregory and Augustine, but there was little they could do to prevent it because the Saxons had already driven them from the region where Augustine landed. Apologetic Church history records that his mission was designed to convert the Saxon invaders but, according to the 8th-century priest Bede of Jarrow, Augustine's papal brief was to subjugate 'all the bishops of Britain'.[8] The intention is made transparent because the Saxons had no bishops. Some time before this event, in 540, the Welsh priest Ambrose Telesina wrote his warning of things to come:

> Woe to hym thatt doth not keepe
> From Romish wolves thy flockes of sheepe,
> And preach hys charge amonge;
> That will nott watch his fold alwai
> As toe hys office doth belong.
> Woe to Hym thatt doth not keepe
> From Romish wolves thy flockes of sheepe
> With staff and weapon strong.[9]

At the 1545 Council of Trent in Northern Italy, the bishops formally agreed to withdraw all Druid-based material from the public domain. In the 10th century, 30 volumes of Celtic manuscripts were catalogued at the Abbey library of St Gall in Switzerland, but only one survives today.[10] The story of loss and destruction is the same throughout Western Europe, and constitutes the reason why the era became known as the Dark Ages; its history was literally plunged into darkness. Within the Britannic Church communities of those times there had been prominent adepts of the old wisdom – abbots and culdees such as St Ninian, St David, St Patrick, St Columba and St Kentigern, all of whom were denounced by the Roman Church for their so-called wizardry and pagan beliefs. Even the later papal establishment regarded them as necromancers and sorcerers, but this is not the way things are currently portrayed. The teachings of these men were so firmly cemented in society that the Church was

Columba and Augustine 1997 Commemorative Stamps

obliged to pursue a tactical strategy of incorporation. A thousand years after their lifetimes, the Vatican officials elected to bring them posthumously into the orthodox saintly fold so that the truth of their establishment would be lost to history. Recently, in 1997, the British Post Office and the Anglican Church joined forces to promote St Columba alongside his bitter Catholic rival St Augustine of Rome, who came to England with an express papal brief to destroy the Celtic movement immediately after Columba's death in 597. The 1,400th anniversary postage stamps and the allied promotional material portrayed these two arch-enemies as if they had been blood-brothers in a mutual Catholic cause.

The period of Anglo-Saxon conquest in pre-Augustinian times was the era in which King Arthur rose to fame in British history. He was born into an environment of battles and conflict as the traditional kings fought to preserve their boundaries and religion against attack and incursion. In the western and northern domains, these kings were all bloodline descendants in two original 2nd-century Arimatheac strains from Mordrains the Avallach, and from King Lucius.

Merlin and the Warlords

After Vortigern's death in AD 464, his son Cunedda had remained in North Wales. He succeeded as Pendragon, also becoming the supreme military commander of the Britons. The holder of this latter post was called the Guletic (or in Welsh, the *Wledig*). The Pendragons were not necessarily dynastic; they were appointed from parallel families of the royal stock by a Druid council of elders to be the Guardians of the Celtic Isle (*Pen Dracos Insularis*). In effect a Pendragon was an elected King of Kings. When Cunedda died, Vortigern's son-in-law, Brychan of Brecknock in Wales, became Pendragon, and Ceretic of Strathclyde became the military Guletic. Meanwhile, Vortigern's grandson Aurelius, a man of considerable military experience, returned from Brittany to take up arms against the Saxons, and it was he who ordered the execution of Hengist after his seizure.[11] In his capacity as a druidic priest, Aurelius was the designated Prince of the Sanctuary – a monastery known as the Cloister of Ambrius near Caer Caradduc (Salisbury).[12] The Ambrius guardians were individually styled Ambrosius and wore a scarlet mantle called the *pesrud*. From his fort in Snowdonia, Aurelius Ambrosius maintained the military defence of the West and succeeded as the Guletic when Brychan died.

In the early 500s, Brychan's son (also named Brychan) moved to the Firth of Forth in the north country as Prince of Manau Gododdin. There he founded another region of Brecknock in Forfarshire, which the Welsh people referred to as Breichniog of the North. His father's seat had been at Brecon in Wales, and so the northern fortress was similarly called Brechin. Brychan II's daughter' Lluan, married Prince Gabràn of Scots Dalriada, as a result of which Gabràn (eventually King of Scots and the father of Aedàn) became Lord of the Forth, inheriting a castle at Aberfoyle.

Adding weight to the Celtic heritage of Britain, the ancestors of Gabràn had arrived in the Western Highlands from north-eastern Ireland in AD 498. Born of Gaelic royalty in descent from High King Conaire Mór of Tara, they were three Scots princes of Irish Dal Riàta who left their native soil to settle in the land that became known as Argyll. They were the sons of King Erc and, once established, they created the new kingdom of Scots Dalriada. The middle-born son, Fergus, reigned as the senior king until 501, and from him the subsequent Kings of Scots descended. His elder brother, Loarn, governed northern Dalriada, which became Lorne, while the younger brother, Aonghus, controlled the kingdom of Islay and the Western Isles.[13]

Ireland's northern province of Dal Riàta (meaning 'Riàta's share') was situated in Antrim between modern Portstewart and Ballyclare. It was but a short passage to Kintyre and the Firth of Clyde, where some Dalriadan settlements already existed before the royal brothers arrived. As the tribal population of Irish Dal Riàta grew, it over-spilled into a less populated region across a short stretch of sea. By this means, the kingdom of the Scots was expanded, and in time the overall name of Scotland emerged within the greater realm of Caledonia, as the Pictish country north of the Forth-Clyde isthmus was called.

Neither Ireland nor Caledonia had been penetrated by the Romans, and there were no vestiges of Roman government as in England and Wales. In fact, having failed to subdue the fearsome Picts of Caledonia, the Romans had built great walls across the land to keep them from moving south. Emperor Hadrian's Wall (AD 122) extended from Tynemouth to the Solway Firth, while the Antonine Wall of Emperor Antonius (AD 142) crossed the higher land between the Clyde Estuary and the Firth of Forth.

In the Lowland and Border areas below the Scottish and Pictish territories, the regions of Galloway, Lothian, Tweeddale and Ayrshire were all governed by Welsh princes of the *Gwyr-y-Gogledd* (Men of the North) and the tribe of the Votadini. One of these local rulers in the early 6th-century, with his hill-fort at Traprain Law,[14] was King Loth, from whose name Lothian (the Edinburgh region) derived. It was to his grandson, also Loth (or Lot) of Lothian, that Arthur's sister Morgause was married.

Despite the eventual alliance between the Scots and the Britons against the Saxons, there was a dispute in the early 5th century between the Brychan house and that of King Cairill of Antrim. Cairill attempted to expand his Irish rule into Brychan's territory, and launched an assault against the Manau region in 514. The invasion was successful and the Forth area was brought under Irish control. Brychan duly called for assistance from his son-in-law, Prince Gabràn of Scots, and from the military commander Aurelius Ambrosius. Rather than attempt to remove the Irish from Manau, the leaders decided to launch a direct sea offensive against Antrim. In 516, Gabràn's Scots fleet sailed from the Sound of Jura with the Guletic troops of Aurelius. Their objective was the castle of King Cairill, the formidable hill-fort of Dun Baedàn (Badon Hill). The Guletic forces were victorious, and Dun Baedàn was overthrown (*see* also 'The Battles', page 342). In 560, the chronicler Gildas III

(516–570) wrote of this conflict in his *De Excidio Britanniae*, and the great battle features in both the Scots and Irish chronicles.[15] Some years after the Battle of Dun Baedàn, Gabràn became King of Scots in 537, with his West Highland court at Dunadd (Dun Add), near Loch Crinan.

At that time, the Pendragon was Cunedda's great-grandson, the Welsh king, Maelgwyn of Gwynedd. He was succeeded in this appointment by King Gabràn's son, Aedàn of Dalriada, who became Pendragon in 548 and King of Scots in 574. The Scottish Lowlands (below the Forth) consisted of thirteen separate kingdoms and they bordered on the Northumbrian realm to the south and on the Pictish domain to the north. One of these regions above Hadrian's Wall was that of the *Gwyr-y-Gogledd*, whose chief was King Gwenddolau.

Shortly before Aedàn's kingly installation by St Columba, King Rhydderch of Strathclyde had killed Gwenddolau in battle at Arderydd near Carlisle. Strathclyde was a tribal region of the Damnonii and, because of the similarity of names, Damnonii has often been confused with Dumnonia. This in turn has given rise to the mistaken concept that so much Arthurian activity occurred in the far south of the country. The battle of the northern warlords at Arderydd was an unfortunate and unusual territorial encounter because both kings were of the Arimatheac succession: Gwenddolau was descended (via Coel Hen) from Avallach, and Rhydderch was descended (via Ceretic) from King Lucius. The *Gwyr-y-Gogledd* were closely allied to the Scots kings, and the Rheghed relationship with them appears to have become strained because of the Dalriadic control of entry into the Firth of Clyde, a vital trading route for Strathclyde. The battlefield was at the Moat of Liddel, between the River Esk and Liddel Water, above Hadrian's Wall.[16] It was here that the Arthurian tale of *Fergus and the Black Knight* was set.

Gwenddolau's chief adviser, the Merlin of Britain, was Emrys of Powys, a son of Aurelius Ambrosius and his wife Niniane. On Gwenddolau's death, Merlin fled the battlefield to Hart Fell Spa, near Moffat in the Caledonian wood north of Carlisle, and then sought refuge at King Aedàn's court of Dunadd. As a succeeding

Druid guardian of the Ambrius, Merlin was in a position to request that the Prince of Scots take action against Gwenddolau's killer. Aedàn complied and duly demolished Rhydderch's Court of Alcut at Dumbarton.[17]

The most important urban centre in the north of Britain at that time was Carlisle, the dominant bastion of the *Gwyr-y-Gogledd*.[18] It had been a prominent Roman garrison town and by AD 369 was one of the Roman provincial capitals, each of which was designated as a *Caerleon* (City of the legion. In Latin: *Urb legionum*). Along with Carlisle, others included Chester, Caerleon-on-Usk and York. In his *Life of St Cuthbert*, Bede referred to a Christian community in Carlisle long before the Anglo-Saxons penetrated the area. A little south of Carlisle, near Kirkby Stephen in Cumbria, stands the medieval ruin

The Ruin of Pendragon Castle at Kirkby Stephen

of a later built Pendragon Castle. The city of Carlisle was also called Cardeol, Cardoil or Caruele, and it was here that Grail writers such as Chrétien de Troyes located King Arthur's royal court. In the Dark Ages, it was the military headquarters of the Guletic (the *Dux Bellorum*: Lord of Battles). *The High History of the Holy Grail* refers throughout to King Arthur's court at Carlisle, which also features in the French *Suit de Merlin* and in the British tales, *The Avowing of King Arthur* and *Sir Gawain and the Carl of Carlisle*:[19]

> King Arthur lives in merry Carlisle,
> And seemly is to see;
> And there with him Queen Guenever,
> That bride so bright of blee.[20]

Meanwhile in Rome

The 5th century was a time of monumental change for the Church of Rome and, as the Western Empire fell into decline, so the Eastern Orthodox Church rose to prominence in Constantinople, Alexandria, Antioch and Jerusalem. Each of these centres, alongside Rome, was recognized as being equally pre-eminent by the Council of Chalcedon in AD 451. The increasing menace of invasions from across Italy's northern frontiers caused Rome to become ineffectual as an administrative capital, and the more northerly city of Milan became the main seat of government. By the middle 400s Rome had been sacked by Alaric the Goth, Atilla the Hun and Gaiseric the Vandal. Then in AD 455 another massive Vandal assault signalled the total collapse of the Roman Empire, which was just 21 years away.[21]

Following a period of weak papal leaders, Rome was fortunate for a while, having gained Leo I, the Great, as *Pontifex Maximus* in AD 440. He protested strongly when the Patriarch of Constantinople emerged as the head of the Eastern Church, but his opposition was fruitless and the two Churches were separated for all time. Leo's

Roman branch, within a crumbling Empire, was threatened with annihilation, especially when the Merovingian Franks gained control in Gaul. Some years after Leo's death in AD 461, the Church's position was saved when King Clovis was baptized into Catholicism (*see* page 295). But, for the time being, and with the feeble Emperor Valentinian III in his shadow, Leo was left with the unenviable task of managing the political intrigue of Rome as well as the Church.

Valentinian had become Emperor in AD 425 at the minority age of six. Imperial affairs were conducted by his mother and a self-indulgent general named Flavius Aëtius, who had switched allegiance after being a leader of the invading Huns. Aëtius was eventually murdered by Valentinian, who was then assassinated by the general's supporters in AD 455. This turbulent period was marked by the dismemberment of the Western Empire, which terminated in AD 476 when the 13 year-old Emperor Romulus Augustulus abdicated after his military defeat by the German chieftain Odoacer.

In AD 452, shortly before Valentinian's assassination, a further invasion of Rome by Attila the Hun was somehow averted by Pope Leo. Along with an unarmed body of monks, Leo confronted the fearsome Attila and his army by the River Po in northern Italy. At that time, Attila's empire stretched from the Rhine across into Central Asia. His well-equipped hordes were ready with chariots, ladders, catapults and every martial device to sweep on towards the capital. The conversation between Leo and Attila lasted no more than a few minutes, but the outcome was that Attila ordered his men to vacate their encampments and retreat northwards. What actually transpired between the men was never revealed, but afterwards Leo the Great was destined to wield supreme power.[22]

It was this event which cemented a future role for the popes as national leaders in their own right but for more than a century most of Leo's successors were mainly incompetent. Not until 590 was another pontiff distinguished by the Church as being called 'the Great'. He was Pope Gregory I, a hitherto lawyer who changed the course of Church history and forged the newly styled Catholicism of the West as distinct from the composite of Eastern and Western traditions which had prevailed before his time.[23] In 591, Pope Gregory maligned Mary Magdalene, giving rise to her non-biblical representation as a sinful harlot. He subsequently amended the original Catholic Mass, invented the concept of a horned devil, sacked all lay staff from the Lateran Palace, redefined matters of ecclesiastical discipline, and took overall control of the military.[24] Then, in 597, he sent St Augustine to England with a brief to overawe and decimate the Celtic Church. From the time of Gregory I, the Church and the Roman State became one again, as it had been in high imperial times, and a new form of empire began – an international realm of absolute spiritual dominion by the popes.

The Beleaguered Kingdoms

The period between the death of Leo the Great in AD 461 and the death of Gregory the Great in 604 was the era which incorporated the lives of those from Gralon Mawr in Brittany to King Arthur in Britain. The Grail and Arthurian romances relate to events that seem to have occurred within this time-frame, but the stories of the Round Table knights and their Quest did not emerge until the Middle Ages. The earliest written mention of Arthur comes from his own lifetime, with other accounts following in the 7th to 9th centuries. They detail his battles and adventures, but make no mention of the Grail Quest, which was attached to his legacy in later times. It appears that Arthur's knights were used as literary vehicles to convey the need for a quest that was caused by an event, or events, that occurred during the intervening period. Hence it was that his 6th-century Celtic warriors were dubbed with the mantle of medieval armoured knights in a chivalric environment, thereby giving a romantic and timeless quality to the *Sangréal* tradition.

In Arthurian lore, the Quest of the *Sangréal* relates to an ambition to heal the wound of the maimed Fisher King, to reinstate the kingdom and return the barren wasteland to fertility. In British terms, the various Celtic kingdoms of the desposynic bloodline were demolished by the Saxon invaders whose reigns began in the 6th century. By the 9th century there were some very fine kings from this Saxon stock, Alfred the Great of the House of Wessex being a good example. They were themselves usurped by the invading Normans under Duke William (the Conqueror) in 1066. Contrary to common belief, the Normans were not French in origin; they were Norsemen who had previously invaded Neustria in northern France, giving rise to the new territorial name of Normandy. William's ancestral forebear was Hrolf (Rollo), who had gained title to Normandy from King Charles III at the Treaty of St Clair-sur-Epte in 912. Under King William I and the Normans, many of the Saxon shires of England became redesignated as counties subject to the authority of appointed counts, with shire reeves (sheriffs) supervising the shires. An overall class-structured feudal system was implemented, and the era saw the erection of many of the nation's prized castles and churches.

Strictly speaking, Norman rule did not last for long, however, and within a century of the conquest, Matilda (the heiress of King Henry I) married Geoffrey Plantagenet, the Count of Anjou. Their son, Henry II (1154–89), married Eleanor of Aquitaine and, by virtue of these marital alliances, two of the Faramund strains from the original Sires of France were embodied in the succeeding Plantagenet kings – the dynasty of Richard the Lionheart and Henry V. The installation of Henry II was the first undisputed succession to the English throne in more than a century, and he became the lord of an empire that stretched from the Scottish border to the French Pyrenees. As the Duke of Aquitaine, Duke of Normandy and Count of Anjou, Henry spent 21 years of his 34-year reign in France, and commerce between his two countries flourished as never before.[25] From the time of Henry's marriage to Queen Eleanor, his chancellor Walter Map and others began writing stories of the Holy Grail (*see* page 252); Eleanor's daughter Marie began liaising with the Grail writer, Chrétien de Troyes, and eventually the Age of Chivalry was born.

In June 1162, Henry appointed the churchman Thomas Becket to the post of Archbishop of Canterbury, but from the outset Becket went out of his way to oppose the King. The worst of the disputes was over a matter of Church regulation which considered clerics to be exempt from sentence and punishment by secular law courts for criminal actions. Henry proclaimed at Westminster in October 1163 that, in his view, churchmen who committed crimes should be handed over to the lay courts for trial like anyone else. Thomas Becket opposed this and so did the Pope. Maintaining his right to decide the law of his own realm, Henry then forefeited Becket's estates and the discredited archbishop fled to France.

After some years and a threat from Pope Alexander to have Henry excommunicated, Becket returned to England. He not only renewed his hostility towards the King by condemning him on Mary Magdalene's feast day,[26] but also denounced many of England's churchmen, whereupon the exasperated Henry exclaimed, 'Who will rid me of this turbulent priest?'. In a misguided attempt to gain royal favour, four knights (Reginald Fitzurse, Hugh de Moreville, William de Tracy, and Richard le Breton) hurried to Canterbury where, on 29 December 1170, they slew Becket at the foot of the altar steps.[27] The unfortunate event had little effect on Henry's reputation or general popularity outside the Church, and he remained the most powerful king in Europe, but his dispute with Becket had been in vain. Based on the terms of the *Donation of Constantine* (*see* page 319), even King Henry was subject to the Rule of Rome, and churchmen within all the Catholic realms remained outside the jurisdiction of secular law until the 16th-century Protestant Reformation.

It was during the course of Henry II's reign – so heavily influenced by Eleanor of Aquitaine and her daughter Marie of Champagne – that Britain's Arthurian history became attached to the French tales of the Grail Quest. In the days of old Provence and later Brittany, the desposynic strains of Britain and France had been entwined, but their senior successions had departed from the regnal scene long before Plantagenet times. The Saxons had dismantled their kingdoms in England, but in France the destroyer had been the

Church. The route by which the Vatican achieved this destruction in 751 led to an enforced new practice whereby kings and queens within the Catholic domain were henceforth crowned by, and made subordinate to, the Pope. The effects of this were felt not only in France, but also in England which (subsequent to the arrangement between St Augustine and King Aethelbert) had also become a Catholic realm. In earlier times, monarchs on both sides of the water had reigned by virtue of bloodline inheritance, but this desposynic tradition was curtailed when the rules of hereditary status were dogmatically changed by a strategy that has since become known as the greatest documentary fraud in sovereign history.

Clovis the Merovingian had been persuaded by the bishops that, following his agreement to baptism in AD 496, his successors would be supported in turn by the Church of Rome (*see* page 295). For a while this appears to have been the case, but as the popes became more ambitious they sought control over secular as well as spiritual matters. A foremost subject of ecclesiastical debate about heritable interests from the latter 5th century was that of royal dynastic progression in contrast to the Vatican's own Apostolic Succession. Although the Roman Church had found the means to gain supremacy over other church movements, it still had to contend with kingly lines that gained their right of succession by way of bloodline inheritance. Singled out for particular scrutiny in this debate were the Merovingian Kings of the Franks.[28]

A Holy Empire

In order to tackle the problem of heritable interest, Pope Zachary came up with a plan to gain supremacy over all the kings and queens of Christendom. In the year 751, without revealing his source, he produced a previously unknown document that was purported to be more than 400 years old and carried the signature of Emperor Constantine. It proclaimed that the Pope was Christ's personally elected representative on Earth, with a palace that ranked above all the palaces in the world. His divinely granted dignity was stated to be above that of any earthly ruler and that only he, the Pope, had the power and authority to 'create' kings and queens as his subordinates. The charter made it forcefully clear that the Pope held a vicarious office as Christ's chosen deputy, granting him the style *Vicarius Filii Dei* (Vicar of the Son of God).

The document became known as the *Donation of Constantine*, and its provisions were immediately enforced by the Vatican as being an edict from Jesus Christ himself. Consequently, the whole nature and structure of monarchy changed from being an office of community guardianship to one of absolute rule. Henceforth, European monarchs were crowned by the Pope, becoming servants of the Church instead of being champions of the people.[29]

Zachary's plan was to change all kingly tradition by granting territorial dominion to future kings who would operate under his supreme authority. The defunct Roman Empire was a relic of history, but Zachary had a new concept – a Holy Roman Empire controlled from the Vatican. His first initiative was to depose the long-standing royal house of France: the Merovingians of Gaul. Papal troopers seized King Childeric III and, as a humiliation to signify the loss of his kingship, his hair was cut brutally short. He was then incarcerated in a monastery dungeon, where he died four years later.

Installed in place of the Merovingians was a family of hitherto regional mayors. They were descendants of the renowned Carolus Martel, who had turned back a Moorish invasion near Poitiers in 732, and the kings of the new dynasty were styled Carolingians. In all the 236 following years of Carolingian monarchy, their only king of any significance was Martel's grandson, the legendary Charlemagne. Nevertheless, a new tradition had been born and the so-called Holy Roman Empire begun. Henceforth, European kings were enthroned by the Pope, and in England by his deputy the Archbishop of Canterbury. Scotland, the last bastion of the Celtic realms, stood alone in resisting this Catholic invasion, and her monarchs were never subjected to papal authority.

For all the apparent Carolingian attachment to the Vatican, Charlemagne does not seem to have been wholly committed to the Roman ideal. He appears to have inherited a strong contrary legacy from his mother, who was a daughter of the Merovingian princess Blanche Fleur. Undeterred by the *Donation of Constantine*, which had enabled his father King Pepin to usurp the Merovingian throne under Pope Zachary, Charlemagne retained advocates of both the Grail Church and the Roman Church at his court.[30] He was not too keen on the idea of becoming Holy Roman Emperor as well as King of the Franks, but on Christmas Day in the year 800, when Charlemagne was in the Basilica of St Peter's in the company of several bishops, Pope Leo III crept up behind him and placed the imperial crown on his head without warning.[31]

There was no thought by anyone at the time that the *Donation of Constantine* might be a forgery. Even the anti-papists who sought to criticize its content did not question its authenticity. The best they could do was to maintain that Emperor Constantine had no right to have signed away the Western Empire in this fashion. But the fact was that, although the opening and closing sections of the *Donation* were cleverly constructed in the 4th-century style of Constantine's day, its more central themes, such as the descriptions of imperial and papal ceremony, were representative of a much later era. Its New Testament references relate to the Latin *Vulgate* Bible – an edition translated and compiled by St Jerome, who was not born until AD 340, some 26 years after Constantine supposedly signed and dated the document.[32] Apart from this, the language of the *Donation*, with its numerous anachronisms of form and content, is that of the 8th century and it bears no relation to the writing style of Constantine's day.[33] It is as different as modern English is to that of William Shakespeare – with a similar span of time in between. Also of particular significance is the fact that, at one point in the document, the Byzantine city of Constantinople (named after Constantine) is cited as being in existence, whereas later in the text the idea of founding this city is put forward as a future concept!

The document, known in Latin as the *Constitutum Constantini*, was first declared to be a forgery by the Saxon Emperor Otto III in the year 1001. Intrigued by the fact that Constantine had moved his personal capital from Rome to Constantinople, Otto recognized that this was merely a ruse to pre-empt any Frankish ambition to centre their own operation in Rome so as to oppose the imperial bishops. Although Otto was a German, his mother was an East Roman who was well aware that this fear had existed in the late Merovingian era, at which time Zachary's deception of the *Donation of Constantine* was implemented.

Otto's 11th-century pronouncement came as unwelcome news to the prevailing Pope Sylvester II, but the matter was ignored and did not come to the fore again until the German theologian and philosopher Nicholas of Cusa (1401–64) announced that Constantine had never produced the said *Donation*.[34] However, although a doctor of canon law who decreed that the Pope was actually subordinate to the members of the Church movement, Nicholas was somehow overawed by the bishops and subsequently took up a cardinalate position in 1448, becoming a staunch supporter of the papacy.

The *Donation* was not publicly mentioned again until its authenticity was fiercely attacked by the Italian linguist Lorenzo Valla in the 15th century. Valla (c1407–57) was commissioned by Pope Nicholas V to translate the works of Herodotus and Thucydides from Greek into Latin. Valla was not just an eminent scholar, he was also an ardent spokesman for the reform of education and firmly believed that the spirit of Greco-Roman antiquity had been lost during the Middle Ages. Angered by the fact that the elegance of classical Latin had given way to a clumsy medieval language, as exemplified by the largely incomprehensible style of Church Latin, he was highly critical of the Church's *Vulgate* Bible and its strategic errors in translation from the earlier Greek manuscripts. This led other scholars of the Renaissance, such as the Dutch humanist Desiderius Erasmus (c1466–1536), to revert their Bible studies to the more original texts. Resultantly, in 1516, Erasmus issued his own Latin translation of the Greek New Testament, thereby exposing the

Vulgate as a cleverly mistranslated document, which he called a 'second-hand account'.

The outcome of Lorenzo Valla's investigation into the *Donation of Constantine* was that he discovered it to be an outright forgery compiled some four centuries after Emperor Constantine's death in AD 337. In his related treatise, he wrote: 'I know that for a long time now men's ears are waiting to hear the offence with which I charge the Roman pontiffs. It is, indeed, an enormous one'.[35]

Notwithstanding the debates which ensued from Valla's findings in 1450, the Church managed to survive the Renaissance era of enlightenment, branding many of the great thinkers of the time as heretics. Valla's report (known as the *Declamatio*) was conveniently lost within the Vatican archives, and it was to be more than 100 years before it was once more revealed by the priest Murator who worked in the Vatican Library in the 17th century. Subsequently, the spurious nature of the *Donation* was discussed anew by the Anglican minister Henry Edward Manning (1808–92)[36], but, in the footsteps of Nicholas of Cusa, he was swayed from his original Church to become a Vatican Council member, a cardinal and the Catholic Archbishop of Westminster, publishing his work *The Temporal Power of the Vicar of Jesus Christ* in 1862.

The task of exposing the fraud was subsequently taken up by Christopher B Coleman, a director of the Historical Commission and Historic Bureau at the Indiana State Library from 1924, who produced an updated commentary on *The Treatise of Lorenzo Valla on the Donation of Constantine*.[37] In the event, the very fact that this work came out of North America, and not out of Britain or Europe, made it easy enough for the Church to contain. As a result, very little (outside the occasional encyclopaedic reference) has been written concerning the *Donation* during the past century. But the fact remains that it still exists as the document which has enabled the Church to maintain control of monarchical, political and educational affairs for well over 1,200 years.

The Arthurian Realm

Romantic Tradition

In identifying King Arthur within the genealogical structure of the Grail families, the most important evidence is his name. Despite the nominal variations that we have encountered in respect of other characters (Ygerna/Igraine, Perceval/Peredur, Viviane/Nimue, Lambord/Amlawdd, Urien/Urbgen), the name of Arthur is consistent in all literature. This applies in both history and romance from all linguistic sources.

Over the years many enthusiasts have seized upon specific individuals in their competitive endeavours to portray each of them in turn as the historical King Arthur. These figures include the 2nd-century Roman centurion Lucius Artorius Castus, along with Arthun, a son of the 4th-century Roman governor Magnus Maximus. Others cited are the Welsh lords, Owain Ddantgwyn of Powys and Athrwys ap Meurig of Gwent. Another contender, as we have seen, is King Riathamus of Brittany, and even the 6th-century Saint Armel of Brittany is on the list of presumed Arthurs. But, in the final analysis, it makes little sense to latch on to someone with a vaguely adaptable provenance, and then to claim that the chroniclers all changed his name to Arthur when telling his story. The fact remains that the best way to find an historical king called Arthur is to look for an historical king called Arthur – especially for one who was the son of a Pendragon.

Onwards from the early 1900s, it has been claimed by some that the name Arthur derives from the Romano-Etruscan name Artorius,[1] but such claims are invalid. The Arthurian name was purely Gaelic, emerging from the Milesian-Irish name Artúr. The 3rd-century sons of King Art of Tara, for example, were Cormac and Artúr. The Romans never conquered Ireland and Irish names were not influenced in any way by the Romans. In fact, the root of the name Arthur can be found as far back as the 5th century BC, when Artúr mes Delmann was King of the Lagain. It was long afterwards that Augustus Caesar established the Roman Empire in 44 BC and, by AD 476, the Empire had crumbled to extinction in the West, some time before Arthur of the Britons was born.

In terms of extant literature, the first known reference to Arthur comes from around the year 594 in a lengthy heroic poem called *Y Gododdin*. This was composed by the Celtic writer Aneurin, one of the six poets of Britain mentioned by Nennius in his *Historia Brittonum* (*see* page 186).[2] The poem is a series of elegies for the warriors of Manau Gododdin who fell against the Angles of Deira and Bernicia at the Battle of Catraeth (Catterick) in North Yorkshire.[3] In describing the deeds of Eithinyn the bold, Aneurin (who was himself captured at the battle) wrote that 'his courage was enchanted', but that Eithinyn did not measure up to the battlefield model, and in this respect 'he was no Arthur'.[4] From the same era is a poem attributed to Taliesin and entitled *The Chair of the Sovereign*, which also includes references to Arthur.[5]

The next two mentions of Arthur come from the 7th-century – one in the *Life of Saint Columba* and the other in the *Senchus Fer n'Alban* (Census of the Men of Albany). These works are especially important since they are explicit in their personal identification. Further details are then found in the 9th-century *Historia Brittonum* of Nennius, the 10th-century *Annales Cambriae* (Annals of Wales), and in various medieval chronicles. We shall return to each of these manuscripts shortly but, for the time being, it is better to begin with Arthur's romantic history from the Grail legends.

Arthur's story is given in Geoffrey of Monmouth's *Historia Regum Britanniae* (*c*1147) and it was this work that provided the adventurous backdrop for Arthur's attachment to the Grail tradition. Although earlier texts had given details of Arthur's battles and prowess,

Geoffrey was among the first to explain that the warrior king's mother was called Ygerna. He also identified Arthur's father as being called Uther Pendragon, a name which had never been stated as such in the earlier writings. He confirmed other texts by relating that Arthur's mother and father were not married at the time of Arthur's conception, and gave the name of Ygerna's first husband as Gorlois, the Duke of Cornwall, whose castle was at Tintagel. Furthermore, Geoffrey introduced Arthur's wife as Queen Guanhumara, and described Arthur's sword as being called *Caliburn*.[6]

It is impossible to know whether the historical sword of Arthur was truly dubbed *Caliburn*, but it is an intriguing concept and gives an insight into how Arthurian legends were constructed from separately collected stories. During the Dark Ages, some of the finest blades were made by the Scythian iron-working tribe of the Calybs (or Kalybs), and it is not inconceivable that *Caliburn*, whether in fact or fiction, emanated from this source. The Calybs of the Black Sea region were the upholders of a ritualistic sword culture, and one of their best-known tales relates to the hero Batradz. Having received his death wound, Batradz asked his companions to throw his sword into a lake. Twice they pretended to do so, but Batradz knew they had failed to comply, whereupon they conceded to his wish, at which the water became turbulent.[7] In Sir Thomas Malory's *Morte d'Arthur*, it is the knight Bedevere who twice disobeys the dying King Arthur in precisely the same manner before casting his sword into the lake as instructed. In the earlier *Vulgate Cycle*, the knight featured in this same sequence is Girflet.

In 1155, the Jersey poet Robert Wace (a canon of Bayeux) composed the *Roman de Brut* (Story of Brutus). This was a poetical version of Geoffrey's *Historia*, which began with a tradition that civilization in Britain was founded in around 1130 BC by Prince Brutus of Troy.[8] A copy of Wace's poem, which included the very first reference to the Arthurian Round Table, was presented to Eleanor of Aquitaine. In this notable work, Queen Guanhumara appeared with her name adjusted to Gwynefer (from the Gaelic *gwen-hwyfar*: 'fair spirit') and Arthur's *Caliburn* was renamed *Excalibur*.

In about 1190, the Worcestershire priest Layamon compiled an expanded English version of Wace's poem but, prior to this, a more exciting romance emerged from France. Its author was Chrétien de Troyes, whose mentor was Eleanor's daughter Marie, Countess of Champagne. Chrétien transformed Arthur's already adventurous tradition into thoroughly inspired legend and gave Gwynefer the more poetic name of Guinevere. His five related tales appeared individually from 1170 to 1190,[9] and it was in his account of Lancelot, entitled *Le Chevalier de la Charrette*, that Camelot first appeared as the royal Arthurian court. It was at this stage that British and European writers began amalgamating Arthurian literature with the lore of the Holy Grail. At the request of Count Philippe d'Alsace, Chrétien commenced his famous tale of Perceval in *Le Conte del Graal* (The Story of the Grail). But Chrétien died during the course of this and the work was concluded by other writers. Meanwhile, in England, Henry II's chancellor Walter Map pursued a similar course with the *Grand Saint Graal*. It was King Henry II who, following the disastrous fire of 1184, granted a Charter of Renovation for 'the mother and burying place of the saints' and sponsored the vast new Abbey of Glastonbury (*see* page 163).

Next on the Arthurian scene was the Burgundian poet Robert de Boron. His verses of the 1190s included *Joseph d'Arimathie – Roman l'estoire dou Saint Graal*. However, unlike Chrétien's story of the Grail Quest, Robert's account was not contemporary with King Arthur. It was more concerned with the 1st-century time frame of Joseph of Arimathea, although Arthur's knights were incorporated into the story. From about the same era came the anonymous manuscript entitled *Perlesvaus* (the *High History of the Holy Grail*). This work had Templar origins and also compacted the Joseph and Arthurian story, declaring that Joseph of Arimathea was Perceval's great-uncle. Then, in about 1208, emerged the tale of *Parzival*, a detailed and expanded story of the Grail Family by the Bavarian knight Wolfram von Eschenbach.

King Arthur was brought more fully into the picture by a series of five stories from the period 1215–35, which became known as the

Vulgate Cycle.[10] Written in France by Cistercian monks, these works featured Lancelot's son Galahad, whose mother was the Fisher King's daughter, Elaine le Corbenic. Perceval also remained a central character, and Wace's *Excalibur* was retained as the name of Arthur's sword. Subsequently, from between 1230 and 1240 came the *Post-Vulgate Cycle*, a French prose series also known as the *Lancelot Graal*.[11] These works contain additional details about *Excalibur*, and of how Arthur received the sword from the Lady of the Lake. The story of young Arthur gaining his kingship by drawing a sword from a stone stemmed from an incident in Robert de Boron's *Merlin*, and was repeated (with the sword stuck in an anvil) in Malory's *Morte d'Arthur*. At no time, however, were *Excalibur* and this other sword portrayed as one and the same weapon – a popular theme of some latter-day works from Victorian times.

The English poem *Arthour and Merlin* appeared in the late 1200s, as did the Welsh version of the *Perlesvaus* entitled *Y Seint Greal*. Arthur also made appearances in the *White Book of Rhydderch* (c1325) and the *Red Book of Hergest* (c1400). The Welsh *Triads* included some Arthurian references, as did the *Four Branches of the Mabinogi* which, in the 19th century, were translated from Welsh into English by Lady Charlotte Guest under the revised title of *The Mabinogion*. Other English stories from the 14th century were *The Avowing of King Arthur*, *Sir Gawain and the Green Knight* and *Sir Gawain and the Carl of Carlisle*.

Not until the 15th century (around 900 years after the time of the historical Arthur) did the various legends consolidate into the format that is most familiar today. This occurred in the collected writings of Sir Thomas Malory. Released in 1485 under the title *The Whole Book of King Arthur and His Noble Knights of the Round Table*, it was one of the early books printed by William Caxton, and has since been regarded as the definitive work on the subject. Malory settled Arthur firmly into the medieval period and his characters forsook their Celtic garb for suits of shining armour. In all, there were eight interlaced stories,[12] the last of which, *The Most Piteous Tale of the Morte d'Arthur*, gave rise to the *Morte d'Arthur* (Death of Arthur) title by which Malory's collection has now become better known.

Sir Thomas Malory of Newbold Revell in Warwickshire was wealthily born, knighted in 1442 and served in the Parliament of 1445. But, outside of his extraordinary writing ability, he was either very unlucky or simply incompetent in managing his own life. Caught up in the political intrigue of the Wars of the Roses and the hostilities between the competing Plantagenet houses of Lancaster and York, Malory kept changing sides and managed to spend a good many years in prison. He was never actually brought to trial, nor had any case proved against him, but his enemies accused him of theft, rape, cattle rustling, debt, extortion and the attempted murder of the Duke of Buckingham. At regular intervals from 1451, he was held under lock and key in the cells of Coleshill, Colchester Castle, Ludgate, Newgate and the Tower of London. He became equally renowned for his escapes – on one occasion by swimming a filthy moat, and on another by fighting his way out with a sword and a halberd. Eventually, he conceded to his fate and the *Morte d'Arthur* was completed during his confinement in London's Newgate Gaol. Becoming known as the 'knyghte presoner', he died there on 12 March 1471 and never saw his work in print.[13] According to his Introduction, he finished the book in 1470:

> For this book was ended the ninth year of the reygne of King Edward the Fourth, by Syr Thomas Maleore, knyghte, as Jesu helpe hym for his grete myght, as he is the servaunt of Jesu both day and nyght.

Malory's wonderful tales were a compilation of the most popular traditions from a variety of sources. All the familiar names were brought into play and, in some instances, various lesser-known themes were expanded. Not the least of these was the love affair between Lancelot and Guinevere, which had been introduced in Chrétien's *Le Chevalier de la Charrette* and the *Vulgate Cycle*. For a reason best known to himself, Malory's Camelot was located at Winchester in Hampshire,[14] the 9th-century capital of Alfred the Great where a magnificent 18-ft (5.5 m) Arthurian-style Round Table still hangs in the Castle Hall.[15] The table

The Round Table at Winchester

was first made for the tournaments of Edward III Plantagenet,[16] whose Order of the Garter (based on the supposed Arthurian model) was founded in 1348. The table was repainted in 1522 for the visit of King Henry VIII and the Habsburg Emperor Charles V.

The Histories

Reverting now to the early historical manuscripts, we should first look at the 9th-century *Historia Brittonum* of Nennius. In this work, he details a number of battles at which Arthur was victorious.[17] The locations include:

✠ '*At the mouth of the River Glein*': The River Glen in Northumbria, where the fortified enclosure was the centre of operations from the middle 500s.

✠ '*At another river, by the Britons called Duglas in the region of Linuis*': The River Douglas in the Linuis district of the Novantae tribe, to the north of Dumbarton where Ben Arthur stands at the head of Loch Long.

✠ '*On the River Bassas*': The Bass Rock entrance to the Firth of Forth near North Berwick.

✠ '*In the wood Celidon, which the Britons call Cat Coit Celidon*': The Caledonian wood, now called the Kielder Forest, north of Carlisle.

✠ '*Near Gurnion Castle*': The hill-fort of Vinovia (Guinnion) east of Carlisle.

✠ '*At the City of the Legion, which is called Caer lion*': The city fortress of Caer Ligualid at Carlisle.

✠ '*On the banks of the River Trat Treuroit*': The River Teviot, north of Carlisle near Hadrian's Wall in the Scottish border country.

✠ '*On the mountain of Breguoin, which we call Cat Bregoin*': The Votadini fort of Bremenium in the Cheviot Hills of Northumbria.

✠ '*When Arthur penetrated the Hill of Badon*': [*see* below].

Apart from the Hill of Badon, to which we shall return, all the Arthurian battlefield sites as given by Nennius are in the very north of England and the Scottish borders. Arthur was listed by name in the 7th-century *Senchus Fer n'Alban*, a document which was a royal genealogy and military roster cataloguing the strength of each of the three main tribal groups or *cenéla* of Scots Dalriada. In the context of these warlords of the early 600s, Arthur appears in the census record of King Aedàn mac Gabràn and his sons.[18]

We have seen that Domlech, the daughter of Maelchon-Celidoine, was married to Aedàn (sometimes Aidan).[19] Also that Ygerna's daughter Morgaine is recorded as 'Muirgein, the daughter of Aedàn'. We also know that Aedàn was the overall King of Kings, and was called the *Uthir Pen Draco* – equivalent to the more familiar name of Arthur's father, Uther Pendragon. Throughout the history of Britain's 22 Pendragons – from Cymbeline (died AD 42) to Cadwalader (died 664) – only Aedàn mac Gabràn was ever dubbed with the Gaelic epithet *uthir* (meaning 'terrible').[20]

Additionally, Arthur's sister Morgaine married Urien of Rheghed and Gowrie, and Arthur's maternal half-sister Morgause was married to Lot of Lothian. When the Court of Camelot made its first literary appearance in Chrétien's *Le Chevalier de la Charrette*, it was said to have been at Carlisle, and the original tales of Merlin relate to the nearby region of the Caledonian wood. In all respects, Arthur's primary environment was that of Dalriada and the north of England, as confirmed by the various battlefield sites given by Nennius.

Not only was Arthur listed as Aedàn's son in the *Senchus Fer n'Alban*,[21] but Aedàn is the only Pendragon on record to have had a son named Arthur. The two were mentioned again by name in the *Annals of Tigernach* from the monastery of Clonmacnoise.[22] These *Annals* state that Aedàn's son Arthur fought, along with his brothers, at the battle of Circinn in 598.[23] The Plain of Circinn was near Brechin in Forfarshire – the land of Brychan II, Prince of Manau Gododdin.

Brychan II's daughter, Lluan, was the wife of King Gabràn and the mother of Aedàn (*Lluan, mater Aidan vradauc et vxor Gafran*).[24] Lluan's ancestry, via her grandfather Brychan of Brecknok, traces back to King Lucius and to Anna and Brân the Blessed. Brychan's line, and thereby the maternal line of King Aedàn, was strictly desposynic in the Arimatheac strain.

Aedàn's sons by his wife Domlech included Domangart, the husband of Elaine del Acqs and father of Viviane II, thereby cementing the Celidoine ancestry of Lancelot. By virtue of his maternal descent, Domangart's brother Gartnait (as listed in the *Senchus Fer n'Alban*) became King of the Picts after Bruide in 586.[25] Another brother, Eochaid Buide, succeeded Aedàn as King of Scots Dalriada in 608, and was also dubbed *Rex Pictorum* (King of Picts).[26] Arthur was not, however, the offspring of Aedàn and Domlech; he was the son of Aedàn and Ygerna, who were also the parents of Morgaine.

THE HERITAGE OF AVALLON DEL ACQS
Revision of chart sections from *Bloodline of the Holy Grail*

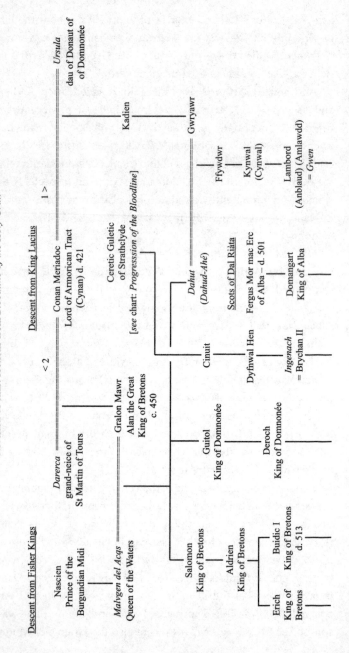

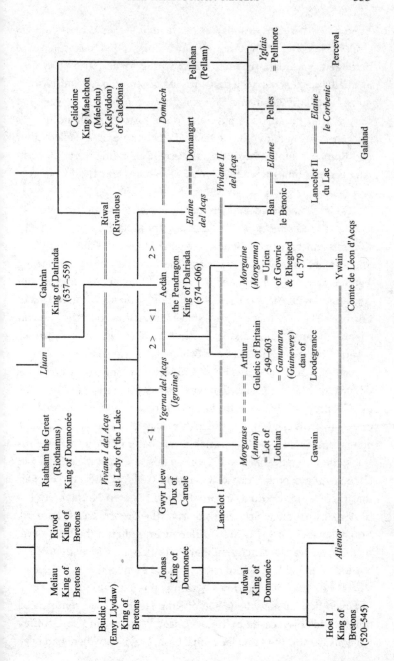

Ygerna had her own desposynic heritage in the Jesus bloodline via Gralon, Nascien and the Sires of France. This, added to Aedàn's own heritage from Lluan, rendered his offspring, Arthur and Morgaine, as dually desposynic – the first such incidents since the 2nd-century marriage of Aminadab and Euergen. It was for this very reason that King Arthur became so important to the history of Britain. It was also the reason why the details of Arthur became veiled after the Roman Church began to destroy Celtic literature in post-Augustinian times after the Synod of Whitby and the *Donation of Constantine*.

Having ascertained the parental heritage of Arthur, we can now look at the *Chronicles of the Scots* as reproduced by the Treasury Commissioners for HM General Register House and the Lord-Clerk Register of Scotland. Here is found the necessary entry concerning Ygerna and the Pendragon. It explains that, at the time of her conception with Arthur, Ygerna was 'another man's wiffe, ye Dux of Caruele'. The document further states that Arthur (born in 559) was eventually proclaimed a king on his 15th birthday.[27] In practice, he became the Sovereign Guletic of Britain: the *Dux Bellorum*.

Ygerna's husband, the Dux of Caruele (Warlord of Carlisle), was Gwyr-Llew – and it is here that we discover a significant error made by Geoffrey of Monmouth in his *Historia Regum Britanniae*. In describing Gwyr-Llew, he called him Gorlois. This is reasonable enough given the spelling variables of the era but, in making his translation from the old texts, Geoffrey misconstrued the title Dux of Caruele as meaning Duke of Cornwall. Geoffrey did not consider that there were no dukes in Britain until his own Norman era – a titular distinction which derived from the French *Duc*. The early British style of *Dux* was quite different from that of the later ducal nobility; it was a strictly military distinction, which denoted a warlord, and held no feudal tenure of land ownership.

At the time of Geoffrey's writing, the 1st Earl of Cornwall, Reginald de Dunstanville (a son of King Henry I), had commenced building his own castle at Tintagel near Padstow, and so Geoffrey gave his Gorlois the same locational base. Previously there had been only a ruined Celtic monastery on the site, and the castle was completed a century after Reginald's lifetime by Richard, a brother of Henry III.[28] In fact, Geoffrey might have been swayed in his report by Reginald's brother Robert, Earl of Gloucester, whose financial patronage enabled him to write the *Historia*.[29]

Even though Arthur's battles were listed at sites in the North Country, there is no reason to disassociate him with Cornwall just because of Geoffrey's error.[30] Neither should Arthur be dismissed from the traditions of Glastonbury or Wales where his legacy also prevails. In his role as the Sovereign Guletic, Arthur's military responsibilities would have encompassed the Celtic realms of Cornwall, Dumnonia, Siluria, Wales and Cumbria, as well as Northumbria and Scotland. As given by Nennius, Arthur led 'all the kings and military force of Britain'.[31] Just as in Carlisle and other northern sites, the spirit of Arthur lives on in places like Tintagel which abounds with the legends of Alfred Tennyson's famous *Idylls of the King*. Even the *High History of the Holy Grail* tells of how Arthur, Lancelot and Gawain came upon this magical place:

> They beheld a chapel that was right fair and rich, and below was a great ancient hall. They saw a priest appear in the midst of the castle, bald and old, that had come forth of the chapel. They are come thither and alighted, and asked the priest what the castle was, and he told them that it was the great Tintagel.[32]

Distractions

Items which serve to confuse the matter of Arthur's heritage are entries which have been presumed to refer to him in the biographical accounts of Welsh saints. However, the Arthur of these texts bears little resemblance to the Arthur of Guletic tradition or Grail lore. In contrast, he features as something of a tyrant and a troublesome interloper in the *Vita Cadoc*, the *Vita Carannog* and elsewhere.[33]

The identity of this other Arthur is found, however, in an allied medieval work called the *Epitome of the History of Britain*. It explains that he was installed as a prince of Dyfed by the Welsh bishop, St Dubricius of Llandaff, at the Cotswold town of Cirencester in 506.[34]

Apart from Arthur mac Aedàn, this character was the only other recorded Arthur of the 6th century, but he was not on good terms with the people of Dyfed, and his forebears were enemies of the native Welsh. Arthur of Dyfed was descended from disinherited Déssi royalty who were expelled from Ireland in the late 4th century.[35] When the Roman troops left South Wales in AD 383, the Déssi leaders came from Leinster to settle in Dyfed (Demetia).[36] According to the 12th-century *Life of St Gildas* (Badonicus) by Caradoc of Llancarfan, this Arthur was known as the *regi rebelli* (rebellious king), and he slew Hueil, the brother of Gildas, on the Isle of Man.

The 10th-century *Annales Cambriae* (Annals of Wales) explain that the Welsh Arthur perished at the Strife of Camlann,[37] and the 15th-century *Red Book of Hergest* (a collection of Welsh legends) states that this battle was fought in 537. The probable location was at Maes Camlan, south of Dinas Mawddwy.[38] If so, then it is quite possible that Arthur of Dyfed fought and died there; he was renowned for leading incursions into both Gwynedd and Powys, and his reputed grave known as the *Carnedd Arthur* (Arthur's Cairn) is in Snowdonia. In about 1140, Geoffrey of Monmouth introduced the *Gueith Camblan* into his *Historia*, but gave it the date of 542 and moved the battlefield to a site by the River Camel in Cornwall in order to comply with his Tintagel sequence.[39]

The name Camel became associated with the Arthurian tradition because of its abbreviated similarity to Camelot, although the word *camel* actually meant 'crooked' in reference to the river's winding course. The name became useful again in 1542 when King Henry VIII Tudor's antiquary, John Leland, identified an enormous Iron Age hill-fort in England's West Country as the Arthurian Court of Camelot.[40] His justification for this was that the South Cadbury site was near to the settlement of Camel in Somerset. From high above sea level, the site commands a wide view of the area, including the Tor at Glastonbury 12 miles away. Latter-day excavations at Cadbury during the 1960s unearthed the remains of a Dark Age feasting-hall but, appealing as it was to the tourist industry, there was absolutely nothing to associate the camp with King Arthur. Indeed, more than 40 constructions of a similar age and type have been found in the immediate area and there are many more elsewhere in the country.[41] Stemming from the name Cadwy-bury, the Cadbury fort appears to have been that of King Cadwy of Dumnonia, the 4th-century brother-in-law of Caradawc Vreichvras of Archenfield.

Unlike the situation with Tintagel, Arthur does not have any direct literary affiliation with Glastonbury. There are brief mentions of the place in the *Morte d'Arthur*, when Bedevere is said to have visited a chapel and hermitage at Glastonbury after Arthur's death, as did Lancelot after the death of Guinevere.[42] The main connection is made by virtue of Glastonbury having long been designated as the Isle of Avalon, to where Arthur was conveyed after being mortally wounded. Another association is provided by the fact that a grave was attributed to Arthur and Guinevere at the site of Glastonbury Abbey.

Avalon appears in Geoffrey's *Historia* as the place of Arthur's healing after his battle against Mordred at Camblan.[43] The theme was progressed in Geoffrey's other work, the *Vita Merlini* (Life of Merlin), wherein Avalon is called *Insula Pomoru* (the Island of Apples). In Celtic lore, this enchanted island was said to lie in the sea between Antrim and Lethet (the stretch of land between the Clyde and the Forth). Known as Arunmore, and now the Isle of Arran, it was the traditional home of Manannan, the sea-god, and was called *Emain Ablach* (the Place of Apples).[44] Geoffrey explained that the sacred isle was governed by nine holy sisters, whose leader was Morgen,[45] and that it was she who received the wounded Arthur into her care. As far back as the 1st century, the geographer Pomponius Mela had written of nine mysterious priestesses living under vows of chastity on the Isle of Sein, off the Brittany coast near

Carnac. Mela told of their powers to heal the sick in much the way that Morgen is portrayed in the *Vita Merlini*. In Grail literature, the Morgen of Geoffrey's account is identified as Morgaine (Morganna or Morgan le Fay), the sister of King Arthur who, along with other queens, carried the dying king on a barge to Avalon.[46] Medieval Christianity had difficulty assimilating a benevolent enchantress, especially one who was reminiscent of the Grail princesses who tended the wounds of the Fisher Kings. Consequently, Morgaine's healing arts became associated in some texts with sorcery and witchcraft.

Although Geoffrey's Avalon was based on the concept of a Celtic otherworld known as *A-val* or *Avilion*, neither he nor any other early writer identified a location for the mystical island. In fact, Avalon did not have to be anywhere in particular, and the nature of its attraction was the enigma itself. The only historical Avallon was in Burgundy, and the only island which carried such a legacy of enchantment was Arran in the Firth of Clyde. The Glastonbury identification of the Isle of Avalon's inland location as an island was justified on the basis that Glastonbury stood amid watery marshland and the nearby lake-villages of Godney and Meare dated from about 200 BC. Nevertheless, because of the geographical anomaly, the name Vale of Avalon emerged as a popular alternative.

Prior to that date there had been no recognized connection between Arthur and Glastonbury except for a passing mention by Caradoc of Llancarfan. In about 1130, he wrote that the Abbot of Glastonbury had been instrumental in Guinevere's release from her capture by King Melwas of Somerset, and that Arthur and Melwas met afterwards at Glastonbury.[47] But he did not suggest that Glastonbury was Avalon. The man who made the connection was the chronicler William of Malmesbury (d c1143). Twice in his *De Antiquitate Glastoniensis Ecclesiae*, he referred to Glastonbury as Avallonia – once in respect of King Lucius, and again in respect of St Patrick.[48]

In 1191 the monks of Glastonbury made use of William's comments in a way that transformed the fortunes of the Abbey.

Following the death of King Henry II, who had begun to fund restoration work after the great fire of 1184, his son and successor from 1189 was Richard I, the Lionheart. But Richard was more concerned with applying Treasury resources to the Holy Land Crusade. As a result, the Abbey funding was terminated, leaving the abbot and his monks in a difficult situation. Conveniently, however, when digging between a couple of Saxon monuments south of the Lady Chapel, they found the supposed remains of King Arthur and Queen Guinevere. Unearthed in a hollowed length of oak were the bones of a tall man, along with some smaller bones and some strands of fair hair. Such a find was of little consequence in its own right, but the monks were in luck, for buried not far above the log coffin there was said to have been a leaden cross embedded in stone. Upon the cross was inscribed *Hic Iacet Sepultus Inclytus Rex Arthurius In Insula Avallonia Cum Uxore Sua Secunda Wenneveria* (Here lies interred the renowned King Arthur in the Isle of Avalon with his second wife Guinevere).

Not only had the monks found Arthur's grave; they had also conveniently found written proof that Glastonbury was the Isle of Avalon. The Roman Church officials were far from happy that Guinevere was described as the king's second wife and it was asserted that the inscription was obviously incorrect. Undeterred, the monks decided that such an error could easily be remedied, and soon afterwards the legend reappeared, miraculously amended in both spelling and format. This time it dispensed with Guinevere altogether, so that it was far more in keeping with requirement: *Hic Iacet Sepultus Inclitus Rex Arturius In Insula Avalonia* (Here lies interred the renowned King Arthur in the Isle of Avalon).[49]

Quite why the monks should have dug in that particular spot is unclear. William of Malmesbury mentioned that Arthur had been conveyed to Avallonia after the battle of Camba, but he did not indicate that there was any grave to be found.[50] In fact, he wrote in his 1127 *Gesta Regum Anglorum* (Deeds of the English Kings) that 'the tomb of Arthur is nowhere beheld'. There is, however, a passage in his subsequent *De Antiquitate Glastoniensis Ecclesiae* which relates to the discovery of the Arthurian grave. Since William died about 48 years before the excavation, this item is clearly a later interpolation by another hand, but it does describe the two Saxon monuments. They were said to have been tall pyramid-shaped tombstones, each marked with a number of heavily weathered names, which stood at the edge of the monks' cemetery.[51] It is, therefore, not surprising that bones were found in the immediate vicinity.

According to the *Speculum Ecclesiae*, written in 1216 by the churchman Gerald of Wales (Giraldus Cambrensis), the dig was inspired by Bishop Henry of Worcester. But the 13th-century *Chronicle of Margam Abbey* in Llandaff contradicts this, stating that the monks were simply digging to bury one of their companions. Whatever the case, when the monks found the bones there was no tombstone or monument above the site, and there was nothing to associate the contents with King Arthur except for the inscription on the leaden cross. The Latin was, however, plainly of the Middle Ages, and differed from Dark Age Latin to the extent that today's English differs from that of Tudor times. The incident, as it evolved, was clearly a purposefully designed subterfuge, but the monks' purpose was well served and, following a successful publicity campaign, pilgrims flocked in their thousands to Glastonbury. The Abbey was substantially enriched with their donations and the complex was rebuilt as planned. As for the alleged bones of Arthur and Guinevere, they were deposited in two painted chests and placed in a black marble tomb before the high altar in 1278.

The entombed remains proved to be such a popular attraction that the monks determined to benefit further from their new-found tourist enterprise. It was apparent that if Arthur's bones created such a stir, then the relics of a saint or two would have a significant impact, so they took to their spades once more, and other discoveries were soon announced: the bones of St Patrick and St Gildas, along with the remains of Archbishop Dunstan, which most people knew had lain at Canterbury Cathedral for 200 years.

By the time of Henry VIII's Dissolution of the Monasteries, Glastonbury Abbey was boasting dozens of relics, including a

The Ruin of Glastonbury Abbey
(The chained area is the site of the old altar)

thread from Mary's gown, a sliver from Aaron's rod, a pair of cruets belonging to Joseph of Arimathea, and a stone that Jesus had apparently refused to turn into bread. But at the Dissolution in 1539, the Abbey's days of monastic activity were done and the relics all disappeared without trace, including the inscribed leaden cross. Since that time, no one has seen the supposed bones of Arthur and Guinevere; all that remains today is a notice marking the site of the 13th-century marble tomb in its position before the altar.

The Battles

The Scottish and Irish records provide details of the Battle of Camlann (variantly, Camblan, Camlan and Camba) as well as giving a full account of the battle that took place when 'Arthur penetrated the Hill of Badon', as described by Nennius.

In 516 Aurelius Ambrosius and Prince Gabràn of Scots launched a sea offensive against the hill-fort of King Cairill, known as Dun Baedàn (Badon Hill) in Antrim (see page 310). Gildas Badonicus wrote about this conflict in his *De Excidio Britanniae*, and correctly named Aurelius Ambrosius as the Guletic commander of the era.[52] Yet Nennius, writing at a later date, credited the battle of Badon Hill to King Arthur. Gildas Badonicus died in 572, but the battle to which Nennius referred did not take place until 575 – a second battle at Dun Baedàn. It is described in the *Bodleian Manuscripts*, the *Book of Leinster*, the *Book of Ballymote* and the *Chronicles of the Scots*. On that occasion, however, the Scots were defeated and Arthur's father, King Aedàn, was obliged to submit to Prince Baedàn mac Cairill at Ros-na-Righ on Belfast Lough.[53] Individual annals cite different names for this conflict and its location. The battle site is generally referred to as *Mons Badonicus* (Mont Badon) or *Dun Baedàn* (Badon Hill). Names for the battle include *Cath Badwn*, *Bellum Badonis* and *Obsessio Badonica* (the first suggests a battle, the second a war, and the third a siege).

Subsequently, in 581, King Aedàn managed to expel the Irish from Manau-Gododdin and the Forth.[54] Later, in 598, Arthur's cavalry drove the Irish out of Breichniog. King Aedàn was present at the battles, but Arthur's younger brothers Bran and Domangart were killed at Brechin on the Plain of Circinn. This was the battle at which Arthur and his brothers were said to have been present in the *Annals of Tigernach*.

The records denote that Aedàn was a close friend of Saint Columba, who installed him as King of Scots in 574.[55] When the saint's eventual successor, Abbot Adamnan of Iona (627–704), wrote the *Life of St Columba*, he referred to an occasion when Aedàn had consulted Columba about his due inheritor in Dalriada. The record states that he asked, 'Which of my three sons is to reign: Arthur, or Eochaid Find, or Domangart?' Columba replied:

> None of these three will be ruler, for they will fall in battle, slain by enemies; but now if thou hast any other younger sons, let them come to me ... A fourth son, Eochaid Buide, was summoned and the saint blessed him, saying to Aedàn, 'This is thy survivor'.[56]

Adamnan further confirmed that the prophecy was accurate, for Arthur was killed in battle a few years after Columba's own death in 597. His account continues:

> And thus it was that afterwards, in their season, all things were completely fulfilled; for Arthur and Eochaid Find were slain after no long interval of time in the Battle of the Miathi. Domangart was killed in Saxonia; and Eochaid Buide succeeded to the kingdom after his father.

Whether this consultation and prophecy actually took place as stated is not particularly important – Adamnan would clearly have known of the intervening events that he detailed – but the relevant fact is that Arthur was recorded as a likely successor in Dalriada. The rest of the account is entirely accurate: Eochaid Buide did succeed as King of Scots, and the battles at which Arthur and his brothers were killed (including the battle at Circinn) are detailed in the Scottish annals. Moreover, they reveal Adamnan's Battle of the Miathi as being the historical Battle of Camlann.

The Miathi (*Maeatae*) were a warlike tribe who settled in two separate groups, north of the Antonine and Hadrian Walls respectively. In 559 the Angles had occupied Deira (Yorkshire) and had driven the Miathi northwards from their original eastern domain. By 574, the Angles had also pushed up into Northumbrian Bernicia. Some of the Miathi decided to stay by the lower wall and make the best of it, while others moved further north to settle beyond the upper wall. The main stronghold of the northern Miathi was at Dunmyat, on the border of modern Clackmannanshire, in the district of Manau on the Forth.[57] Here, they had cast their lot with the Irish settlers, which made them none too popular with the Scots and Welsh. Despite King Cairill's 516 Badon Hill defeat in Antrim, the Irish remained boisterously obstructive in Manau, as a result of which the Guletic forces made their second, but unsuccessful, attack on Dun Baedàn in 575.

In subsequently defeating the Irish at Manau in 581, the Guletic troops also had to face the northern Miathi, whom they met in battle at the fort of Camelon (Camelyn), west of Falkirk, above the Antonine Wall.[58] In this event, the Scots were victorious and the Miathi were driven northwards, where they and their Irish confederates were further decimated by Pictish warriors. Afterwards, a nearby foundry construction on the River Carron was dubbed *Furnus Arthuri* (Arthur's Fire) to mark the Camelon event.[59] It was a long-standing attraction and was not demolished until the 18th-century Industrial Revolution.

A few years after subduing the remaining Irish in Breichniog, the Scots then had to face the southern Miathi, who had joined forces with the Northumbrian Angles on the Scottish Border. This confrontation was a protracted affair fought on two battlegrounds – the second conflict resulting from a short-term Scots retreat from the first. The forces initially met at Camlanna, an old Roman hill-fort at Castleheads by Hadrian's Wall.[60] Unlike the previous encounter, the Battle of Camlanna was a complete fiasco for the Guletic army. Falling for a diversionary tactic by the Miathi, they allowed the Angles to move behind them in a concerted north-westerly push towards Galloway and Strathclyde.

Only a few months earlier, the Angle king, Aethelfrith of Bernicia, had defeated King Rhydderch at Carlisle, thereby acquiring new territory along the reaches of the Solway Firth. The Dalriadan forces under Aedàn and Arthur were therefore under some pressure to intercept and halt the Angles' northward advance. They were said to have assembled immense forces drawn from the ranks of the Welsh princes, and they even gained support from Maeluma mac Baedàn of Antrim, the son of their erstwhile enemy. By that time, the Irish were themselves daunted by the prospect of an Anglo-Saxon invasion.

The Guletic troops faced King Aethelfrith, the Angles and the Miathi at Camlanna in 603. The initial affray was short-lived and the Celtic warriors were obliged to chase after the Angles, who had swept past them. They caught up again at Dawston-on-Solway (then called Degsastan in Liddesdale) and the *Chronicles of Holyrood* and of *Melrose* refer to the battle site as Dexa Stone.[61] It was here that Arthur (aged 44) fell alongside Maeluma mac Baedàn.

The battle, which began at Camlanna and ended at Dawston, was one of the fiercest in Celtic history. The *Annals of Tigernach* call it 'the day when half the men of Scotland fell', and it was a complete disaster for King Aedàn.[62] Although Aethelfrith was victorious, heavy losses were sustained by all. His brothers Theobald and Eanfrith were slain, along with all their men,[63] and King Aedàn left the field having lost two sons, Arthur and Eochaid Find.

Aethelfrith never reached Strathclyde, but his success at Dawston enabled the Northumbrian territory to be extended northwards to the Firth of Forth, incorporating the Lothians.[64] Ten years later, in 613, Aethelfrith besieged Chester and brought Cumbria fully under Angle control.[65] This drove a permanent geographical wedge between the Welsh and the Strathclyde Britons. The Mercian Angles then pushed westwards, forcing the Welsh behind what was eventually to be the line of Offa's Dyke,[66] while the Wessex Saxons encroached beyond Exeter, annexing the South West peninsula.

In time, the once conjoined Celtic lands of Strathclyde, Northumbria, Wales and Dumnonia were totally isolated from each other. King Aedàn of Dalriada died within three years of the Camlanna disaster, which was said to have opened the door to the final conquest of Britain by the Anglo-Saxons. In the years following the defeats at Camlanna and Dawston (jointly called *di Bellum Miathorum*: the Battle of the Miathi), the old kingdoms of the Britons began to expire.

Once and Future Kings

The Book of Descent

Quite apart from Arthur's historical demise and his imagined grave sites at Glastonbury and elsewhere, his legendary departure to Avalon is attached to a strange and nearly unique mythology. In relating the last of King Arthur, Geoffrey of Monmouth did not mention his death in the *Historia Regum Britanniae*. He stated only that:

> Arthur himself, our renowned king, was mortally wounded and was carried off to the Isle of Avalon, so that his wounds might be attended to.

In the *Vita Merlini* it was added that Arthur's sister Morgen:

> placed the king on a golden bed and with her own hand she uncovered his honourable wound … At length she said that health could be restored to him if he stayed with her for a long time and made use of her healing art.

When compiling his *Roman de Brut*, Robert Wace embellished the Arthurian content with the introduction of *Excalibur* and the Round Table, but a most significant addition came at the end of the story. In respect of Arthur's wounding, Wace put forward an intriguing new concept:

He had himself carried to Avalon for the treatment of his wounds.
He is still there awaited by the Britons, as they say and believe,
and will return and may live again.

Layamon, a priest of Areley Kings in Worcestershire, took up the
theme in his *Brut* – a work that had a significant impact on the writing of medieval history in England. Still within the 12th-century
time-frame of Geoffrey and Wace, and long after Arthurian times,
Layamon related in respect of Arthur:

The Britons yet believe that he is alive, and dwells in Avalon …
and the Britons still await the time when Arthur will come again.

The suggestion in these works was that, by virtue of Morgaine's
healing powers, Arthur's wound was not fatal, and that he lived on
through the centuries in Avalon, awaiting the day of his return. And
so the various accounts continued down to Malory's *Morte d'Arthur*,
which claimed:

Yet some men say in many parts of England that King Arthur is
not dead, but had by the will of our Lord Jesu into another place;
and men say that he shall come again, and he shall win the holy
cross … Many men say that there is written upon his tomb this
verse: *Hic jacet Arthurus Rex, quondam Rex, Rex que futurus* (Here
lies King Arthur, King Once, King in the Future).[1]

In some cases Arthur is depicted as somehow immortal, while in
others his return is seen as a resurrection. Not since the time of Jesus
Christ had such a prophecy or hoped for occurrence been portrayed
within the sentimental realm of Christendom. Both Jesus and
Arthur, in their individual ways, had been perceived as semi-divine
opposers of enforced subjugation, and it was said that they would
each rise and come again in the future. In Arthur's case, the
prophecy did not emerge in his own historical era, but more than
500 years later during the reign of King Henry II of England, the first

monarch of the House of Plantagenet and the husband of Eleanor of Aquitaine.

Subsequent to Arthur's unsuccessful final attempt against the Anglo-Saxons, the land became known as England under their rule. The nation evolved well during their era, with such notable kings as Alfred of Wessex (871–899), who defended the realm against invading Vikings. With his famous statue now at Winchester, Alfred was the only English king ever to be called 'the Great'. In later times, however, following the death of Alfred's descendant King Edward the Confessor in 1066, Harold Godwinson lost his crucial battle against the invader William of Normandy at Hastings on the south coast. England was then plunged into a feudal regime and the Saxon era was over. But it was not Alfred or Harold, nor any other warrior-king of the Saxon period who became the icon of later Plantagenet times; it was King Arthur whose legacy prevailed from a long distant era. It was the romantic notion of the Arthurian court and its ideal of the Round Table which cemented the Age of Chivalry in England.

Three centuries later, when Henry Tudor defeated Richard III at Bosworth Field, and usurped the throne as King Henry VII in 1485, the memory of Arthur was heightened when Sir Thomas Malory's work was published in that very same year. The questions that must therefore be asked are: Why Arthur? Why was it that, from the 12th-century reign of Henry II, writers attached to the House of Anjou in Britain and France introduced the concept of Arthurian knights questing for the Holy Grail?

The answers to these questions lie in the fact that the Grail was stated in the very first instance by Robert de Boron in *Joseph d'Arimathie* to be a chalice containing the blood of Jesus known as the *Sangréal*. It was also given in the 8th-century tradition of Waleran as representing a 'book of descent' – the descent of the Fisher Kings and the Grail Family, whose 'roots and branches' were further defined in Wolfram's *Parzival* from the registry of Anjou.

Plainly, the Quest of the Grail had nothing to do with a desired reversion to the old kingdoms of Celtic Britain. The concept of the perceived Wasteland, as caused by the loss of the Grail, had a much wider significance in France as well as in Britain. All Grail tradition was based on the notion that the original guardian of the sacred heritage was Joseph of Arimathea (Jesus' brother James), and that the barren land would only return to fertility when the wound of the original Fisher King (Jesus) was healed. This wound was seen to be perpetuated through the generations of the maimed Fisher Kings – the *Desposyni* heirs of the *Sangréal*. Despite all references to the various Fisher Kings in succession, Arthur (the son of Aedàn the Pendragon and Ygerna del Acqs) emerged as a unique kingly descendant in the conjoined bloodlines of both Jesus and James. Thus the Grail and its guardian were seen to be inherent in the same man.

The wound of Jesus, as applied to the Fisher Kings, was determined as the spear thrust of the centurion in order to test whether or not he was dead on the cross. It became known as the *Dolorous Stroke*, but the gospels do not suggest that this action was fatal in itself. In literary terms, the emblematic wound of Grail lore was indicative of the loss of Jesus' dignity by way of the Roman persecution of the *Desposyni* heirs. It related to their overthrow by way of a contrived Apostolic Succession and the papal denouncement of Mary Magdalene in 591. This was just a few years before the death of Arthur, whose family mentor St Columba of the Celtic kindred died in 597. The last six years of Arthur's life until 603 saw not just the final throes of Anglo-Saxon conquest, but also the crushing of the Celtic Church of his ancestry by St Augustine of Rome throughout Angle-land. Then, to complete the crucifixion of the *Desposyni*, the true *Dolorous Stroke* that sliced into their messianic heritage was the fraudulent *Donation of Constantine*, enforced throughout Christendom by papal decree in 751.

Achieving the Sangréal

In the early 12th century, the ailing remnant of the Celtic Church in Scotland was financially assisted by the Cistercian abbot St Bernard de Clairvaux, patron and protector of the Knights Templars of Jerusalem. In 1128, Bernard's cousin Hugues de Payen, founder and Grand Master of the Templars, met with King David I in Scotland, and a firm bond was cemented between the Cistercians and the Celtic Church. In 1203, a new Cistercian abbey was established on Iona, where Columba's original monastery had been demolished by Vikings in 807, and at length all the Celtic abbacies became Cistercian.

With a belief structure that was independent of the Church of Rome, the Cistercian brotherhood was closer to the Celtic fraternity than any other monastic movement of the Middle Ages. St Bernard had likened Mary Magdalene's historic predicament to that of the lost bride in the Song of Solomon.[2] His English counterpart, the Lincolnshire abbot Gilbert de Hoyland, had associated Galahad with the family of Jesus, whilst claiming that the flocks of the Church had become separated from the truth.[3] Then, just a few decades later, Cistercian monks produced the *Vulgate Cycle* of Arthurian and Grail texts, which brought Galahad centre stage as the knight who achieved the *Sangréal*. Even his father Lancelot, the bravest knight in the world, could not succeed in the Quest, and a central theme of the *Vulgate* is that purity and nobility are the required qualities of a chivalrous Grail knight, not battlefield and tournament honours.

Of all the Grail works, the Cistercian *Vulgate* collection is undoubtedly the most spiritual in terms of its biblical teaching. The *Queste del Saint Graal* in particular focuses many times on chapter 6 of the gospel of John in which Jesus discusses the bread of heaven: the *manna* of Moses. The *Queste* cites this bread as being the key to the divine mystery of the Holy Grail.[4] In this regard, Jesus foreshadowed his Last Supper address when he announced that the eucharistic bread represented his own body, the *cors benicon*, which became the *Corbenic* of Grail lore. In association with this, Jesus defined the wine as symbolic of his own royal blood, the *Sang Réal*.

Jesus Washing Peter's Feet, by Julius Schnorr von Carolsfeld (1794–1872)

Alongside these aspects of the Grail Mass, as instituted by Josephes in the *Queste*, was the ultimate reference to the desired humility of chivalric behaviour, which became known as the Grail Code. It was a parable for the human condition which asserted that the primary quest of life must be to achieve through service to others. It is not by chance that, from the Middle Ages, the motto of Britain's Princes of Wales (the senior heirs to the throne) has been *Ich dien* (I serve). The motto was first granted to Edward the Black Prince, the son of Edward III Plantagenet, during the Age of Chivalry. It was this princely concept that the lay disciples of Jesus found so hard to comprehend in their messianic leader. This is well demonstrated in John 13:4–11, when Jesus washed the apostles' feet at the Last Supper. Peter queried the action, saying, 'Thou shalt never wash my feet', but Jesus was insistent, replying with finality, 'I have given you an example that ye should do as I have done to you'.

There is nothing in history to suggest that King Arthur's 6th-century warriors ever quested for the Holy Grail. There was no need for any such quest during Arthur's lifetime. The *Sangréal* was not considered lost until the Church's destruction of the bloodline inheritance was complete. This act of injury and betrayal was paralleled in the *Vulgate Cycle* and other accounts by way of the adulterous affair between Lancelot and Arthur's wife Guinevere. Their illicit liaison caused the breakdown of the fellowship of the Round Table, the decline of the kingdom of Camelot, and the loss of the dignity of the Holy Grail. Thereby, some time before the affray at Camlanna and his physical wound from the treacherous Mordred, Arthur received his spiritual wound in an act of betrayal that we are told 'began with a kiss'. This betrayal of Arthur by Lancelot is a reflection of the gospel story of Jesus wherein Judas, a trusted member of his apostolic circle, betrayed Jesus with a kiss in the Garden of Gethsemane as a precursor to his physical ordeal.[5]

The Court of Love

It is not insignificant that the linking of Arthurian history with legends of the Holy Grail took place during the Consort reigns of Eleanor of Aquitaine, first as Queen of France and then as Queen of England. During this overall period, 1137–1204, Grail romance was born and flourished, although Eleanor's own life was far from tranquil. Having divorced Louis VII and married Henry II in 1152, she soon began to tire of his philanderings and, in 1169, she instigated a separation and established her own court at Poitiers. But, in 1173, Henry had Eleanor seized in France and she spent the next 10 years in various English prisons including a dungeon at Winchester Castle. During the first three years of these confinements, Henry's favourite mistress was Rosamund Clifford, but in 1176 she died mysteriously, and tradition relates that Eleanor (although herself restrained under guard) was accused of poisoning Fair Rosamund.

In reality, the first historical mention of this accusation comes from an anonymous 14th-century manuscript which actually referred to Eleanor of Provence (Henry II's daughter-in law), not his wife Eleanor of Aquitaine.[6] From 1183 until Henry's death in 1189, Eleanor was maintained in better circumstances under house arrest, but she eventually gained her freedom and was still the richest and most influential woman in Western Europe until she finally retired to the Sanctuary of St Mary Magdalene in Fontevrault[7] and died in 1204.

Eleanor's life was very much like a Grail adventure in itself, and her court at Poitiers became known as the Court of Love.[8] The concept of Courtly Love (*Amour Courtois*) was a legacy of her family's troubadour culture in Aquitaine and Provence. It was a medieval system of attitudes, myths and etiquette that spawned several genres of medieval literature, including Grail romance. The principle of *Amour Courtois* was that a knight would dedicate his professional life to the love of a lady whom he would champion, but that such a love could not exist within marriage. In general terms it might apply to a knight's love for the wife of his liege lord – precisely as depicted in the tale of Lancelot and Guinevere, although they broke the rules and pushed the boundaries of acceptable etiquette with disastrous results.

Despite the romantically conceived ideal behind this chivalric form of worship, it was pronounced ungodly by the Church because it placed womanhood on a pedestal of veneration. Even worse in the eyes of the bishops was the fact that the women always controlled the relationships, and could dictate whether or not they accepted the knightly devotions. This level of female status was declared by the Church as blasphemous and contrary to the will of God. By the early 13th century, the ideas of courtly tradition were formally condemned as being heretical, and it is no coincidence that the cult of the Virgin Mary grew rapidly during this period to counter the secular perception of women in noble society. Meanwhile, the troubadours had long revered their own Great Lady (*la Dompna del Aquae*) in Mary Magdalene, whom they called the Grail of the World.

Just four years after Eleanor's death, Pope Innocent III decided to take action against the Magdalene culture of Provence. In 1208, he admonished the people of Languedoc for their heretical beliefs, and in the following year he sent 30,000 troops into the region with the instruction to exterminate the sect of the *Cathari* (the Pure Ones). According to Dominican annals held at the Historical Institute in Rome, the Cathars believed that 'Mary Magdalene was in reality the wife of Christ'.[9]

More than 450 years after the *Donation of Constantine*, and despite all efforts to suppress such a belief, the desposynic legacy of Mary and Jesus persisted in the land of the troubadours. The slaughter in Languedoc continued for 35 years, claiming tens of thousands of lives and culminating in the hideous massacre at the fortress seminary of Montségur II, where more than 200 hostages were set up on stakes and burned alive in 1244. In defence of the Cathars, Queen Eleanor's colleague St Bernard de Clairvaux had stated some time earlier that 'No sermons are more Christian than theirs, and their morals are pure'. And yet still the papal armies came, in the outward guise of a holy mission, to eradicate their community from the landscape in what became known as the Albigensian Crusade.[10]

The reason why the invasion and assault was left until 1209 was specifically because of Eleanor of Aquitaine. She was so prominent and popular that even the Pope dared not cross swords with her. It was Eleanor's ancestor, William I de Toulouse, who had established the original Languedoc monastery of St Guilhelm-le-Désert long before in about the year 800.[11] Although the Magdalene traditions of the Provençal territories had been a constant problem for the papal establishment, Cathar society was perceived as a positive threat to the Church during Eleanor's lifetime. They were fervent Christians of an old style, who spoke their own language (the *langue d'oc*) and would not acknowledge the Catholic bishops. This 12th-century period had also seen the rise of the Cistercian brotherhood and St Bernard's inauguration of the Knights Templars, whose required obedience from 1128 was to the Bethany foundation of Mary Magdalene and Martha.[12] Above all, there had been a widespread awareness of the *Desposyni* culture in the public domain by way of the Arthurian and Grail romances. These had largely been instigated by Queen Eleanor and her daughter, Countess Marie of Champagne, in liaison with the Templars, the Cistercians and the Court of Anjou.

Thus it was that, following Eleanor's death at the age of 82, the Pope and his staunchly Catholic ally King Philippe II of France laid their plans to decimate her legacy by using whatever measures of force were necessary. Albeit the Church had appropriated the chalice of Grail tradition for its own eucharistic bread and wine ceremony, Grail lore was itself proclaimed a heresy. Catholic literature states: 'The Grail legend contained the elements of which the Church could not approve. Its sources are not in canonical scripture, and the claims of sanctity made for the Grail were refuted by their very extravagance'.[13]

Thereafter, the bishops maintained such a tight control over published literature that, onwards from the 13th century, very little was added to the Grail collection in Europe apart from some new translations and a few retellings. In Britain, there emerged some independent tales concerning Gawain and Merlin, but the next major work appeared when Sir Thomas Malory took up the cause with his *Morte d'Arthur* in 15th-century England. Subsequently, notable writers such as John Dryden, Sir Richard Blackmore and Richard Hole entered the Arthurian arena, but it was not until Victorian times that a revived Grail fever took hold with works from Sir Walter Scott, Howard Pyle, Lord Lytton and Alfred, Lord Tennyson. The Pre-Raphaelite brotherhood, along with Gustave Doré and others introduced a wealth of new pictorial art, and the operas *Tristan and Isolde* and *Parsifal* by Richard Wagner brought the old Grail cycle to the musical stage.

Camelot

In more recent times, the best known Arthurian work is probably *The Once and Future King* by the English author T[erence] H[anbury] White.[14] Published in 1958, the novel's success became assured when it was transposed by Alan Jay Lerner and Frederick Loewe into the 1960s stage musical and subsequent cinema movie *Camelot*. Initially, the story relies largely on comedy aspects relating to Merlin's incompetence with magic and Pellinore's obsessive hunt for the mysterious Questing Beast. But the tale becomes gradually darker and more deeply psychological as the individual motives of the various characters are examined. In the course of this, Merlin somehow lives backwards in time, while at the end of the tale young Thomas Malory of Warwick makes an out-of-time cameo appearance. Arthur (whom Merlin calls Wart) insists that Malory should preserve the tragic story of the kingdom of Camelot for posterity.

The most important focus of White's account is not the storyline itself, which is reconstructed and does not follow any traditional format, but the manner in which the principles of the original Grail Code are subtly conveyed throughout. Whereas writers such as Malory had glorified the military aspects of Arthur and his knights, White implies that Arthur is a great king not because of his strength on the battlefield, but because of his achievement in translating Merlin's moral judgements into a just system of governance. The story concentrates on the ultimate relationship between strength and justice, which Arthur calls 'Might and Right', and he learns that they are not synonymous. He therefore becomes successful because he does not use force to maintain a balanced political system, but he fails to realize that treachery can exist within any establishment, no matter how well founded. Ultimately, his ideal of equality for all, as symbolized by the Round Table, collapses within the fraternity of his own court, and the kingdom of Camelot falls into ruin.

Just as in the earlier Grail stories, the parallel between the idealistic missions of Jesus and Arthur is drawn – missions that eventually

Achieving the Sangréal, by Aubrey Beardsley, 1893

failed because there are always others with opposing vested interests. In Roman times, Arthurian times, the Middle Ages and the modern day, leaders like Jesus and Arthur have had to confront an avaricious society complex based on the survival of the fittest. In the real courtroom and battlefield world of this competitive arena, Right is rarely seen to prevail over Might, and if the latter does not exist as an effective defence mechanism, the kingdoms of individuals and nations fall.

In such instances therefore, Grail lore reflects the precept that although Right and Might are not synonymous, perhaps the greatest strength of success exists in Right backed by Might. The most noble of quests are fraught with obstacles and setbacks – the dragons and adversaries of the way, which have to be faced and overcome if the quests are to succeed. Neither Jesus nor Arthur have ever been perceived to have failed in their ambitions because they were wrong; they lost their battles simply because their enemies were stronger. Whether from history, myth or legend, they are both remembered and admired because of a majority opinion that their causes were right. The spirit of their ideals lives on, and whatever interpretations might be placed on the speculative notions of their prophesied returns, their mutual legacy remains in their shared identification as the Once and Future Kings.

End of the Reigns

With the death of Arthur, the potentially dual desposynic heritage of 6th-century Britain was terminated. History relates that Arthur's half-sister Morgause had a son called Mordred. Some traditions claim that Arthur was his father; others tell that Mordred was the son of Lot of Lothian. But either way, Modred was slain at Dawston along with Arthur, and there is no further record of his family. Lot and Morgause are also listed as having been the parents of the knights Gareth and Gawain, but there are no recorded descendants in their lines. The desposynic posterity of Urien and Arthur's sister Morgaine succeeded via their only known son, Ywain, in Brittany, and his line cannot be traced beyond two more generations.

The kingly branches of Arimatheac descent ceased to be operative in England from the middle 7th century, and the registers give way thereafter to the Anglo-Saxon monarchs. There will have been many families who evolved from the various branches along the way, but the generations are not individually recorded. In Wales, a branch of the succession from Cadwaladr (the last Pendragon) continued to reign through the Saxon and Norman periods until finally overthrown by England's House of Plantagenet, which had its own desposynic root in the Anjou tradition from Faramund.

In Scotland, the desposynic legacy from Brychan was retained by Aedàn's son Eochaid Buide, progressing through the early Kings of Scots into the noble families of Moray and Lochaber. Meanwhile in France, a desposynic cousin line of the Merovingians in descent from Faramund became the Senechals of Dol in Brittany. Marrying into the Lochaber strain, they became the High Stewards of Scotland in the 12th century. Then, by way of a further marriage into the House of Bruce, they became the Stewart Kings of Scots from 1371.[15] It can therefore be said that, although many centuries of marital dilution had occurred in the interim, these kings emerged distantly from two ultimately desposynic strains.

Given that Emperor Charlemagne of the Franks had a Merovingian grandmother, it can equally be said that the Carolingians of France had desposynic ancestry in the female line. But, although the Merovingians were themselves deposed in 751, their own lines of descent continued alongside. These families can be traced through the centuries, marrying into other French houses, onwards to Godefroi de Bouillon and the 12th-century Crusader Kings of Jerusalem. In parallel, the Capetian and Valois monarchs of France inherited a remnant of Merovingian heritage in their female lines.

The overall picture of traceable generations in Britain and France is extremely complex, even without considering all the many branches and offshoots that are not in the registers. With nearly 2,000 years of descent from the time of Jesus and Mary Magdalene, or indeed from any couple in the 1st century, the possible number of desposynic descendants at the present time, although now vague, obscure and dynastically quite irrelevant, would run into millions. There is neither any merit nor uniqueness in the fact that anyone today might be descended from a person that far back in time. Vast numbers of people could trace their lines back into the family strains cited in this book, and eventually we all stem from common ancestors.

Heirs of the Lord

As related at the beginning of this book, 'history' is not necessarily an expression of fact; it is a compilation of documented record. By its very nature, it does not amount to proof of anything; it constitutes written evidence of past characters and events. The content of the Bible is not in itself a proof of its inherent fact, but it is documentary evidence of what its writers believed to be true at the time. The same can be said of all other chronicles, annals and books of historical record including the many primary sources given in the Notes and References section of this work. What we do know for a fact – whether dealing with Boudicca, Charlemagne, Joan of Arc, or whoever – is that the currently accessible records of history are the best and the only records that we have. Whether or not we elect to believe them is a matter of personal choice. Only the Church has enforced dogma; history does not. Whether presented as hard or circumstantial evidence, history is always open to interpretation, and clearly its authors are not consistently objective. Just as in modern news reporting, there have always been personal, national, social, political or religious opinions to consider.

Within the context of all this fall the accounts of the persecution and generational records of the *Desposyni* heirs. Onwards from the 1st century, they were recorded by historians such as Hegesippus, Africanus and Eusebius. Their stories were progressed through the Dark Ages into medieval and later times, with a legacy that prevailed especially in Britain and France to become romanticized in the legends of the Holy Grail. None of the individual or conjoined accounts of the characters concerned can be proven as historically accurate any more than can the existence of Jesus himself. On the other side of the scales, the evidence might not be overwhelming, but it is solid and it is consistent. It is also apparent from centuries of Vatican records that the Church believed these various generational accounts to be true even if the characters' deeds were often fictional. The bishops never denied the fact; they simply proclaimed such supportive beliefs to be heretical, stating that 'the claims of sanctity made for the Grail were refuted by their very extravagance'. It was, after all, the Vatican hierarchy who themselves described the *Desposyni* inheritors as being the Heirs of the Lord, 'those persons in the bloodline with Jesus through his mother'.[16]

Without the long-standing tradition of descendants from Jesus and his brother James, who ultimately became known as the Grail Family, the Apostolic Succession of Rome would never have been questioned; Mary Magdalene need never have been denounced; the *Donation of Constantine* would never have been deemed necessary, neither would the Church's condemnation of the troubadours or the papal annihilation of the Cathars. Over and above these things, the very idea of the *Sangréal* heritage of the messianic 'blood royal' and the emergent quest for its reinstatement into the Christian doctrine would never have been conceived. All things considered, maybe the evidence is overwhelming after all.

Notes and References

Chapter 1: Forging the Testament

1 *The Concise Oxford Dictionary of Current English*, Oxford University Press, Oxford, 1995 – History: 'A continuous, usually chronological, record of important or public events.'

2 Cornelius Tacitus, *The Annals of Imperial Rome* (trans, Michael Grant), Penguin, London, 1996, ref AD 64, p 365.

3 Flavius Josephus, *The Antiquities of the Jews* in *The Works of Flavius Josephus*, (trans, William Whiston), Milner & Sowerby, London, 1870, bk XX, ch IX:1.

4 *Ibid*, bk XVIII, ch III:3.

5 The term was first recorded in Antioch, Syria, in AD 44. *See* Establishment of the Antioch Christian movement in Norman J Bull, *The Rise of the Church*, Heinemann, London, 1967, ch 3, pp 58–9.

6 By AD 397, Constantine was long departed and Emperor Honorius was on the throne, along with Pope Sicirius, the 6th imperial Bishop of Rome.

7 Tacitus, *The Annals of Imperial Rome*, ref AD 64, p 365.

8 Eusebius of Caesarea, *Ecclesiastical History* (trans, CF Crusè), George Bell, London, 1874, bk III, ch 4, p 69.

9 Luke 1:3 and Acts 1:1.

10 Luke 1:1–4.

11 *The Catholic Encyclopedia*, Robert Appleton, New York, NY, 1910, vol X, *see* Gospel of St Matthew.

12 The codex was acquired by the Vatican in 1209. It includes both the Old and New Testaments.

13 *The Catholic Encyclopedia*, vol IV, *see* Codex Vaticanus.

14 *Ibid*, vol IX, *see* Gospel of St Mark.

15 Many thousands of other Greek manuscripts of New Testament books have been discovered in the past 100 years, but none is as old as the Vatican and Sinai codices.

16 *The Catholic Encyclopedia*, vol IV, *see* Codex Sinaiticus.

17 1 Corinthians 15:1.

18 A striking example occurs in Matthew 9:6, Mark 2:10 and Luke 5:24 which all contain the parenthesis ('saith he to the sick of the palsy'). This would be an uncanny coincidence if they were independently produced.

19 James M Robinson (ed) and the Coptic Gnostic Project, *The Nag Hammadi Library*, Institute for Antiquity and Christianity, EJ Brill, Leiden, 1977, 'The Gospel of Thomas', item 77, p 126.

20 *Ibid*, item 114, p 130.

21 *Ibid*, intro, p 117.

22 NJ Bull, *The Rise of the Church*, ch 4, p 84.

23 For information concerning 'Q', *see* Marcus Borg (ed), *The Lost Gospel Q*, Ulysses Press, Berkeley, CA, 1996.

24 NJ Bull, *The Rise of the Church*, ch 4, p 84.

25 *The Catholic Encyclopedia*, vol V, *see* Ecclesiastical Art.

26 *See*, for example, 'The Wine Press' by John Spencer Stanhope: plate 12 in
    Laurence Gardner, *Bloodline of the Holy Grail*, HarperCollins, London, 2002.

27 Matthew 26:26–9.

28 In ancient Israel, grapes were also indicative of peace. James Hastings (ed),
    Dictionary of the Bible, T&T Clark, Edinburgh, 1909, *see* Vine and Vineyard.
    The Omer Cup was designed to hold fruit, notably grapes, not liquid.
    Although an *omer* is a dry-weight measurement, the original cup capacity is
    obscure. It was said to be equivalent to 1/10th of an *ephah*, which equates
    roughly with 22 litres of liquid. Hence an omer cup would hold about 2.2
    litres (around 3.8 imperial pints).

29 The English translated text for this work is currently published as Wolfram
    von Eschenbach, *Parzival* (trans, AT Hatto), Penguin , London, 1980.

Chapter 2: From Rags to Riches

1 *Encyclopaedia Judaica*, Keter Publishing, Jerusalem, 1906, under Bar Kokba
   and Bar Kokba War.

2 Malachi Martin, *The Decline and Fall of the Roman Church*, Secker & Warburg,
   London, 1982, ch 1, p 21.

3 Celsus, *Alethès Lógos* (the True Discourse), AD 178 – *see* in *The Catholic
   Encyclopedia*, vol III, under Celsus the Platonist.

4 Irenaeus, *Adversus Haereses*, AD c175, vol I, bk I, ch 26:2. *See* also *The Catholic
   Encyclopedia*, vol V, under Ebionites.

5 A dramatic account of the persecutions is given in Eusebius, *Ecclesiastical
   History* (1838 edn), bk V, ch 1, pp 150–62.

6 The experiences of these women are told in WH Shewring (trans), *The
   Passion of Perpetua and Felicity*, Sheed and Ward, London, 1931.

7 *The Catholic Encyclopedia*, vol III, under Celsus the Platonist.

8 Marcus Minucius Felix, *The Octavius of Marcus Minucius Felix*, Paulist Press,
   New York, NY, 1974, item 9. By virtue of translation difficulties from ancient
   Latin, there are some variations in individual editions of this work. For
   example in GW Clarke (trans), *The Octavius of Marcus Minucius Felix*,
   Newman Press, New York, NY, 1974. Here the word 'flour' is used instead
   of 'meal'; the word 'pontiff' instead of 'priest', etc. Essentially, however, the
   content is the same, as is the case in the further translation, JH Freese
   (trans), *The Octavius of Marcus Minucius Felix*, Macmillan, New York, 1919.
        Even earlier than the *Octavius*, the Christian apologist Justin Martyr had
   written in the 2nd century about accusations of Christians consuming
   human flesh. The Church Father, Clement of Alexandria, also wrote on this
   subject in the 3rd century, disassociating Christians at large with references
   to debauchery at Christian love feasts. And in the 4th century Epiphanius of
   Salamis wrote of a Christian group eating babies in representation of the
   body of Christ. *See* Robert L Wilken, *The Christians as the Romans Saw Them*,
   Yale University Press, New Haven, CT, 1984, ch 1, pp 19–20.

9 M Martin, *The Decline and Fall of the Roman Church*, ch 1, p 22.

10 Richard E Reubenstein, *When Jesus Became God*, Harcourt, Orlando, FL, 1999, ch 2, p 33.

11 According to the contemporary Roman writer Lactantius, Galerius suffered and died from a painful bowel disease. Before his demise, he became obsessed with the frightful deaths of other Christian persecutors such as Nero, Domitian, Decius, Valerian, Aurelian and Diocletian. Lactantius (a prosecutor of Christians for Diocletian) wrote in his *De Mortibus Persecutorum* (On the Deaths of the Persecutors) that the bad ends were attributed by Galerius to the persecutions. In an attempt to ease his own fate, he relaxed his edict of February AD 303, and issued a cancellation edict of toleration in April AD 311, just before his death in the May.

12 *Ibid*, ch 1, p 35.

13 George F Jowett, *The Drama of the Lost Disciples*, Covenant Books, London, 1961, ch 12, pp 125–6. Also *see* Gladys Taylor, *Our Neglected Heritage*, Covenant Books, London, 1974, vol I, pp 40–45.

14 *Ibid*, vol I, p 33. In attempts to veil the royal heritage of Linus, he has often been portrayed as if he were a lowly slave, but this has not removed the thorn from the Church's side and, because of it, the papal doctrine has to be considered 'infallible' when emanating from the throne. Without this doctrine, the whole concept of a structured progression of high bishops in Apostolic Succession from Peter would collapse, since Peter was neither a Bishop of Rome, nor of anywhere else.

15 Three British bishops attended the Council of Arles in 314: those of London, York and Caerleon.

16 *The Catholic Encyclopedia*, vol IV, under Archaeology of the Cross.

17 *The Catholic Encyclopedia*, vol X, under Holy Nails. The Iron Crown of Lombardy is both a reliquary and one of the most ancient royal insignia of Europe. A narrow band of iron about one centimetre (three-eighths of an inch), set within the crown, is said to be beaten from a crucifixion nail of Jesus. The first to possess the crown was Queen Theodelinda of the Lombards, 570–628. Holy Roman Emperors such as Charlemagne, Otto I, Henry IV, and Frederick I Barbarossa were crowned with Lombardy relic.

18 *See* Geoffrey of Monmouth, *The History of the Kings of Britain* (trans, Lewis Thorpe), Penguin London, 1966, part III:vi, pp 131–2.

19 *The Compact Oxford English Dictionary*, Oxford University Press, Oxford, 1971, under Propaganda.

20 For example in David Farmer (ed), *Oxford Dictionary of the Saints*, Oxford University Press, Oxford, 1997.

21 PJ Chandlery, *Pilgrim Walks in Rome*, Manresa Press, London, 1905.

22 The Roman document most commonly cited to uphold the anti-Colchester message is a manuscript written in the late 4th century (after Helena's death) by Ammianus Marcellinus, from which the original information concerning Helena (AD c248–328) has gone missing. There is, nevertheless, a spuriously entered margin note from the 1600s, which gives the newly

devised Church-approved details on which the Gibbonites and others based their subsequent opinions.

23 Caesar Baronius, *Annales Ecclesiastici a Christi nato ad annum 1198*, Hieronymi Scoti, Venice, 1612.

Chapter 3: Feuds and Fragments

1   F Josephus, *The Antiquities of the Jews*, bk XX, ch IX:1.

2   *Ibid*, bk XVIII, ch III/3. This extract is often referred to as the *Testimonium Flavianum* (Testimony of Flavius).

3   Timothy Freke and Peter Gandy, *The Jesus Mysteries*, Three Rivers, New York, NY, 2001, ch 7, p 137.

4   NJ Bull, *The Rise of the Church*, ch 6, p 155.

5   *Ibid*, ch 5, p 125.

6   For recommended study concerning the early Christians, *see* RL Wilken, *The Christians as the Romans Saw Them*.

7   *The Life of Flavius Josephus* is published in F Josephus, *The Works of Flavius Josephus* as an introduction to *The Antiquities and Wars of the Jews*.

8   AN Wilson, *Jesus*, Sinclair-Stevenson, London, 1992, ch 4, p 89.

9   Geza Vermes, 'The Josephus Portrait of Jesus Reconsidered' in *Occident and Orient: A Tribute to the Memory of A Schieber*, Akademiai Kiado, Budapest, EJ Brill, Leiden, 1988, p 373. *See* also AN Wilson, *Jesus*, ch 4, p 89.

10 Origen, 'Commentaries on the Gospel of St Matthew: The Brethren of Jesus' in Rev Alexander Roberts and James Donaldson (eds), *The Ante-Nicene Fathers – The Writings of the Fathers down to* AD *325*, T&T Clark, Edinburgh, 1867, vol X, ch 17.

11 Origen, 'Against Celsus' in *Ibid*, vol I, ch 47.

12 Robert Eisler, *The Messiah Jesus and John the Baptist according to Flavius Josephus* (trans, Alexander H Krappe), Methuen, London, 1931.

13 Albert Bell, *An Historical Analysis of the Exido Hierosolymitano*, University of North Carolina, Chapel Hill, NC, 1977.

14 Lucas Osiander, *Epitomes Historiae Ecclesiasticae Centuria*, Tübingen, 1592, vol I, lib 2, ch 17.

15 For a discussion of the arguments in this debate, *see* Shirley Jackson Case, *The Historicity of Jesus*, University of Chicago Press, Chicago, IL, 1912, ch 8, pp 238–70.

16 There are good references by GJ Goldberg, on the Flavius Josephus website http://members.aol.com/FLJOSEPHUS/home.htm. Also *see* Henry Thackery, *Josephus, the Man and the Historian*, KTAV, Jerusalem, 1968.

17 Luke 2:52–3:2 and F Josephus, *The Antiquities of the Jews*, bk XVIII, ch III:1–3.

18 Luke 2:1–3 and F Josephus, *The Antiquities of the Jews*, bk XVIII, ch I:1.

19 Matthew 14:3–11, Mark 6:17–28.

20 F Josephus, *The Antiquities of the Jews*, bk XVIII, ch V:4.

21 *Ibid*, bk XVIII, ch V:2.

22 *See* David Hendin, *Guide to Biblical Coins*, Amphora Books, Amsterdam, 2001.

23 Exodus 20:4.

24 David Keys, 'Coins Show Cultural Split' in *BBC History Magazine*, Origin Publishing, Bristol, vol 66, no 7, July 2005, pp 8–9.

25 For details of the coinage survey, *see* Christopher Howgego, Volker Heuchert and Andrew Burnett (eds), *Coinage and Identity in the Roman Provinces*, Oxford University Press, Oxford, 2005.

26 For full details of the discovery and subsequent analysis, *see* Morton Smith, *The Secret Gospel*, Victor Gollancz, London, 1974.

27 Otto Stählin and Ursula Treu, *Clemens Alexandrinus Register*, Akademie-Verlag, Berlin, 1980, 2nd edn, vol 4:1, pp 17–18.

28 Irenaeus, 'Doctrines of Carpocrates' in *Adversus Haereses*, AD *c*175, item I, 25:6.

29 Elaine Pagels, *The Gnostic Gospels*, Weidenfeld and Nicolson, London, 1980, ch 3, p 60.

30 *See* also Shawn Eyer 'The Strange Case of the Secret Gospel According to Mark' in *Alexandria: The Journal for the Western Cosmological Traditions* (ed, David Fideler), Phanes Press, 1995, vol 3, pp 103–29.

31 John 11:1–45.

32 Michael Baigent, Richard Leigh and Henry Lincoln, *The Holy Blood and the Holy Grail*, Jonathan Cape, London, 1982, ch 12, p 296.

33 Carsten Peter Theide and Matthew D'Ancona, *The Jesus Papyrus*, Weidenfield & Nicolson, London, 1996, intro, pp 1–7.

34 For further details *see* Kurt Aland, 'The Significance of the Papyri for Progress in New Testament Research' in *The Bible in Modern Scholarship: Papers Read at the 100th Meeting of the SBL, December 28–30, 1964* (ed, JP Hyatt) Abingdon, Nashville, TN, 1965, pp 325–46.

35 CP Theide and M D'Ancona, *The Jesus Papyrus*, ch 3, pp 56–69.

Chapter 4: Marriage of the Messiah

1 John 11:47–53.

2 John 2:1–11.

3 John 20:11–17.

4 John 21:1–13.

5 *The Catholic Encyclopedia*, vol IX, under Mark.

6 Barbara Thiering, *Jesus the Man*, Transworld/Doubleday, London, 1992, ch 14, p 75.

7 NJ Bull, *The Rise of the Church*, ch 4, p 85.

8 Matthew 1:22.

9 Matthew 5:1–7:29.

10 Matthew 5:3–12.

11 *The Catholic Encyclopedia*, vol VIII, under Gospel of John.

12 The earliest date postulated for the gospel of John is AD 37. *See* B Thiering, *Jesus the Man*, ch 14, p 75.

13 Revelation 1:4.

14 John 21:24.

15 John 11:5.
16 John 19:26–7.
17 John 20:2.
18 John 21:7, 21:20.
19 Matthew 26:6–7.
20 Mark 14:3.
21 John 12:2–3.
22 B Thiering, *Jesus the Man*, ch 20, p 98 and app III, p 333.
23 Luke 16:20–31.
24 Mark 15:40.
25 Mark 16:1.
26 Luke 10:40 and John 12:2.
27 Bishop John Shelby Spong, *Born of a Woman*, HarperSanFrancisco, San Francisco, CA, 1992, ch 13, pp 187–99.
28 6 June at 6.00 pm. *See* B Thiering, *Jesus the Man*, app I, Chronology, p 211.
29 Dynastic wedlock, as in kingly and priestly strains, was quite unlike the Jewish family norm as explained in Rev J Fleetwood (ed), *The Life of Our Lord and Saviour Jesus Christ*, William MacKenzie, Glasgow, 1900, ch 1, pp 10–11 which outlines the customary rules of 1st-century Jewish matrimony.
30 Luke 7:37–8.
31 Mark 14:3.
32 John 11:1–2 and 12:1–3.
33 As related in 1 Kings 2:13–25.
34 Bernard de Clairvaux, *Patrologia Latina* (ed, JP Minge), Paris, 1854, vol 183, cols 1050–55.
35 Origen, *The Song of Songs, Commentary and Homilies* (trans, RP Lason) Newman Press, New York, NY, 1956, bk 2, ch 6, pp 160–61.
36 Song of Solomon 1:12.
37 Matthew 26:7, Mark 14:4, John 12:2–3.
38 The ceremony was inherited directly from the *Hieros Gamos* (Holy Matrimony) of the Shepherd-king. The imagery is also found in the Old Testament Psalm 23:5, 'The Lord is my shepherd …', where it is said of the female aspect of the deity, 'Thou preparest a table before me … thou anointest my head with oil; my cup runneth over'.
39 Exodus 30:23–5.
40 J Hastings (ed), *Dictionary of the Bible*, under Anointing.
41 Mark 14:9.
42 Margaret Starbird, *The Woman with the Alabaster Jar*, Bear, Santa Fe, NM, 1993, ch 2, pp 40–41.
43 Mark 14:8.
44 Mark 16:1.
45 The Institute of Assyriology and Ancient Near Eastern Studies is affiliated to Bar-Ilan University, Tel Aviv, Israel.
46 Samuel Noah Kramer, *The Sacred Marriage Rite*, Indiana University Press, Bloomington, AL, 1969, ch 5, pp 85–6.
47 J Hastings (ed), *Dictionary of the Bible*, under Shulamite.

48 For a detailed account of Mary Magdalene's life and ancestry, *see* Laurence Gardner, *The Magdalene Legacy*, HarperCollins, London, 2005.

49 Samuel Macauley Jackson (ed), *The Schaff-Herzog Encyclopedia of Religious Knowledge*, Baker Book House, Grand Rapids, MI, 1953, under Song of Solomon.

50 J Hastings (ed), *Dictionary of the Bible*, under Song of Solomon.

51 M Starbird, *The Woman with the Alabaster Jar*, ch 11, pp 35–6.

52 AM Hocart, *Kingship*, Oxford University Press, Oxford, 1927, ch 8, p 103.

53 Ahmed Osman, *The House of the Messiah*, HarperCollins, London, 1992, ch 28, p 152, and p 230, bk 3, note 7.

54 *Diatessaron*: Late Latin, from Greek: *dia tessaron khordon sumphonia* – 'concord through four notes', from *dia* (through) + *tessares* (four). For details, *see* WL Peterson 'Taitan's Diatessaron' in Helmut Koester, *Ancient Christian Gospels: Their History and Development*, SCM Press, London, 1990, pp 403–30.

55 John 1:13–14.

56 *See* NJ Bull, *The Rise of the Church*, ch 4, pp 93–4. Also in *The Catholic Encyclopedia*, vol VI, under Gospel and Gospels.

57 The main among them (apart from the canonical gospels) included the Gospels: of Peter, of the Hebrews, of the Nazarenes, of Matthias, of the Egyptians, of Mary, of Philip, of Thomas, of Nicodemus, of the Apostles, of Basilides, of Valentius, of Marcion, of Eve, of Judas.

Chapter 5: A Conflict of Interests

1 *The Catholic Encyclopedia*, vol I, under Apostolic Fathers.

2 The early Bishops of Rome (Popes) from Linus in AD 58 down to the time of Constantine are recorded in the *Liber Pontificalis* (Book of Pontiffs), Raymond Davis, *The Book of Pontiffs (Liber Pontificalis)*, University of Liverpool Press, Liverpool, 1989. This work also shows their years of service and the corresponding emperors. From the 4th century, it was updated at various stages through the next 1,000 years.

3 St Clement of Rome, *The Clementine Homilies* (trans, Rev Alexander Roberts and James Donaldson), The Ante-Nicene Christian Library, T&T Clark, Edinburgh, 1870, pp 6–16.

4 *The Catholic Encyclopedia*, vol III, under St Ignatius of Antioch.

5 *Ibid*, vol XII, under St Polycarp.

6 Rev J Tixeront, *A Handbook of Patrology* (trans, S A Raemers), B Herder, St Louis, MO, 1920, sectn I, item 4, p 18.

7 *Ibid*, sectn I, item 5, pp 19–20.

8 *Ibid*, sectn I, item 7, pp 23–5.

9 *Ibid*, sectn I, item 8, pp 27–8. *See* also *The Catholic Encyclopedia*, vol XI, under St Papias.

10 Rev J Tixeront, *A Handbook of Patrology*, sectn II, General Survey, p 31.

11 *The Catholic Encyclopedia*, vol I, under Apologetics.

12 *Ibid*, vol XIV, under Tertullian.

13 Rev J Tixeront, *A Handbook of Patrology*, sectn III, item 1, pp 52–4.

14 *Ibid*, sectn II, item 2, pp 54–60.

15 *The Catholic Encyclopedia*, vol VII, under St Hippolytus of Rome.

16 *Ibid*, vol XV, under The Blessed Trinity.

17 NJ Bull, *The Rise of the Church*, ch 7, p 195.

18 *The Catholic Encyclopedia*, vol VII, under St Gregory of Neoceasarea.

19 Matthew 12:32.

20 Matthew 1:18.

21 Matthew 28:18.

22 John 14:28.

23 *The Catholic Encyclopedia*, vol XI, under The First Council of Nicaea.

24 RE Rubenstein, *When Jesus Became God*, ch 3, pp 54–5.

25 Michael Baigent, Richard Leigh and Henry Lincoln, *The Messianic Legacy*, Jonathan Cape, London, 1986, ch 3, p 49.

26 NJ Bull, *The Rise of the Church*, ch 7, p 197.

27 The following is a literal translation of the Greek text of the *Nicene Creed* as decreed in AD 381 at Constantinople. The brackets indicate the words altered or added for the Western liturgical form in present use:

'We believe [I believe] in one God, the Father Almighty, maker of heaven and earth, and of all things visible and invisible. And in one Lord Jesus Christ, the only begotten Son of God, and born of the Father before all ages. [God of God] Light of light, true God of true God. Begotten not made, consubstantial to the Father, by whom all things were made. Who for us men and for our salvation came down from heaven. And was incarnate of the Holy Ghost and of the Virgin Mary and was made man; was crucified also for us under Pontius Pilate, suffered and was buried; and the third day rose again according to the Scriptures. And ascended into heaven, sits at the right hand of the Father, and shall come again with glory to judge the living and the dead, of whose Kingdom there shall be no end. And [I believe] in the Holy Ghost, the Lord and Giver of life, who proceeds from the Father [and the Son], who together with the Father and the Son is to be adored and glorified, who spoke by the Prophets. And one holy, catholic, and apostolic Church. We confess [I confess] one baptism for the remission of sins. And we look for [I look for] the resurrection of the dead and the life of the world to come. Amen'.

28 NJ Bull, *The Rise of the Church*, ch 7, p 201.

29 *Ibid*, ch 7, pp 201–2.

30 M Martin, *The Decline and Fall of the Roman Church*, ch 1, pp 55–6.

31 Notwithstanding the practicalities of the break between Rome and Constantinople, the fact that it resulted in two separate and independent Churches was not formalized by the denominations concerned until as late as 1945.

32 The Constitution *Ineffabilis Deus* of 8 December, 1854. *The Catholic Encyclopedia*, vol VII, under Immaculate Conception.

Chapter 6: Heirs of the Bloodline

1 For transcript, *see* Philip Schaff and Henry Wace (eds), *Nicene and Post-Nicene Fathers, Second Series,* Oxford University Press, Oxford, 1894, vol 6.

2 *The Catholic Encyclopedia,* vol XV, under Virginity.

3 AN Wilson, *Jesus,* ch 4, p 79.

4 Origen, 'Contra Celsus' in Rev A Roberts and J Donaldson (eds), *The Ante-Nicene Fathers,* vol IV, bk I, ch 34:1.

5 Nancy Qualls-Corbett, *The Sacred Prostitute,* Inner City Books, Toronto, ON, 1988, ch 2, p 58.

6 *The Catholic Encyclopedia,* vol XV, under Virgin Birth of Christ.

7 *Ibid,* vol XV, under The Blessed Virgin Mary.

8 M Martin, *The Decline and Fall of the Roman Church,* pp 42–3.

9 Rev J Tixeront, *A Handbook of Patrology,* sectn IV, item 1, p 76.

10 *Ibid,* sectn V, item 4, p 101.

11 *The Catholic Encyclopedia,* vol I, under Abdias of Babylon.

12 Eusebius of Caesarea, *An Ecclesiastical History* (trans, Rev CF Crusè), Samuel Bagster, London, 1838, bk III, ch XII, p 84.

13 Eusebius of Caesarea, *The History of the Church from Christ to Constantine,* Penguin, London, 1989, bk 1, p 22.

14 C Tacitus, *The Annals of Imperial Rome,* ref AD 64, p 365.

15 Eusebius, *The History of the Church from Christ to Constantine,* bk 3, p 81.

16 *Ibid,* bk 3, p 82.

17 M Martin, *The Decline and Fall of the Roman Church,* ch 1, p 42.

18 WE Vine (ed), *Vine's Expository Dictionary of Old and New Testament Words,* Thomas Nelson, London, 1996, under Peter.

19 John 1:41–2.

20 The Gospel of Thomas in JM Robinson (ed), *The Nag Hammadi Library* item 12, p 119.

21 M Martin, *The Decline and Fall of the Roman Church,* pp 42–4.

22 Irenaeus, *Adversus Haereses,* AD c175, vol I, bk I, ch 26:2.

23 B Thiering, *Jesus the Man,* app III: Hierarchy, p 371.

24 Flavius Josephus, *The Jewish Wars* (trans, GA Williamson), Penguin, London, 1959, bk II, ch VIII: 6.

25 Philo Judaeus, *Quod Omnis Probus Liber Sit* (That Every Good Man is Free), in CD Yonge (ed), *The Works of Philo Judaeus,* HG Bohn, London, 1854–90, ch XII, item 91.

26 A Osman, *The House of the Messiah,* ch 5, p 31.

27 An Arabic alternative is *en Nusara – see* Rev John Fleetwood, *The Life of Our Lord and Saviour Jesus Christ,* ch 1, p 10.

28 R McL Wilson, *The Gospel of Philip* (translated from the Coptic Text), AR Mowbray, London, 1962, 110:10–15, p 38.

29 A Osman, *The House of the Messiah,* ch 5, pp 30–32.

30 *The Jewish Encyclopedia,* Funk and Wagnalls, New York, NY, 1906, under Nazareth.

31 Judges 13:3–5.

32 Luke 1:26.

33 Numbers 6:3, 5, 13.

34 John Allegro, *The Dead Sea Scrolls*, Penguin, London, 1964, ch 7, p 131; ch 12, p 164; ch 13, p 168.

35 *Scroll of The Rule*, Annex II, 17–22. For the citation as given, *see* the *Messianic Rule* within the *Community Rule*: Geza Vermes, *The Complete Dead Sea Scrolls in English*, Penguin, London, 1998, ($_1$QSa=$_1$Q$_2$8a), pp 159–60.

36 F Josephus, *The Antiquities of the Jews*, bk XVIII, ch I:5, in particular footnote, p 390.

37 Philo, *Quod Omnis Probus Liber Sit*, in CD Yonge (ed), *The Works of Philo Judaeus*, ch XII, item 76.

38 Matthew 21:9.

39 Luke 19:36–9. The strewing of the palm fronds was intended to remind people of the triumphant entry into Jerusalem of Simon Maccabaeus, the deliverer of Palestine from the yoke of Syrian oppression in 142 BC.

40 John 12:37 further explains that Jesus spoke to some people in the street, following which, 'though he had done so many miracles before them, yet they believed not on him'.

41 The definition 'Sabbath day's journey', as given in The Acts, refers to a law of the Torah in Exodus 16:29 wherein Jews were forbidden to travel out of a city, or from one city to another on the Sabbath. From within the Jerusalem city wall, one could travel out to the city's pasture lands (about 2,000 cubits) but no further. If starting a journey from outside the boundary, however, there was no limitation of distance, only a rule that one must not travel into another city. The 2,000 cubit distance was doubled during the 1st century AD, and then increased yet again. Tents pitched outside city limits constitued a new city boundary. If tents were on common ground between cities – say, midway in the 2 miles between Jerusalem and Bethany, then the overlapping would cause Jerusalem and Bethany to become a single encampment, and Sabbath travel between the cities was permitted.

42 F Josephus, *The Antiquities of the Jews*, bk XV, ch X:4.

43 F Josephus, *The Wars of the Jews*, bk II, ch VIII:2.

44 F Josephus, *The Antiquities of the Jews*, bk XVIII, ch I:3.

45 *The Jewish Encyclopedia*, under Jesus.

46 Proselytes were Gentile converts to Judaism.

47 Matthew 23:15.

48 Matthew 23:2–4.

49 Acts 24:5–14.

50 *The Catholic Encyclopedia*, vol V, under Ebionites.

51 James Montague Rhode (ed), *The Apocryphal New Testament*, Clarendon Press, Oxford, 1924, pp. 8–10.

52 G Vermes, *The Complete Dead Sea Scrolls in English*, Scroll 4Q246, pp 576–7.

53 Luke 7:19–20.

54 Matthew 5:3–12.

55 G Vermes, *The Complete Dead Sea Scrolls in English*, Scroll 4Q525, p 424.

56 Matthew 27:33.

57 Deuteronomy 23:10–14. *See* also B Thiering, *Jesus the Man*, ch 24, p 113.

58 The Judaean earthquake of 31 BC is described in F Josephus, *Antiquities of the Jews*, bk XV, ch V:2, p 331.

59 B Thiering, *Jesus the Man*, app II, Locations, p 312.

60 Matthew 2:13–14.

61 Willis Barnstone, (ed), *The Other Bible*, HarperSanFrancisco, San Francisco, CA, 1984, p 334.

62 *See* J M Rhode, *The Apocryphal New Testament*, pp 1–8. Further information is found in Burton H Throckmorton (ed), *Gospel Parallels*, Thomas Nelson, London, 1949.

63 Ernest A Wallis Budge, *Miscellaneous Coptic Texts in the Dialect of Upper Egypt*, British Museum, London, 1915, pp 626–50.

64 R McL Wilson, *The Gospel of Philip*, 103:20–25, p 31.

Chapter 7: The Virgin and the Whore

1 Daniel 8:16, 9:21–2.

2 F Josephus, *The Wars of the Jews*, bk II, ch VIII:7.

3 G Vermes, *The Complete Dead Sea Scrolls in English*, (4Q201), pp 513–14.

4 J Allegro, *The Dead Sea Scrolls*, ch 6, p 104. *Kittim* was ostensibly a name for Mediterranean coastal people. It was also used to denote the ancient Chaldeans, whom the Old Testament describes as 'that bitter and hasty nation which shall march through the breadth of the land to possess dwelling places that are not theirs' (Habakkuk 1:6). The Essenes resurrected the old word for use in their own time and enlightened readers knew that *Kittim* always stood for Romans.

5 War Scroll 9:15–17 in G Vermes, *The Complete Dead Sea Scrolls in English*, p 172. *See* also André Dupont-Sommer, *The Essene Writings From Qumrân* (trans, G Vermes), Basil Blackwell, Oxford, 1961, sectn V, p 183 regarding Angelic Shields.

6 2 Samuel 15:29.

7 2 Samuel 20:25.

8 B Thiering, *Jesus the Man*, app III, pp 335–8, 340. The name Michael means 'Who is like God'. The name Gabriel means 'Man of God'. Also, Rev J Fleetwood, *The Life of Our Lord and Saviour Jesus Christ*, ch 1, p 4, confirms that the name Gabriel in this context represents a title corresponding to angelic office, as defined in Dr William Smith, *Smith's Bible Dictionary* (1868 revised), Hendrickson, Peabody, MA, 1998, under Gabriel.

9 Luke 1:9.

10 Luke 1:26.

11 Matthew 1:20.

12 F Josephus, *Wars of the Jews*, bk II, ch XIII:2.

13 B Thiering, *Jesus the Man*, ch 8, p 44.

14 F Josephus, *Wars of the Jews*, bk II, ch XIII:13.

15 *Ibid.*

16 B Thiering, *Jesus the Man*, ch 8, p 45 and note 9, p 412 extract from Josephus: 'They give their wives a three years' probation, and only marry them after they have by being three times pure given proof of being able to bear'.

17 *Ibid*, ch 8, p 47, and app I, p 177.

18 Luke 7:37–8.

19 Matthew 26:7, Mark 14:3, John 12:3.

20 Matthew 1:19–20.

21 Leviticus 16:29–31 and 23:27–8. Settled always on a Sabbath, the precise date for *Yom Kippur* varies slightly each year between latter September and early October in the Gregorian calendar. For example:
    2005 (Jewish Year 5766) from sunset 12 October to nightfall 13 October.
    2006 (Jewish Year 5767) from sunset 1 October to nightfall 2 October.
    2007 (Jewish Year 5768) from sunset 21 September to nightfall 22 September.
    2008 (Jewish Year 5769) from sunset 8 October to nightfall 9 October.
    2009 (Jewish Year 5770) from sunset 27 September to nightfall 28 September.

22 This calendar was not adopted in Britain until 1752.

23 The precise length of time depends on which point of the sun's ecliptic one chooses: starting from the (northern) vernal equinox (one of the four cardinal points along the ecliptic) yields the vernal equinox year, while averaging over all starting points on the ecliptic yields the mean tropical year.

24 B Thiering, *Jesus the Man*, app I, Chronology, pp 161–284.

25 Twelve other works dating from and related to the last part of the Old Testament era constitute the *Apocrypha* (Hidden things). Although included in the Greek *Septuagint*, they were not contained in the Hebrew canon. They originated in the Hellenist Judaism of Alexandria, but are not accepted by orthodox Jews. The books are, nevertheless, included in St Jerome's Latin *Vulgate* (AD c382) as an extension to the Old Testament, and are recognized by the Roman Catholic Church. They are omitted, however, by almost all Protestant Bibles, having been sidelined by the reformer Martin Luther (1483–1546) and largely ignored by translators. The twelve books are: Esdras, Tobit, Judith, the Rest of Esther, the Wisdom of Solomon, Ecclesiasticus [of Jeremiah], Baruch with the Epistle of Jeremy, the Song of the Three Holy Children, the History of Susanna, Bel and the Dragon, the Prayer of Manasses, and Maccabees.

26 JT Milik, *Ten Years of Discovery in the Wilderness of Judaea* (trans, J Strugnell), SCM Press, London, 1959, ch 1, pp 11–19.

27 In the New Testament, 2 Corinthians 4:3–7 similarly states: 'If our Gospel be hid, it is hid to them that are lost ... But we have this treasure in earthen vessels'.

28 B Thiering, *Jesus the Man*, app I, p 209.

29 Frank Williams (ed), *The Panarion of Epiphanius of Salamis*, EJ Brill, Leiden, 1994, ch 78 'Against the Antidicomarians', items 1:1–3, 6:4, 7:1, 21:5, 221, 24:3.

30 B Thiering, *Jesus the Man*, ch 78 7:1.

31 Prior to 1860, all Bibles used the correct translation 'cousin' for *suggenhs* and *cognata* in respect of Elizabeth – for instance, the Douay Reims Bible (Catholic) 1609, the King James Version (Protestant) 1611 and the Noah Webster Bible 1833. Then followed a series of 'updated' Bibles which corrupted much of the original content. In respect of Elizabeth, the less explicit word 'kinswoman' became popular, as in the American Standard Version 1901, Darby's English Translation 1890 and the Jerusalem Bible (Catholic) 1966. Subsequently, further revisions were made to the point where the language was amended to suit what was called the 'modern era'. In such Bibles as these, Elizabeth has become a loosely defined 'relative', as in the World English Bible 1997. The so-called Revised versions of the early 1900s have now been superseded by New Revised versions, which have progressed the text into a quite unrecognizable format. From 1860, however, there has been no revision which reflects accurately the language of the original Greek *Septuagint* or the Latin *Vulgate*.

32 *Constitutions of the Holy Apostles*, T&T Clark Edinburgh, 1870, bk III, p 96.

33 The Gospel of Philip in JM Robinson (ed), *The Nag Hammadi Library*, item 59:6–11, p 136.

34 *Protevangelion of James* 19:3–20; 4; *See* also in Richard Bauckham, *Jude and the Relatives of Jesus in the Early Church*, T&T Clark, Edinburgh, 1988, ch 1, p 37.

35 Epiphanius, *Panarion* (trans, F Wilkins), EJ Brill, Leiden, 1989–93, 78:8:1 & 78:9:6; *Ancoratus* (trans, Karl Hol), Walter de Gruyter, Berlin, 2002–4, 60:1.

36 This segment of the list in Matthew contains 22 ancestors, against 20 in Luke.

37 There is some minor dispute over the entry of Zerubbabel as the son of Shealtiel. Whereas the Old Testament books of Ezra 3:2 and Haggai 1:1 confirm that Zerubbabel was born into Shealtiel's family, there could have been a generation between the two – a possible son of Shealtiel named Pedaiah, who would then have been Zerubbabel's father. The account in 1 Chronicles 3:19 is confusing in this regard.

38 Matthew 1:16.

39 Luke 3:23.

40 B Thiering, *Jesus the Man*, ch 5, p 29. The genealogical list in Matthew, from David to Jacob–Heli (spanning about 1,000 years) contains 25 generations at 40 years each. Luke, on the other hand, gives 40 generations at 25 years each. Hence, Luke places Jesus in the 20th generation from Zerubbabel, whereas Matthew places him in the 11th. Through this latter period of around 530 years, the Matthew list supports a 53-year generation standard, while Luke is more comprehensible with its 28-year standard.

41 Eusebius of Caesarea, *Ecclesiastical History*, 1874 edn, bk I:7. Also some extant writings of Julius Africanus can be found in Rev A Roberts and J Donaldson (eds), *The Ante-Nicene Fathers*, vol VI.

42 1 Chronicles 3:10–17.

43 Hebrews 7:12.

44 Matthew 26:63–4.

45 Luke 22:70.

46 As in Matthew 26:63–4.

47 For example, John 20:31 states: 'But these things are written, that ye might believe that Jesus is the Christ, the son of God'. Similarly in Acts 9:20 when Paul is said to have preached that Christ was the son of God.

48 Matthew 27:11, 37; Mark 15:2, 26; Luke 23:3, 28; John 18:32, 19:19.

49 Didache 9:6.

50 Luke 2:25–35.

51 John 1:15–16.

52 1 Kings 25:38–9.

53 John 1:32, Mark 1:10, Matthew 3:16.

54 *The Catholic Encyclopedia*, vol VII, under Holy Ghost.

55 *See* R McL Wilson, *The Gospel of Philip*, item 107:5, pp 35, 97. In some *Gospel of Philip* translations, the Greek word *koinonôs* has been translated as 'companion'. Linguistic scholars have pointed out however that, although not wholly incorrect in the broader sense, *koinonôs* is a singular term with conjugal connotations that should more correctly be translated as 'consort'. *The Oxford Compact English Dictionary* (Oxford Word Library Micrographic), Oxford University Press, Oxford, 1971, states 'consort' as deriving from *con* (together) + *sortem* (lot), the noun 'consort' relates to 'holding title in common'. In Nathan Bailey (ed), *Nathan Bailey's Universal Etymological Dictionary*, T Cox at The Lamb, Royal Exchange, London, 1721, the term 'consort' is given as 'The wife of a sovereign prince'.

56 The Gospel of Philip in JM Robinson (ed), *The Nag Hammadi Library*, items 63–4, p 138.

57 Dialogue of the Saviour in *Ibid*, item 139, p 235.

58 The Gospel of Philip in *Ibid*, items 63–4, pp 138–9.

59 David Farmer (ed), *Oxford Dictionary of Saints*, under Mary Magdalene.

60 Homily on the Dormition in EAW Budge (trans), *Miscellaneous Coptic Texts in the Dialect of Upper Egypt*, pp 626–50.

61 *The Catholic Encyclopedia*, vol VIII, under St John Damascene.

62 *Ibid*, vol VII, under Immaculate Conception.

Chapter 8: The Myth of Succession

1 *The Catholic Encyclopedia*, vol I, under Apostolicity.

2 *Ibid*, under Apostolic Succession.

3 *The Concise Oxford Dictionary of Current English* (1995), under 'pontificate'.

4 Ephesians 5:23.

5 The full text of Zachary's proclamation is given in Christopher B Coleman, *The Treatise of Lorenzo Valla on the Donation of Constantine*, University of Toronto Press, Toronto, ON, 1993.

6 'St Paul's Tomb' by John Thavis, Catholic News Service, Washington, DC, 10 March 2005.

7 *The Catholic Encyclopedia*, vol I, under Apostolic Succession.

8 F Josephus, *The Antiquities of the Jews*, bk XX, ch XIII:5.

9   *Ibid*, bk XX, ch XIII:6.

10 Acts 21–3.

11 Acts 24. Also see, *The Catholic Encyclopedia*, vol XI, under St Paul.

12 Acts 25–6.

13 Acts 27–8.

14 Acts 12:1–19.

15 It is not known if the New Testament's two epistles carrying Peter's name were written by him or simply ascribed to him. Either way, they make no mention of Rome or Romans.

16 *The Catholic Encyclopedia*, vol XI, under St Peter.

17 Irenaeus, 'Adversus Haereses' in Rev A Roberts and J Donaldson (eds), *The Ante-Nicene Fathers*, vol I, bk III, ch III:2.

18 Tertullian, 'The Prescription Against Heretics' in *Ibid*, vol II, ch 36.

19 *The Catholic Encyclopedia*, vol XI, under St Peter.

20 Eusebius, *Ecclesiastical History*, 1874 edn, bk III, ch 1, p 67.

21 Referring to Genesis 6:1–4.

22 Tertullian, 'On the Apparel of Women' in Rev A Roberts and J Donaldson (eds), *The Ante-Nicene Fathers*, vol IV, bk I, ch 1:1.

23 1 Corinthians 9:5. Simon Peter is referred to here as Cephas, the name given to him by Jesus in John 1:42.

24 Henry C Lea, *History of Sacerdotal Celibacy in the Christian Church*, Watts & Co, London 1932, ch 2, p 20 and ch 3, p 33.

25 *Ibid*, ch 4, p 43.

26 *Ibid*, ch 5, p 58.

27 Christopher Witcombe, 'The Chapel of the Courtesan and the Quarrel of the Magdalens' in *The Art Bulletin*, College Art Association, New York, NY, vol 84, no 2, pp 273–92.

28 For the toleration of prostitution in ancient Rome and later, *see* Thomas AJ McGinn, *Prostitution, Sexuality, and the Law in Ancient Rome*, Oxford University Press, New York, NY, 1998, pp 343–5; and James A Brundage, *Law, Sex, and Christian Society in Medieval Europe*, University of Chicago Press, Chicago, IL, 1987, pp 105–7.

29 Nigel Cawthorne, *Sex Lives of the Popes*, Prion, London, 2004, ch 2, p 32.

30 *Ibid*, ch 6, p 65.

31 HC Lea, *History of Sacerdotal Celibacy in the Christian Church*, ch 10, p 115.

32 N Cawthorne, *Sex Lives of the Popes*, ch 7, p 76.

33 *Ibid*, ch 13, p 166.

34 Following Lucrezia, Pope Alexander's other children by Vannozza dei Cattanei were Giovanni, born in 1474, Cesare, born in 1476, and Goffredo, born in 1481.

35 Nigel Cawthorne, *Sex Lives of the Popes*, ch 15, pp 222–3.

36 *The Catholic Encyclopedia*, vol III, under Celibacy in the Church.

37 1 Timothy 3:2–5.

Chapter 9: The Age of Corruption

1 This professorship was expressed by deed in December 1663 at Cambridge University, England, as a result of a gift from Henry Lucas, Minister of Parliament for the University. King Charles II Stuart signed the letter of acceptance of the deed on January 18, 1664. The Lucasian professorship of mathematics is perhaps the most reputed academic chair in the world.

2 Frank E Manuel, *The Religion of Isaac Newton* (The Freemantle Lectures 1973), Clarendon Press, Oxford, 1974, ch 1, p 7.

3 *Ibid*, ch 3, p 67.

4 Michael White, *Isaac Newton, The Last Sorcerer*, Fourth Estate, London, 1998, ch 7, p 149 and ch 12, p 302.

5 *Ibid*, ch 7, pp 152–3.

6 The full transcript of Isaac Newton's letter to John Locke, along with the original letter itself, is held by the Newton Project in Cambridge. The work is entitled, Isaac Newton, *Paradoxical Questions Concerning the Morals and Actions of Athanasius and his Followers*, Nov 1690 (trans, Stephen Snobelen, April 1998), MS 10, Kings College, Cambridge.

7 Sometimes called the *Johannine Comma*.

8 *See* 'Liber Apologeticus' in RP Vaggione, *Eunomius: The Extant Works*, Oxford Early Christian Texts, Oxford, 1987, pp 34–74.

9 Now held at the Bodleian Library in Oxford.

10 The *Textus Receptus* (Received Text) was compiled by the Dutch Catholic scholar, Desiderius Erasmus.

11 The story of the translation of the King James Version is well told in Adam Nicolson, *Power and Glory*, HarperCollins, London, 2003.

12 RE Rubenstein, *When Jesus Became God*, ch 4, pp 79–82.

13 *Ibid*, ch 6, p 106–7.

14 *The Catholic Encyclopedia*, vol II, under St Athanasius.

15 Comments from Eusebius in this regard are found in Eusebius of Caesarea, *Ecclesiastical History*, 1874 edn, bk III:15, pp 94–5.

16 An annual pastoral letter that fixed and announced the movable feasts of the current year.

17 GM Hahneman, 'The Muratorian Fragment and the Origins of the New Testament Canon' in LM McDonald and JA Sanders (eds), *The Canon Debate*, Hendrickson, Peabody, MA, 2002, pp 405–15.

18 BM Metzger, *The Canon Of The New Testament: Its Origin, Significance and Development*, Clarendon Press, Oxford, 1997, p 246.

19 The Catholic Church had long prevailed in England from the time of St Augustine in the 7th century, but King Henry VIII Tudor separated the English Church from Roman control to aid his divorce from Catherine of Aragon and to acquire Church property in England. The *Thirty-nine Articles* of the Anglican Communion were subsequently implemented by Henry's daughter, Queen Elizabeth I, in 1570. This established the Protestant Church of England as distinct from that of Rome, at which time Elizabeth was excommunicated by Pope Pius V.

20 Born in France, John Calvin (Jean Cauvin) emerged as one of the most important figures of the Protestant Reformation. Having studied for the Catholic priesthood in Paris, he became exposed to the ideas of Martin Luther (*see* below) and switched to the Protestant camp by 1533. Subsequently, he established a Protestant movement in Geneva.

21 In October 1517, Martin Luther, an Augustinian monk and professor of theology at the University of Wittenberg, Germany, nailed his written protest against the sale of Indulgences to the door of his local church. This act of formal objection was destined to split the Western Church permanently in two. On receiving a papal reprimand, he publicly set fire to it and was excommunicated for his pains. His fellow protesters became known as Protestants.

22 *The Catholic Encyclopedia*, vol III, under Canon of the New Testament.

23 *Ibid*.

24 William Whiston, *Primitive Christianity Revived* (Cambridge University MSS, 5 vols), London, 1711, vol III, containing the epistles of Ignatius, the Apostiolic Constitutions in Greek and English; essay on the Apostiolic Constitutions; account of the Primitive Faith concerning the Trinity, and the Recognition of Clement.

25 *The Catholic Encyclopedia*, vol I, under Apostolic Constitutions.

26 *See* W Barnstone, (ed), *The Other Bible*.

27 *See* translated collection in JM Robinson (ed), *The Nag Hammadi Library*.

28 Catalogued at the British Museum as *Piste Sophia Coptice*, MS Add. 5114.

29 Jean Doresse, *The Secret Books of the Egyptian Gnostics* (trans, Philip Mairet), Hollis & Carter, London, 1960, ch 2, p 64. It was not until the 10th century that Coptic gave way to the Arabic language, although it is still used by the Coptic branch of the Egyptian Church.

30 GRS Mead (trans) *Pistis Sophia: A Gnostic Miscellany* (1921), reprint: Kessinger, Kila, MT, 1992, bk 1, ch 1, p 1.

31 *Ibid*, bk 1, ch 36, p 47.

32 *Ibid*, bk 2, ch 72, p 135. This is sometimes rendered as '… hateth our sex'.

33 *Ibid*, bk 1, ch 17, p 20.

34 The Gospel of Thomas in JM Robinson (ed), *The Nag Hammadi Library*, item 114, p 130.

35 The Gospel of Mary in *Ibid*, item 10, p 472.

36 R McL Wilson, *The Gospel of Philip*, item 107:5–10, p 35.

37 *Ibid*, item 111:30–112:35, pp 39–40.

38 Plate 50 in L Gardner, *The Magdalene Legacy*. Leonardo da Vinci's *The Last Supper* and artists' depictions of John are discussed in this book.

39 The painting is at the Musée des Beaux-Arts, Chambery.

40 Tertullian, 'On the Veiling of Virgins' (*De virginibus velandis*) in Rev A Roberts and J Donaldson (eds), *The Ante-Nicene Fathers*, vol IV, ch 9.

41 1 Timothy 2:11–2.

42 1 Corinthians 11:3.

43 *Constitutions of the Holy Apostles*, bk III, sectn VI, p 96.

44 *Ibid*, bk III, sectn VI, p 100.
45 E Pagels, *The Gnostic Gospels*, ch 3, p 60.
46 1 Timothy 2:13–14.
47 J Wijngaards, *No Women in Holy Orders?* Canterbury Press, Norwich, 2002, app: The Texts, pp 156–205.
48 *The Catholic Encyclopedia*, vol XI, under St Olympias.
49 *Ibid*, vol IV, under Deaconesses.
50 *Ibid*. This work is published as James Cooper and Arthur John Maclean (trans), *Testament of Our Lord*, T&T Clark, Edinburgh, 1902.
51 Romans 16:1–2.
52 Romans 16:15.
53 Romans 16:3–4.
54 1 Timothy 3:2–5.
55 1 Corinthians 9:5. Also *see* John Shelby Spong, *Born of a Woman*, ch 13, pp 187–99.

Chapter 10: Pagan Origins

1 *Anno Domini Nostri Iesu Christi* (In the Year of our Lord Jesus Christ). This dating structure was adopted in parts of Western Europe during the 8th century.
2 Correct English usage follows the Latin by placing the AD abbreviation before the number of the year, but after the number for BC years (eg, 64 BC, but AD 64). In the North American variant, AD and BC more commonly both come after the number. In terms of AD years it is recognized practice to cease AD usage from the year 500 in situations where the period is otherwise made apparent – ie, AD 499, but 501.
3 In Latin this was determined as *Ante Christum* (AC): Before Christ.
4 In the Christian year 3760 BC.
5 F Josephus, *The Antiquities of the Jews*, bk XVII, ch VIII:1.
6 As for example in 'The Oxford Concordance to the Bible' in *The Holy Bible*, Oxford University Press, Oxford – under Christ, Date of Birth.
7 *The Catholic Encyclopedia*, vol III, under Biblical Chronology.
8 *Ibid*, under Christmas.
9 From the Old English *nativiteo*.
10 In the southern hemisphere the Yuletide date corresponds to the northern feast of Midsummer.
11 D Farmer (ed), *Dictionary of Saints*, under Nicholas, p 364.
12 *The Times* newspaper reported on 21 December 1996 that Belgian children are more confused than ever this Christmas by the duelling Santas. Like their cousins in The Netherlands, they know that St Nicholas is an austere, thin, white-bearded old man in a bishop's mitre who turns up with presents on a boat from Spain on 5 December … He is, however, increasingly rivalled by the jolly, fat, red-clad man who flies in three weeks later'. The concept of Nicholas coming from Spain doubtless arose because Holland was ruled from Spain in the 16th century.

13 Jacob Grimm, *Teutonic Mythology*, Thoemmes Press, London, 1999, ch 17, pp 105, 115.

14 F Josephus, *The Antiquities of the Jews*, bk XVII, ch 13:5, and bk XVIII, ch I:1.

15 S Perowne, *The Later Herods*, Hodder & Stoughton, London, 1958, ch 5, pp 26–9.

16 B Thiering, *Jesus the Man*, ch 8, p 48.

17 Hugh J Schonfield, *The Original New Testament*, Waterstone, London, 1985, p 136; Luke 2:45–50. In the King James Bible, the word 'teachers' is translated as 'doctors', as would be those with academic doctorates.

18 AN Wilson, *Jesus*, ch 4, p 80.

19 *The Oxford Concise English Dictionary*, under Manger.

20 *The Catholic Encyclopedia*, vol III, under Christmas.

21 *Ibid*, vol IV, under Crib.

22 *Ibid*, vol V, under Easter.

23 Eusebius, *Ecclesiastical History*, 1874 edn, bk V, chs 23–6.

24 *The Catholic Encyclopedia*, vol V, under Easter.

25 Leviticus 23:4–6. The Passover celebrates the Israelites' exodus from Egypt, and is followed from the 15th *Nissan* by the seven days of unleavened bread.

26 Exodus, 12:3–11.

27 John 1:29.

28 Gordon Strachan, *Jesus the Master Builder*, Floris, Edinburgh, 1998, ch 1, p 19.

29 Bede, *The Ecclesiastical History of the English People*, Oxford University Press, Oxford, 1969, bk III, ch 25, pp 152–9. According to Bede, Whitby was then called *Streanæshealh*: the Bay of the lighthouse.

30 It is from Eostre that the name for the female hormone oestrogen (USA: estrogen) derives.

31 Rev Lionel Smithett Lewis, *Joseph of Arimathea at Glastonbury*, AR Mobray, London, 1927, pp 15–16.

32 Some commentators have suggested that a younger Aristobulus (the second husband of the deadly dancer, Salome) was Mary's confederate, but he was acting as Regent for the King in Lesser Armenia at the time.

33 Verulamium in Hertfordshire was renamed St Albans after a 4th-century martyr, the Roman soldier Alban, was beheaded by his military superiors in AD 303 for sheltering a Christian priest.

34 Gildas, *De Excidio Britanniae* (trans, JA Giles), G Bell, London, 1891, part II, item 8.

35 Middle English, from Late Latin *neophytus*; from Greek *neophutos*: *neo* + *phutos* – planted (from *phuein*, 'to bring forth').

36 Sir Henrici Spelman, *Concilia, Decreta, Leges, Constitutiones, in re Ecclesiarum Orbis Britannici*, Richardus Badger, London, 1639, pp 5, 108, 109.

37 Rev Cyril C Dobson, *Did Our Lord Visit Britain?* Avalon Press, Glastonbury, 1938, p 26.

Chapter 11: The Crystal Isle

1 Rev LS Lewis, *Joseph of Arimathea at Glastonbury*, p 59.

2 Edward Conybeare, *Roman Britain*, SPCK, London, 1911, p 254.

3 Rev CC Dobson, *Did Our Lord Visit Britain?* p 36.

4 Currently available as William of Malmesbury, *The Antiquities of Glastonbury*, JMF Books, Llanerch, 1992.

5 G Strachan, *Jesus the Master Builder*, ch 2, p 26.

6 James P Carley, *Glastonbury Abbey – The Holy House at the Head of the Moors Adventurous*, Gothic Image, Glastonbury, 1992, ch 3, p 82.

7 William of Malmesbury, *The Antiquities of Glastonbury*, intro, p xiii.

8 Rev LS Lewis, *Joseph of Arimathea at Glastonbury*, p 37.

9 *Ibid*, p 67.

10 William of Malmesbury, *De Antiquitate Glastoniensis Ecclesiae*, Talbot, London, 1908, pp 139–40. Referenced also in *Proceeding of the Somerset Archaeological and Natural History Society*, vol XXXV, 1889, pp 121–6.

11 JP Carley, *Glastonbury Abbey – The Holy House at the Head of the Moors Adventurous*, ch 4, pp 109–10.

12 Matthaei Parisiensis, Monachi Sancti Albani, *Chronica Majora* (ed, HR Luard), Rolls Series lvii, 7 vols, Master of the Rolls, Court of Chancery, 1872–83.

13 William of Malmesbury, *The Antiquities of Glastonbury*, ch 1, pp 2–3.

14 John W Taylor, *The Coming of the Saints*, Covenant Books, London, 1969, ch 7, p 138.

15 Rev CC Dobson, *Did Our Lord Visit Britain?* pp 9–12.

16 Rev LS Lewis, *Joseph of Arimathea at Glastonbury*, pref, p 8.

17 William of Malmesbury, *The Antiquities of Glastonbury*, ch 1, p 3.

18 Extracted from the work of Capgrave is a text known as *Joseph of Armathy*. This (as printed in England by Wynkyn de Worde, *c*1500) is reproduced in Rev Walter W Skeat, *Joseph of Arimathea*, N Trubner and the Early English Text Society, London, 1871, pp 27–32.

19 G Strachan, *Jesus the Master Builder*, ch 1, p 17.

20 Also known as Polydore Virgil.

21 Polidoro Virgilio, *Anglicae Historicae*, Basle, 1534, lib II, ch 7.

22 The Roman poet Martial referred in AD 68 to her as 'Claudia peregrina et edita Britannis' (Foreign Claudia, native of the Britons), and cites her as 'Claudia caeruleis cum sit Rufina Britannis' in Martialis, *Epigrammaton* (ed, W Heraeus) J Borovskij, Leipzig, 1976–82, VII, lib XI, LIII

23 Rev LS Lewis, *Joseph of Arimathea at Glastonbury*, p 16.

24 Eusebius of Caesarea, *An Ecclesiastical History*, 1838 edn, bk III, ch XII, pp 84, 86.

25 GF Jowett, *The Drama of the Lost Disciples*, ch 9, p 86.

26 *See* Michael Wood, *In Search of the Dark Ages*, BBC Books, London, 1981, ch 2, p 50.

27 Helaine Newstead, *Brân the Blessed in Arthurian Romance*, Columbia University Press, New York, NY, 1939, ch 2, p 13. *Cymbeline* (Cunobelinus) and Llyr (*King Lear*) were each the subject of plays by William Shakespeare.

28 'Genealogies of the Welsh Princes' in Harleian MS 3859 confirms that Anna
    was the daughter of Joseph of Arimathea. Anna is sometimes loosely
    referred to as a '*consobrina*' of the Blessed Mary (that is Jesus' mother, Mary).
    Because Joseph has sometimes been wrongly portrayed as Mary's uncle, the
    word *consobrina* has often been taken to denote a cousin. In practice,
    however, the word denoted no more than a junior kinswoman. It was,
    therefore, the perfect word to use when a genealogical relationship was
    unspecific, or when it was deemed necessary for it to remain veiled.

29 Beli Mawr and his grandson Brân are sometimes muddled with the earlier
    brothers Belinus and Brennus (Beli and Bren), who contended for power in
    northern Britain in around 390 BC and were regarded as gods in the old
    Celtic tradition. Brân the Blessed is often cited as the father of Caractacus,
    but Caractacus' father was Cymbeline, whereas Brân's father was King Llyr.
    The reason for the muddle is that, some generations later, the three names
    were repeated during the 3rd and 4th centuries when the Welsh chief Llyr
    Llediath was the father of another Brân, whose son was named Caradoc (a
    variant of Caractacus). Hence, the names Llyr, Brân and Caradoc appear
    successively in two different progressions.

    Penardun, the wife of Marius, is similarly confused on occasions with a
    Penardun who appears in the *Mabinogion* tradition as a daughter of Beli
    Mawr. *See* 'Branwen, Daughter of Llyr' in Jeffrey Gantz (trans), *The
    Mabinogion*, Penguin, London, 1976, p 67. Historically, this other Penardun
    was not a daughter, but a sister of Beli. *See* Hector Munro Chadwick (ed),
    Studies in Early British History, Cambridge University Press, Cambridge,
    1954, ch 5, p 103, note 5.

    Another discrepancy occurs by way of straightforward Church
    corruption. Rather than admit in later times that Linus (Lleyn), the son of
    Caractacus, had been the first Bishop of Rome, a revised story was invented
    in the 885 *Liber Pontificalis* (Book of Popes). This medieval work asserted
    that Linus was a slave from Tuscany, but even the *Catholic Encyclopedia*
    states, 'We cannot discover the origin of this assertion'. *See* in *The Catholic
    Encyclopedia*, vol IX, under Saint Linus.

30 William of Malmesbury, *De Antiquitate Glastoniensis Ecclesiae* (Talbot edn),
    p 135.

31 Johannes Glastoniensis, *Cronica sive Antiquitates Glastoniensis Ecclesiae*,
    Boydell & Brewer, Woodbridge, 1985.

32 Roger Sherman Loomis, *The Grail: From Celtic Myth to Christian Symbolism*,
    University of Wales Press, Cardiff, 1963, ch 15, p 262.

33 Rev CC Dobson, *Did Our Lord Visit Britain?* p 15.

34 Deuteronomy 21:22–3.

35 Hugh Serenus Cressy, *Church History of Brittany or England from the
    Beginning of Christianity to the Norman Conquest*, Rouen, 1668.

36 *The Times Atlas of the Bible*, Times Books, London, 1994, p 147.

37 In modern terms of Western monarchical structure, this would be
    equivalent to the princely style, His Royal Highness.

38 B Thiering, *Jesus the Man*, app III, p 353.

39 *Ibid*, app III, p 363.

40 Rev LS Lewis, *Joseph of Arimathea at Glastonbury*, p 58.

41 F Josephus, *The Antiquities of the Jews*, bk XX, ch IX:1 and note p 439.

42 W Whiston, *Primitive Christianity Revived*, vol III, chs 43–6.

43 As detailed in Acts 15:1–29.

44 John Strype, *Stow's Survey of London*, London, 1720, ch VI:4.

45 G Strachan, *Jesus the Master Builder*, ch 2, p 30.

46 Rev LS Lewis, *Joseph of Arimathea at Glastonbury*, p 15. Following the union of Scotland with England and Wales in 1603, the King's title was adjusted to the less pious 'His Britannic Majesty'.

47 *Disputatio Super Dignitatem Angliae et Galliae in Concilio Constantiano*, Theodore Martin, Lovan, 1517.

48 Rev LS Lewis, *Joseph of Arimathea at Glastonbury*, p 35.

Chapter 12: The Holy Relic

1 G Jowett, *Drama of the Lost Disciples*, ch 2, p 17.

2 Rev CC Dobson, *Did Our Lord Visit Britain?* p 19.

3 JW Taylor, *The Coming of the Saints*, ch 8, p 143.

4 Rev CC Dobson, *Did Our Lord Visit Britain?* p 18.

5 Kenneth O Morgan (ed), *Oxford History of Britain*, Oxford University Press, Oxford, 1988, ch 1, p 16.

6 AN Wilson, *Jesus*, ch 4, p 83; ch 6, pp 122–3.

7 The Aramaic equivalent of *ho tekton* was *naggar*, which denoted a 'scholar' or 'learned man'. *See* Geza Vermes, *Jesus the Jew*, SCM Press, London, 2001, ch 1, p 5.

8 G Strachan, *Jesus the Master Builder*, ch 11, p 141.

9 Sometimes called the *Acts of Pilate*. *See* Gospel of Nicodemus, chs IX–XI in Rutherford H Platt (ed), *The Lost Books of the Bible*, World Publishing, New York, NY, 1963, pp 74–8.

10 Gregory of Tours, *A History of the Franks* (trans, Lewis Thorpe), Penguin, London, 1964, bk 1, item 22, p 82.

11 RS Loomis, *The Grail: From Celtic Myth to Christian Symbolism*, ch 14, pp 223–6.

12 *Ibid*, ch 14, pp 227–8.

13 Riane Eisler, *The Chalice and the Blade*, Harper & Row, New York, NY, 1987, p 72.

14 Harold Bayley, a leading authority on the paper trade, wrote in 1912 that these Provençal watermarks are like 'thought fossils in which lie enshrined aspirations and traditions … They are historical documents of high importance, throwing light not only on the evolution of European thought, but also upon many obscure problems of the past. They are explicable by a code of interpretation'. *See* Harold Bayley, *The Lost Language of Symbolism*, Williams & Norgate, London, 1912, ch 1, p 2.

15 Recommended reading in respect of the Troubadours and the Grail, and for further study with regard to early watermarks is Margaret Starbird, *The Woman with the Alabaster Jar*.

16 Dondaine (1898–1987) was famed for his informative work *Les Heresies et L'Inquisition*.

17 Istituto Storico Domenicano, established as the *Collegium Historicum* in Rome on 2 February 1930.

18 Yuri Stoyanov, *The Hidden Tradition in Europe*, Arkana/Penguin, London, 1994, ch 6, pp 222–3.

19 'Hec Scriptura Testatur Quod Rex Arthurus de Stirpe Ioseph Descendit' in Johannes Glastoniensis, *Cronica sive Antiquitates Glastoniensis Ecclesiae*, XXI.

20 Sebastian Evans (trans), *The High History of the Holy Grail* (*Perlesvaus*), Everyman, London, 1912, branch I, title 1, p 2.

21 RS Loomis, *The Grail: From Celtic Myth to Christian Symbolism*, ch 14, p 232.

22 M Paulin Paris, *Le Romans de la Table Ronde*, Paris, 1877, vol 1, p 91. Also *see* Norma Lorre Goodrich, *King Arthur*, Harper Perennial, New York, NY, 1989, bk III, ch 4, p 234.

23 Wolfram von Eschenbach, *Parzival* (trans, AT Hatto), Penguin, London, 1980, fwd, p 10; ch 8, p 213; ch 9, p 232.

24 Currently published as Geoffrey of Monmouth, *The History of the Kings of Britain*.

25 Matthew Paris, *The Illustrated Chronicle of Matthew Paris*, Alan Sutton, Stroud, and Corpus Christie College, Cambridge, 1993, pp 37–8.

26 PM Matarasso (ed), *The Quest of the Holy Grail*, Penguin, London, 1969, intro, p 10.

27 B Thiering, *Jesus the Man*, app I, pp 325–30.

28 Sebastian Evans (ed), *The High History of the Holy Grail*, James Clarke, Cambridge, 1969, branch II, title 4, p 29.

29 PM Matarasso (ed), *The Quest of the Holy Grail*, ch 1, p 37.

30 1 Chronicles 5:14.

31 Genesis 31:21–5.

32 Genesis 31:46–8.

33 RS Loomis, *The Grail: From Celtic Myth to Christian Symbolism*, ch 12, p 179.

34 Hugh J Schonfield, *The Passover Plot*, Element Books, Shaftesbury, 1985, ch 12, p 168.

35 Other references are: Matthew 16:21, Matthew 17:22, Matthew 17:23, Mark 9:31, Mark 10:34, Luke 9:22, Luke 18:33, Luke 24:7.

36 M Smith, *The Secret Gospel*, ch 7, p 48.

37 B Thiering, *Jesus the Man*, ch 20, p 98.

38 Robert Eisenman and Michael Wise, *Dead Sea Scrolls Uncovered*, Penguin, London, 1992, intro, p 10; ch 6, p 216.

39 G Vermes, *The Complete Dead Sea Scrolls in English*, Temple Scroll, LXIV:10–13, p 217.

Chapter 13: Conquest and Concession

1 C Suetonius Tranquillus, *The Lives of the Twelve Caesars*, Loeb Classical Library, Harvard University Press, Cambridge, MA, 1914, 'The Life of Claudius', 25:4–5.

2 G Jowett, *Drama of the Lost Disciples*, ch 10, p 89.

3 Isabel Hill Elder, *Celt, Druid and Culdee*, Covenant Books, London, 1947, ch 5, p 49.

4 Geoffrey of Monmouth, *The History of the Kings of Britain*, part III:iv, p 111.

5 LA Waddell, *The Phoenician Origin of the Britons, Scots and Anglo-Saxons*, Luzac, London, 1931, ch 8, p 69.

6 Cornelius Tacitus, *Agricola* (trans, M Hutton and W Peterson), Loeb Classical Library, Harvard University Press, Cambridge, MA, 1969, item 13.

7 Geoffrey of Monmouth, *The History of the Kings of Britain*, part III:iv, p 121.

8 C Tacitus, *The Annals of Imperial Rome*, ref AD 51, p 267.

9 Rev RW Morgan, *St Paul in Britain*, Covenant, London 1925, ch 2, p 56.

10 Percy E Corbett, *Why Britain?* RJ Press, Newbury, 1984, p 21. This druidic college is known alternatively as Caer Eurgen.

11 *Ibid*, ch 12, p 126.

12 2 Timothy 4:21.

13 C Tacitus, *The Annals of Imperial Rome*, AD 60, p 330.

14 Galatians 1:19.

15 F Josephus, *The Antiquities of the Jews*, bk XX, ch IX:1.

16 Epiphanius, *Panarion* 78:8:1 & 78:9:6, and *Ancoratus* 60:1.

17 R McL Wilson, *The Gospel of Philip*, 107:10, p 35.

18 *Constitutions of the Holy Apostles*, bk III, p 96.

19 G Jowett, *Drama of the Lost Disciples*, ch 18, p 215.

20 Geoffrey of Monmouth, *The History of the Kings of Britain*, part III:v, p 132.

21 Acts 8:1.

22 Acts 9:1–2.

23 Acts 13:9.

24 AN Wilson, *Jesus*, ch 2, p 26.

25 M Baigent, R Leigh and H Lincoln, *The Messianic Legacy*, ch 6, p 67.

26 Acts 9:13.

27 Acts 9:17.

28 B Thiering, *Jesus the Man*, ch 30, p 139.

29 The doctrinal theme of the Qumrân community was called 'The Way', and those who followed The Way were the 'Children of Light'. In this context, those who were unsympathetic to the doctrine were 'blind to The Way', Symbolically, his instruction in Hellenist principles enabled him to 'see The Way' and, as the English metaphor has it, to 'see the Light'.

30 Daniel 7:13–14.

31 AN Wilson, *Jesus*, ch 2, pp 18–19.

32 1 Thessalonians 4:16–17.

33 AN Wilson, *Jesus*, ch 2, pp 22–3.

34 2 Thessalonians 2:2.

35 JR Porter, *The Illustrated Guide to the Bible*, Duncan Baird, London, 1995, p 239.

36 *Ibid*, p 241.

37 NJ Bull, *Rise of the Church*, ch 4, pp 79–80.

38 The Gospel of Thomas in JM Robinson (ed), *The Nag Hammadi Library*, item 77, p 120.

39 *Ibid*, item 12, p 119.

Chapter 14: A Royal Family

1 *See* chap 13, note 1: Suetonius, *The Lives of the Twelve Caesars*.

2 B Thiering, *Jesus the Man*, ch 31, p 144.

3 C Tacitus, *The Annals of Imperial Rome*, ref AD 57, p 299.

4 Miles Dillon and Nora Chadwick, *The Celtic Realms*, Weidenfeld & Nicolson, London, 1967, ch 1, p 7.

5 Henry Hubert, *The Greatness and Decline of the Celts*, Kegan Paul, London, 1934, ch 3, item 2, p 229.

6 Dom Louis Gougaud, *Christianity in Celtic Lands* (trans, Maud Joynt), Four Courts Press, Dublin, 1932, ch 6, pp 201–4.

7 H Hubert, *The Greatness and Decline of the Celts*, ch 3, item 2, p 228.

8 B Thiering, *Jesus the Man*, ch 15, p 79, and app: People and Events, pp 395–6.

9 For example in Eusebius, *Ecclesiastical History*, 1874 edn, bk II, ch 13, pp 48–9.

10 Steve Richards, *Levitation*, Thorsons, Wellingborough, 1980, ch 5, pp 66–7.

11 Matthew 10:4, Mark 3:18.

12 M Dillon and NK Chadwick, *The Celtic Realms*, ch 1, p 15.

13 IH Elder, *Celt, Druid and Culdee*, ch 5, p 46.

14 Diogenes Laërtius, *The Lives and Opinions of Eminent Philosophers* (trans, CD Tonge), Bohn, London, 1853, intro, item V.

15 A primary work in this regard is Miranda Green, *The Gods of the Celts*, Alan Sutton, Stroud, 1986.

16 H Hubert, *The Greatness and Decline of the Celts*, ch 3, item 5, p 236.

17 Miranda J Green, *Exploring the World of the Druids*, Thames & Hudson, London, 1997, p 78.

18 Dom L Gougaud, *Christianity in Celtic Lands*, ch 10, pp 348–9.

19 Geoffrey Higgins, *Celtic Druids*, Rowland Hunter, London, 1829, ch 4, p 130.

20 H Hubert, *The Greatness and Decline of the Celts*, ch 3, item 5, p 231.

21 F Josephus, *The Antiquities of the Jews*, bk XV, ch X:4.

22 The Second Treatise of the Great Seth in JM Robinson (ed), *The Nag Hammadi Library*, items 55–6, p 332.

23 Details from this Codex are available in Majella Franzmann, *Jesus in the Manichaean Writings*, Continuum International, New York, NY, 2003.

24 Matthew 27:49, Mark 15:37, Luke 23:46, John 19:30.

25 Genesis 25:8, Genesis 25:17, Genesis 35:29.

26 Luke 23:46.

27 Matthew 27:46, Mark 15:34.

28 John 19:36. Alternatively in Matthew 21:4, 'All this was done that it might be fulfilled which was spoken by the prophet'.

29 H Schonfield, *The Passover Plot*, ch 11, p 156.

30 Luke 24:13–31.

31 John 20:19–28.

32 John 21.

33 Acts 1:9–12.

34 B Thiering, *Jesus the Man*, ch 27, p 128.

35 *See* plate 14 in L Gardner, *The Magdalene Legacy*.

36 Since Eostre was a pagan goddess of Britain, Mary Magdalene became the new symbol of Easter in the Christian world. In relating the fertility of Eostre to the gospel tradition, it was said that Mary went from Judaea to Rome for an audience with Emperor Tiberius. Presenting an egg as a gift, she told him of how Jesus had come back to life, whereupon Tiberius remarked that it was as impossible as it would be for the egg to turn red – at which the egg in Mary's hand turned red. Despite all pagan tradition, it is explained that this is why Easter eggs became a popular tradition! But this does not explain why Mary would travel 1,500 miles across the Mediterranean Sea to give the Emperor an ordinary egg in order to prove the resurrection.

37 Hebrews 7:12–20.

38 F Josephus, *The Wars of the Jews*, bk II, ch VIII:3.

39 B Thiering, *Jesus the Man*, ch 27, p 127.

40 Exodus 13:21–2.

41 Exodus 19:16.

42 B Thiering, *Jesus the Man*, app II, p 297; app III, pp 363–4.

43 Acts 1:10–11.

44 B Thiering, *Jesus the Man*, app III, p 177.

45 Acts 3:20–21.

46 B Thiering, *Jesus the Man*, ch 33, p 151; app I, p 251.

47 Elizabeth AM Wilson, *Shostakovich: A Life Remembered*, Faber & Faber, London, 1994, p 317.

48 *Ibid*, ch 29, p 133.

49 Mark 4:11–12.

50 Mark 4:8.

51 R McL Wilson, *The Gospel of Philip*, item 129:14–20, p 57.

52 B Thiering, *Jesus the Man*, ch 31, p 141; app I, p 262.

53 Barbara Thiering, *Jesus of the Apocalypse*, Doubleday, London, 1996, ch 3, pp 25–30.

54 Revelation 19:10–13.

Chapter 15: Legacy of the Bride

1 Simon is honoured as the first missionary priest in Cyprus. The main church in Larnaca, where his is said to have been the first bishop, is dedicated to him under his other New Testament name, Lazarus.

2 Catalogued at the British Museum as *Piste Sophia Coptice*, MS Add. 5114.

3 *Pistis Sophia*, bk 1, ch 36, p 47.

4 The Gospel of Philip, items 63–4, pp 138–9; The Gospel of Thomas, item 114, p 130; The Gospel of Mary, item 10, p 472 – all in JM Robinson (ed), *The Nag Hammadi Library*.

5 The Dialogue of the Saviour in *Ibid*, item 139, p 235.

6 Susan Haskins, *Mary Magdalen, Myth and Metaphor*, Harcourt Brace, New York, NY, 1994, ch 3, pp 63–7.

7 *Ibid*, ch 3, pp 58–9.

8 Acts 12:23 states that Herod-Agrippa was smote by an angel and 'eaten of worms'. *See also*, Stewart Perowne, *The Later Herods*, Hodder & Stoughton, London, 1958, ch 10, p 83.

9 The story, as told in Acts 12:3–10, is that Peter subsequently escaped with the aid of an angel.

10 In respect of his pronouncements concerning divorce and separation, Paul stated, 'to the rest speak I, not the Lord' (1 Corinthians 7:10–12).

11 Luke 8:2–3.

12 The view that Mary decided to leave Jesus of her own accord because she did not agree with his doctrine is postulated in B Thiering, *Jesus the Man*, ch 32, p 146.

13 Origen, *The Song of Songs, Commentary and Homilies*, bk 2, ch 6, pp 160–1.

14 Bernard de Clairvaux, *Patriologia Latina*, vol 183, cols, 1050–55.

15 The Gospel of Thomas in JM Robinson (ed), *The Nag Hammadi Library*, item 12, p 119.

16 *Pistis Sophia*, bk 1, ch 17, p 20.

17 B Thiering, *Jesus the Man*, 'People and Events', p 395.

18 F Josephus, *The Wars of the Jews*, bk II, ch VII:3.

19 The language of Marseilles (Massilia) and the Provençal region in general was Greek until the 5th century. *See* G Taylor, *Our Neglected Heritage*, vol 1, p 17.

20 The Proselytes were Gentile converts to the Jewish faith.

21 C Witcombe, 'The Chapel of the Courtesan and the Quarrel of the Magdalens' in *Art Bulletin*, vol 84, no 2, pp 273–92.

22 JW Taylor, *The Coming of the Saints*, ch 6, p 103.

23 *The Catholic Encyclopedia*, vol XII, under Rabanus Maurus.

24 JW Taylor, *The Coming of the Saints*, ch 5, p 90.

25 Ean CM Begg, *The Cult of the Black Virgin*, Arkana, London, 1985, ch 4, p 98.

26 Voragine is now Varazze, near Genoa in Italy.

27 Jacopo di Voragine, *Légenda Aurea (Golden Legend)*, (trans, William Caxton, 1483; ed, George V O'Neill), Cambridge University Press, Cambridge, 1972.

28 The Abbey of St Maximus is around 30 miles (48 km) from Marseilles.

29 Marseilles subsequently became a recognized monastic centre, and was the birthplace of the Candlemas ritual which succeeded the earlier torchlight procession of Persephone of the Underworld. Culminating at the harbour, near the fortress-style Abbey of St Victor, the event (with its long green fertility candles) still takes place on 2 February each year. It coincides with the Imbolc spring festival of the pagan calendar and, in recognition of Mary Magdalene's sea voyage, the Abbey bakery produces orange flavoured, boat-shaped biscuits called *navettes*. St Victor's contains John Cassian's sarcophagus and a medieval Black Madonna (*Notre Dame de Confession*), while an ancient altar in the crypt is inscribed with Mary Magdalene's name.

30 Père Lacordaire, *St Mary Magdalene*, Thomas Richardson, Derby, 1880, ch VII, p 99.

31 Song of Solomon 4:15. It had also been prophesied in Zechariah 14:8 that the 'living waters shall go out from Jerusalem, half of them toward the former sea, and half of them toward the hinder sea'. The monks considered this to be manifest in the two aspects of Christianity, with Mary's sea voyage representing the fount of the *Desposyni*.

32 Albert Dauzat and Charles Rostaing (eds), *Dictionnaire étymologique des noms de lieux en France*, Guénégaud, Paris, 1963, under Aix.

33 JW Taylor, *The Coming of the Saints*, ch 5, p 83.

34 The chief sources for the Hasmonaeans are the apocryphal books of Maccabees. *See* in Sir Lancelot CL Brenton (trans), *The Septuagint with Apocrypha*, Samuel Bagster, London, 1851. They also feature in F Josephus, *The Antiquities of the Jews*.

35 M Starbird, *The Woman with the Alabaster Jar*, ch 3, pp 50–1.

36 G Jowett, *Drama of the Lost Disciples*, ch 15, p 164.

37 For a fuller description of the Church of Saint Martha, *see* JW Taylor, *The Coming of the Saints*, ch 10, pp 195–7.

38 St Caesarius was abbot of a pre-Benedictine monastery at Arles in Southern France in Merovingian times. *See* David Farmer (ed), *Oxford Dictionary of Saints*, under Caesarius.

39 *Sermo 26 de Verbis Domini*, from *Homilia sancti Augustini Episcopi* – A Homily by St Augustine the Bishop.

40 JW Taylor, *The Coming of the Saints*, ch 10, pp 194–5.

41 P Lacordaire, *St Mary Magdalene*.

42 *The Catholic Encyclopedia*, vol VIII, under Lacordaire.

43 *The Hutchinson Encyclopedia*, Hutchinson, London, 1997, under Saracens.

44 *The Macmillan Encyclopedia*, Macmillan, London, 1996, under Moors. The designation derived from 'Mauritania', the Roman name for NW Africa.

45 P Lacordaire, *St Mary Magdalene*, ch 7, p 103.

46 ECM Begg, *The Cult of the Black Virgin*, ch 4, p 103. The reference to a castle stems from an item in the 9th-century *Life of Mary Magdalene* by Raban Maurus, which eventually found its way into the *Golden Legend* of Jacopo di Voragine. The entry states that 'Mary with her brother Lazarus, and her sister Martha, possessed the castle of Magdalo at Bethany. In such wise that Mary had the castle, whereof she had her name Magdalene'. It actually related to a high community station (a castle or tower) of community guardianship, as in Micah 4:8, the *Magdal-eder* (Watchtower of the flock) rather than to a building as such.

47 *Ibid*, ch 7, p 107.

48 Eudes, as mentioned in the inscription, was Eudes of Aquitaine, who had declared his independence from the attempt by the Carolingian, Pepin the Short (Charlemagne's father), to take control from the Merovingians in France. Eudes was considered regionally to be King of France south of the Loire.

49 See plate 53 in L Gardner, *The Magdalene Legacy*.

50 At that stage Charles's successor, Bene, was King of Naples and Provence.
51 *The Catholic Encyclopedia*, vol XII, under Friars Preachers.
52 Edgcumbe Staley, *King René d'Anjou and his Seven Queens*, John Long, London, 1912, ch 9, p 334.
53 *Ibid*.
54 P Lacordaire, *St Mary Magdalene*, ch VII, p 120.
55 Philippe VI of France, Alfonso IV of Aragon, Hugh IV of Cyprus, John of Bohemia, Robert of Sicily.
56 John XXII, Benedict XII, Clement VII, Urban V, Gregory XI, Urban VI, Boniface IX, Innocent VII.
57 S Haskins, *Mary Magdalene, Myth and Metaphor*, ch 5, pp 158–9.
58 Jean Evenou, 'La messe de Sainte Marie Madeleine au Missel romain (1570–1970)' in Robert SJ Godding, *Grégoire le Grand et la Madeleine in Memoriam soctorum venerantes – Miscellanea in onore di Mgr Victor Saxer*, The Vatican, Rome, 1992, pp 353–65.
59 'De nativitate sancti Johannis Baptiste, et de beaetis apostolic Petro et Paulo, et de beata maria Magdalena fiat festum totum duplex; et magister ordinis cures de sequentiis providere' in B Reichert (ed), *Acta Capitulorum Generalium Ordinis Praedicatorum*,The Vatican, Rome, 1898, p 283.
60 S Haskins, *Mary Magdalene, Myth and Metaphor*, ch 5, p 147.
61 R McL Wilson, *The Gospel of Philip*, item 107:5, pp 35, 97.

Chapter 16: The Greater Quest

1 The *Sone de Nansi* suggests alternatively that Joseph's wife was a princess of Norway (RS Loomis, *The Grail: From Celtic Myth to Christian Symbolism*, ch 10, p 142), but this does not refer to the Norse country. It translates from *Nor Wegia*: the 'Northern Way'.
2 B Thiering, *Jesus the Man*, ch 8, p 47.
3 Innogen's name was corrupted in William Shakespeare's play, *Cymbeline*, to Imogen.
4 Matthew 1:24–5, Luke 2:7.
5 M Martin, *The Decline and Fall of the Roman Church*, pp 42–3.
6 John 19:25.
7 R Bauckham, *Jude and the Relatives of Jesus in the Early Church*, ch 2, p 79.
8 Eusebius, *The History of the Church from Christ to Constantine*, ch 3:32, p 95.
9 R Bauckham, *Jude and the Relatives of Jesus in the Early Church*, ch 2, pp 97–100.
10 Eusebius of Caesarea, *Ecclesiastical History*, 1838 edn, bk III, ch 4, p 69.
11 A selection of ancient Welsh writings published by the Welsh Manuscripts Society from the library of Edward Williams (1747–1826), better known by his bardic style of Iolo Morgannwg.
12 Rev Lionel Smithett Lewis, *Glastonbury, The Mother of Saints*, St Stephen's Press, Bristol, 1925, p 2. This was confirmed from Roman records at the Council of Constance.
13 William J Watson, *The History of the Celtic Place Names of Scotland*, William Blackwood, Edinburgh, 1926, ch 13, p 457.

14　Harleian MS 3859. Also *see* PC Bartrum, *Early Welsh Genealogical Tracts*, University of Wales Press, Cardiff, 1966, p 9.

15　WAS Hewins, *The Royal Saints of Britain*, Chiswick Press, London, 1928, p 20. *See* also Rev WJ Rees, *Lives of the Cambro British Saints*, Welsh MSS Society, Llandovery, 1853, ch III, p 400 and *passim* regarding Beino, Cadoc, Carannog, Dewi and Gwynllyw.

16　Helaine Newstead, *Brân the Blessed in Arthurian Romance*, ch 3, p 30.

17　Bede, *The Ecclesiastical History of the English People*, bk I, ch 4, p 14.

18　GO Harry, *The Genealogy of the High and Mighty Monarch James*, chart B, p 20.

19　Geoffrey of Monmouth, *The History of the Kings of Britain*, part III:iv, pp 125–6.

20　The Gildas anomaly is discussed in Richard Barber, *The Figure of Arthur*, Longman, London, 1972, ch 4, pp 45–6.

21　Michael Swanton (trans), *The Anglo-Saxon Chronicle*, JM Dent, London, 1997, Peterborough MS (E) 62, 167, p 9.

22　*The Catholic Encyclopedia*, vol V, under St Eleutherius.

23　G Jowett, *Drama of the Lost Disciples*, ch 9, p 80.

24　A transcript of Eleutherius' reply to King Lucius in AD 177 is given in JW Taylor, *The Coming of the Saints*, app K.

25　G Jowett, *Drama of the Lost Disciples*, ch 15, p 175.

26　*See* chapter 19, section: Pagans and Wizards regarding this transfer.

27　References in Roman martyrology to the burial of Lucius at Chur in Switzerland are inaccurate on two counts. They actually relate to King Lucius of Bavaria (not to Lucius the Luminary of Britain). Moreover, the Bavarian Lucius died at Curia in Germany, not at Chur in Switzerland.

28　Geoffrey of Monmouth, *The History of the Kings of Britain*, part III:v, pp 131–2.

29　GO Harry, *The Genealogy of the High and Mighty Monarch James*, chart A, p 24.

30　*See* this genealogy in 'Dynasty of Dumnonia' in HM Chadwick (ed), *Studies in Early British History*, ch 3, p 52.

31　*The Catholic Encyclopedia*, vol XV, under St Veronica.

32　D Farmer, *Oxford Dictionary of Saints*, under Veronica.

33　Revelation 12:17.

34　*See* B Thiering, *Jesus of the Apocalypse*, ch 1, p 25, *passim*.

35　NJ Bull, *The Rise of the Church*, ch 4, pp 97–8.

36　B Thiering, *Jesus the Man*, ch 33, p 151.

37　Dan Brown, *The Da Vinci Code*, Bantam Press, London, 2003, ch 60, p 255.

38　Her story is recounted in Jean-Paul Clébert, *The Gypsies* (trans, Charles Duff), Visita Books, London, 1963, *passim*.

39　Charles Sigisbert Sonnini: 1751–1812 (trans), *The Long Lost Chapter of the Acts of the Apostles*, Covenant, London, 1920.

40　Rev RW Morgan, *St Paul in Britain*, ch 4, pp 107, 116.

41　Arthur Edward Waite, *The Hidden Church of the Holy Grail*, Rebman, London, 1909, bk I, ch 4, p 57. The *Grand Saint Graal* is alternatively called the *Book of the Holy Graal*.

42　He was also a Prebend of St Paul's and a Canon of Lincoln.

43 RS Loomis, *The Grail: From Celtic Myth to Christian Symbolism*, ch 14, p 228.

44 For example, Jessie L Weston, *From Ritual to Romance*, Cambridge University Press, Cambridge, 1920, ch 14, p 183.

45 'From the Beginnings to the Cycles of Romance' in *The Cambridge History of English and American Literature*, vol I, Putnam, New York, NY, 1907–21, item 4: Walter Map.

46 AE Waite, *The Hidden Church of the Holy Grail*, bk I, ch 4, p 59.

47 Roger Sherman Loomis, in *The Grail: From Celtic Myth to Christian Symbolism*, ch 14, pp 234–5, makes the point that proper names in manuscript transmission sometimes lose their initial letter – although mutation of the initial letters of names is a feature of the Celtic languages. By this process, Morgaine is sometimes found as Orguein and, with specific relevance to the present case, Galains (Galaain) became Alain (Alaain).

48 S Evans (ed), *The High History of the Holy Grail*, 1969 edn, branch I, title 1, p 2.

49 *See* B Thiering, *Jesus of the Apocalypse*, ch 3, p 31. This work details the full sequence of events in respect of the messianic family history as recounted in The Revelation.

50 The *Roman l'Estoire dou Saint Graal* also confirms that, on the death of Alain, the Lordship of the Grail passed to Josue – although defining him as Alain's brother rather than his cousin. Frederick J Furnival (ed), *The History of the Holy Grail* – from *Roman l'Estoire dou Saint Graal* by Sires Robert de Boron (trans, Henry Lonelich Skynner), Early English Text Society and N Turner, London, 1861.

51 AE Waite, *The Hidden Church of the Holy Grail*, bk V, ch 2, pp 306–7; ch 3, p 313. Calaphas is sometimes listed as Alphasan.

52 *Ibid*, bk V, ch 2, pp 291–3.

53 PM Matarasso (ed), *The Quest of the Holy Grail*, ch 15, pp 275–6.

54 Sir Thomas Malory, *Tales of King Arthur*, Guild Publishing, London, 1980, bk II, p 188.

55 WAS Hewins, *The Royal Saints of Britain*, pp 18–19.

56 AE Waite, *The Hidden Church of the Holy Grail*, bk V, ch 2, p 298.

57 Johannes Glastoniensis, *Cronica sive Antiquitates Glastoniensis Ecclesiae*, p 68.

58 Exodus 6:23.

59 Song of Solomon 6:5. Cited as 'Galaad' in the Latin *Vulgate*, and 'Gilead' in the *KJV*.

60 Given in Latin as the 'quadrigas Aminadab', from *quadri*: four, and *jungere*: to yoke – thus *quadriga*: a four-horse chariot.

61 Marion Meade, *Eleanor of Aquitaine*, Frederick Muller, London, 1978, pref, p 3.

62 Duc de Castries, *The Lives of the Kings and Queens of France*, (trans, Anne Dobell for the Académie Française), Weidenfeld & Nicolson, London, 1979, p 64.

63 *The Catholic Encyclopedia*, vol XII, under Abby of Saint Denis.

64 Alison Weir, *Eleanor of Aquitaine*, Pimlico, London, 2000, ch 3, p 44.

65 Sometimes called Honorius of Autun.

66 The only surviving ancient quadriga is the Triumphal Quadriga in Venice. Well-known quadriga statues are those at the Brandenburg Gate in Berlin, the Arc du Triomphe du Carrousel in Paris, the monument of Victor Emmanuel II in Rome, Wellington Arch in London, and the Minnesota State Capitol, Saint Paul.

67 For descriptions of Suger's designs, *see* Erwin Panofsky and Gerda Panofsky-Soergel (eds), *Abbot Suger on the Abbey Church of St. Denis and Its Art Treasures*, Princeton University Press, Princeton, NJ, 1979. Also *see* William Henry, *Mary Magdalene: The Illuminator*, Adventures Unlimited, Kempton, IL, 2006, pp 235–9.

68 Émile Mâle, *Religious Art in France of the Thirteenth Century*, Dover, Mineola, NY, 2000, bk IV, ch VII, p 171.

69 AE Waite, *The Hidden Church of the Holy Grail*, bk V, ch 2, pp 291–2.

70 *Ibid*, bk V, ch 2, p 299.

71 S Evans (ed), *The High History of the Holy Grail*, 1969 edn, branch II, title IV, p 31.

72 *Ibid*, branch II, title I, p 23.

73 RS Loomis, *The Grail: From Celtic Myth to Christian Symbolism*, ch 9, pp 106–7.

74 Bernard de Clairvaux, *Patriologia Latina*, vol 183, cols 1050–55.

75 *The Catholic Encyclopedia*, vol VI, under Symbolism of the Fish.

76 AE Waite, *The Hidden Church of the Holy Grail*, bk V, ch 3, p 313.

77 Johannes Glastoniensis, *Cronica sive Antiquitates Glastoniensis Ecclesiae*, p 68.

78 AE Waite, *The Hidden Church of the Holy Grail*, bk V, ch 3, pp 313–14.

79 RS Loomis, *The Grail: From Celtic Myth to Christian Symbolism*, pp 44, 56, 109, 156–7.

80 His father is given as Lancelot, and his mother as Elaine, the daughter of King Pelles.

Chapter 17: Descent of the Grail

1 Johannes Glastoniensis, *Cronica sive Antiquitates Glastoniensis Ecclesiae*, p 68.

2 GO Harry, *The Genealogy of the High and Mighty Monarch James*, chart B/C, p 24.

3 Geoffrey of Monmouth, *The History of the Kings of Britain*, part VI:viii, p 205.

4 NL Goodrich, *King Arthur*, intro, p 13.

5 RS Loomis, *The Grail: From Celtic Myth to Christian Symbolism*, ch 14, pp 246–7.

6 Including Emma Jung and Marie-Louise von Franz, *The Grail Legend*, Princeton University Press, Princeton, NJ, 1998, and Walter Johannes Stein, *The Ninth Century*, Temple Lodge, London, 1991.

7 The history of Montségur is given in A Czeski, JP Erard, and Marie-Elects Gardel, *Montségur: 13 Years of Archaeological Research, 1964–1976*, Group of Archaeological Research of Montségur and Environs, Lavelanet, 1981.

8 Wolfram von Eschenbach, *Parzival*, ch 9, p 232.

9 AE Waite, *The Hidden Church of the Holy Grail*, bk VI, ch 1, p 395, explains that there is a mysterious Grail tradition that when the knights require

bread they receive a stone called the *lapis exilii*. This alchemical subject is covered in depth in Laurence Gardner, *Lost Secrets of the Sacred Ark*, HarperCollins, London, 2003.

10 RS Loomis, *The Grail: From Celtic Myth to Christian Symbolism*, ch 13, p 201.

11 AE Waite, *The Hidden Church of the Holy Grail*, bk VI, ch 1, p 394.

12 M Starbird, *The Woman With the Alabaster Jar*, ch 4, p 86.

13 Luke 7:37–8.

14 DR Howlett, 'Two Panels on the Ruthwell Cross' in the *Journal of the Warburg and Courtauld Institutes*, vol XXXVII, 1972, p 334. *See* also 'The Religious Meaning of the Ruthwell Cross' in Meyer Shapiro, *Late Antique, Early Christian and Medieval Art*, George Braziller, New York, NY, 1979, vol III, pp 150–95.

15 S. Haskins, *Mary Magdalene*, ch 4, p 112.

16 Nora K Chadwick, *Early Brittany*, University of Wales Press, Cardiff, 1969, ch 6, p 194.

17 Merlin's life is recounted in Geoffrey of Monmouth, *The Vita Merlini* (trans, John Jay Parry), University of Illinois, Urbana, IL, 1925.

18 Keith Spence, *Brittany and the Bretons*, Victor Gollancz, London, 1978, ch 4, pp 52–3.

19 NK Chadwick, *Early Brittany*, ch 6, p 221. *See* also HM Chadwick (ed), *Studies in Early British History*, ch 8, p 252.

20 'The British Immigration' in NK Chadwick, *Early Brittany*, ch 6, pp 193–237.

21 WAS Hewins, *The Royal Saints of Britain*, chart, p 9.

22 Geoffrey of Monmouth, *The History of the Kings of Britain*, part VII:xi, p 258.

23 Whitley Stokes (ed), *Félire Óengusso Céli Dé (The Martyrology of Oengus the Culdee)*, Dublin Institute for Advanced Studies, Dublin, 1984, item: January, note 27, p 53.

24 Urien is most renowned for establishing a coalition of Strathclyde rulers against the Northumbrian Angles of Bernicia.

25 In *The Book of Taliesin* eight poems are addressed to Urien Rheged, whose kingdom was centred in the region of the Solway Firth on the borders of present-day England and Scotland. One poem was addressed to Owain, son of Urien.

26 The later Welsh romance entitled *Owein, or The Lady of the Fountain* (as in the *White Book of Rhydderch*, the *Red Book of Hergest* and the *Mabinogion*) was directly based on Chrétien's poem.

27 Withur was a Basque name, derived from the Irish Witur, whose Cornish equivalent was Gwythyr.

28 Geoffrey of Monmouth, *The History of the Kings of Britain*, part VII:ix, p 217.

29 The name Excalibur first appeared in the 1155 *Roman de Brut* by Robert Wace, at which time Arthur's wife Guanhumara was renamed Gwynefer (from the Gaelic *gwen-hwyfar*: 'fair spirit'). At that stage, the story of Arthur's drawing a sword from a stone had nothing whatever to do with Excalibur. This stemmed from a quite separate incident in Robert de Boron's *Merlin*, as taken up by Thomas Malory in *Morte d'Arthur*. It was not until the 19th-century writings of Alfred, Lord Tennyson, that Excalibur

and the sword on the stone were brought together as being one and the same.

30 Ygerna also appears as Eigyr in the *Brut Dingestow* (c1300), a Middle Welsh translation of Geoffrey of Monmouth's *Historia Regum Britanniae*, which was written originally in Latin.

31 Viviane (Vivien) or Nimue is sometimes called Niniane or Nyneve.

32 The Welsh text is discussed in S Evans (ed), *The High History of the Holy Grail*, 1969 edn, intro, pp vii–viii.

33 RS Loomis, *The Grail: From Celtic Myth to Christian Symbolism*, ch 12, pp 182–3.

34 AE Waite, *The Hidden Church of the Holy Grail*, bk V, ch 7, p 360.

35 Rev WW Skeat, *Joseph of Arimathea*, p 31.

36 The most comprehensive account of the Septimanian princedom is in Arthur J Zuckerman, *A Jewish Princedom in Feudal France*, Columbia University Press, New York, NY, 1972.

37 *See* James King Hewison, *The Isle of Bute in the Olden Time*, William Blackwood, Edinburgh, 1895, Chart XXIII.

38 *See* James Anderson, *Royal Genealogies*, London, 1732–36, tables CCCLXXI, CCCLXXIII, pp 612, 614.

39 AE Waite, *The Hidden Church of the Holy Grail*, bk V, ch 7, p 333.

40 *Ibid*, bk V, ch 7, p 334–5.

41 *Ibid*.

42 *Ibid*.

43 S Evans (ed), *The High History of the Holy Grail*, 1969 edn, branch I, title 1, p 2.

44 *See* Sir Thomas Malory, *Tales of King Arthur*, bk II, p 213.

45 PM Matarasso (ed), *The Quest of the Holy Grail*, ch 10, pp 214–15, 220–1.

46 John 19:34.

47 The term 'dolorous' relates to an act which causes grief and sorrow as in the Dolorous Passion of Jesus Christ.

48 In the *Morte d'Arthur*, Pellehan (the father of Pelles) is identified as Pellam, and suffered his assault from the lance of the knight Balyn.

49 Gralon, son of Conan Meriadoc, is sometimes recorded as Urbein or Urban.

50 Lewis Spence, *Legends and Romances of Brittany*, George G Harrap, London, 1917, p 189.

51 Rev Sabine Baring-Gould, *A Book of Brittany*, Methuen, London, 1932, ch 1, pp 4–5.

52 Peter Berresford Ellis, *A Brief History of the Druids*, Constable and Robinson, London, 2002, p 104.

53 WAS Hewins, *The Royal Saints of Britain*, chart, p 9. *See* also *The Catholic Encyclopedia*, vol IV, under St Darerca. Darerca of France is not to be confused with Darerca of Ireland, whose husbands were Restitutus the Lombard and Chonas the Briton.

54 A letter from the Roman prefect Sidonius Apollinaris, requesting the aid of Riatham, is published in OM Dalton (ed), *The Letters of Sidonius Apollinaris*, Clarendon Press, Oxford, 1915, p.76.

55 Charles C Mierow (ed), *The Origin and Deeds of the Goths* (from Jordanes, 551), Princeton University Press, Princeton, NJ, 1915, ch 45, p 237.
56 Geoffrey Ashe, *Avalonian Quest*, Methuen, London, 1982, ch 2, part 3, pp 34–5. Also *see* Geoffrey Ashe, *Kings and Queens of Early Britain*, Methuen, London, 2000, ch 7, part 4, pp 128–37.
57 K Spence, *Brittany and the Bretons*, ch 3, p 41. Also see NK Chadwick, *Early Brittany*, ch 6, p 221.
58 Nennius, *History of the Britons* (trans, John Morris), Phillimore, Chichester, 1980, item 62. The five poets were Tallhaearn Tad Awen (Talhaiarn Cataguen), Aneirin (Neirin), Taliesin, Bluchbard and Cian (Gueinth Guaut). [Aneirin wrote *The Book of Aneurin* and the poem *Y Goddodin*.] The bracketed names are as given in the translation: 'History of the Britons' in Nennius, *Six Old English Chronicles* (trans, John Allan Giles), George Bell, London. 1891.
59 Nikolai Tolstoy, *The Quest for Merlin*, Hamish Hamilton, London, 1985, ch 11, p 184.
60 *Ibid*, ch 10, p 136.
61 The *Book of Taliesin*, known as the Peniarth 2 MS, in the National Library of Wales, Aberwystwyth.
62 National Library of Wales MS 5276.
63 The work includes the *Hanes Taliesin*, as translated by Lady Charlotte Guest in her 1848 edition of *The Mabinogion*.
64 Robert Graves, *The White Goddess*, Faber & Faber, London, 1961, ch 5, p 74.
65 *Ibid*, ch 5, p 83. Line 25 of the *Hanes Taliesin*.
66 *Ibid*, ch 5, p 85. From *Y Gofeisws Byd* (A Sketch of the World) in the *Red Book of Hergest*.
67 Robert Graves, *King Jesus*, Cassell, London, 1946, ch19, pp 223–6.
68 Cotton Vespasian MS A1, item I. Also *see* HM Chadwick (ed), *Studies in Early British History*, ch 3, p 58 and note 3.
69 PC Bartrum, *Early Welsh Genealogical Tracts*, Bonedd yr Arwr, item 31, p 94.
70 Rev S Baring-Gould, *A Book of Brittany*, ch 1, p 5.
71 NK Chadwick, *Early Brittany*, ch 6, pp 206, 209, 211–12.
72 'Vie de St Efflam' in Albert le Grand, *Les Vies des Saintes de la Bretagne Armorique*, Paris, 1901.
73 S Evans (ed), *The High History of the Holy Grail*, 1969 edn, branch XXXV, title 9, p 363.
74 AE Waite, *The Hidden Church of the Holy Grail*, bk V, ch 7, p 334–5.

Chapter 18: The New Kingdoms

1 AE Waite, *The Hidden Church of the Holy Grail*, bk V, ch 2, pp 291–3.
2 The concept was brought to public attention in M Baigent, R Leigh and H Lincoln, *The Holy Blood and the Holy Grail*.
3 The Sicambrians took their name from their tribal queen, Cambra, in about 380 BC. Apart from the *Royal Genealogies* (*see* note 6 below), information concerning the Sicambrian and Frankish generations is given in Herman L

Hoeh, *Compendium of World History*, Ambassador College, Pasadena, CA, 1963, vol II, ch XII:A.

4 *Oxford Compact English Dictionary*, under Frank.

5 JM Wallace-Hadrill, *The Long Haired Kings*, Methuen, London, 1962, ch 4, p 78.

6 *See* J Anderson, *Royal Genealogies*, tables CCCLXXI, CCCCLXXVIII, pp 612, 731.

7 AE Waite, *The Hidden Church of the Holy Grail*, bk IV, ch 1, p 375.

8 Edouard Sandoz, 'Tourneys in the Arthurian Tradition' in *Speculum*, Medieval Academy of America, Cambridge, MA, Nov 1944, vol 19, pp 389–420. For Arthurian heraldry, *see* also Michel Pastoureau, *Armorial des Chevaliers de la Table Ronde*, Léopard d'Or, Paris, 1983.

9 The *Prose Tristan* is attributed to either Luces de Gast, or Helie de Borron.

10 P Lacordaire, *St Mary Magdalene*, ch VII, p 120.

11 M Baigent, R Leigh, H Lincoln, *The Holy Blood and the Holy Grail*, ch 9, pp 202–3.

12 R Graves, *The White Goddess*, ch 5, p 85. From *Y Gofeisws Byd* (A Sketch of the World) in the *Red Book of Hergest*.

13 The name Clovis was later adapted to become Louis.

14 RHC Davis, *A History of Medieval Europe*, Longmans, London, 1957, ch 6, p 109.

15 Claudus appears in the *High History of the Holy Grail* (*Perlesvaus*) chapters XXVII and XXXIV.

16 J Anderson, *Royal Genealogies*, table CCCLXX, p 611.

17 JM Wallace-Hadrill, *The Long Haired Kings*, ch 7, pp 156–7.

18 RHC Davis, *A History of Medieval Europe*, ch 6, p 109.

19 Gregory of Tours, *A History of the Franks*, bk II, item 9, p 125.

20 RHC Davis, *A History of Medieval Europe*, ch 6, p 115.

21 Sir Samuel Dill, *Roman Society in Gaul in the Merovingian Age*, Macmillan, London, 1926, bk I, ch 4, p 113.

22 JM Wallace-Hadrill, *The Long Haired Kings*, ch 7, p 204.

23 Sir S Dill, *Roman Society in Gaul in the Merovingian Age*, bk I, ch 3, p 78.

24 Gregory of Tours, *A History of the Franks*, bk II, item 30, pp 143–4.

25 An overall view of the Franks and later Merovingians is given in Margaret Deanesly, *A History of Early Medieval Europe 476–911*, Methuen, London, 1956, ch 4, pp 54–74; ch 15, pp 260–84.

26 St Martin's life is recounted in Gregory of Tours, *A History of the Franks*, bk X, item 31, pp 594–5.

27 Dom L Gougaud, *Christianity in Celtic Lands*, ch 2, p 33.

28 HM Chadwick (ed), *Studies in Early British History*, ch 7, p 175.

29 *The Catholic Encyclopedia*, vol XIII, under St Samson.

30 Columba's life, as written in the 7th century, is recounted in St Adamnan, *A Life of Saint Columba (Columb-Kille) 521–597* (trans, Wentworth Huyshe), George Routledge, London, 1908.

31 Bede, *The Ecclesiastical History of the English People*, bk I, ch 15, p 27.

32 KO Morgan (ed), *Oxford History of Britain*, ch 2, p 62.

33 HM Chadwick (ed), *Studies in Early British History*, ch 2, pp 21–33.
34 Penairth MS 45, entitled *Bonedd Gwyr y Gogledd*, gives the descent of the Men of the North.
35 William Forbes Skene, *The Four Ancient Books of Wales*, Edmonston and Douglas, Edinburgh, 1868, ch 6, p 82.
36 R Cunliffe Shaw, *Post Roman Carlisle and the Kingdoms of the North-West*, Guardian Press, Preston, 1964, part I, p 11.
37 M Swanton (ed), *The Anglo Saxon Chronicle*, Peterborough MS (E), ref AD 449–56, p 13.
38 The Anglo-Saxon incomers did not penetrate the Celtic western peninsula, to which they gave the name Wales (*weallas* meaning 'foreigners').
39 AE Waite, *The Hidden Church of the Holy Grail*, bk V, ch 7, pp 334–5.
40 *Ibid*, bk V, ch 2, p 305.
41 Rev WW Skeat, *Joseph of Arimathea*, pp 67–8.
42 Bede, *The Ecclesiastical History of the English People*, bk III, ch 4, p 115.
43 A *belach* or *bealach* relates to a pass or lowland route. *See* WJ Watson, *The History of the Celtic Place Names of Scotland*, pp 482–3.

Chapter 19: The Church and the Quest

1 NL Goodrich, *King Arthur*, bk I, ch 4, p 100.
2 *The Catholic Encyclopedia*, vol XV, under Synod of Whitby.
3 G Taylor, *Our Neglected Heritage*, vol 2, p 69.
4 Bede, *The Ecclesiastical History of the English People*, bk I, ch 25, pp 39–40.
5 JW Taylor, *The Coming of the Saints*, app L, pp 243–4.
6 The O'Donnells claimed ownership of the *Cathach* from the 11th century, when it was enclosed in a shrine and carried into battle as a saint's relic. The *Cathach* was taken to France in 1691 and forgotten for a long time, until its shrine was opened in 1813. The O'Donnell family then reclaimed the Cathach and it was presented to the Royal Irish Academy in 1842.
7 The work is published as Rev HJ Lawlor, *The Cathach of St Columba*, Royal Irish Academy, Dublin, 1916.
8 Bede, *The Ecclesiastical History of the English People*, bk I, ch 29, p 56.
9 G Taylor, *Our Neglected Heritage*, vol 2, pp 67–8.
10 Diana Leatham, *They Built on Rock: Stories of the Celtic Saints*, Hodder & Stoughton, London, 2000, ch 9, p 155.
11 Geoffrey of Monmouth, *History of the Kings of Britain*, part VI:viii, p 195.
12 *Ibid*, index note 'Ambrius', p 293.
13 Hector Munro Chadwick, *Early Scotland – The Picts, Scots and Welsh of Southern Scotland*, Cambridge University Press, Cambridge, 1949, ch 9, pp 120–22.
14 NL Goodrich, *King Arthur*, intro, part 3, pp 32–3.
15 The battle is cited in the *Bodleian Manuscripts*, the *Book of Leinster*, the *Book of Ballymote* and the *Chronicles of the Scots* – and all give the date as 516. The Scots commander is generally named as Aedàn mac Gabràn of Dalriada, but Aedàn had not yet been born. The leader was actually his father, Prince

Gabràn, who became King of Dalriada in 537. Aedàn and his eldest son, Arthur, fought at the second battle of Dun Baedàn, which took place in 575. Despite the definitive date of 516 quoted in the chronicles, there has been a great deal of speculation about the first battle, much of which has arisen because researchers have been directed to the wrong historian Gildas. All too often it is Gildas I Albanius who is mistakenly identified as the author of *De Excidio*. But he lived AD 425–512, and was thus already dead when Gildas III Badonicus was born in 516 – the very year of the battle, as he made a point of stating in his text (*see* Gildas, *De Excidio Britanniae*, part II, item 26), and the very reason why he was dubbed Badonicus.

16 Alan Orr Anderson, *Early Sources of Scottish History* (ed, Marjorie Anderson), Paul Watkins, Stamford, 1990, vol I, part II, ref 573, p 74.

17 Joseph Loth, *Les Mabinogion*, Fontemoing Et Cie, Paris, 1913, vol 2, p 248.

18 RC Shaw, *Post Roman Carlisle and the Kingdoms of the North-West*, part 3, p 24.

19 Richard Barber, *King Arthur in Legend and History*, Cardinal, London, 1973, ch 7, p 105.

20 'Sir Gawaine and the Carle of Carlisle' in Thomas Hahn (ed), *Sir Gawain: Eleven Romances and Tales*, Western Michigan University Medieval Institute, Kalamazoo, MI, 1995.

21 NJ Bull, *The Rise of the Church*, ch 9, pp 256–7.

22 M Martin, *The Decline and Fall of the Roman Church*, pp 63–5.

23 F Homes Dudden, *Gregory the Great, His Place in History and in Thought*, Longmans Green, London, 1905, vol 1, ch 1, p 5.

24 *The Catholic Encyclopedia*, vol VI, under Pope St Gregory I.

25 KO Morgan, *The Oxford History of Britain*, ch 3, pp 141–4.

26 S Haskins, *Mary Magdalene*, ch 4, p 123.

27 *Ibid*, ch 5, p 145.

28 HC Lea, *History of Sacerdotal Celibacy in the Christian Church*, ch 5, p 58.

29 An English transcript of the *Donation of Constantine* is given in Ernest F Henderson (trans), *Select Historical Documents of the Middle Ages*, G Bell, London, 1925, pp 319–29.

30 WJ Stein, *The Ninth Century*, ch 7, p 282. Roman Christianity was allied with the progressive powers of State politics, whereas Grail Christianity was concerned with human development.

31 Duc de Castries, *The Lives of the Kings and Queens of France*, part 2, p 41.

32 In the late 4th century (from AD 382), St Jerome made a Latin translation of the Bible from the earlier Hebrew and Greek texts for subsequent Christian usage. It was called the *Vulgate* because of its 'vulgar' (general) application – from *vulgata editio* (common edition). Emperor Constantine died before this in AD 337.

33 The earliest known manuscript of the Donation is in the *Codex Parisiensis Lat. 2778* in the *Collectio Sancti Dionysii*, found in the monastery of St Denis in France. *See* CB Coleman, *The Treatise of Lorenzo Valla on the Donation of Constantine*, p 6.

34 *Ibid*, p 3. Nicholas of Cusa (Nicholas Cusanus) published his critical appraisal of the *Donation* in his *De Concordantia Catholica*.

35 *Ibid*, p 25.

36 Details of Henry Edward Manning's life and Catholic conversion are given in David Newsome, *The Convert Cardinals*, John Murray, London, 1993, *passim*.

37 CB Coleman, *The Treatise of Lorenzo Valla on the Donation of Constantine*, p 20, ff, presents the *Laurentii Vallensis* as a translated discourse. At the time of Coleman's publication, he was Professor of History at Allegheny College, Meadville, Pennsylvania, compiling his work with assistance from that College and from Columbia University, New York.

Chapter 20: The Arthurian Realm

1 The presumed etymology was put forward in Kemp Malone, 'Artorius' in *Modern Philology*, University of Chicago Press, Chicago, IL, vol 22, no 4, May 1925, pp 367–74.

2 Nennius, *History of the Britons*, item 62 in both Morris and Giles translations.

3 The poem is discussed in John T Koch (ed), *The Gododdin of Aneirin: Text and Context from Dark Age North Britain*, University of Wales Press, Cardiff, 1997.

4 Richard Barber, *The Figure of Arthur*, ch 2, p 22.

5 'The Book of Taliesin' in WF Skene, *The Four Ancient Books of Wales*, ch XV, Poems B VI, *The Chair of the Sovereign*, p 259.

6 Geoffrey of Monmouth, *The History of the Kings of Britain*, part VI:viii, pp 205–8; part VII:ix, pp 217–21.

7 Ronan Coghlan, *The Illustrated Encyclopaedia of Arthurian Legends*, Element Books, Shaftesbury, 1993, p 221.

8 Brutus (died *c*1103 BC) was the grandson of Ascanius Julius, son of Aeneas and Creusa (daughter of King Priam of Troy.) After the fall of Troy in about 1184 BC, the royal house of Dardanos was scattered. The Trojan Cycle, as listed by Proclus in the 2nd century AD, records that Aeneas went to Italy with 88,000 Trojans in a fleet of 332 ships. Brutus led another party to Britain, where, as cited in Nennius' *Historia*, he founded London, calling it Trinovantium. The Brutus Stone, from which royal accessions were traditionally proclaimed, is at Totnes in Devon. *See* G Taylor, *Our Neglected Heritage*, bk III, ch 4, pp 28–9.

9 Chrétien's stories were: *Erec and Enide* (*c*1170), *Cligès* (*c*1176), *Yvain, the Knight with the Lion*, and *Lancelot, the Knight of the Cart* (each between 1177 and 1181), and *Perceval, the Story of the Grail* (1181–90, unfinished).

10 The *Vulgate Cycle* includes the *Estoire del Saint Grail* (History of the Holy Grail), the *Estoire de Merlin* (also called the Prose Merlin) to which is attached the *Suite du Merlin* (a Merlin continuation), the *Lancelot Propre* (Lancelot Proper), the *Queste del Saint Graal* (Quest for the Holy Grail), and the *Mort Artu* (Death of Arthur).

11 The *Post-Vulgate* sections are similar to those of the original *Vulgate Cycle*, being the *Estoire del Saint Graal*, the *Estoire de Merlin*, the *Suite du Merlin* (also known as the *Huth-Merlin*), and the *Prose Tristan*.

12 Malory's stories are: *The Tale of King Arthur, The Noble Tale of King Arthur and Emperor Lucius, The Noble Tale of Sir Lancelot du Lake, The Tale of Sir Gareth, The Book of Sir Tristram de Lyonesse, The Tale of the Sangréal, The Book of Sir Lancelot and Queen Guinevere* and *The Most Piteous Tale of the Morte Arthur.*

13 PJC Field, *The Life and Times of Sir Thomas Malory*, DS Brewer, Cambridge, 1993, pp 115–30.

14 Sir Thomas Malory, *Tales of King Arthur*, bk 12, p 249.

15 The Great Hall is now the only existing remnant of Winchester Castle.

16 Sir Thomas Malory, *Tales of King Arthur*, intro, p 13.

17 Nennius, *History of the Britons* (Giles). In the Morris translation, the *'mountain of Breguoin'* is given as *'the hill called Agned'*. The Arthurian battle locations as given by Nennius are discussed in William Forbes Skene, *The Four Ancient Books of Wales*, ch IV, pp 52–8.

18 John Bannerman, *Studies in the History of Dalriada*, Scottish Academic Press, Edinburgh, 1974, pp 91, 154–6. *See* also *Senchus Fer n'Alban* in AO Anderson, *Early Sources of Scottish History*, intro, pp cl–cli.

19 The name of Aedàn (Aidan) mac Gabràn (Gabrain/Gafran) is sometimes rendered in old texts as Edhan mac Goueran. *See* WA Cummins, *The Age of the Picts*, Alan Sutton, Stroud, 1995, ch 16, p 123.

20 Richard Barber, *Arthur of Albion*, Boydell Press, London, 1971, ch 3, p 31.

21 Artúr mac Aedàn is supported as being King Arthur of the Britons by various scholars of Celtic history. *See* Nora K Chadwick, 'The Lost Literature of Celtic Scotland' in *Scottish Gaelic Studies*, University of Aberdeen, Old Aberdeen, vol II, 1953, part II, pp 115–83.

22 Compiled 1017–88 by Tigernach Ua-Broein of Clonmacnoise.

23 Whitley Stokes (ed) *The Annals of Tigernach* (for the *Revue Celtique*, 1896), Llanerch Publishers, Felinfach, 1993, vol 1, p 160. Also *see* AO Anderson, *Early Sources of Scottish History*, vol 1, part V, p 118.

24 PC Bartrum, *Early Welsh Genealogical Tracts*, 'Cognatio Brychan 15', p 18.

25 J Bannerman, *Studies in the History of Dalriada*, pp 93–4.

26 Marjorie O Anderson, *Kings and Kingship in Early Scotland*, Scottish Academic Press, Edinburgh, 1980, p 151.

27 William Forbes Skene (ed), *Chronicles of the Picts and Scots*, HM General Register House, Edinburgh, 1867, Chronicle MCCCCLXXXIJ–MDXXX, p 382.

28 The subject of Tintagel Castle is discussed in Paul Broadhurst, *Tintagel and the Arthurian Mythos*, Pendragon Press, Launceston, 1995, ch 2, pp 36–41.

29 From the time of Edward, the Black Prince, son of King Edward III Plantagenet in 1337, the Duchy of Cornwall has been held in the royal line. The current Duke of Cornwall is HRH Charles, Prince of Wales, the eldest son of the British monarch, HM Queen Elizabeth II.

30 *See* a report concerning Geoffrey's errors of location in NL Goodrich, *King Arthur*, ch 1, pp 12–13.

31 Nennius, *History of the Britons*, item 50.

32 S Evans (ed), *The High History of the Holy Grail*, branch XX, title X, p 242.

33 Rev WJ Rees, *Lives of the Cambro-British Saints*, ch 3, pp 312, 340–42; ch 4, p 398.

34 *Ibid*, ch 10, p 615.
35 Kuno Meyer (ed), 'The Expulsion of the Déssi' in *Y Cymmrodor 14*, Cymmrodorion Record Society, Cardiff, 1901, pp 101–25.
36 R Barber, *The Figure of Arthur*, ch 3, pp 34–6.
37 AO Anderson, *Early Sources of Scottish History*, vol I, part I, 'Annales Cambriae', p 9.
38 The Camlan Valley at Eifionydd on the old border between Gwynedd and Powys, west of Dolgellau.
39 Geoffrey of Monmouth, *History of the Kings of Britain*, part VII:x, pp 259–61.
40 G Ashe, *Avalonian Quest*, ch 2, p 35.
41 M Wood, *In Search of the Dark Ages*, ch 2, p 50.
42 Sir Thomas Malory, *Tales of King Arthur*, bk 13 (*Morte d'Arthur*), pp 343–4.
43 Geoffrey of Monmouth, *History of the Kings of Britain*, part VII:xi, p 261.
44 WJ Watson, *The History of the Celtic Place Names of Scotland*, ch 3, p 97.
45 Only seven of her eight sisters are named: Moronoe, Mazoe, Gliten, Glitonea, Gliton, Tyronoe and Thitis.
46 Sir Thomas Malory, *Tales of King Arthur*, bk 13 (*Morte d'Arthur*), pp 338–9.
47 G Ashe, *Avalonian Quest*, ch 3, p 48.
48 William of Malmesbury, *The Antiquities of Glastonbury*, ch 2, p 7; ch 10, p 23.
49 G Ashe, *Avalonian Quest*, ch 4, p 65–9.
50 William of Malmesbury, *The Antiquities of Glastonbury*, ch 31, p 59.
51 William of Malmesbury, *The Antiquities of Glastonbury*, intro, pp vi–vii; ch XXXI, pp 58–9; ch XXXII, pp 60–61.
52 Gildas, *De Excidio Britanniae*, part II, item 26.
53 'Tract on the Tributes Paid to Baedàn, King of Ulster' in WF Skene, *Chronicles of the Picts and Scots*, ch XV, p 127.
54 Thomas O'Rahilly, *Early Irish History and Mythology*, Dublin Institute for Advanced Studies, Dublin, 1946, notes p 504.
55 M Dillon and NK Chadwick, *The Celtic Realms*, ch 4, p 77.
56 Saint Adamnan of Iona, *The Life of Saint Columba*, ch IX, pp 29–30.
57 AO Anderson, *Early Sources of Scottish History*, vol I, part IV, 'Adamnan', p 97.
58 The battle, known as *Cath Manau*, is recorded in the *Annals of Tigernach*: *Ibid*, vol I, part III, pp 89–90; in the *Annals of Inisfallen*: WF Skene, *Chronicles of the Picts and Scots*, ch XXVIII, p 167, and in the *Annals of Ulster*, *Ibid*, ch XLVIII, p 345. Also *see* HM Chadwick, *Early Scotland*, ch 9, pp 124–5.
59 WF Skene, *The Four Ancient Books of Wales*, ch 4, p 60.
60 *See* M Wood, *In Search of the Dark Ages*, ch 2, p 58. Camlanna or Camboglanna means 'crooked glen'. The Castleheads site is on a sharp curve of the River Irthing close to another old fort called Birdoswald.
61 AO Anderson, *Early Sources of Scottish History*, vol I, part V, 'Chronicle of Holyrood', p 123.
62 Elizabeth Sutherland, *In Search of the Picts*, Constable, London, 1994, part II, p 53.
63 M Swanton (ed), *The Anglo-Saxon Chronicle*, MS: Peterborough E, ref 603, p 21.

64 NJ Higham, *The Kingdom of Northumbria*, Alan Sutton, Stroud, 1993, ch 3, pp 99, 111.

65 AO Anderson, *Early Sources of Scottish History*, vol I, part V, note 3 'Tigernach Annals', p 141.

66 The great dyke separating Wales from Mercia was built in the late 700s by Offa the Bretwalda (King of Kings) as a fortified boundary between Wales and his English realm. M Wood , *In Search of the Dark Ages*, ch 4, pp 78, 94–6.

Chapter 21: Once and Future Kings

1 Sir Thomas Malory, *Tales of King Arthur*, bk 13, p 339.

2 Bernard de Clairvaux, *Patriologia Latina*, vol 183, cols 1050–55.

3 RS Loomis, *The Grail: From Celtic Myth to Christian Symbolism*, ch 9, pp 106–7.

4 This subject is discussed at length in Laurence Gardner, *Lost Secrets of the Sacred Ark*.

5 Matthew 26:48–9, Mark 14:44–5, Luke 22:47–8.

6 Eleanor of Provence was married to Henry III. *See* M Meade, *Eleanor of Aquitaine*, p 287.

7 S Haskins, *Mary Magdalene*, ch 5, p 174.

8 A Weir, *Eleanor of Aquitaine*, ch 10, p 181.

9 Y Stoyanov, *The Hidden Tradition in Europe*, ch 6, pp 222–3.

10 For recommended reading on the subject, *see* Jonathan Sumption, *The Albigensian Crusade*, Faber & Faber, London, 1978, and Zoé Oldenbourg, *Massacre at Montségur* (trans, Peter Green), Pantheon, New York, NY, 1961.

11 Marion Meade, *Eleanor of Aquitaine*, pref, p 3.

12 ECM Begg, *The Cult of the Black Virgin*, ch 4, p 103.

13 *The Catholic Encyclopedia*, vol VI, under The Holy Grail.

14 TH White, *The Once and Future King*, Collins, London, 1958. The novel was compiled from three previously published works: *The Sword in the Stone* (1938), *The Witch in the Wood*, later renamed *The Queen of Air and Darkness* (1939) and *The Ill-Made Knight* (1940). Added to the 1958 compilation was a further section entitled *The Candle in the Wind*, and White also wrote a fifth book that was separately published, *The Book of Merlyn*.

15 A more complete account of these various descents in Scotland is related in L Gardner, *Bloodline of the Holy Grail*, ch 19, pp 224–5.

16 M Martin, *The Decline and Fall of the Roman Church*, pp 42–3.

Bibliography

Adamnan, St, *A Life of Saint Columba (Columb-Kille) 521–597*, (trans, Wentworth Huyshe), George Routledge, London, 1908

Albert le Grand, *Les Vies des Saintes de la Bretagne Armorique*, Paris, 1901

Allegro, John, *The Dead Sea Scrolls*, Penguin, London, 1964

Anderson, Alan Orr, *Early Sources of Scottish History* (ed, Marjorie Anderson), Paul Watkins, Stamford, 1990

Anderson, James, *Royal Genealogies*, London, 1732–36

Anderson, Joseph, *Scotland in Early Christian Times*, David Douglas, Edinburgh, 1881

Anderson, Marjorie O, *Kings and Kingship in Early Scotland*, Scottish Academic Press, Edinburgh, 1980

Ashe, Geoffrey, *Avalonian Quest*, Methuen, London, 1982

— *Kings and Queens of Early Britain*, Methuen, London, 2000

Baigent, Michael, with Richard Leigh and Henry Lincoln, *The Holy Blood and the Holy Grail*, Jonathan Cape, London, 1982

— *The Messianic Legacy*, Jonathan Cape, London, 1986

Bailey, Nathan (ed), *Nathan Bailey's Universal Etymological Dictionary*, T Cox at The Lamb, Royal Exchange, London, 1721

Bannerman, John, *Studies in the History of Dalriada*, Scottish Academic Press, Edinburgh, 1974

Barber, Richard, *Arthur of Albion*, Boydell Press, London, 1971

— *The Figure of Arthur*, Longman, London, 1972

— *King Arthur in Legend and History*, Cardinal, London, 1973

Baring-Gould, Rev Sabine, *A Book of Brittany*, Methuen, London, 1932

Barnstone, Willis (ed), *The Other Bible*, HarperSanFrancisco, San Francisco, CA, 1984

Baronius, Caesar, *Annales Ecclesiastici a Christi nato ad annum 1198*, Hieronymi Scoti, Venice, 1612

Bartrum, PC, *Early Welsh Genealogical Tracts*, University of Wales Press, Cardiff, 1966

Bauckham, Richard, *Jude and the Relatives of Jesus in the Early Church*, T&T Clark, Edinburgh, 1988

Bayley, Harold, *The Lost Language of Symbolism*, Williams & Norgate, London, 1912

Bede, *The Ecclesiastical History of the English People*, Oxford University Press, Oxford, 1969

Begg, Ean CM, *The Cult of the Black Virgin*, Arkana, London, 1985

Bell, Albert, *An Historical Analysis of the Exido Hierosolymitano*, University of North Carolina, Chapel Hill, NC, 1977

Bernard de Clairvaux, *Patriologia Latina* (ed, JP Minge), Paris, 1854

Blair, Peter Hunter, *The Origins of Northumbria*, Northumberland Press, Gateshead, 1948

Borg, Marcus (ed), *The Lost Gospel Q*, Ulysses Press, Berkeley, CA, 1996

Bowen, EG, *The Settlements of the Celtic Saints in Wales*, University of Wales Press, Cardiff, 1956

Brandon, SGF, *The Fall of Jerusalem and the Christian Church*, SPCK, London, 1951

— *Jesus and the Zealots*, Charles Scribner's Sons, New York, NY, 1967

Brenton, Sir Lancelot CL (trans), *The Septuagint with Apocrypha*, Samuel Bagster, London, 1851

Broadhurst, Paul, *Tintagel and the Arthurian Mythos*, Pendragon Press, Launceston, 1995

Bromwich, Rachel (trans), *The Welsh Triads*, University of Wales Press, Cardiff, 1961

Brown, Dan, *The Da Vinci Code*, Bantam Press, London, 2003

Brundage, James A, *Law, Sex, and Christian Society in Medieval Europe*, University of Chicago Press, Chicago, IL, 1987

Bryant, Nigel (trans), *Perlesvaus*, DS Brewer, Cambridge, 1978

Budge, Ernest A Wallis, *Miscellaneous Coptic Texts in the Dialect of Upper Egypt*, British Museum, London, 1915

Bull, Norman J, *The Rise of the Church*, Heinemann, London, 1967

Burns, Jane E (ed), *The Vulgate Cycle*, Ohio State University Press, 1985

Cambridge History of English and American Literature, Putnam, New York, NY, 1907–21

Capellanus, Andreas, *The Art of Courtly Love*, (trans, JJ Parry), Columbia University Press, New York, NY, 1941

Carley, James P, *Glastonbury Abbey – The Holy House at the Head of the Moors Adventurous*, Gothic Image, Glastonbury, 1992

Carpenter, Clive, *The Guinness Book of Kings, Rulers and Statesmen*, Guinness Superlatives, Enfield, 1978

Case, Shirley Jackson, *The Historicity of Jesus*, University of Chicago Press, Chicago, IL, 1912

Castries, Duc de, *The Lives of the Kings and Queens of France*, (trans, Anne Dobell for the Académie Française), Weidenfeld & Nicolson, London, 1979

Catholic Encyclopedia, Robert Appleton, New York, NY, 1910

Cawthorne, Nigel, *Sex Lives of the Popes*, Prion, London, 2004

Chadwick, Hector Munro, *Early Scotland – The Picts, Scots and Welsh of Southern Scotland*, Cambridge University Press, Cambridge, 1949

— *Studies in Early British History*, Cambridge University Press, Cambridge, 1954

Chadwick, Nora K, *Early Brittany*, University of Wales Press, Cardiff, 1969

Chandlery, PJ, *Pilgrim Walks in Rome*, Manresa Press, London, 1905

Chrétien de Troyes, *The Story of the Grail*, (trans, RW Linker), North Carolina Press, Chapel Hill, NC, 1952

— *Le Conte del Graal*, (trans, Ruth Harwood Cline), University of Georgia Press, Atlanta, GA, 1985

Clarke, GW (trans), *The Octavius of Marcus Minucius Felix*, Newman Press, New York, NY, 1974

Clébert, Jean-Paul, *The Gypsies*, (trans, Charles Duff), Visita Books, London, 1963

Clement, St of Rome, *The Clementine Homilies*, (trans, Rev Alexander Roberts and James Donaldson), The Ante-Nicene Christian Library, T&T Clark, Edinburgh, 1870

Coghlan, Ronan, *The Illustrated Encyclopaedia of Arthurian Legends*, Element Books, Shaftesbury, 1993

Coleman, Christopher B, *The Treatise of Lorenzo Valla on the Donation of Constantine*, University of Toronto Press, Toronto, ON, 1993

Compact Oxford English Dictionary, Oxford University Press, Oxford, 1971

Concise Oxford Dictionary of Current English, Oxford University Press, Oxford, 1995

Constitutions of the Holy Apostles, T&T Clark, Edinburgh, 1870

Conybeare, Edward, *Roman Britain*, SPCK, London, 1911

Cooper, James, and Arthur John Maclean (trans), *Testament of Our Lord*, T&T Clark, Edinburgh, 1902

Copley, Gordon K, *The Conquest of Wessex in the Sixth Century*, Phoenix House, London, 1954

Corbett, Percy E, *Why Britain?*, RJ Press, Newbury, 1984

Cressy, Hugh Serenus, *Church History of Brittany or England from the Beginning of Christianity to the Norman Conquest*, Rouen, 1668

Cummins, WA, *The Age of the Picts*, Alan Sutton, Stroud, 1995

Czeski, A, with JP Erard, and Marie-Elects Gardel, *Montségur: 13 Years of Archaeological Research, 1964–1976*, Group of Archaeological Research of Montségur and Environs, Lavelanet, 1981

Dalton, OM (ed), *The Letters of Sidonius Apollinaris*, Clarendon Press, Oxford, 1915

Dauzat, Albert, and Charles Rostaing (eds), *Dictionnaire étymologique des noms de lieux en France*, Guénégaud, Paris, 1963

Davis, Raymond, *The Book of Pontiffs (Liber Pontificalis)*, University of Liverpool Press, Liverpool, 1989

Davis, RHC, *A History of Medieval Europe*, Longmans, London, 1957

Deanesly, Margaret, *A History of Early Medieval Europe 476–911*, Methuen, London, 1956

Delaney, Frank, *Legends of the Celts*, Hodder & Stoughton, London, 1989

— *The Celts*, Grafton/Collins, London, 1989

Dill, Sir Samuel, *Roman Society in Gaul in the Merovingian Age*, Macmillan, London, 1926

Dillon, Miles, and Nora Chadwick, *The Celtic Realms*, Weidenfeld & Nicolson, London, 1967

Disputatio Super Dignitatem Angliae et Galliae in Concilio Constantiano, Theodore Martin, Lovan, 1517

Dobson, Rev Cyril C, *Did Our Lord Visit Britain?*, Avalon Press, Glastonbury, 1938

Doresse, Jean, *The Secret Books of the Egyptian Gnostics*, (trans, Philip Mairet), Hollis & Carter, London, 1960

Dudden, F Homes, *Gregory the Great, His Place in History and in Thought*, Longmans Green, London, 1905

Dupont-Sommer, André, *The Essene Writings From Qumrân*, (trans, G Vermes), Basil Blackwell, Oxford, 1961

Ehler, Sidney Z, and John B Morral (eds), *Church and State through the Centuries*, Burns & Oates, London, 1954

Eisenman, Robert, and Michael Wise, *Dead Sea Scrolls Uncovered*, Penguin, London, 1992

Eisler, Riane, *The Chalice and the Blade*, Harper & Row, New York, NY, 1987

Eisler, Robert, *The Messiah Jesus and John the Baptist according to Flavius Josephus*, (trans, Alexander H Krappe), Methuen, London, 1931

Elder, Isabel Hill, *Celt, Druid and Culdee*, Covenant Books, London, 1947

Ellis, Peter Berresford, *A Brief History of the Druids*, Constable and Robinson, London, 2002

Encyclopaedia Judaica, Keter Publishing, Jerusalem, 1906

Epiphanius, *Panarion*, (trans, F Wilkins), EJ Brill, Leiden, 1989–93

Epiphanius, *Ancoratus*, (trans, Karl Hol), Walter de Gruyter, Berlin, 2002–4

Eusebius of Caesarea, *An Ecclesiastical History*, (trans, Rev CF Crusè), Samuel Bagster, London, 1838

— *Ecclesiastical History*, (trans, CF Crusè), George Bell, London, 1874

— *The History of the Church from Christ to Constantine*, Penguin, London, 1989

Evans, Sebastian (trans), *The High History of the Holy Grail* (*Perlesvaus*), Everyman, London, 1912

— *The High History of the Holy Grail*, James Clarke, Cambridge, 1969

Farmer, David (ed), *Oxford Dictionary of the Saints*, Oxford University Press, Oxford, 1997

Felix, Marcus Minucius, *The Octavius of Marcus Minucius Felix*, Paulist Press, New York, NY, 1974

Field, PJC, *The Life and Times of Sir Thomas Malory*, DS Brewer, Cambridge, 1993

Fleetwood, Rev J (ed), *The Life of Our Lord and Saviour Jesus Christ*, William MacKenzie, Glasgow, 1900

Franzmann, Majella, *Jesus in the Manichaean Writings*, Continuum International, New York, NY, 2003

Frappier, Jean, *Chrétien de Troyes and his Work*, (trans, Raymond Cormier), Ohio State University Press, 1982

Freese, JH (trans), *The Octavius of Marcus Minucius Felix*, Macmillan, New York, 1919

Freke, Timothy, and Peter Gandy, *The Jesus Mysteries*, Three Rivers, New York, NY, 2001

Furnival, Frederick J (ed), *The History of the Holy Grail* – from *Roman l'Estoire dou Saint Graal* by Sires Robert de Boron, (trans, Henry Lonelich Skynner), Early English Text Society and N Turner, London, 1861

Gantz, Jeffrey (trans), *The Mabinogion*, Penguin, London, 1976

Gardner, Laurence, *Bloodline of the Holy Grail*, HarperCollins, London, 2002
— *Lost Secrets of the Sacred Ark*, HarperCollins, London, 2003
— *The Magdalene Legacy*, HarperCollins, London, 2005
Geoffrey of Monmouth, *The Vita Merlini*, (trans, John Jay Parry), University of Illinois, Urbana, IL, 1925
— *The History of the Kings of Britain*, (trans, Lewis Thorpe), Penguin London, 1966
Gildas, *De Excidio Britanniae*, (trans, JA Giles), G Bell, London, 1891
Godding, Robert SJ, *Grégoire le Grand et la Madeleine in Memoriam soctorum venerantes – Miscellanea in onore di Mgr Victor Saxer*, The Vatican, Rome, 1992
Goodrich, Norma Lorre, *King Arthur*, Harper Perennial, New York, NY, 1989
Gougaud, Dom Louis, *Christianity in Celtic Lands*, (trans, Maud Joynt), Four Courts Press, Dublin, 1932
Grant, M, *Herod The Great*, Weidenfeld & Nicolson, London, 1971
— *The Jews in the Roman World*, Weidenfeld & Nicolson, London, 1973
Graves, Robert, *King Jesus*, Cassell, London, 1946
— *The White Goddess*, Faber & Faber, London, 1961
Green, Miranda, *The Gods of the Celts*, Alan Sutton, Stroud, 1986
Greenia, Conrad, *Bernard de Clairvaux Treatises*, Cistercian Publications, Kalamazoo, MI, 1977
Gregory of Tours, *A History of the Franks*, (trans, Lewis Thorpe), Penguin, London, 1964
Grimm, Jacob, *Teutonic Mythology*, Thoemmes Press, London, 1999
Guest, Lady Charlotte (trans), *The Mabinogion*, John Jones, Cardiff, 1977
Gurney, Robert, *Celtic Heritage*, Chatto & Windus, London, 1969

Hahn, Thomas (ed), *Sir Gawain: Eleven Romances and Tales*, Western Michigan University Medieval Institute, Kalamazoo, MI, 1995
Halsberghe, GS, *The Cult of Sol Invictus*, EJ Brill, Leiden, 1972
Harry, George Owen, *The Genealogy of the High and Mighty Monarch James*, Simon Stafford and Thomas Salisbury, London, 1604
Harvey, John, *The Plantagenets*, BT Batsford, London, 1959
Haskins, Susan, *Mary Magdalen, Myth and Metaphor*, Harcourt Brace, New York, NY, 1994
Hastings, James (ed), *Dictionary of the Bible*, T&T Clark, Edinburgh, 1909
Hervey, Thomas K, *The Book of Christmas*, Frederick Warne, London, 1888
Henderson, Ernest F (trans), *Select Historical Documents of the Middle Ages*, G Bell, London, 1925
Hendin, David, *Guide to Biblical Coins*, Amphora Books, Amsterdam, 2001
Henry, William, *Mary Magdalene: The Illuminator*, Adventures Unlimited, Kempton, IL, 2006
Hewins, WAS, *The Royal Saints of Britain*, Chiswick Press, London, 1928
Hewison, James King, *The Isle of Bute in the Olden Time*, William Blackwood, Edinburgh, 1895
Higgins, Geoffrey, *Celtic Druids*, Rowland Hunter, London, 1829
Higham, NJ, *The Kingdom of Northumbria*, Alan Sutton, Stroud, 1993

Hocart, AM, *Kingship*, Oxford University Press, Oxford, 1927

Hodgkin, RH, *A History of the Anglo-Saxons*, Oxford University Press, Oxford, 1952

Hoeh, Herman L, *Compendium of World History*, Ambassador College, Pasadena, CA, 1963

Howgego, Christopher, with Volker Heuchert and Andrew Burnett (eds), *Coinage and Identity in the Roman Provinces*, Oxford University Press, Oxford, 2005

Hubert, Henry, *The Greatness and Decline of the Celts*, Kegan Paul, London, 1934

Hulme, Edward F, *Symbolism in Christian Art*, Swann Sonnenschein, London, 1891

Hutchinson Encyclopedia, Hutchinson, London, 1997

Hutton, Ronald, *The Pagan Religions of the British Isles*, Basil Blackwell, Oxford, 1991

Jacopo di Voragine, *Légenda Aurea (Golden Legend)*, (trans, William Caxton, 1483; ed, George V O'Neill), Cambridge University Press, Cambridge, 1972

Jackson, Samuel Macauley (ed), *The Schaff-Herzog Encyclopedia of Religious Knowledge*, Baker Book House, Grand Rapids, MI, 1953

James, BS, *Saint Bernard of Clairvaux*, Harper, New York, NY, 1957

Jewish Encyclopedia, Funk and Wagnalls, New York, NY, 1906

Johannes Glastoniensis, *Cronica sive Antiquitates Glastoniensis Ecclesiae*, Boydell & Brewer, Woodbridge, 1985

Josephus, Flavius, *The Antiquities of the Jews* and *The Wars of the Jews* in *The Works of Flavius Josephus*, (trans, William Whiston), Milner & Sowerby, London, 1870

— *The Jewish Wars*, (trans, GA Williamson), Penguin, London, 1959

Jowett, George F, *The Drama of the Lost Disciples*, Covenant Books, London, 1961

Jung, Emma, and Marie-Louise von Franz, *The Grail Legend*, Princeton University Press, Princeton, NJ, 1998

Kingsland, William, *The Gnosis or Ancient Wisdom in the Christian Scriptures*, Allen & Unwin, London, 1937

Knox, Wilfred, *Sources of the Synoptic Gospels*, Cambridge University Press, Cambridge, 1959

Koch, John T (ed), *The Gododdin of Aneirin: Text and Context from Dark Age North Britain*, University of Wales Press, Cardiff, 1997

Koester, Helmut, *Ancient Christian Gospels: Their History and Development*, SCM Press, London, 1990

Kramer, Samuel Noah, *The Sacred Marriage Rite*, Indiana University Press, Bloomington, AL, 1969

Lacordaire, Père, *St Mary Magdalene*, Thomas Richardson, Derby, 1880

Laërtius, Diogenes, *The Lives and Opinions of Eminent Philosophers*, (trans, CD Tonge), Bohn, London, 1853

Lawlor, Rev HJ, *The Cathach of St Columba*, Royal Irish Academy, Dublin, 1916

Lawrence, DH, *The Man Who Died*, Martin Secker, London, 1931

Layamon, *Arthurian Chronicles* (trans, Eugene Mason), Dent, London, 1972

Lea, Henry C, *History of Sacerdotal Celibacy in the Christian Church*, Watts & Co, London, 1932

Leatham, Diana, *They Built on Rock: Stories of the Celtic Saints*, Hodder & Stoughton, London, 2000

Leland, John, *The Itinerary of John Leland in or about the Years 1535–1543*, (ed, L Toulmin Smith), London, 1906–10

Lewis, Rev Lionel Smithett, *Glastonbury, The Mother of Saints*, St Stephen's Press, Bristol, 1925

— *Joseph of Arimathea at Glastonbury*, AR Mobray, London, 1927

Lindsay, Jack, *The Normans and Their World*, Purnell, London, 1974

Loomis, Roger Sherman, *The Grail: From Celtic Myth to Christian Symbolism*, University of Wales Press, Cardiff, 1963

Loth, Joseph, *Les Mabinogion*, Fontemoing Et Cie, Paris, 1913

Mackie, JDA, *A History of Scotland*, Pelican, London, 1964

Macmillan Encyclopedia, Macmillan, London, 1996

MacNeill, Eoin, *Celtic Ireland*, (Martin Lester, Dublin, 1921), Academy Press, Dublin, 1981

Mâle, Émile, *Religious Art in France of the Thirteenth Century*, Dover, Mineola, NY, 2000

Malory, Sir Thomas, *Morte D'Arthur*, New York University Books, New York, NY, 1961

— *Tales of King Arthur*, Guild Publishing, London, 1980

Manuel, Frank E, *The Religion of Isaac Newton*, (The Freemantle Lectures 1973), Clarendon Press, Oxford, 1974

Martialis, *Epigrammaton*, (ed, W Heraeus), J Borovskij, Leipzig, 1976–82

Martin, Malachi, *The Decline and Fall of the Roman Church*, Secker & Warburg, London, 1982

Matarasso, PM (ed), *The Quest of the Holy Grail*, Penguin, London, 1969

McDonald, LM, and JA Sanders (eds), *The Canon Debate*, Hendrickson, Peabody, MA, 2002

McGinn, Thomas AJ, *Prostitution, Sexuality, and the Law in Ancient Rome*, Oxford University Press, New York, NY, 1998

Mead, GRS (trans), *Pistis Sophia: A Gnostic Miscellany*, (1921), reprint: Kessinger, Kila, MT, 1992

Meade, Marion, *Eleanor of Aquitaine*, Frederick Muller, London, 1978

Metzger, BM, *The Canon Of The New Testament: Its Origin, Significance and Development*, Clarendon Press, Oxford, 1997

Mierow, Charles C (ed), *The Origin and Deeds of the Goths* (from Jordanes, 551), Princeton University Press, Princeton, NJ, 1915

Milik, JT, *Ten Years of Discovery in the Wilderness of Judaea*, (trans, J Strugnell), SCM Press, London, 1959

Morgan. Kenneth O (ed), *Oxford History of Britain*, Oxford University Press, Oxford, 1988

Morgan, Rev RW, *St Paul in Britain*, Covenant, London 1925

Morris, John, *Annales Cambriae: The Annals of Wales*, Phillimore, Chichester, 1980

Nennius, *Six Old English Chronicles*, (trans, John Allan Giles), George Bell, London. 1891

— *History of the Britons*, (trans, John Morris), Phillimore, Chichester, 1980

Newsome, David, *The Convert Cardinals*, John Murray, London, 1993

Newstead, Helaine, *Brân the Blessed in Arthurian Romance*, Columbia University Press, New York, NY, 1939

Nicolson, Adam, *Power and Glory*, HarperCollins, London, 2003

Norgate, Kate, *England Under the Angevin Kings*, Macmillan, London, 1887

Oldenbourg, Zoé, *Massacre at Montségur*, (trans, Peter Green), Pantheon, New York, NY, 1961

Oman, Sir Charles, *England Before the Norman Conquest*, Methuen, London, 1938

O'Rahilly, Cecile, *Ireland and Wales*, Longmans Green, London, 1924

O'Rahilly, Thomas, *Early Irish History and Mythology*, Dublin Institute for Advanced Studies, Dublin, 1946

Origen, *The Song of Songs, Commentary and Homilies*, (trans, RP Lason), Newman Press, New York, NY, 1956

Osiander, Lucas, *Epitomes Historiae Ecclesiasticae Centuria*, Tübingen, 1592

Osman, Ahmed, *The House of the Messiah*, HarperCollins, London, 1992

Oxford Compact English Dictionary, (Oxford Word Library Micrographic), Oxford University Press, Oxford, 1971

Pagels, Elaine, *The Gnostic Gospels*, Weidenfeld and Nicolson, London, 1980

Panofsky, Erwin, and Gerda Panofsky-Soergel (eds), *Abbot Suger on the Abbey Church of St. Denis and Its Art Treasures*, Princeton University Press, Princeton, NJ, 1979

Paris, M Paulin, *Le Romans de la Table Ronde*, Paris, 1877

Parisiensis, Matthaei, Monachi Sancti Albani (Matthew Paris), *Chronica Majora*, (ed, HR Luard), Rolls Series lvii, 7 vols, Master of the Rolls, Court of Chancery, 1872–83

— *The Illustrated Chronicle of Matthew Paris*, Alan Sutton, Stroud, and Corpus Christie College, Cambridge, 1993

Pastoureau, Michel, *Armorial des Chevaliers de la Table Ronde*, Léopard d'Or, Paris, 1983

Perowne, Stewart, *The Life and Times of Herod the Great*, Hodder & Stoughton, London, 1956

— *The Later Herods*, Hodder & Stoughton, London, 1958

Planché, JR, *The Conqueror and his Companions*, Tinsley Bros, London, 1874

Platt, Rutherford H (ed), *The Lost Books of the Bible*, World Publishing, New York, NY, 1963

Porter, JR, *The Illustrated Guide to the Bible*, Duncan Baird, London, 1995

Qualls-Corbett, Nancy, *The Sacred Prostitute*, Inner City Books, Toronto, ON, 1988

Rees, Rev WJ, *Lives of the Cambro British Saints*, Welsh MSS Society, Llandovery, 1853

Reichert, B (ed), *Acta Capitulorum Generalium Ordinis Praedicatorum*, The Vatican, Rome, 1898

Reubenstein, Richard E, *When Jesus Became God*, Harcourt, Orlando, FL, 1999

Rhode, James Montague (ed), *The Apocryphal New Testament*, Clarendon Press, Oxford, 1924

Richards, Steve, *Levitation*, Thorsons, Wellingborough, 1980

Richey, Margaret Fitzgerald, *Studies of Wolfram Von Eschenbach*, Oliver & Boyd, London, 1957

Roberts, Rev Alexander, and James Donaldson (eds), *The Ante-Nicene Fathers – The Writings of the Fathers down to* AD *325*, T&T Clark, Edinburgh, 1867

Roberts, G, *Aspects of Welsh History*, University of Wales Press, Cardiff, 1969

Robinson, James M (ed), and the Coptic Gnostic Project, *The Nag Hammadi Library*, Institute for Antiquity and Christianity, EJ Brill, Leiden, 1977

Round, J Horace, *Calendar of Documents Preserved in France 918–1206*, Eyre & Spottiswoode, London, 1899

Rutherford, Ward, *The Druids and Their Heritage*, Gordon & Cremonesi, London, 1978

Schaff, Philip, and Henry Wace (eds), *Nicene and Post-Nicene Fathers, Second Series*, Oxford University Press, Oxford, 1894

Schonfield, Hugh J, *The Original New Testament*, Waterstone, London, 1985

— *The Passover Plot*, Element Books, Shaftesbury, 1985

Shapiro, Meyer, *Late Antique, Early Christian and Medieval Art*, George Brazillier, New York, NY, 1979

Shaw, R Cunliffe, *Post Roman Carlisle and the Kingdoms of the North-West*, Guardian Press, Preston, 1964

Shewring, WH (trans), *The Passion of Perpetua and Felicity*, Sheed and Ward, London, 1931

Skeat, Rev Walter W, *Joseph of Arimathea*, N Trubner and the Early English Text Society, London, 1871

Skeels, Dell (trans), *Didot Perceval*, University of Washington Press, Seattle, WA, 1966

Skene, William Forbes (ed), *Chronicles of the Picts and Scots*, HM General Register House, Edinburgh, 1867

— *The Four Ancient Books of Wales*, Edmonston and Douglas, Edinburgh, 1868

Smith, Dr William, *Smith's Bible Dictionary*, (1868 revised), Hendrickson, Peabody, MA, 1998

Smith, Morton, *The Secret Gospel*, Victor Gollancz, London, 1974

Sonnini, Charles Sigisbert: 1751–1812 (trans), *The Long Lost Chapter of the Acts of the Apostles*, Covenant, London, 1920

Spelman, Sir Henrici, *Concilia, Decreta, Leges, Constitutiones, in re Ecclesiarum Orbis Britannici*, Richardus Badger, London, 1639

Spence, Keith, *Brittany and the Bretons*, Victor Gollancz, London, 1978

Spence, Lewis, *Legends and Romances of Brittany*, George G Harrap, London, 1917

Spong, Bishop John Shelby, *Born of a Woman*, HarperSanFrancisco, San Francisco, CA, 1992

Stählin, Otto, and Ursula Treu, *Clemens Alexandrinus Register*, Akademie-Verlag, Berlin, 1980

Staley, Edgcumbe, *King René d'Anjou and his Seven Queens*, John Long, London, 1912

Starbird, Margaret, *The Woman with the Alabaster Jar*, Bear, Santa Fe, NM, 1993

Stein, Walter Johannes, *The Ninth Century*, Temple Lodge, London, 1991

Stenton, FM, *Anglo-Saxon England*, Oxford University Press, Oxford, 1950

Stokes, Whitley (ed), *Félire Óengusso Céli Dé (The Martyrology of Oengus the Culdee)*, Dublin Institute for Advanced Studies, Dublin, 1984

— *The Annals of Tigernach* (for the *Revue Celtique*, 1896), Llanerch Publishers, Felinfach, 1993

Stoyanov, Yuri, *The Hidden Tradition in Europe*, Arkana/Penguin, London, 1994

Strachan, Gordon, *Jesus the Master Builder*, Floris, Edinburgh, 1998

Strype, John, *Stow's Survey of London*, London, 1720

Sumption, Jonathan, *The Albigensian Crusade*, Faber & Faber, London, 1978

Sutherland, Elizabeth, *In Search of the Picts*, Constable, London, 1994

Swanton, Michael (trans), *The Anglo-Saxon Chronicle*, JM Dent, London, 1997

Tacitus, Cornelius, *Agricola*, (trans, M Hutton and W Peterson), Loeb Classical Library, Harvard University Press, Cambridge, MA, 1969

— *The Annals of Imperial Rome*, (trans, Michael Grant), Penguin, London, 1996

Taylor, Gladys, *Our Neglected Heritage*, Covenant Books, London, 1974

Taylor, John W, *The Coming of the Saints*, Covenant Books, London, 1969

Thackery, Henry, *Josephus, the Man and the Historian*, KTAV, Jerusalem, 1968

Theide, Carsten Peter, and Matthew D'Ancona, *The Jesus Papyrus*, Weidenfield & Nicolson, London, 1996

Thiering, Barbara, *Jesus the Man*, Transworld/Doubleday, London, 1992

— *Jesus of the Apocalypse*, Doubleday, London, 1996

Throckmorton, Burton H (ed), *Gospel Parallels*, Thomas Nelson, London, 1949

Times Atlas of the Bible, Times Books, London, 1994

Tixeront, Rev J *A Handbook of Patrology*, (trans, S A Raemers), B Herder, St Louis, MO, 1920

Tolstoy, Nikolai, *The Quest for Merlin*, Hamish Hamilton, London, 1985

Topsfield, LT, *A Study of the Arthurian Romances of Chrétien de Troyes*, Cambridge University Press, Cambridge, 1981

Tranquillus, C Suetonius, *The Lives of the Twelve Caesars*, Loeb Classical Library, Harvard University Press, Cambridge, MA, 1914

Vaggione, RP, *Eunomius: The Extant Works*, Oxford Early Christian Texts, Oxford, 1987

Vermes, Geza, *The Complete Dead Sea Scrolls in English*, Penguin, London, 1998

— *Jesus the Jew*, SCM Press, London, 2001

Vine, WE (ed), *Vine's Expository Dictionary of Old and New Testament Words*, Thomas Nelson, London, 1996

Virgilio, Polidoro, *Anglicae Historicae*, Basle, 1534

Waddell, LA, *The Phoenician Origin of the Britons, Scots and Anglo-Saxons*, Luzac, London, 1931

Wade-Evans, Arthur W, *Welsh Christian Origins*, Alden Press, Oxford, 1934

Waite, Arthur Edward, *The Hidden Church of the Holy Grail*, Rebman, London, 1909

Wallace-Hadrill, JM, *The Long Haired Kings*, Methuen, London, 1962

Watson, William J, *The History of the Celtic Place Names of Scotland*, William Blackwood, Edinburgh, 1926

Weir, Alison, *Eleanor of Aquitaine*, Pimlico, London, 2000

Weston, Jessie L, *From Ritual to Romance*, Cambridge University Press, Cambridge, 1920

Whiston, William, *Primitive Christianity Revived*, (Cambridge University MSS, 5 vols), London, 1711–12

White, Michael, *Isaac Newton, The Last Sorcerer*, Fourth Estate, London, 1998

White, TH, *The Once and Future King*, Collins, London, 1958

Wijngaards, J, *No Women in Holy Orders?*, Canterbury Press, Norwich, 2002

Wilken, Robert L, *The Christians as the Romans Saw Them*, Yale University Press, New Haven, CT, 1984

William of Malmesbury, *De Antiquitate Glastoniensis Ecclesiae*, Talbot, London, 1908

— *The Antiquities of Glastonbury*, JMF Books, Llanerch, 1992

Williams, Frank (ed), *The Panarion of Epiphanius of Salamis*, EJ Brill, Leiden, 1994

Wilson, AN, *Jesus*, Sinclair-Stevenson, London, 1992

Wilson, Elizabeth AM, *Shostakovich: A Life Remembered*, Faber & Faber, London, 1994

Wilson, R McL, *The Gospel of Philip*, (trans from the Coptic Text), AR Mowbray, London, 1962

Wolfram von Eschenbach, *Parzival*, (trans, AT Hatto), Penguin , London, 1980

Wood, Michael, *In Search of the Dark Ages*, BBC Books, London, 1981

Yonge, CD (ed), *The Works of Philo Judaeus*, HG Bohn, London, 1854–90

Zuckerman, Arthur J, *A Jewish Princedom in Feudal France*, Columbia University Press, New York, NY, 1972

Picture Credits

Thanks must go to those below for courtesies and reproduction permissions in respect of the following photographic illustrations and copyright images:

Bridgeman Art Library: 1, 2, 4, 6, 9, 10, 12, 13, 14, 15, 17, 19, 21, 22, 25, 26, 28. Colin Palmer www.buyimage.co.uk: 8. Brendon Arts Resources: 3, 5, 7, 11, 16, 18, 20, 23, 24, 27, 29.

While every effort has been made to secure permissions, if there are any errors or oversights, we apologize and will make suitable acknowledgement in any future edition of this book.

Index